POLITICS IN THE GUTTERS

POLITICS IN THE GUTTERS

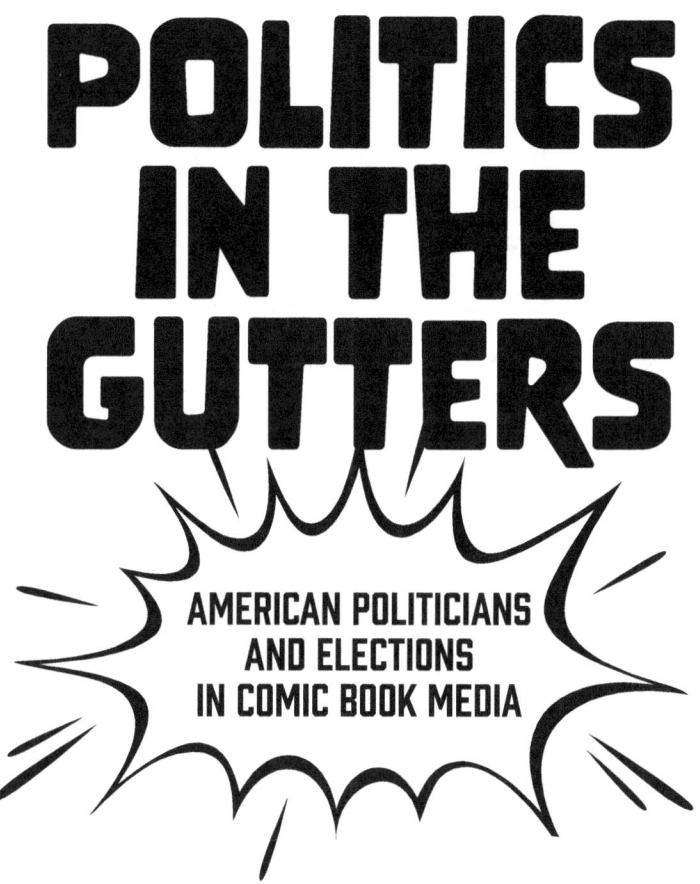

AMERICAN POLITICIANS AND ELECTIONS IN COMIC BOOK MEDIA

CHRISTINA M. KNOPF

UNIVERSITY PRESS OF MISSISSIPPI / JACKSON

The University Press of Mississippi is the scholarly publishing agency of
the Mississippi Institutions of Higher Learning: Alcorn State University,
Delta State University, Jackson State University, Mississippi State University,
Mississippi University for Women, Mississippi Valley State University,
University of Mississippi, and University of Southern Mississippi.

www.upress.state.ms.us

The University Press of Mississippi is a member
of the Association of University Presses.

Copyright © 2021 by University Press of Mississippi
All rights reserved

First printing 2021
∞

Library of Congress Cataloging-in-Publication Data

Names: Knopf, Christina M., 1980- author.
Title: Politics in the gutters: American politicians and elections in
comic book media / Christina M. Knopf.
Description: Jackson: University Press of Mississippi, 2021. | Includes
bibliographical references and index.
Identifiers: LCCN 2021008847 (print) | LCCN 2021008848 (ebook) | ISBN
978-1-4968-3422-5 (hardback) | ISBN 978-1-4968-3423-2 (trade paperback) | ISBN
978-1-4968-3424-9 (epub) | ISBN 978-1-4968-3425-6 (epub) | ISBN 978-1-4968-3426-3
(pdf) | ISBN 978-1-4968-3427-0 (pdf)
Subjects: LCSH: Comic books, strips, etc.—Political aspects. | Comic
books, strips, etc.—History and criticism. | United States—Politics
and government. | LCGFT: Literary criticism.
Classification: LCC PN6714 .K58 2021 (print) | LCC PN6714 (ebook) | DDC
741.5/3581—dc23
LC record available at https://lccn.loc.gov/2021008847
LC ebook record available at https://lccn.loc.gov/2021008848

British Library Cataloging-in-Publication Data available

FOR MOM AND DAD,
WITH LOVE AND GRATITUDE.

CONTENTS

ix		Acknowledgments
xi		Preface: Origin Stories
xiii		Introduction: The Political is Pop Cultural
3	1	Hey, Voters! Comics! Campaign Comics, Election Specials, and Graphic Biographies
20	2	Cold Conflicts, Comics Codes, and Congressional Committees
38	3	Great Superheroic Powers and Great Presidential Responsibilities
56	4	The Nixon PREZidency and the Rise of the Politically Cynical Comic Book
75	5	Reagan's Raiders, Trump's Titans, and Political Parody
94	6	The Fall of the Towers and the Rise of Political Comics Journalism
113	7	Comic Book Versions of Presidential Campaigns
132	8	The Difference Between a Superhero and a Female Politician is a Cape
150	9	Zombamas, Sopapillas, Dark Horses, and Other Politicians of Color
168	10	The Very Stable Evil Genius of Luthor, Loki, Doom, and Donald
186	11	Ex-Presidents and Days of Futuristic Pasts
203		Conclusion: The Art of the People, By the People, For the People

209	Postscript: Political Picks and Pandemics
215	Notes
221	Works Cited
265	Index

ACKNOWLEDGMENTS

This book would not have been possible without the encouragement and aid of many wonderful people. I especially want to thank: Rebecca Townsend, for making a special trip to Mount Holyoke to help me gather campaign comics; Vijay Shah, for his interest in this project; Michael Churchill at Pulp Nouveau Comix, for the recommendations and trivia; Mary L. Kahl, Kathleen Kendall, Josh Heller, and Sandy Camillo, for being inspirational role models and mentors; the anonymous readers of the original manuscript, as well as assorted reviewers in ECA and NCA, for their positive feedback and constructive criticism; and, Paul van der Veur, chair of the SUNY Cortland Communication and Media Studies Department, and Maryalice Griffin, the department's administrative assistant extraordinaire, for their support. I also want to give special thanks to my family: Boneau the Dog, for forcing me to get out of the house and away from the computer every day, and Donald and Sandra Knopf, for supporting me always and in every possible way. Lastly, a tip of my hat to the creators of comics and cartoons who speak truth to power in difficult times.

PREFACE
ORIGIN STORIES

In July 2019, an Op-Ed from *Al Jazeera* decried "the death of the political cartoon," and an Op-Ed in the *Washington Post* proclaimed that "political cartooning is becoming a lost art" (Gathara 2019, headline; Daniels 2019, headline). This came just a few weeks after the *New York Times* ended publication of political cartoons in its international edition (Dunn 2019). It came just a month after a Canadian political cartoonist, Michael de Adder, was fired from his contract with Brunswick News shortly after one of his anti-Trump cartoons went viral (Yancey-Bragg 2019). Just a little more than a year before that, cartoonist Rob Rogers, a Pulitzer Prize finalist, was fired from his twenty-six-year position with the *Pittsburgh Post-Gazette*, following the rejection of multiple cartoons by the paper (Lyons 2018).

In August 2019, concerns surrounding politics in comics were refocused when Marvel Comics chairman Isaac "Ike" Perlmutter was criticized for supporting Donald Trump (Dumaroag 2019). Days later, it was revealed that Pulitzer Prize-winning author and comics creator Art Spiegelman (*Maus*, *In the Shadow of No Towers*) withdrew his introduction for a Marvel Comics historical collection after the publisher demanded he remove a reference to "an Orange Skull" in Washington, DC (MacDonald 2019). Spiegelman's introductory essay, which subsequently went viral after being shared in the *Guardian*, discussed the anti-fascist roots of superhero comic books. Spiegelman (2019) observed,

> The young Jewish creators of the first superheroes conjured up mythic—almost god-like—secular saviours to deal with the threatening economic dislocations that surrounded them in the great depression and gave shape to their premonitions of impending global war. [. . .]
>
> Auschwitz and Hiroshima make more sense as dark comic book cataclysms than as events in our real world. In today's all too real world, Captain America's most nefarious villain, the Red Skull, is alive on screen and an Orange Skull haunts America. International fascism again looms large (how quickly we humans forget—study

these golden age comics hard, boys and girls!) and the dislocations that have followed the global economic meltdown of 2008 helped bring us to a point where the planet itself seems likely to melt down. (para. 20–21)

The essay, in conjunction with Amazon's adaptation of Garth Ennis's dark superhero satire *The Boys* (2019) and Spider-Man's killing spree in *Avengers: Endgame* (2019), prompted rhetoric professor Shaun Treat (2019) to call superheroes "the original AntiFa"—symbols of militant opposition to fascism. A couple of weeks later, Marvel was again scrutinized for depoliticizing a speech for the *Marvel Comics* #1000 anniversary issue, replacing writer Mark Waid's discussion of loving a "deeply flawed" country to a more generic statement about "Captain America isn't a man. It's an idea" (in Maveal 2019).

All in all, the Marvel controversies indicate that politics in cartoon form are not dead, nor do they sleep. The *New York Times* might have ceased publication of traditional editorial cartoons, but it has opened itself up to more forms of visual storytelling, such as the comics journalism found in Wendy MacNaughton's (2019) column, "Behind Bars, and Pixels Too: How Technology Makes Jail Even Bleaker." *MAD Magazine* might no longer be providing punditry through parody, but we can find a similarly twisted take on culture in Ahoy Comics' *Edgar Allan Poe's Snifter of Terror* and read snappy social satire in the likes of DC Comics' *The Flintstones*. If we want to see candidate caricatures by our favorite cartoonists, we can follow them online if not in print, or turn to the parodic and satiric comic books produced by Antarctic, Keenspot, or numerous independent artists on Kickstarter.

Sequential art has long had a tumultuous kinship with politics, ebbing and flowing from the mainstream. For several years during the 1950s, Walt Kelly's *Pogo*, a funny-animal strip set in the Okefenokee Swamp, "was the only comic strip to dare poke its readers in their political ribs" (Black 2016, 168–69). That meant that at least one comic strip *was* tackling politics in the heated domestic climate of the Cold War.[1] Even Marvel's recent efforts at being apolitical are political. As Spiegelman (2019) observed, the first comic book superheroes were created by Jewish immigrants as mythic saviors to combat the Nazi threat. Comic books have always been political, and whether it is Marvel's chairman Ike Perlmutter making a campaign contribution to Donald Trump in 2016, or Marvel's character Howard the Duck running for president during America's bicentennial in 1976, the politics of comics have overlapped with the politics of campaigns and governance.

INTRODUCTION

THE POLITICAL IS THE POP CULTURAL

During a speech at a political fundraising dinner in October 2008, Senator Barack Obama alluded to the story of Superman, saying, "Contrary to the rumors you have heard, I was not born in a manger. I was actually born on Krypton and sent here by my father, Jor-El, to save the planet Earth" (CBS/AP 2008, para. 2). In the early months of his presidential bid in 2015, Donald Trump told a nine-year-old boy during a campaign stop in Iowa, "I am Batman," in an apparent comparison between his wealth, showcased by the customized Sikorsky S-76B helicopter in which he arrived, and the wealth and technology commanded by billionaire Bruce Wayne, aka Batman (Lake 2015, para. 30). These moments highlighted what numerous news, media, and academic sources have proclaimed: US politics is not merely intertwined with popular culture, it *is* popular culture (Thompson 2018; Moses 2017; Seaquist 2017; Grady 2017; Taveira 2016; Berthiaume 2015; Rubin 2013). As Trevor Parry-Giles and Shawn J. Parry-Giles (2006), in *The Prime-Time Presidency*, note, "Politics comes from a variety of sources; political meaning is derived from a myriad of texts and discourse" (5). The comments of Obama and Trump suggest that some of these sources of political meaning include comic books and their multimedia adaptations.

Recognizing what political scientist Murray Edelman referred to as the "multivocal" aspect of American politics, a growing number of political communication and media scholars are pursuing a more complete understanding of American political processes and institutions, particularly the presidency, by giving attention to political texts and discourses that circulate and contribute to cultural meaning beyond the campaigns, news media, and academe (Edelman 1995, 66; Parry-Giles and Parry-Giles 2006; also, Holbert, Pillion et al 2003; Holbert, Tschida et al 2005). These studies ably demonstrate that the public receives political information and democratic sensibilities from a variety of news *and* entertainment content, mostly agreeing that there is considerable democratic value in the inextricable link between politics and popular culture (Foy 2008). They find that pop culture artifacts open broader dialogues on civic matters and thus motivate, educate, and connect the public to political issues and systems (e.g., Brewer and Cao 2006; Eveland Jr. 2002; Holbert, Shah, and Kwak 2004; Holbert, Shah, and Kwak 2003; Moy and Pfau 2000; Niven, Lichter, and Amundson 2003; Pfau, Moy, and Szabo 2001; Shah 1998; Young 2004).

Fictional or fictionalized presidencies found in film, television, and print "regularly engage serious issues and define presidential leadership in powerful and meaningful ways, reflecting the cultural preoccupation with this [government] institution and its place in our national culture" (Parry-Giles and Parry-Giles 2006, 2). Representations of the presidency "frequently offer audiences new realities of this political institution or new renditions of the biographies of the men who have served as America's chief executive," contributing to the range of representational texts that exist in political and public discourse (Parry-Giles and Parry-Giles 2006, 4). Fictional presidencies are thought to both epitomize and shape Americans' views of a model leader, while also revealing the histories of the nation and people (Smith 2009). This leader is honorable yet personable, effective yet flawed, historically aware yet relationally sensitive, trusting yet shrewd, and decisive yet reflective, who acts predominately like a chief executive rather than a private citizen or political candidate (Phalen, Kim, and Osellame 2012; Holbert, Tschida et al 2005). And, even if this person is female, their presidency reinforces the White, militaristic masculinity that has always been central to the executive branch of the US government (Parry-Giles and Parry-Giles 2006; Semmler, McKay-Semmler, and Robertson 2013). Such entertainment further provides audiences with a rare behind-the-scenes look at the Oval Office (Holbert, Pillion et al 2003). Meanwhile, fictionalized accounts of real presidents often suggest popular sentiments and concerns of the time (Smith 2009).

These compelling presidential depictions are seen in feature films, such as *Dave, My Fellow Americans, The American President, Air Force One,* and *Independence Day.* They are also seen in television programming, such as *The West Wing, House of Cards, Commander in Chief, Veep,* and *1600 Penn.* Writing in the *International Journal of Communication,* Cornelia Brantner and Katharine Lobinger claimed that "comics representing a new form of interrelation between political content and popular culture have [recently] emerged" in which political actors serve as the primary protagonists and/or political issues comprise the foundation for the story (2014, 250). They highlight 2008 election comics from IDW featuring Barack Obama and John McCain, but such political comics emerged long before the twenty-first century.

One of the earliest full-length political comic books known is *Centennial Congress—1876 Democratic House of Representatives Illustrated by Cash Thomas* (BOOT 2016; see figure 0.1). In 1928, the Hoover campaign benefitted from the use of a biographical comic book, *Picture Life of a Great American,* by Bob "Sat" Satterfield (Dinschel n.d.). The same year, Augustus Mutt, of Bud Fisher's *Mutt and Jeff* became the first comics character to run for president (Cronin 2016). The likes of Pogo, Superman and Lex Luthor, Wonder Woman, Howard the Duck, Captain America and Red Skull, Thor and Loki, Dr. Doom, Alvin of Alvin and the Chipmunks, Bullwinkle Moose, and Daffy Duck joined Mutt as presidential candidates in the decades that followed. Since 1942, actual presidents, too, have been depicted in numerous types of comics, from propaganda and biographies to superhero and fantasy, and in numerous ways, from cameos to central characters, and from supporting players to heroic leads (Weiner and Barba 2012). According to the ComicVine wiki, as of June 2020, the White House appears in more than 950 comic book titles. Despite this, Brantner and Lobinger are correct in their assessment that while "a vast literature exists on ideological and political messages in comics" and "on social and political commentary in editorial cartoons," explicit representations of politics in comics and strategic uses of comics as political communication have received comparatively little scholarly attention (2014, 248–49). Other studies of strategic use of comics as political communication include Wodak and Forchter (2014), Mahrt (2008/2009), and Scott and Parks (1992).

The studies that exist on the intersection of politics and comics effectively demonstrate the culturally significant capacity of comics to present ideologies and compelling political dramas with the ability to garner mass media attention and a broad audience. Research further indicates that comics, particularly superhero comics, act as proxies for particular geopolitical identities and

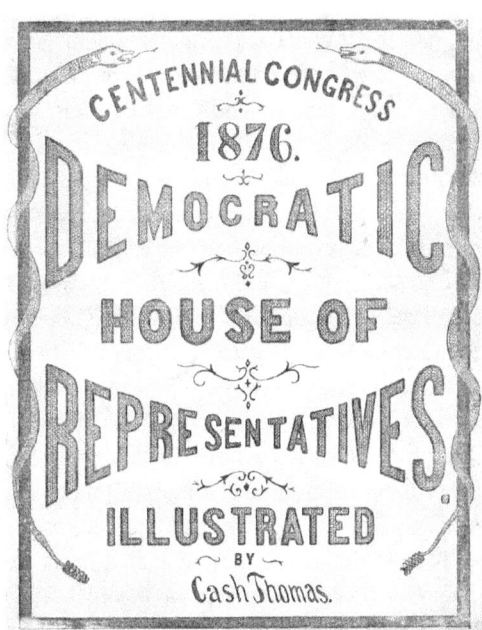

Figure 0.1. The cover of an early politically focused comic book, the *Centennial Congress—1876 Democratic House of Representatives Illustrated by Cash Thomas*.

civic virtues (Dittmer 2013). "Superheroes are routinely represented as models of right action and feeling. [. . .] anti-heroes illustrate what thoughtful citizens concerned with justice should do" (Wanzo 2009, 93). Their physiques and appearances embody their ideals and environments (Round 2008).

As Marc DiPaolo (2011) observes in *War, Politics, and Superheroes*, while the multimedia texts produced from comic book narratives have often been marketed to "children and adolescents, their content is often far more serious than their reputations would suggest." In fact, DiPaolo notes, since the publishing debut of *Superman* in 1938, "comic books have always been political, and have taken stands on controversial issues such as the death penalty, abortion, gay rights, and the environment," while reflecting the public's mood of an era and also serving as a voice for the minority (loc. 390–95).

Solidifying the political importance of comic books, well-known comic book characters and titles are regularly lent to certain causes for raising funds and/or awareness, such as the 2016 Orlando Pulse nightclub shooting, the Deepwater Horizon oil spill, and UNICEF, as well as to presidential initiatives for physical fitness and drug prevention. Wonder Woman even briefly served as an honorary ambassador to the United Nations for the empowerment of women and girls. "During election years, grass-roots campaigners like to co-opt copyrighted superhero imagery, largely because superheroes are so iconic and recognizable, as a means of making a political point" (DiPaolo 2011, loc. 471–72). In 2004, John Kerry supporters illegally used an image of Marvel's Spider-Man on buttons distributed in Manhattan. In 2008, a website supported and promoted the fictional Batman for the actual presidency; eight years later, Batman received a notable number of write-in votes in both Florida and Indiana. In 2016, supporters of Libertarian presidential candidate Gary Johnson created a YouTube video/ad that compared America to Batman's home of Gotham City, casting Hillary Clinton as the mob and Donald Trump as the villain Joker, with Johnson as "freaking Batman." In 2018, a hotly contested election in Ontario, Canada, saw lawn signs promoting the election of *Superman* villain General Zod for the province's premier. And in 2020, police donned the iconic skull logo of Marvel's antihero vigilante the Punisher during the George Floyd and Black Lives Matter protests (DiPaolo 2011; Kennedy 2016; Evans 2016; Stanley 2016; Couto 2018; Drum 2020).

In early 2019, freshman congressional representative Alexandria Ocasio-Cortez (D-NY), better known as AOC, caused a Twitter stir when she quoted the Rorschach character from *Watchmen* when responding to an article in *Politico* about the frustration her older colleagues felt about her outspoken tendencies. AOC quipped, "To quote Alan Moore: 'None of you understand. I'm not locked up in here with YOU. You're locked up in here with ME'" (in Papenfuss 2019, para. 3). And 2020 Democratic presidential candidate and bestselling self-help book author Marianne Williamson posted a *Neon Genesis Evangelion* meme on

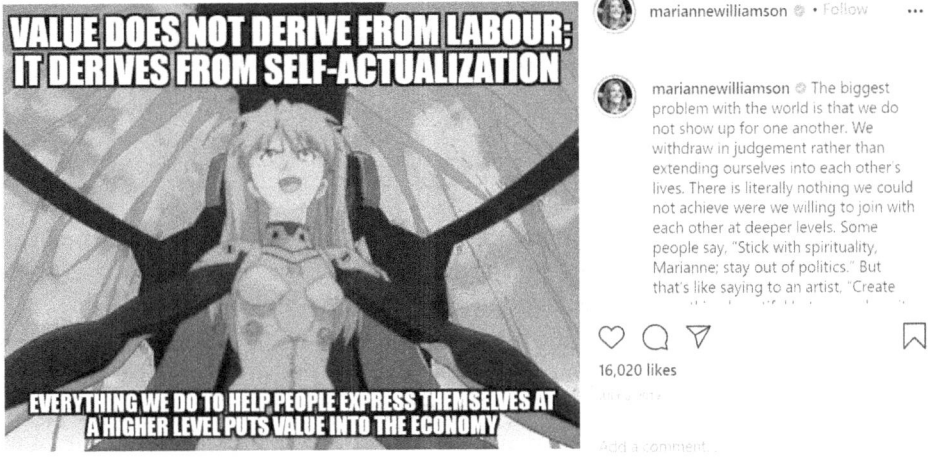

Figure 0.2. Screenshot of 2020 Democratic presidential candidate Marianne Williamson's *Neon Genesis Evangelion* meme posted on Instagram in early July 2019.

Facebook and Instagram, in which Williamson set her own words to an image of the Japanese mecha anime's character Asuka within a blood-spattered cockpit during a fight (see figure 0.2).

Paste Magazine observed a "certain kind of mentality in American politics" rising on the liberal left that perceives politics as a comic book narrative of conflict between villains in the opposing party and heroes of anyone who stands up to them (Ryan 2019, para. 2). The Trump campaign seemingly embraced the role of the villain in this ideological conflict. In December 2019, the campaign's "Trump War Room" Twitter account responded to the impeachment probe against the president with a a video mashup featuring Trump as Thanos—Marvel's genocidal antagonist to Captain America and the Avengers superhero team. The *New York Post* described the video:

> [. . .] instead of wiping out half the universe with the snap of a finger—like [Thanos] at the end of "Avengers: Infinity War"—Team Trump's version of the fictional character wipes out the Democrats leading the impeachment proceedings. [. . .]
>
> When the Trump-Thanos hybrid snaps his finger, the clip cuts to the [. . .] press conference where the House Democrats announced their articles of impeachment against the president.
>
> House Speaker Nancy Pelosi is seen behind the podium, saying, "On this solemn day, I recall the first order of business to members of . . ." before her voice gets drowned out by a growing gust of wind accompanied by a dark mass.
>
> The ominous mass then sweeps across the screen, leaving nothing in its wake. (Garger 2019, paras. 1–6).

Six months earlier, Thanos actor Josh Brolin had appeared on *The Late Show with Stephen Colbert* to read some of Donald Trump's tweets in the voice of Thanos, the "Mad Titan," complicating questions of political intent and actual impact (Graham 2018).

◆ ◆ ◆

The purpose of this volume is to contribute to the literature of politainment/entertaining politics studies by demonstrating the rich and relevant political content of comic books and their related media. It is written largely for scholars, teachers, and students of politics and campaigns in communication and political science, designed to familiarize audiences with the presidential and campaign content of comics and/or to prompt those audiences toward recognition of how comics reflect and shape our political knowledge and attitudes. As such, it makes efforts to explain or situate characters and genres for those who may be unfamiliar with these aspects of popular culture. It is also written for comics studies scholars and students, offering the perspective of rhetoric and political communication to the interpretation of comics content. As such, it tries to avoid belaboring explanations of major comics characters, genres, and tropes. It is also a book that will hopefully be of interest to political junkies and comics fans, potentially offering some interesting trivia, historical context, and suggested readings. As such, spoilers are avoided whenever possible, but this overview should serve as a spoiler warning.

The titles, themes, and genres explored and analyzed in this volume are many. It is certainly not all-inclusive of politically focused or politically important comic texts; indeed, during the creation of the volume, new comics were being regularly released starring Donald Trump, Bernie Sanders, Alexandria Ocasio-Cortez, Barack Obama, and Michael Mueller, and the politically-charged environment of 2017 through 2020 meant that many more fictional characters were entering the presidential fray as the book was completed in 2020. Despite not being fully inclusive, the study does strive to be wide-ranging, including as many genres, characters, creators, politicians, and decades as possible, though no doubt there are comics fans reading this who will be dismayed by something that was omitted. The broad focus is meant to be both introductory for those unfamiliar with the variety of comics content and aesthetics, as well as indicative of the significance of presidential and campaign politics in the medium. Decisions about which texts received more or less attention in given chapters were often subjective judgements based on the perception of which plots were easier to explain, which books were more exemplary of the themes, and which titles were more accessible for thorough research.

Unpacking the political ideologies of comic books is complex. Many comics are created by teams, and the creative forces will change on long-running series.

Not all writers and artists make their political leanings public. What's more, readers are free to interpret stories in their own way (DiPaolo 2011). Even critics are undecided as to whether comic books more often project conservative or liberal ideologies, or whether they uphold or challenge the status quo (McAllister 1990). The visuals have the trappings of right-wing masculine power fantasies with White, muscle-bound male heroes, though many stories are underpinned with progressive ideals, such as equity and inclusion, and/or are written by self-described liberals (DiPaolo 2011). Matthew J. Costello referred to this combination as "liberalism with a fascist aesthetic" (2009, 215). This book, however, focuses less on ideologies and more on what comics have to say about political structures and processes. Comics under consideration are those wherein political actors serve as major protagonists or antagonists of the narrative.

Comic books are an art form and a mass medium with considerable reach. Since 1997, sales of the top 300 comic book titles have ranged from 4,402,000 copies per month to an excess of 9,360,000 copies in a single month. Sales for all comic titles in a single month have passed 10,260,000 ("Industry Wide Records" n.d.). Comic book-based multimedia expands the medium's reach through video games, television and streaming service programs, and major motion pictures; the Marvel Comics film *Black Panther* earned nearly $700 million in the domestic box office (Mendelson 2018). Furthermore, comic books have an established place within public dialogue and political discourses. From a critical standpoint, they offer a popular yet complicated vision of the American political tableau. This project examines the political myths, moments, and mimeses in comic books—from nonfiction to science-fiction, superhero to horror, dramatic to satirical, Golden Age to present day—to consider how they represent, re-present, underpin, and/or undermine ideas and ideals about American electoral politics.

Ideological criticism will guide the discussion, premised on Parry-Giles and Parry-Giles's argument that "to completely appreciate the ideological meaning of the presidency requires engagement with the vast collection of discourses that also figure in the cultural meaning of the office and the people who occupy it" (2006, 3). Ideological criticism may be "broadly defined as criticism that begins from motivational warrants" (Crowley 1992, 452). Recognizing implicit, powerful vested interests at work in communication, the critic seeks to "demystify the discourse of power" (McKerrow 1989, 91; Wander 1983). Works that can be understood as dramatizing a social or political conflict are appropriate for ideological analysis, keeping in mind how the text fits into the wider context—though any and every rhetorical artifact arguably has an evaluative position on some subject simply because of the choices made in its creation. "The most basic assumption of ideological analysis of comics may simply be that the characters, places, and events in fictional comic book stories can *represent* actual people, places and events," artistically taking sides in, and perhaps imagining resolution to, conflict (Rifas 2012, 225).

Ideological criticism is not bound to a standardized approach, and in practice is multiple kinds of criticisms. There are, however, some structural elements that provide a framework for analysis. Ideologies are composed of three interrelated components: cognition, involving systems of ideas shared in groups; society, referring to how idea systems promote group interests; and discourse, comprising the communication of those ideas (Van Dijk 1998). For the ideological critic, discourse may be understood as presented elements, the basic observable features of an artifact, and suggested elements, the references and concepts associated with those features. By identifying patterns, considering imbedded logic, or examining aspects of group practices and structures revealed in the suggested elements, the critic can articulate the inherent ideology of an artifact (Foss 2009).

Critical postmodern rhetorical theory contends that texts can be playful with various meanings and are open to multiple forms of understandings, allowing the critic to make sense from the various appropriations of discourses on the postmodern experience (Ceccarelli 1998; McKerrow 1991). Furthermore, comics must be understood in light of both their verbal and visual content, as well as the interplay between the words and images. Given the wide variety of texts considered in the analysis here, multiple critical approaches are engaged, as appropriate. Therefore, the ideological critique is further informed by image function analysis, semiotics, intertextual analysis, and generative criticism.

Image function analysis recognizes that images work in comics not only as a means of showing the story, but also as commentary on, direction to, or insight into the story. It is guided by the further assumptions that images on the page result from creator intention and that the meaning an audience derives from the images may not coincide with that intention. There are three categories of images that accomplish these tasks. Sensory diegetic images show the physical reality of the story world. Non-sensory diegetic images show the internal reality of the story's characters. Hermeneutic images are separate from the story world; they are the author's commentary on the story, often attempting to influence reader interpretation. Because these hermeneutic images are an important agency/technique for conveying subtext, they are the focus of image function analysis (Duncan 2012). Hermeneutics acknowledges the integrative nature of analysis, wherein the critic recognizes the significance and relationships of noted elements (Bontekoe 1996). The first step in image function analysis is to identify the significant hermeneutic images, as suggested by frequency or by significance to pivotal story points. Hermeneutic images, or their variation, that are repeatedly used become a visual motif, often relevant to the narrative's theme. Once these images have been identified, the second step of analysis is determining how they function in contributing to the meaning of the story (Duncan 2012).

tion, environmental destruction, international strife, domestic terrorism, and impeachment, *Prez*, in just four issues, presented a bleak outlook on American politics, one that resonated across four decades with nine different iterations of the Prez character. Prez's themes of alienation and disaffection, competing with themes of hope and commitment, further resonate throughout major deconstructionist comic works of the 1980s, such as *Watchmen*, and became integral to much of the work of writer Mark Russell in the 2010s.

Chapter five continues the exploration of critical comic book commentary by focusing on satirical comics, or modern "funny books," with explicitly political subject matter. Arguing that the polyvalent nature of satire makes many political comics ineffective modes of persuasion, it highlights the 1986 series *Reagan's Raiders* and its 2017 takeoff, *Trump's Titans*, as examples of satire so absurd that readers cannot decipher its meaning. By comparison, the single-paneled editorial cartoon is lauded, even as it loses ground as an industry, for its ability to offer new visions of campaigns and candidates, clarifying obscure values and images, with impact and resonance.

The intermedia phenomenon of the 9/11 terrorist attacks provide the basis for chapter six, which examines graphic novel adaptations of government reports, including the so-called 9/11 Report, Torture Report, Mueller Report, Trump-Russia Memos, and Warren Commission Report, as well as other examples of comics journalism that have focused on campaigns and presidential politics. Building on studies of comics journalism, the chapter argues that graphic reportage offers readers context to aid in the consumption and comprehension of complex and emotionally challenging material and that the medium is particularly adept at enabling underrepresented voices and gaining recognition for narrative as a mode of knowing.

The 2004 election became infamous for widespread voter disenfranchisement and fraud, leading to the creation and publication of *Cheated!*, which chronicled voter experiences in Ohio. Chapter seven subsequently looks at *Cheated!* and other comics that engage with voting, elections, and civic responsibilities. Relating these themes to "good government" and activist comics of the 1950s and 1960s, the chapter explores representations of American elections as related to narratives of quests and conspiracies that express the realization or frustration of political ideals.

Women took center stage during the 2008 presidential election with the campaigns of Hillary Clinton and Sarah Palin, sparking a cottage industry of comic books that are the focus of chapter eight. Drawing on metaphoric clusters used by the media to frame female politicians, the chapter provides a historical look at real and imagined political women of comics and cartoons, from Victoria Woodhull to Betty Boop, and from Wonder Woman to Michelle Obama. Recognizing that both American comic book culture and American political culture have historically been male-dominated spaces, these females are doubly disadvantaged.

American comics culture and political culture are not only traditionally masculine realms, but they are also traditionally White realms. Yet, in 2008, Barack Obama, a Black man, took both by storm. Chapter nine discusses the politician of color, both real and fictional, in comic books, analyzing how the Whiteness of the presidency interacts with the Whiteness of the superhero genre when the protagonist is not White. The chapter considers some of Obama's many comic book appearances and cameos, as well as the non-White presidencies featured in *Treasure Chest*, *Saucer State*, *Prez*, and *Eagle*, plus other politicians of color to appear in comics, including Herman Cain, Condoleezza Rice, Colin Powell, John Lewis, and Marco Rubio.

Chapter ten brings the discussion up to the end of the 2010s, looking at the Donald Trump presidency and the many comparisons in popular media made between Trump and comic book supervillains. Whereas chapter three considers the mythmaking of presidents-as-superheroes, and superheroes-as-presidents, this chapter critiques the allure of toxic leaders through the many successful attempts by villains, such as Lex Luthor, Red Skull, and Loki, to assume the mantle of president. The chapter suggests that villains and other toxic leaders are appealing because of their ambition and because right and wrong, good and bad, are often matters of perspective and context.

In chapter eleven, comics look back at American political history through presidential allohistories—fictionalized, reimagined, or reinterpreted versions of historical record in forms that can be considered speculative fiction. The chapter primarily focuses on several "punk" histories: steampunk, dieselpunk, and biopunk accounts of wartime presidents and eras, among them Abraham Lincoln, Theodore Roosevelt, Woodrow Wilson, and the Cold War of Franklin D. Roosevelt through Lyndon B. Johnson. It argues that nostalgia plays a large role in the shape of these accounts, and in current political debates, continuing to reinforce the American presidency as an inherently White and masculine institution.

These chapters, the topics they represent, and the texts they consider are not mutually exclusive. Readers will encounter some comics discussed across several chapters, so involved are their political narratives and so numerous are their political lessons. Likewise, some analytical themes recur throughout, and these may perhaps be the book's key findings, as discussed in more detail in the book's conclusion. Across decades and genres, comic book audiences will encounter: depictions of the presidency specifically and the American political arena more broadly as a distinctly White, masculine realm in which women, nonbinary individuals, and people of color are oddities at best and suspect or un-American at worst; and, political cynicism and disaffection, tempered by hope and optimism, frequently expressed through conspiracy narratives that work to uncover the truth and/or achieve justice. These findings are consistent with previous research on politics in entertainment media finding that pop culture artifacts open broader dialogues on civic matters and thus motivate, educate, and connect the public to political issues and systems (Foy 2008); that fictional presidencies epitomize and shape Americans' views of a model leader, while also revealing the histories and present concerns of the nation (Smith 2009); that this vision of the president is of a person who is, essentially, both hero and villain and both representative and individual (Phalen, Kim, and Osellame 2012; Holbert, Tschida et al 2005); and that the president either embodies or enacts tough, White masculinity (Parry-Giles and Parry-Giles 2006; Parry-Giles and Parry-Giles 2002; Semmler, McKay-Semmler, and Robertson 2013).

So, if comics are just offering more of the same, then, why do they matter and why should we care about them? The answer is because audiences will learn these messages differently through comics. Comics engender a different kind of literacy that improves both verbal intelligence and visual skills while strengthening the mind (Riggs 2016). Research points specifically to how comics enable political learning. A 2019 article in *PS: Political Science and Politics* found that civics students better understood complex political information with visual, rather than just verbal, depictions of difficult texts (Owens, Eno, Abrams, and Bedney 2019). Comics are also important because they are as often proactive as they are reactive in their political content. From the time Captain America punched Hitler in the face nine months *before* Pearl Harbor and the United States' entrance into World War II, comics have not only depicted current trends but also the trajectory of those trends. In the chapters that follow, for example, you will discover comics that portrayed foreign interference in presidential elections forty years before Russia's influence in the 2016 election, comics that featured Donald Trump's *The Art of the Deal* months, even years, before his 2015 campaign announcement, and comics that made Mexican immigration the central focus of elections years before anyone chanted "build that wall" at a political rally.

POLITICS IN THE GUTTERS

HEY, VOTERS! COMICS!
CAMPAIGN COMICS, ELECTION SPECIALS, AND GRAPHIC BIOGRAPHIES

During the 1948 presidential campaign, the polls, the pundits, and the news outlets all agreed that the Republican nominee, New York Governor Thomas Dewey, would defeat incumbent President Harry S. Truman. Even Bess Truman believed her husband would lose the election. Nevertheless, the Democratic National Committee (DNC) worked to build support for their candidate through branding and storytelling. As part of their strategy, they issued a sixteen-page graphic biography of Truman's life, *The Story of Harry S. Truman*. The DNC released more than three million copies in October, just weeks before the election, targeting farmers, African Americans, labor unions, and veterans—the groups most likely to swing their vote to Truman. The comic, written by Malcolm Ater, summarized Truman's life from his birth in 1884 to his role as president towards the end of World War II and after. Although there is no way to know the extent of influence the comic book had, Truman's win by a margin of 1,188,054 votes is conceivably covered by the three million recipients of the graphic biography (Truman Library Institute 2016).

Truman was not the first political candidate, nor even the first president, to use a comic book as part of his campaign strategy. In 1928, Bob "Sat" Satterfield produced a prototype comic book for Herbert Hoover's presidential bid. A series of eighteen pages, each containing a four-panel narrative about Hoover's life, was published by Allied Printing in Washington, DC, as *Picture Life of a Great American*—though it was more likely read by many Americans serialized in their local newspapers (Scott and Parks 1992; Dinschel n.d.). Four years later, an anti-Hoover political comic book by cartoonist Frederick Opper promoted the election of Franklin Delano Roosevelt, *'Erbie and 'Is Playmates*, featuring Opper's famous characters Happy Hooligan, Alfonse, and Gaston (BOOT 2016). Truman's 1948 comic book message, however, was the first to truly recognize and tap into the potential of the medium. The comic book format was popularized in 1938 with the creation of Superman in *Action Comics*, and World War II helped contribute to a large and eager marketplace for the medium.[1] By 1948, more than sixty million comic books were being sold each month, and many of the readers were veterans who used comic books as entertainment in the war and were now key votes for politicians (Scott and Parks 1992; Truman Library Institute 2016). By 1950, one out of four adults read comics, and four out of every five *urban* adults read comics; comic audiences were spread throughout all levels of society, though a higher percentage of the college-educated read them than those with a grade-school education; and comic book readers were also more likely to spend more time listening to the radio, reading magazines, and attending movies than those who did not read comics (Dirksen Congressional Center Staff n.d.).

Recognizing comics' reach, the Truman comic was used as a model for US Senator Scott Lucas's (D-IL) 1950 campaign against Republican challenger Everett M. Dirksen. The Illinois Democratic State Central Committee produced a sixteen-page graphic biography that told a story of Lucas's ancestors, his early life of hardship, his education and law practice, and his public service, from election to the House and then Senate to his role as US Senate Majority Leader and his stance on campaign issues. Scripted by Malcolm Ater and produced by Commercial Comics, just like Truman's graphic biography, the comic had a press run of one million at a cost of $13,250—well beyond the means of the Dirksen campaign. In the ensuing years, at least twenty more politicians—in races ranging from lieutenant governor of Louisiana to president of the Philippines—had campaign comics created by Ater's Commercial Comics. Alabama Governor John Patterson used comics twice, supposedly convincing his opponent George Wallace to eventually team with Ater to create "Alabama Needs the Little Judge, George Wallace for the Big Job" (Dirksen Congressional Center Staff n.d.; Christopher n.d.). This comic, with a strong pro-segregation message, is credited as a key factor in Wallace's win and his rise to become one of the South's most iconic opponents to civil rights (Persoff 2007). By one account, seven out of ten candidates who used Ater's Commercial Comics as part of their campaign messages won their elections (BOOT 2016). The medium was so popular during the 1950s and into the early 1960s that Dwight Eisenhower used at least four comics in his two bids for president and, in Arkansas, even candidates for county-level seats had graphic biographies created and published by local newspapers (Scott and Parks 1992). Some of these comics, such as one for Richard Hughes in his bid for New Jersey governor, even had Spanish-language editions (Christopher n.d.).[2]

In the United States, comic books as campaign propaganda fell to the wayside as television gained in popularity. Sequential art, however, continued to be a powerful means of campaign communication. Political cartoons, recognized for their ability to offer new visions of campaigns or candidates, are part of the composite of political messages received by the public and have thus been embraced by politicians (Conners 2005; Morrison 1969). Not only did President Bill Clinton invite cartoonist Mike Luckovich aboard Air Force One during his 1996 re-election campaign, but President Donald Trump tweeted political cartoons as part of his communication with the public on multiple occasions (Conners 2005; Borchers 2018). In 2004, both the Republican and the Democratic National Committees issued political cartoons mocking their opponents (Conners 2005). Comic books, too, are still engaged in the electoral process, though they now more likely come from commercial entities separate from the candidates' official messages. Though there are presently relatively few studies that focus on comic books explicitly used for political communication, those that do adeptly demonstrate the potential of the medium as a culturally significant means of presenting compelling political dramas with the ability to garner a broad audience (Brantner and Lobinger 2014; Scott and Parks 1992; Weiner and Barba 2012; Yanes 2012; Dawe 2013; Mahrt 2008/2009). Moreover, comics studies regularly prove the capacity of comics to both challenge and legitimize political identities and ideologies (e.g., Berlatsky 2015; Devarenne 2008; Diebler 2006; DiPaolo 2011; Dittmer 2013; Wanzo 2009).

Beginning in 2009, TidalWave Productions (formerly Bluewater Productions), an independent comic book/graphic novel press based in Portland, Oregon, led the market with political biography titles. Mostly unauthorized, TidalWave's biographies attempted to leverage the power of celebrity in order to broaden their distribution reach. Their first foray into political biographies started in 2009 with the creation of *Female Force*, a series celebrating influential women in politics, media, and society, and *Political Power*, featuring past and present opinion leaders in politics, government, and media from the United States and around the world.

In 2015, TidalWave Productions started a special run of *Political Power* issues featuring the 2016 presidential candidates—from those that "also-ran" to those that voters wished had run, including Donald Trump, Hillary Clinton, Rand Paul, Jeb Bush, Marco Rubio, and Elizabeth Warren (Capps 2015). TidalWave publisher Darren Davis explained, "As a reluctant reader, I found the comic book form easy to access, so I always believed comics could both entertain and teach," thus he followed up on the 2016 Republican focus with attention to the Democrats in 2020 (in Marston 2020, para. 3). TidalWave both released new stories featuring candidates from the 2020 Democratic primary, including New York Mayor Michael Bloomberg and South Bend Mayor Peter Buttigieg, and promoted its older comics for candidates Vice President Joe Biden, Senator Elizabeth Warren, and Senator Bernie Sanders.

IDW, Antarctic Press, and BOOM! Studios have also been active publishers of political comics. BOOM! Studios created a special limited series entitled *Decision 2012*. Issues were planned for biographies of incumbent Barack Obama and potential Republican challengers Michelle Bachmann, Herman Cain, Newt Gingrich, Jon Huntsman, Sarah Palin, Ron Paul, Rick Perry, Mitt Romney, and Rick Santorum. The initiative was designed to engage voters in a comic book-driven straw poll whose winner was determined by preorders; those candidates earning fewer than 1,500 votes/orders were dropped from the race/publication (Khouri 2011). The poll resulted in the release of issues with nonpartisan biographies of Obama, Bachmann, Paul, and Palin. In 2008, IDW also created informative biography comics for the election: a two-volume set of comic biographies/graphic novellas in 2008 called *Presidential Material*. Written by Andrew Helfer from thorough research in public records, the books were released in October 2008, just a month before the election, to "provide a straight and unbiased look at the two presumptive party nominees"—Barack Obama and John McCain (IDW n.d.). Likewise, Antarctic Press, known more for political parody comic books such as *President Evil, Tremendous Trump*, and *Steampunk Palin*, Antarctic Press released *McCain: The Comic Book* and *Obama: The Comic Book* in 2008, with a special "inauguration edition" of *Obama* in 2009.

GOLDEN AGE CAMPAIGN COMICS

Campaign-produced graphic biographies frequently follow the same basic narrative formula: as observed by researchers Kim Allen Scott and Susan Parks, campaign comics of the 1950s and '60s typically offered a revelation of a candidate's humble origins, work ethic, athletic prowess, and military service. Humble origins were demonstrated through images of a rural life. A solid work ethic was established by showing the candidates doing both tough and menial labors, working as coal miners and lumberjacks or washing dishes to earn their way through school. Sports achievements and military service both provided campaign comics with action sequences (Scott and Parks 1992). Another common theme among many of the comics was an indication of the candidate's religious faith. Beyond these shared characteristics, comics varied in their presentation, responding to contemporary issues, sociopolitical climates, and biographical distinctions of their moments and subjects. Typically, the campaign comics opened with a vignette that established the importance of the civic moment and/or the unique accomplishments or strengths of the candidate.

President Hoover's 1928 campaign comic established his Quaker heritage, modest origins, athletic abilities, and responsible work ethic by the time he was ten—or, to put it another way, within just the first five of its eighteen pages. The first two pages, or eight panels, however, were not about Hoover but about his family and ancestry—Quakers from France and Holland who settled on farms in Maryland and eventually migrated to Iowa, founding the town of West Branch and making a "hard-earned living from the soil." Such qualities were shown to be both part of his heritage as well as America's. Such an opening was representative of Hoover's social philosophy, political principles, and historical place. He had an acute perception of the difference between the Old World, which he equated with the imperialism and social hierarchies of Europe, and the New World, which he saw as a place of equality and opportunity in accordance with his own upward mobility from rural orphan to engineer, humanitarian, and statesman (Nash 2003). Moreover, as Kendrick A. Clements (2010) suggests, Hoover served as a bridge between the nineteenth and twentieth centuries, shaped by a rural small-town life and working in the modern profession of engineering. All of this is reflected in the way *Picture Life of a Great American* establishes Hoover's family as hard-working European immigrant farmers before introducing Hoover himself as an enterprising youth (see figure 1.1).

Figure 1.1. These scenes from the Hoover campaign comic *Picture Life of a Great American* (1928) help to establish Hoover as a bridge between the nineteenth and twentieth centuries.

By comparison, President Truman's 1948 comic recognized the impact World War II had on comic book content and readership, opening not with Truman's ancestry or even his youth but with battle scenes from 1945, reflecting the imagery of mainstream comics in the years during and immediately following the

Figure 1.2. Scenes from *The Story of Harry S. Truman* (left) echo those of popular war comics of the era, such as that seen on the cover of *True Comics* #18 (right).

war (see figure 1.2). Against this action-packed setting, readers were taken to the announcement of Franklin D. Roosevelt's death and Truman's ascension from vice president to president. From there, the comic asked, "And what was the background of the new President?" and thusly introduced readers to Truman's forefathers who settled in western Missouri, where Truman himself was born and raised on a farm, attended church on Sundays, and became a bank clerk before enlisting to fight in the Great War. Truman's military experience provided two more action-packed pages of battle scenes highlighting Truman's own heroic derring-do. Such dramatic presentations of warfare, and candidates' participation in it, was a prominent feature of postwar campaign comics. This strategy responded to an electorate comprised of politically aware and engaged veterans who read comic books (Scott and Parks 1992; Duncan, Smith, and Levitz 2015).

George Wallace was elected governor of Alabama in 1962 (and made three unsuccessful bids for the presidency) and was known for supporting "segregation now, segregation tomorrow, segregation forever." Like the Truman comic's opening war sequence, Wallace's campaign comic opened with a vignette focused on the pressing political concerns of the election, the sociopolitical worldview of the readers, and the defining characteristic of the candidate: Wallace's comic began with a conversation between two citizens that offers a flashback to Wallace's fight for state rights, in order to uphold segregation in Alabama, against the federal government's civil rights commission in 1959. Following three and a half pages celebrating Wallace's defense of Alabama and segregation, the comic then became more biographical, telling readers about Wallace growing up in a Christian family, working on his father's farm, being a star student and multisport athlete in high school, and then flying combat missions in the Air Force when "Japan was being softened up for America's great victory" (Friends of George C. Wallace n.d.).

The campaign comic for Robert Meyner's 1953 New Jersey gubernatorial bid broke with the standard biographical formula. Rather than focusing solely on Meyner, it both named and attacked his opponents, going so far as to link them to organized crime (Christopher n.d.). Similarly, in Massachusetts, Governor Paul Dever's campaign produced a comic biography to tell his own story but also had comics designed to undermine his opponents. In 1950, the Dever campaign used *Man Against the People: The True Record of Arthur W. Coolidge*, which offered a comparison of the lives and political records of Dever and his opponent, former Massachusetts lieutenant governor Arthur Coolidge. The comic was prepared by a coalition of labor groups supporting Dever's reelection bid (Mount Holyoke n.d.). The cover described Arthur Coolidge as "a selfish politician who hides his true feelings behind a cloak of deception ... who pretends to work for the people but who really works only for his own 'state street' gang." The comic book then presented Coolidge voting against an investigation of unethical practices by electric companies, against regulating the rates of loan sharks, against simpler wording of questions on ballots, against absentee ballots for incapacitated voters, against increased unemployment benefits, against protection for pregnant workers, against increased worker disability payments, and against an array of veteran benefits—before losing the gubernatorial race to Paul Dever. Next, the comic contrasted Coolidge's negative actions with Devers's positive record in favor of working people. A similar campaign comic book was released on behalf of Dever in 1952: *The Career of a Reactionary in Politics: A Life Story of Christian Archibald Herter*. The comic, published by Massachusetts United Labor, criticized Herter's political record, encouraging readers to vote for Dever instead (Conolly 2017).

The US government also occasionally used biographical comic books to introduce politicians to readers. During World War II, a comic book telling the life story of President Franklin Delano Roosevelt was produced by the Office of War Information in at least six different languages for distribution to American allies (BOOT 2016; Kimble and Goodnow 2017). In 1961, the government distributed *John F. Kennedy: New U.S. President* to US embassies to introduce the newly elected president to the worldwide public (BOOT 2016). The comic revealed Kennedy's childhood, upbringing, activities, education, military service during World War II, and entrance into politics.

CONTEMPORARY ELECTION COMICS

A modern twist on campaign comics occurred in a 2017 race for a seat in the New York State Assembly. Democratic candidate Keith Batman, from Cayuga County in Assembly District 126, capitalized on the spelling of his last name to promote himself as a crusader and a hero for the people. A series of campaign mailers were designed with comic book style elements: frames and gutters, speech balloons, explosive borders, and pointillistic backgrounds reminiscent of the four-color printing process originally used in comic production. Headlines proclaimed, "Batman is the hero we need" and "A hero we can count on." The campaign logo resembled the Bat signal: a pale yellow oval behind bold black lettering declaring, "Elect Keith Batman." Yard signs used yellow font on a black background, mimicking the modern costume colors of DC's Batman. Keith Batman's campaign website, www.batmanforassembly.org, opened with the candidate's explanation "I don't have a cave lair or rocket propelled batmobile. I'm not that kind of Batman"—though the site *did* boast a digital "batcave" which offered voters Batman-inspired images to show their support, with iconography and illustrations based on the 1966 television version of Batman, *Lego Batman*, *Batman the Animated Series*, and more.

Two years later, Jaime Harrison (2019) announced his candidacy for the US Senate in South Carolina with a YouTube ad called "Character." The three-minute commercial opened with the following words: "Comic books. That's how I learned to read." In the first thirty-seconds of the ad, the visuals blended black-and-white drawings, full-color illustrations, photographs—some of which were colorized to give them a newsprint look—and video footage. Images were framed by heavy black borders and transitions moved from one frame to another, mimicking the reading of a comic page. The voiceover was duplicated in a narration box at the bottom of the screen (see figure 1.3). Following a brief cut to Harrison, the comic book aesthetic returned at the one-minute mark, when the ad framed Harrison's opponent, Lindsey Graham (R-SC), as a comic book villain. By using colorized footage of Graham with animated effects, all set within the frames of a comic page, the ad highlighted the politician's pandering as villainy.

Most modern political comics, however, are not produced by the campaigns but are instead commercial enterprises. BOOM! Studios' *Decision 2012* comic books frequently offered content similar to the elements found in campaign comics of the 1950s. For example, the first pages of the book for Ron Paul, a

Figure 1.3. A series of screen shots from the 2019 Jaime Harrison Senate campaign video "Character" show how Harrison used comic book aesthetics to tell his story.

retired congressional representative from Texas and 2012 presidential candidate, introduced him as the son of a dairy farmer who earned money in his youth by finding dirty milk bottles, delivering newspapers, mowing lawns, painting, and delivering furniture. At school, he was president of the student council, a wrestler, a football player, a baseball player, a swimmer, and a runner; the comic's visuals underscored his athleticism with a panel depicting his win of 220-yard dash in a state track championship. The comic also featured Ron Paul wearing his air force and then air national guard uniform, before quickly introducing his work in public service, indicating that "after three presidential campaigns and 12 terms in Congress, Ron Paul continues to make an effort to ensure that his ideas match his actions as closely and consistently as possible" (Kotz and Moore 2011). The Barack Obama edition likewise gave a nod to the challenges of Obama's youth and humble beginnings, to his athletic ability in basketball, and to his life in public service.

The issues for Republican politicians Michele Bachman and Sarah Palin in the *Decision 2012* series followed a similar format, noting humble origins: Palin's working-class parents, Bachmann's broken family and financial hardships, athleticism, and public service. Bachmann's comic even worked in a nod to the military by showing her father in an air force uniform. There was, however, a notable difference in how the athleticism of the women was depicted compared to their male counterparts. Palin's noted athletic activities included childhood and teenage pastimes of game hunting, ice fishing, hiking, running, and basketball. However, whereas Ron Paul was depicted actively running, and winning, a race, and Obama was portrayed making a jump shot over the head of an opposing player, Palin was shown standing still while holding up fresh-caught fish and, again, standing poised to take a foul-shot on the basketball court. Active panels of *others*—hockey and football players—were reserved for a discussion of Palin's push, as mayor of Wasilla, Alaska, for the construction of a multi-use sports complex. Similarly, Michele Bachmann's edition of *Decision 2012* remarked that Bachmann was a cheerleader, but it showed her only striking a pose in her cheerleading uniform for a photograph rather than actively cheering.

Overall, commercial comics are longer and tend to offer more context than their campaign counterparts. The election comics of 2008 published by IDW, for example, focused on the biographical elements most central to the creation of the political careers and public personas of Democratic nominee Obama and Republican nominee McCain. Such featured traits included Obama's biracial, international heritage and McCain's military service. *Presidential Material: Barack Obama* was structurally reminiscent of the campaign comics of the 1950s in that it opened in the contemporary moment, offering a seemingly private glimpse of Obama on Super Tuesday during the primary elections, and used that event as the impetus to look back at how he had gotten there, starting with his birth on August 4, 1961. *Presidential Material: John McCain* did not open in the present-day but still resembled Golden Age campaign comics in that it drew from McCain's naval service during America's war in Vietnam to offer action-packed panels—thirteen pages of them. Both books were written from research in news sources as well as the candidates' own autobiographies and examined their political strengths and weaknesses as candidates. Antarctic's 2008 election comics more directly engaged candidate platforms by providing a bulleted list of the candidates' goals on the inside front covers, while the main storylines still featured standard biographies focusing on McCain's military service and Obama's biracial heritage.

The *Political Power* series, both contemporary/election-focused and historical/retrospective, frequently emphasized familial influences on politicians: the teachings of New Jersey Governor Chris Christie's mother, Senator Marco Rubio's (R-FL) Cuban grandfather, Herman Cain's inspirational father, Florida Governor Jeb Bush's dynastic political family, the connections among Representative Michele Bachmann's (R-MN) roles as wife, mother, and politician, Senator Rand Paul's (R-KY) upbringing, the relationship between Donald Trump and his father, Vice President Al Gore's childhood inside the Washington, DC, political universe. While some aspects of *Political Power* are similar to campaign comic biographies—such as scenes depicting Gore's military service in Vietnam, a mention of Trump's work ethic and an action panel of him dribbling a basketball down court, an image of a young Christie in a baseball uniform, and panels filled with text and images of Rubio's football aspirations and career—the stories were often framed with dramatic and fantastic vignettes comparable to mainstream superhero comic book genres.

The Obama issue of *Political Power* opens with a depiction of the president as "an idealized superman" lifting the entire Capitol building over his head, his appearance an allusion drawn from Superman's red and blue cape and tights and Alex Ross's "Time for a Change" portrait (Ward and Akberali 2009). Bachmann's issue refers to her as "something of a superhero," calling on the cultural ideal of the supermom juggling a family with a law career (Cooke and Kars 2012). Both the Rand Paul and the FBI Director James Comey comic books were described in the press as superheroic, establishing Rand Paul's "moral arc" and Comey's "origin story" (Capps 2015, para. 4; Hibbard 2018, headline). Gore's story begins with a narrator in an alternate universe in which Gore won the 2000 election, ratified the Kyoto Treaty, put programs in motion to minimize the impact of climate change, provided universal healthcare, and saw the development of flying cars powered by water. The Jeb Bush comic opens in 1918 with Prescott Bush participating in mysterious and macabre rites of the Skull and Bones Society. Christie's story is told through a conversation he has with the ghost of New Jersey and her companion, Stephen Crane's specter of the black hound, in the aftermath of Hurricane Sandy. Special collections for the 2012 and 2016 elections brought together the individual issues of candidates in special volumes: *Political Power: Romney Obama 2012* and *Political Power: Election 2016—Clinton, Bush, Trump, Sanders, Paul*.

Female Force, from the same publication company as *Political Power*, was similar in style and substance, but with a deliberate "female empowerment angle" (CBS 2016, para. 5). Inspired by the 2008 election comics on McCain and Obama, the first four *Female Force* biographies featured Alaska Governor Sarah Palin, Secretary of State and former Senator (D-NY) Hillary Clinton, First Lady Michelle Obama, and First Daughter Caroline Kennedy. The comics were intended to be biographical, not fictional or political, focused on providing "as much information and journalism [. . .] as possible," drawn from cited research (CBS 2016, para. 8). The original series writer, Neal Bailey observed, "All four of these women, to be frankly honest, were people I underestimated before I studied them. Why? Because I live, and you live, and we live in a world of sound bytes [sic]" (Bailey and Howe 2009).

Eventually, the series encompassed female entertainers and authors, such as Cher and J.K. Rowling, but it also continued to highlight politicians, including Representative Gabrielle Giffords (D-AZ), Supreme Court Associate Justice Ruth Bader Ginsberg, Speaker of the House Nancy Pelosi (D-CA), First Lady Nancy Reagan, and Secretary of State Condoleezza Rice. In February 2020, *Female Force* also featured Stormy Daniels, the adult-film star at the center of one scandal of the Donald Trump presidency. Daniels and TidalWave also teamed up to develop the satirical comic *Stormy Daniels: Space Force*, described as a "*Barbarella*-meets-*Star Trek*-meets-*Stripperalla*" story in which Daniels served Earth's leader, who resembled Trump (quoted in Turnquist 2020).

Female Force issues on Sarah Palin, Michelle Obama, Hillary Clinton, and Senator Elizabeth Warren (D-MA) all earned sequels. The sequels, however, belied the publisher's claims that the books avoided politics. The writer of the Palin sequel, as part of the comic, indicated that he was a liberal and did not like Palin or her Tea Party movement while he offered his perspective on Palin's skills as a politician and her appeal to the people (Rafter and Carson 2010). Michelle Obama's sequel was written by a clear fan and showcased the underreported accomplishments of her first year as First Lady.

Female Force: Elizabeth Warren #2 was partly a redux of #1 but with greater focus on her 2012 US Senate campaign, her rise to power, and her fight in Congress to ease the burden of student loan debt. It was also published with support from the Progressive Change Campaign Committee. The first Clinton book focused on her professional accomplishments, especially those overshadowed by her husband's political career and public scandals. The second one, *The Road to Secretary of State*, which is identical to the issue of *Political Power* featuring Clinton, looked at her failed presidential bids in 2004 and 2008. A third Clinton issue, *The Road to the White House*, explored how the investigation of Clinton's actions surrounding a terrorist attack on a US diplomatic compound in Benghazi, Libya, dogged her 2012 run. Pelosi's issue was also particularly political, filled with anthropomorphized elephants and donkeys telling her story.

A variety of political graphic biographies also exist, separate from campaigns and elections, designed to simply entertain or educate readers. Political cartoonist and columnist Ted Rall released two graphic novels in 2016 about two different candidates: Senator Bernie Sanders (D-VT) and Donald Trump, each focusing on the socioeconomic, cultural, and partisan forces that precipitated their respective presidential bids. Historical biographies of past presidents, including Barack Obama, Ronald Reagan, John F. Kennedy, Abraham Lincoln, Franklin D. Roosevelt, Theodore Roosevelt, and George Washington, alongside graphic biographies of important political activists such as Edward Snowden, Martin Luther King Jr., and Malcolm X, and contemporary biographies of pundits from Glenn Beck and Rush Limbaugh to Barbara Walters and Jon Stewart, all explore the lives, legends, and legacies of their subjects.

Some of the more unique histories are found within Rick Geary's *A Treasury of Victorian Murder* series. In the installment entitled *The Fatal Bullet: The Assassination of President James A. Garfield* (1999), Geary presents parallel histories of Garfield and his assassin Guiteau, set to black-and-white comic illustrations that mimic old wood engravings. Geary also chronicles the last sixty-two days of Lincoln's life and presidency, beginning on inauguration day in 1865, in *The Murder of Abraham of Lincoln* (2005).

Congressman John Lewis penned his own autobiographical comic series, detailing his work in the civil American rights movement in *March*, with a series about his rise as a politician rumored to be in the works under the title *Run* (Rothman 2018). The "Action Presidents" graphic novel series from Harper offers a "dissenting side of the story of our country, which paradoxically uses the comics medium to tell a much truer story of our first executives than what you get in textbooks" (quoted in McMillan 2015, para. 3). Other educational resources can be found from Colorful History through the Pop Culture Classroom. Designed as free, downloadable resources for teachers, these short historical comics are coupled with lesson plans that focus on, among other subjects, President John F. Kennedy's role in the development of NASA, President Richard Nixon's Watergate scandal and impeachment, and President Dwight Eisenhower's life events and key achievements.

Some political biographies have been overtly critical, blending biography and satire to offer commentary on politicians (see chapter five), such as Matt Tolbert's *Read My Lips: The Unofficial Cartoon Biography of George Bush* (1992) and Bill Kieffer's *Great Morons in History featuring Dan Quayle* (1992). The former provided a fairly straightforward and factual biography of George H. W. Bush, enhanced with caricaturized artwork, sight gags, one-liners, and puns. The latter was also premised on fact, but it focused more on making fun of Vice President Dan Quayle's public and political gaffes, using humorous devices such as a political cartoon-filled maze and a parody of the 1989 comedy *Bill and Ted's Excellent Adventure*.

FROM PANELS TO FRAMES

Campaign comics share much in common with other forms of political advertising, whose primary rhetorical purposes are to praise the candidate, condemn the opponent, or respond to criticisms (Trent and Friedenberg 2008). Political advertisements may extoll the candidates' virtues, defining the candidate and/or explaining their positions—as did the self-congratulatory comic of Alabama Governor George Wallace, which lauded Wallace's defense of state rights and segregation. Political ads may question opponents—as did the comics for Massachusetts Governor Paul Dever and New Jersey Governor Robert Meyner, who both criticized the commitment and ethics of their opponents. But campaign comics, and even their commercial successors the election comic and historical graphic biography, also tell stories, and, in this way they most closely resemble the presidential candidate film.

There are several similarities between the form of comics and the form of films—such as the use of frames, camera angles, "shots," dialogue, and scripts—that support a comparison of campaign comics to candidate films (McCloud 1993; Groensteen 2007; Lefèvre 2012; Wolk 2007). Furthermore, the campaign film emerged during the same decade in which campaign comics were their most prevalent. Joanne Morreale (1991) traces these films back to the 1952 election when both candidates, Republican Dwight Eisenhower and Democrat Adlai Stevenson, used documentary-style films in their campaigns. In more recent decades, the candidate film is usually premiered and featured at presidential nominating conventions, with clips and excerpts used in subsequent political advertising leading into the general election. Like the campaign comic book, the candidate film offers unique potential for visually oriented storytelling that provides candidates with a means for (re)casting their character and record (Timmerman 1996). Both media "trace the trajectories of candidates' lives and careers"; both present candidates as "self-made men who rise from humble beginnings" and are good students and able athletes; and both "link the candidate to the rural heartland of America" in order to construct and condense all the attributes candidates want voters to know and recall (Morreale 1996, 8–9; Strachan and Kendall 2004). Such narrative features are endemic of the images established by American politicians as far back as the country's founding—as fruitful farmers, courageous conquerors, and tenacious trailblazers (Melder 1989).

While campaign comics are part of candidates' efforts to construct a favorable image of themselves through such storytelling, commercial graphic biographies are more likely reflecting not only these established images but also the American ideals and myths on which the images depend. The heroic leader, called by a sense of civic duty, who rises to take on great responsibilities, is patterned after the mythologized ideal of George Washington (Morreale 1996). The President John F. Kennedy comic book distributed to US embassies, for example, presents him as a natural-born leader who had an innate love of learning, was raised to be competitive, and took an active interest in world affairs. Visuals reinforce his leadership strength through images of Kennedy commanding a scene and situation (see figure 1.4).

A record of military service, such as that depicted in battle action sequences in the postwar campaign comics, helps to present candidates as individuals who can rise above the ordinary to lead. In lieu of a military record, bravery may be constructed from ordinary events, such as boldness on a playing field (Morreale 1996). Athleticism speaks to a man's discipline, physicality, skill, and aggression, thus establishing both heroism and masculinity. As Nick Trujillo (1991) wrote, "Perhaps no single institution in American culture has influenced our sense of masculinity more than sport. Throughout our history, dominant groups have successfully persuaded many Americans to believe that sport builds manly

Campaign Comics, Election Specials, and Graphic Biographies

Figure 1.4. This scene in *John F. Kennedy: New U.S. President* (1961) visually places Kennedy as a leader by virtue of his height over others in the room and stop-action of him talking and gesturing, while those around him just appear to listen.

character, develops physical fitness, realizes order, promotes justice, and even prepares young men for war" (291).

Since the presidential election of 1840 when William Henry Harrison triumphed over Martin Van Buren by emphasizing his manly virtues and feminizing Van Buren, masculinity has been a keystone of the American presidency. From this point on, Michael Kimmel observes, "the president's manhood has always been a question, his manly resolve, firmness, courage, and power equated with the capacity for violence, military virtues, and a plain-living style that avoided cultivated refinement and civility" (2011, 29). The significance of athleticism and the cultural connections between sports and masculinity and between masculinity and politics is particularly evident in the commercial graphic biographies of Ronald Reagan.

Reagan's life story did not lack in examples of either military service or athletic achievement. A member of his high school swim team, Reagan worked as a lifeguard in his youth and had seventy-seven rescues credited to him. After the Japanese bombed Pearl Harbor, he was assigned to the First Motion Picture Unit of the Army Air Force, acting in training and morale-boosting films, giving him virtual, if not actual, combat experience. But no part of Reagan's past so perfectly built on the cultural myths of masculinity than Reagan's performance as football legend George Gipp in *Knute Rockne All American* (1940, Warner Bros.). The role was featured in both *Political Power: Ronald Reagan* (2009) and in *Ronald Reagan: A Graphic Biography* (2007). American football, and its growing popularity, "has reinforced a form of masculinity which emphasizes sanctioned aggression, (para)militarism, the technology of violence, and other patriarchal values" (Trujillo 1991, 291). The role of Gipp connected Reagan to this tradition in a way that swimming did not and became an integral part of Reagan's political image. As Andrew Helfer indicated in *Ronald Reagan: A Graphic Biography*, "Decades later, the film's stirring call to action, 'Go out and win one for the Gipper,' would inspire the supporters of not Reagan the actor, but Reagan the politician [. . .] so seamlessly did the roles blur together" (Helfer, Buccellato, and Staton 2007, 23).

Whether the sport was football (e.g., Gore, Nixon), swimming (e.g., J. F. Kennedy, Reagan), baseball (e.g., G. W. Bush, Christie, Hoover), basketball (e.g., Obama, Sanders, Trump), running (e.g., Ron Paul), wrestling (e.g., Franken), boxing (e.g., Wallace), body building (e.g., Schwarzenegger), shooting (e.g., Palin), rock climbing (e.g., T. Kennedy), figure skating (e.g., Rice), or cheerleading (e.g., Bachmann), allusions to athleticism are a consistent part of political graphic biographies, underscoring their significance to the creation and consumption of political images.

Humble origin stories are another means of showing a candidate rising beyond the ordinary by overcoming life challenges (Morreale 1996). Such hardships that were showcased in campaign and other biographical comics include loss (e.g., Hoover, Biden), poverty (e.g., Bachmann), domestic abuse (e.g., B. Clinton), and racism (e.g., Obama, Rice). Particularly in Golden Age campaign comics, humble origins were equated with rural settings and/or agricultural work, evoking myths that equate American virtue with American land (Morreale 1996). Even the commercial comic biography of Al Gore, who grew up in the Embassy Row of Washington, DC, includes two panels of him working on a farm in Tennessee: one where he is surrounded by hogs, and another in which he sits among a clearing after felling trees with an axe. Images and narratives of farm work, small towns, immigrant ancestry, and public schooling connect politicians to America's "heartland." Thomas Jefferson first developed the philosophy of American agrarianism by envisioning farming as essential to democratic citizenship (Thompson 1990). As Lynn M. Harter notes, "Jefferson's oft quoted remarks about farmers as the most independent of citizens have taken on mythic qualities" that are often "coupled with frontier images and hegemonic constructions of masculinity" (2004, 91). Such ideas are amplified in the campaign and commercial biographies through stories of politicians as self-made men, whose strong work ethics—often instilled through the necessity of surviving on a farm—ensured their successes throughout life. *Political Power: Herman Cain* offers an excellent example of this mythology, building on the Protestant work ethic that helped to establish early America, ideal of the American Dream, and the Horatio Alger Myth. Although Cain's story offers no glimpses at rural America, it exemplifies both the American Dream and democratic independence of the Jeffersonian farmer by depicting Cain's rise and reinvention through business and corporate America. Work within such American institutions as Coca-Cola and Pillsbury—whose names and logos are synonymous with baseball, apple pie, and mom's kitchen—represent American heartland in 2012 the way that Hoover's farming ancestry did in 1928.

Such political representations suggest the nation's history, and they further both epitomize *and* shape Americans' views of a model leader: it is someone honorable yet personable, effective yet flawed, ordinary yet superior, empathetic yet masterful. The politician's military experience represents not only their character, but the might of the nation. Their time on a farm suggests not only their work ethic, but the foundations of the country. Their athleticism indicates not only their own stamina, but the virility of the people. Their rise to success proves not only their ability, but the possibilities of success for all. Likewise, such imagery reinforces the White, militaristic, masculinity that has always been central to the executive branch of the US government.

CONCLUSION

Comic books and graphic novels represent just one channel of many through which the voting, and nonvoting, public receives political messages. They, however, offer a unique verbal-visual rhetoric in a medium that is marked by, even equated with, heroism. Superheroes dominate the mainstream American comic book industry, and they routinely embody patriotic ideals and represent model citizenship (Duncan, Smith, and Levitz 2015; Wanzo 2009). While they may lack the archetypal capes and tights, politicians are the superior heroes of their own graphic biographies, as so clearly captured in the opening images of *Political Power: Barack Obama*, wherein Obama, who *is* wearing cape and tights, hoists the Capitol Building over his head, symbolizing the weight of responsibility on his shoulders and his ability to carry the burden and overhaul the process. "In the political arena, it is important to note that images are often intended to symbolize far more than candidates' most attractive personal traits," note J. Cherie Strachan and Kathleen E. Kendall. "Instead, they have often been constructed to imbue candidates with mythical, larger-than-life qualities that stand for not only the candidate, but the nation itself" (2004, 135–36). Just as Superman, larger than life, clad in patriotic red, blue, and gold, stands for "truth, justice, and the American way," so, too, do politicians, rising above the ordinary, clad in the uniforms of their military or their school football team. Just as Superman's sense of duty was forged by his idyllic childhood on a farm in rural Kansas, so, too, were politicians shaped by their humble beginnings and agrarian work. Indeed, Superman and superheroes in general have an intricate relationship with the presidency, as will be explored in subsequent chapters.

COLD CONFLICTS, COMICS CODES, AND CONGRESSIONAL COMMITTEES

As President Harry S. Truman prepared to leave the Oval Office in 1953, police prepared to raid the offices of E. C. Comics in New York City for violating the New York Penal Law section 1141, which governs obscene prints and articles, following the sale of *Panic* magazine, which had depicted Christmas as pagan, Santa Claus as a divorcee, and Santa's reindeer as an eclectic and untraditional cast of characters (Sergi 2013). A few months later, in the spring of 1954, the Senate Subcommittee on Juvenile Delinquency held sensational televised hearings to investigate the comic book industry in response to ongoing charges that comics were harmful to impressionable people, particularly children. The concerns centered on comic consumption stunting reading ability, nurturing disrespect for law and authority, and engendering loose sexual mores. The face of the anti-comics crusade was psychiatrist Fredric Wertham, author of *Seduction of the Innocent*, a controversial tract that indicted comics as a leading cause of juvenile delinquency (Hajdu 2009; Nyberg 1998).

The first attack on comics came in 1940 when a literary critic charged that the medium was a strain on youthful eyes and nervous systems with bad art and bad stories. In the ensuing years, local civic and religious groups sought to impose informal, market-based pressures and controls on comics' content and reach, while efforts at the state and national levels sought to achieve governmental controls through censorship. More than a hundred acts of legislation were introduced at state and municipal levels to regulate or limit the sale of comics, with dozens of titles being banned in New York, Connecticut, Maryland, Massachusetts, and other states. Congress's ultimate involvement was perceived as nearly destroying the comic book industry, with more than eight hundred

Figure 2.1. E. C.'s "Are You a Red Dupe?" advertisement compared efforts to censor American comic books to Communism, and contributed to making E. C. owner Bill Gaines an iconic, and notorious, figure in the eventual creation of the Comics Code Authority.

people—working comics artists, writers, and editors—losing their jobs, many of whom would never publish again (Hajdu 2009; Nyberg 1998; Sergi 2013).

One of the more high-profile publishers in the investigations was E. C. Comics, Educational/Entertaining Comics, which specialized in horror, science-fiction, dark fantasy, crime, war, and irreverent satire titles throughout the late 1940s to the mid-1950s. With many of its titles at the center of complaints against the medium, E. C. became a vocal opponent of censorship and an outspoken critic of the government. In one particularly sensational move, E. C. placed a full-page advertisement with the headline "Are You a Red Dupe?" (see figure 2.1). It depicted censorship in Russia and included a three-panel illustration of a man being hanged for publishing comics. Below the graphics, the ad indicated that there was a movement in the United States to suppress comic books and claimed, "The group most anxious to destroy comics are the communists!" It included a call-to-action:

> So the next time some joker gets up at a P.T.A. meeting, or starts jabbering about the "naughty comic books" at your local candy store, give him the once-over. We're not saying he is a communist! He may be innocent of the whole thing! He may be a dupe! [...] It's just that he's swallowed the red bait ... hook, line and sinker! (quoted in Nyberg 1998, 74; see also Sergi 2013)

E. C. owner Bill Gaines also encouraged comic book readers, and/or their parents, to write to congresspersons in defense of comics, and for adults to use the power of their vote to put counter-pressure on the politicians who were creating "a wave of hysteria" that "seriously threatened the very existence of the whole comic magazine industry" (quoted in Nyberg 1998, 120).

Ultimately, Gaines's penchant for spectacle destroyed his reputation, undermined the effectiveness of pro-comic testimony in the Senate hearings, and helped to usher in the industry's Comics Code, which ultimately doomed his own company, along with Comic Media, Fiction House, Eastern Color Printing Company, United Features, Sterling Comics, Star Publications, Ace Magazines, Avon Comics Group, and Quality Comics Group (Nyberg 1998; Nyberg 2017). The Comics Code Authority (CCA) was implemented to ensure that comic book content was wholesome for children by providing and enforcing "a set of rules for cartoonists to obey or rebel against," and, in cases of the latter, to correct those acts of rebellion before comics hit the stands (Wolk 2007, loc. 641). The Code included guidelines such as: "Inclusion of stories dealing with evil shall be used or shall be published only where the intent is to illustrate a moral issue and in no case shall evil be presented alluringly, nor so as to injure the sensibilities of the reader" (quoted in Wolk 2007, loc. 644) and "[r]idicule or attack on any religious or racial group is never permissible" (quoted in York and York 2012, loc. 94). It thereby enforced a safe banality across mainstream comics throughout the 1950s and 1960s, accompanied by a downturn in comics sales, vestiges of which continued until the CCA was finally disbanded in 2011 (Nyberg 2017).

These Cold War-era restrictions are captured in Darwyn Cooke's 2004 *DC: The New Frontier*. Considered an ambitious "Elseworlds" narrative, the generations-spanning story chronicles a reimagined Silver Age of DC Comics. The story, told from the perspective of the heroes who experienced it, features the individual and cultural impact of a time when Cold War paranoia resulted in laws banning the masked vigilantes and caped crusaders who were the heroes of the Golden Age of World War II. Thus, *New Frontier*'s depiction of Batman changing his costume and adopting a ward to soften his image and appeal to children is analogous to the comics industry developing friendlier, more family-oriented heroes under the Comics Code.

Despite such self-censorship, which began in the film industry back in 1916, American media continued to face intense scrutiny and censure from the government, especially Congress, throughout the 1950s. While Gaines and E. C. Comics suggested that calls for censorship were communist, critics of the media feared that without censorship, communist sympathies and ideologies might proliferate. The 1954 comic book hearings occurred in the wake of Senator Joseph McCarthy's "Red Scare" and the House Un-American Activities Committee (HUAC) congressional hearings that scrutinized the entertainment industry for communist influences. Investigations into the film industry reached a peak in 1947 when the "Hollywood Ten"—a group of writers and directors called to testify—refused to cooperate and used their testimony to denounce HUAC. All ten not only received prison terms but were blacklisted from working in Hollywood (Doherty 2018). One of the blacklisted writers, Adrian Scott, struggled to make a living writing comic books until finding success as a television writer in the mid-1950s (Woo 2012). HUAC's influence was felt throughout the cartooning industry in other ways, too. In 1951, a HUAC inquiry resulted in a devastating staff purge at the United Productions of America animation studios, a purge that included artist Bill Melendez, known for his work with Disney, Warner Bros., and Peanuts productions. Three years later, in 1954—the same year that ushered in the CCA—Tempo Productions animation studios succumbed to HUAC's allegations and influence (Cohen 1997).

By the 1960s, counterculture comics creators delighted in subverting the bland expectations of CCA-approved comics, "appropriating the storytelling techniques of text and image used to create wholesome entertainment to produce" underground comics, or "comix," with decidedly adult themes (Nyberg 2017, 27). Around the same time, Marvel Comics and writer Stan Lee also began pushing back on the CCA by releasing a Spider-Man story about the dangers of drug abuse without the CCA Seal of Approval, the idea for which came in the form of a request by the Department of Health, Education, and Welfare. As a result, the Code was revised in 1971. The increased artistic freedom, combined with changes in the distribution of comics that provided more economic freedom, sparked an increasing number of publishers to release comics without the Seal of Approval, and by 2011 the last comic book titles—some of DC's child-friendly series—ceased to use the Code entirely (Nyberg 2017).

Though the establishment of the Comics Code Authority was considered a good public relations move, it stunted the commercial and creative growth of the industry and art form (Nyberg 2017). Distrust of congressional activity—especially investigations, hearings, and special committees—in the wake of HUAC and the televised hearings from the Senate Subcommittee on Juvenile Delinquency is reflected across the media impacted by the moral panic of the 1940s and 1950s with "subtext in which political, social, and moral issues were engaged and debated with intensity and passion" (Murphy 1999, 3). The world of theater responded with Arthur Miller's *The Crucible*, a 1953 allegorical play of Congress's communist hunts through Salem's witch trials, as well as Miller's World War II parable *Incident at Vichy* and Saul Levitt's Civil War-era *The Andersonville Trial*. Film slapped back with *High Noon* (1952), written by the blacklisted Carl Foreman, about a single courageous sheriff surrounded by cowardly townspeople; *12 Angry Men*, a 1954 teleplay about one man holding out with his convictions against the majority; *On the Waterfront* (1954), directed by cooperative HUAC witness Elia Kazan, which told the story of a conflicted longshoreman who must decide between being loyal to his union or informing on the corrupt union boss; *Advise and Consent* (1962), which follows political machinations under a powerful senator reminiscent of Joseph McCarthy; and, *The Front*, a 1976 comedy-drama about the film industry set against the HUAC hearings, created and performed by once-blacklisted talents. Hollywood also presented such stories as *Mr. Smith Goes to Washington*, released in 1939, just one year after HUAC was formed, and *Legally Blonde 2: Red, White, and Blonde* (2003), about average, idealistic, citizens taking on a corrupt political system inside the Senate and the House of Representatives, respectively.

In comics, a host of heroes have combated congressional corruption. To name just a few examples: in 1958, Superman ran for Senate to thwart a villainous plot, and Lois Lane ran against him to save Metropolis from what she saw as another instance of "conceited, egotistic, glory-hungry politicians" (Schaffenberger, Dorfman, and Snapinn 1958, 1). In 1964, American Comics Groups' *Herbie*, "the fat fury," stands accused by a Senate Investigations Committee for a crime he did not commit in "Herbie and the Purloined Pops" (O'Shea and Whitney 1964). In 1971, *Captain Marvel* comics inrecreated the McCarthy-era witch-hunts, with aliens standing in for communists and H. Warren Craddock as the head of the Alien Activities Commission standing in for Joseph McCarthy and HUAC. In 1972, Barbara Gordon (the civilian identity of Batgirl) ran for Congress to fix a broken system. A 1979 story featured DC's Justice Society of America disbanding rather than appearing before HUAC. In 1980, Marvel's X-Men faced-off with the anti-mutant agenda of Senator Kelly. In 1988, Doctor Fate thwarted a Senate hearing questioning her morality. In 1998, Iron Man fought the Senate to stop a rogue Pentagon operation. In 2005, Mr. Terrific uncovered a senator's Nazi conspiracy.

And the 2017 Hanna-Barbera Beyond title *Exit Stage Left* imagined Snagglepuss as a gay playwright brought before HUAC for his progressive productions.

MS. BATGIRL GOES TO WASHINGTON

Movies often reflect inequities in functional freedom in America, reinforcing the idea that average citizens are cut out of the political process and system (Franklin 2006). Politicians are frequently "portrayed as male, White, at least middle-aged, overweight, self-important, surrounded both by sycophants and those who really control him, not terribly bright, not terribly well informed" (Gianos 1999, 29). Films like *Mr. Smith Goes to Washington* or *Dave* (1993) depict regular—usually White, usually male—folks making it into office only through irregular, and often accidental, means or as dupes in corrupt machinations. Such films promulgate a sentiment that the only way to fix politics is to get the "real" politicians out of Washington, even if democracy itself must be subverted in the process (Franklin 2006). The sentiment that Washington, DC, needs to be purged of politicians has persisted throughout media and popular discourse; in the science-fiction comedy *Mars Attacks!* (1996), for example, as hostile Martians launch a deadly assault on the world, one woman, watching the atrocities unfold on television, gleefully exclaims and laughs, "They blew up Congress!" More recently, the Donald Trump presidential campaign successfully ran with a slogan of "drain the swamp," referring to the quagmire of DC beltway politics.

News media reinforce this perspective. "By 1992 nine of every ten judgments about Congress aired by the networks were unfavorable. And these sound bites were increasingly provided by critics outside the institution" (Mann and Ornstein 1994, 5). News coverage of Congress tends to focus on the legislative process more than on the legislators, and it normalizes political maneuvering and conflict as part of that process (Morris and Clawson 2005). Indeed, since the 1980s, stories are less likely to focus on policy issues and more likely to focus on scandal (Mann and Ornstein 1994). The news media, like the movies, also reinforces the White, male politician as the standard through narrowly focused coverage that is less fair to African Americans and to women in Congress (Zilber and Niven 2000; Niven and Zilber 2001). Fictional accounts of politicians of color, when they occur, follow a similar format. Trevor Parry-Giles and Shawn J. Parry-Giles noted that *The West Wing* television series tended to portray leaders of color, as represented by the Congressional Black Caucus, "as motivated exclusively by self or group interest and [to] depict their issues in terms of political capital or political landmines" (2006, 108).

During the Great Depression, a number of films, such as *Gabriel Over the White House* (1933) and *Meet John Doe* (1941), expressed "a growing concern about the viability of democracy in the face of fascism, political corruption, and economic decline" (Franklin 2006, 16). By the height of the Cold War, "conspiracy theory gained a new prominence in American popular culture" with public anxieties surrounding spies, sinister plots, and government secrets, advanced by the discovery and electrocution of communist spies Julius and Ethel Rosenberg and the shifting allegiances of Hollywood insiders and government leaders during the HUAC investigations (Arnold 2008, loc. 348). Films like *The Manchurian Candidate* (1962) extended those conspiracies into Congress, especially through the figure of the ferocious and tough-minded senator, and through bureaucracies populated by petty and selfish people using the government to gain personal power and prestige (Arnold 2008). Whether fictional or factual, mediated representations of Congress since 1939 have reaffirmed a vision of legislators as greedy, power hungry, petty, and vainglorious, with a penchant for devising or succumbing to plots of conspiracy or publicity at the expense of average Americans, artists, industries, and, occasionally, superheroes.

Despite their competitive runs for Senate in 1958, neither Superman nor his girlfriend, intrepid *Daily Planet* reporter Lois Lane, won election to Congress. *Superman's Girl Friend Lois Lane* #62, published in January 1958, was touted as "a 3 part novel, complete in this issue!" and asked, "Will it be Senator Lois Lane or The Senator of Steel? There has never been an election like this!" An incredulous Lois was shocked that Superman would allow politicking to interfere with his superheroing, believing the latter to be far more civically minded than the former—especially when his good deeds began resembling publicity stunts. Appalled by his behavior and his apparent arrogance in what appeared to be a bid for power and glory, she took her complaints to the voters by mounting her own campaign premised on the simple platform of defeating Superman (her slogan, featured on the comic's cover, was: "A vote for Superman is a vote in vain! Vote instead for Lois Lane!"). As the competition escalated, Lois discovered that Superman's campaign, and thus effectively hers, was a sham designed to distract and thwart the scheming of the magical mischief-maker Mr. Mxyzptlk. With the villain defeated, neither Lois nor Superman pursued their bid for Senate. It is significant that neither one was truly interested in *serving* as a senator. Both campaigns had ulterior, even selfish, motives. Superman's campaign was merely a mechanism by which he could do his superhero work. The campaign, not the office, was his goal. Lois's campaign was merely about thwarting Superman; she did not want the office but to keep him from it. They both got exactly what they wanted, but they did so at the expense of the voters, wasting the time, resources, emotions, and energies of their teams and supporters.

Fourteen years later, another superhero in the DC Comics Universe took her congressional campaign far more seriously. Barbara Gordon, aka Batgirl, decided in *Detective Comics* #422 to run for Congress in place of her father,

Gotham City Police Commissioner Jim Gordon, who was resentful of being "put up for Congress by the 'Fusion Faction'" (Robbins and Heck 1972 #422, 5). (It is important to note that many women entered politics as surrogates for male family members; see chapter eight.) Her decision was motivated by distress "over her continuing failure to prevent crime as 'Batgirl'" (Robbins and Heck 1972 #423, 1). Her campaign focused on opposing "old-guard candidates" (Robbins and Heck 1972 #423, 2), and she soon earned the nickname "the boot" by appealing "directly to the 'man in the street'" with her message to "boot the rascals out of office" (Robbins and Heck 1972 #423, 2 and 1). The fact that her campaign was decidedly antiestablishment was relevant to the burgeoning youth movement of the era; the Twenty-sixth Amendment, enfranchising over eleven million eighteen-to twenty-year-olds, was added to the Constitution just one year earlier (see also chapter four). Its antiestablishment orientation also spoke to a distrust of politics as usual.[1] Cynicism about the effectiveness and integrity of typical politicians was reflected in a panel of *Batman Family* #1: Representative Barbara Gordon was addressing the House about a matter of national security, but the chamber was nearly empty. The representatives who *were* present were all older White men, two of whom could be seen playing cards in a visual that foreshadowed what the American people would see of their real representatives on C-SPAN in the 1990s (see Gilsinan 2020).

The antiestablishment, anti-politician, sentiment continued, more explicitly, in future issues and years. In the 1977 *Batman Family* #9, Representative Gordon was met with hostility from anti-politician college students with strong opinions on busing and the Equal Rights Amendment. Issues connected to race and gender were the only issues mentioned in the story, further highlighting the gap between the old-guard of the aging, White, male congressional representative, or even, as Carolyn Cocca (2014) has noted, Barbara Gordon's own position of privilege as a well-educated, economically secure, White person, and the rest of the American people.

Barbara Gordon's congressional term in the late 1970s was made more noteworthy by her unremarkable return to congressional politics in a 2019 story arc. As a congressional campaign heated up in Gotham, at least one candidate was the target of masked assassins. Barbara worked as a campaign volunteer with the controversial anti-corruption candidate, Luciano Alejo, to enable Batgirl's investigation of the attacks (*Batgirl* #30–32). Other than some narrative commentary about politics in Gotham being deadly, the campaign was little more than a backdrop for a story about family tensions, old grudges, and typical comic book crime. The most revealing congressional comic book stories were not the ones about elections, but those involving conspiracies, cover-ups, and committees, which reflected the mixture of cooperation and animosity of the HUAC and comics hearings of the 1950s.

Figure 2.2. An excerpt from Craddock's "ferret them out" speech (top) in *The Avengers* #92 (Thomas and Buscema 1971) echoes McCarthy's (1950) "enemies from within" speech (bottom).

While DC's Batgirl became a congresswoman in the 1970s, Marvel's Avengers and Captain Marvel battled rumors about an alien plot to conquer Earth. In 1971, *The Avengers* comics established a government-sponsored "Alien Activities Commission" headed by H. Warren Craddock. Craddock's first public announcement in the comics was a direct paraphrase of the 1950 speech by McCarthy to the Republican Women's Club in West Virginia that marked the start of his anti-communist crusade (Thomas and Buscema 1971) (see figure 2.2). Zorikh Lequidre and Evan Azriliant (2006) argue that Marvel chose to reincarnate McCarthy two decades after his rise as commentary on rising dissatisfaction with the American government brought on by the Vietnam War, racial tensions, political assassinations, and the counterculture movement. Indeed, as the next sections will discuss, such political cynicism and distrust was echoed throughout comics in the years to come.

CODE-ED MESSAGES

One type of superhero-Congress interaction involves the uncovering of nefarious designs involving the government. These schemes may be ones intended to disrupt or overtake the government from the outside, but they also may be internal plots hatched to increase the power and control of an individual. Both may be ideologically driven. An example of external plots against Congress can be found in the *Firestorm* comics of the early 1980s. The supervillain Silver Deer—a shape-shifting, mesmerizing, Cherokee sorceress—participates in a plot to take control of "the senators and congressmen, the bureaucrats and statesmen" attending an embassy function as vengeance for "the injustice done to [her] people—the stealing of [her] land, the theft of [her] heritage" (Conway, Kayanan, and Rodriguez 1984, 22). Despite Silver Deer being cast as the villain, the story nonetheless painted an unflattering picture of congressional politics. As the opening narration of issue #27 stated, "There's a lot that goes on behind closed doors in Washington, D.C., than even the most *jaded* capitol watcher would find *incredible*" (Conway et al 1984, 1). Not only did the Silver Deer story arc highlight US atrocities to indigenous peoples and tribes, but it also included a side story of political conspiracy and corruption with a lobbyist blackmailing and besmirching a rare honest senator.

More recently, DC villain Gorilla Grodd took over the minds of US senators, putting the country on the brink of war with Canada in his ongoing efforts to "inflict chaos—destroy human civilization" (Parker and Mendonca 2020, 5). The Flash quickly put an end to Grodd's plot, but not before being tempted by the potential of Grodd's "power to *change minds*"—envisioning a world free of war and pollution, one that promoted education and rehabilitation for all (Parker and Mendonca 2020, 7). Although the story's main message was one of free will, it nonetheless took some potshots at congressional politics: one of the Flash's first clues that something was amiss in Washington, DC, was the unusualness of all the senators agreeing with each other.

An evil plot from *within* Congress might be something relatively simple, like a senator backing a malevolent presidential candidate with mind-control powers in *Deathlok* #5, or it might be a deeper conspiracy like the Sons of Liberty shadow government at work in the "Capitol Offense/Shellshocked" story of *Superman in Action* #679. Another example is found in the *JSA: Classified* #29–31 story arc "Mr. Horrific" in 2007, which began with the superhero Mr. Terrific at a rally for Senator Enfield, the son of a World War II veteran-turned-senator. After Enfield's daughter showed Mr. Terrific the Nazi shrine in their basement, Terrific was framed for the murder of Senator Dana Wilhoite who was trying to expose a deadly plot. The Justice Society soon uncovered a decades-old conspiracy involving Nazi technology to destroy the Earth and establish a Third Reich colony on the moon, funded by skimming from the Cold War defense budget. The Cold War and related defense research and expenditures was also at the center of government conspiracy in the Hanna-Barbera Beyond miniseries *Dastardly & Muttley*, in which the Senate investigated a secret Air Force initiative to control reality itself through chemical warfare. And, Nazi connections played a role in the conspiracy surrounding allegations of treason against the

Justice Society of America, in a story that exemplified another type of superhero-Congress interaction: the congressional committee hearing.

The four-part miniseries of *America vs. The Justice Society* in 1985 was set on Earth-Two (a "cosmic construct" and narrative device within the DC Comics "multiverse" that enables and explains different iterations of characters over time, with Earth-Two essentially serving as home to the Golden Age heroes) in the then-current period of the mid-1980s. Building on the hoax of the counterfeit Hitler diaries in the early 1980s, the story opened with the posthumous discovery of Batman's diary which accused the Justice Society of America (JSA) of Nazi activities as well as aiding and abetting communists. In general, the book was a means of recounting the JSA's adventures between 1940 and 1985, including "clip shows" in television that use flashbacks to present a montage of a series' past episodes as the basis for a new plot. The JSA's reminiscing is made possible, and necessary, through a congressional hearing to decide if the heroes of the JSA should be charged with treason.

Behind the scenes, the televised hearing of the JSA was the result of collusion between Senator Hopkins, chair of the special committee, and his sizable campaign donor, a media mogul and son of a deceased Senator named O'Fallon, who was conspiring with the time-traveling supervillain Per Degaton. With the backdrop of multiple government conspiracies and conspiracy theories, the book made several jokes at the expense of politics and politicians. As a fellow superhero team watched the hearing unfold, Lyta, Wonder Woman's adopted daughter, remarked of the JSA's complicated history, "If it's hard for us chartered members of Infinity, Inc. to comprehend—think how impossible it's gonna be for a bunch of legislators whose main worries are usually pork-barreling and getting re-elected" (Thomas, Orway, Kayanan et al 2015/1985, 75). As the hero called Dr. Midnight waxed eloquent in his testimony, another hero wondered, "How come the Doc never went into politics?" to which someone replied, "Too many principles" (Thomas, Orway, Kayanan et al 2015/1985, 127). And, when it began to look as if the heroes would be vindicated, the scheming O'Fallon cursed Senator Hopkins, demanding, "What do I make my campaign contributions for every six years, anyway?"—implying that he had "bought" the senator (Thomas, Orway, Kayanan et al 2015/1985, 131).

As the JSA reviewed its history for the congressional committee and the American people, one moment of significance was

> an "invitation" to appear before the Joint Congressional Un-American Activities Committee, under Senator O'Fallon, who'd succeeded to its head after the car crash which killed Sen. Joseph McCarthy. [. . .] It was a special hearing into [the Justice Society's] possible alliance with the head of Eliminations, Inc.—who was accused of being an enemy agent . . . (Thomas, Orway, Kayanan et al 2015/1985, 135).

Whereas the real HUAC was known for asking those called to testify to reveal *other* possible enemy agents to prove their American loyalties, this version of HUAC demanded the heroes unmask *themselves*, revealing their own civilian identities as evidence of being good Americans. Just as the Hollywood Ten refused to name names so, too, did the JSA, which immediately disbanded until the 1960s.[2]

The treason hearing in *America vs. The Justice Society of America* also captured the mood of the real 1950s comics hearing when the racial and gender composition of the JSA was scrutinized, offering a contemporary version of some of the concerns raised by Wertham about comics (Thomas, Orway, Kayanan et al 2015/1985, 64). Additionally, the narrative highlighted the post-Code reality of the comic book industry in the 1950s, when ambiguity surrounding enemies and censorship of crime meant decreased popularity of superhero stories; as the JSA told its history, it recalled that "Superman . . . Batman and Robin . . . Wonder Woman, remained active . . . But it was not a *time* for our kind of hero" (Thomas, Orway, Kayanan et al 2015/1985, 136). Indeed, commentary on the comics industry in the 1950s into the 1960s was so clear as to push against the Fourth Wall by stating, "there's a parallel Earth existing in a dimension next to ours . . . one on which there never was a Justice Society of America, except in comic-books" (Thomas, Orway, Kayanan et al 2015/1985, 137).

Another story premised on testimony for a Senate committee is found in the 1992 *Doctor Fate* #39, billed as "Mrs. Nelson Goes to Washington" and entitled "Testimony to the World." The mystical superhero Doctor Fate (the alter ego of Inza Nelson) was called to testify before the US Senate in defense of benevolent yet troublesome changes she brought to New York City, which reduced crime, rehabilitated drug dealers, and cleaned up neighborhoods by leveraging threats, tinkering with souls, and altering reality. The committee claimed it wanted to "strive with moral force and good will to fulfill the democratic ideals of our ancestors" and argued that Mrs. Nelson should be ashamed of her actions (Messner-Lobe and Gross 1992, 1). She disagreed and launched into a strong indictment of American politics:

> I was raised in the thirties, Senator. It was a *hard* time. People thought the country was coming apart. But we clung together . . . We survived. Capitalist . . . Socialist . . . Communist . . . The titles didn't mean much. Everyone was cooperating to survive. We believed in our government. In *self*-government. And we did survive. We defeated Hitler and our own stumbling economy. Women had worked all through the war, but we went home to celebrate the peace. [. . .] But in the last twenty years the government has turned against us. It has divided us by *race* and *class* and sex. It has produced a false prosperity based on *debt* and a false patriotism based on *war*. (Messner-Lobe and Gross 1992, 8)

While the background visuals, as well as a senator's dialogue, placed the blame on the Reagan and Bush administrations for the country's ills, Mrs. Nelson blamed "the Senate! And the House and the statehouses across this country! [And] everyone in power who used the moral exhaustion of this country to create an underclass of misery and despair" (Messner-Lobe and Gross 1992, 9). Although the bulk of the hearing avoided hints of Cold War politics, Mrs. Nelson's closing remarks called to mind witnesses who did not cooperate with HUAC. She affirmed, "I *know* why I was brought here, Senator! I'm just refusing to go along with it!"—and then she turned every corrupt politician in the chamber into newts . . . which, in fact, was *all* the politicians in the chamber (Messner-Lobe and Gross 1992, 10).

Another superhero that got revenge on the congressional committee that summoned him was Deadpool, "the merc with the mouth." In *Deadpool: Wade Wilson's War*, from Marvel Knights, Deadpool's origin story and select adventures were revealed through his testimony to a special commission for a Senate investigation into war crimes in Mexico. As with the JSA, the commission chair, Senator Benjamin Sevier, insisted that Deadpool remove his mask and reveal his face to the world (his identity, Wade Wilson, was already known). But, the masked mercenary had the upper hand; testifying was all part of an elaborate scheme to assassinate the commission members. As Deadpool explained, "The plan was to wipe out the cartels, and make it *sooooo bloody* that the U.S. Senate would have no choice but to pull us in for a hearing. You know politicians—they love hearings like married guys love the *Champagne Room*" (Swierczynski, Pearson, and Vines 2011).

Even Deadpool's unmasking worked to his favor because the deformities beneath his facial hood distracted the commission members, who were summarily executed by Deadpool.

Such assorted congressional opposition to superheroes is especially familiar to movie-going audiences of the twenty-first century. The *X-Men* cinematic franchise that began in 2000 from Marvel and 20th Century Fox opened in Washington, DC as US Senator Robert Kelly attempted to pass a "Mutant Registration Act" in Congress, which would force mutants to publicly reveal their identities and abilities. This plot echoed themes from the comics back to the 1981 "Days of Future Past" storyline in which the assassination of Senator Kelly would spark a mutant holocaust. A similar concept was at the heart of the Marvel Civil War storyline in which a superpowered tragedy spurs Congress, assisted by Tony Stark/Iron Man to pass the Superhuman Registration Act requiring government registration of all persons with superhuman abilities, whether those abilities are naturally occurring or the result of exotic and sophisticated technology (Jenkins et al 2010). This plot was adapted into the 2016 film *Captain America: Civil War*. Elsewhere in the Marvel Cinematic Universe, the 2010 *Iron Man 2* movie featured a storyline in which US Senator Stern was pressuring weapons and technology manufacturer Tony Stark to turn over the Iron Man armor to the government; this storyline is similar to that of the comics in which Senator Byrd called Stark to testify before a congressional committee about the secrets of Iron Man in hopes of giving the US an advantage in the Cold War (Lee et al 2017). The 2014 *Captain America: Winter Soldier* followed the discovery and fallout of a massive government conspiracy in which HYDRA, a rogue Nazi organization, infiltrated all levels of the US government; Natasha Romanoff/Black Widow was called to testify before a Senate subcommittee as to her knowledge of an involvement in the compromised agencies.[3] DC Comics developed a similar plotline in 2010–2011 with its Vigilante Registration Act, which arced across several episodes (particularly "Harvest," "Patriot," and "Beacon") in season ten of the WB/CW series *Smallville* based on the Superman mythology and characters; notably, in this storyline, Clark's human mother, Martha, was a senator and part of a secret government organization and she used her influence to protect her superhero son in both her official and shadow capacities.

RADICALS AND MALCONTENTS

In all these examples of comics' heroes facing off with congressional commissions and committees, the heroes rise victorious. They save the day. They find vindication. They serve justice. Or, in the case of Deadpool, they at least best the government and complete their mission. Despite the inclusion of cynical and critical commentary into the stories, they might be little more than wish fulfillment; a bit of revenge on an entity that not only hurt the artistic community in and beyond the 1950s, but that is also routinely seen as a necessary evil in the lives of regular Americans. There is, however, at least one notable exception to this: *Exit Stage Left: The Snagglepuss Chronicles*. Part of DC Comics' Hanna-Barbera Beyond initiative launched in 2016, *Exit Stage Left* is a six-part miniseries based on characters from the animated cartoon *The Quick Draw McGraw Show*. It recast the pink thespian cougar as a closeted gay playwright whose Tennessee Williams-esque plays were investigated by the House Un-American Activities Committee during the Red Scare of the 1950s. The series mostly took place during the mid-1950s in New York City. Snagglepuss ("S. P.") lived a double life with a marriage of convenience and a secret relationship with a Cuban refugee in Greenwich Village. His critically acclaimed plays about the social condition placed him in the same social circles as the New York City writers and critics of the famed Algonquin Round Table. In addition to helping launch the careers of Hanna-Barbera's Peter Potomus, Squiddly Diddly, and Auggie Doggy, S. P. also mentored a young Clint Eastwood. In the background, the Rosenbergs were publicly executed for treason, Dorothy Parker struggled with money and alcohol after being blacklisted, Marilyn Monroe and Joe DiMaggio began a tempestuous relationship, the US government tested atomic bombs in the Nevada desert, Fidel Castro fought a revolution in Cuba, and Nikita Khrushchev engaged in a corn battle on an Iowa farm.

While history unfolded, an anti-communist activist assisting HUAC conspired to put political pressure on S. P. Hoping to publicly humiliate him, she ordered a police morality raid on the Stonewall Inn where he and his boyfriend spent time.[4] But S. P. was absent that night and instead of him, the raid caught his friend, Huckleberry Hound. Publicly outed, Huck was placed at odds with his policeman boyfriend Quick Draw McGraw; isolated and ashamed, Huck took his own life. Angered by Huck's death, S. P. defied HUAC and was subsequently blacklisted from show business, until 1959, when he was invited to start a new career as the star of an animated television show.

In *Exit Stage Left*, there was no grand victory for the hero, except in survival, and no comeuppance for the government, except in not being able to break their witness. Despite the anthropomorphic characters interacting regularly with the human characters, this comic was a pop cultural snapshot of heartache and hardship. In the climax of *Exit Stage Left*, a Senator demanded of S. P., "This committee is giving you the chance to prove yourself a *loyal* American. In order to do that, you need to name those in the arts who are engaged in *subversion!*" S. P.'s stirring response rejoined,

> The purpose of art **is** subversion. Art is telling the world how it's killing you. How its institutions have failed you. In the end, any culture worth a damn is made by subversives. Because art is what tells the world it needs to *change*. Power merely redecorates it. (Russell, Feehan, Parsons, and Marzán Jr. 2018)

Snagglepuss's sentiment about the importance of art in society was a point that Bill Gaines himself had made in his opening statement to Senate when testifying about comic books in 1954. He told the committee,

> Two decades ago my late father was instrumental in starting the comic magazine industry. [. . .] My father was proud of the industry he helped found. He was bringing enjoyment to millions of people.
>
> The heritage he left is the vast comic-book industry which employs thousands of writers, artists, engravers, and printers.
>
> It has weaned hundreds of thousands of children from pictures to the printed word. It has stirred their imagination, given them an outlet for their problems and frustrations, but most important, given them millions of hours of entertainment. (Gaines 1954)

Both the real juvenile delinquency testimony of Gaines and the fictional HUAC testimony of Snagglepuss, as well as Doctor Fate's testimony to her own Senate investigation, shed light on a gap between congressional intent of promoting and preserving democracy and the reality of what democracy looks like. There is an inherent tension between a hearing designed to elicit the truth and artistic expression; as Pablo Picasso noted, "We all know that Art is not truth. Art is a lie that makes us realize truth, at least the truth that is given us to understand" (quoted in Borofsky 2003, para. 4).

Whether heroes have triumphed or faltered in the face of congressional scrutiny, whether they have saved congress or saved America from congress, one theme runs through most of the congressional storylines: the intertwined notions of corruption, cover-ups, and conspiracies. "Conspiracy theory," Gordon Arnold writes, "is a staple of American popular culture" that "reveal something about American society" (2008, 78). It encompasses a worldview offering a framework for explaining or a folklore for understanding reality. It is a force that has been enabled by a political culture that promotes ideologies and attacks opposition by any available means and by a proliferation of post-World War II media that has used conspiracy to reflect and shape American political and cultural anxieties and attitudes (Arnold 2008).

According to Arnold (2008), conspiracy theories wove their way into everyday experience beginning with the general paranoia about communism, nuclear war, and rapidly advancing technologies that emerged with the Cold War in the late 1940s—the same era that gave rise to HUAC and the CCA. Since then, "the conspiracy theory theme has passed through at least three evolutionary stages" (Arnold 2008, 2630). The first captured a mood of paranoia, fear, and anxiety, fostered by external threats of the Soviet Union and nuclear annihilation. The second stage of evolution was one that captured a mood of cynicism based on concerns about internal or domestic threats; the Watergate scandal of the 1970s (see chapter four) supported a sense that the American government, or at least people in it, might be untrustworthy and could even engage in deception and murder to advance its secret agenda. By the 1980s, such distrust extended to any, and all, American institutions as being "untrustworthy, ineffective, occasionally criminal, and prone to covering up their misdeeds" (Arnold 2008, 2644). The third evolutionary stage of conspiracy theory themes added disaffection to the cynicism, as by the 1990s, civic disengagement and voter apathy were on the rise with more and more people believing civic involvement was futile because institutions were self, rather than public, serving (Arnold 2008).

All three stages and the emotions of paranoia, cynicism, and disaffection can be found in the congressionally themed comic book stories discussed above. Like the conspiracy theory theme itself, comic books' congressional conspiracies grew from Cold War paranoia and post-World War II anxieties. While films often focused on communist plots, these comic book conspiracies focused on the paranoia created by the government's effort to *flush out* communist plots (as in *Exit Stage Left* and *America vs. the Justice Society of America*). Stories about misguided congressional investigations, secret congressional cabals, and efforts to control Congress all further demonstrated cynicism with both politics and politicians (as in "Mr. Horrific"); even the nonfiction graphic short story "The Man in the Green Hat," found in *District Comics: An Unconventional History of Washington, DC*, focuses on congressional corruption and graft surrounding the country's experiment with prohibition (Fahey, Peña, and Keeling 2012). As such, the stories emphasize a disconnect between the American people and their elected representatives, pointing to individual and public disaffection with the system.

Conspiracy theories are comforting. They offer explanations for the chaos and calamity of modern life that may be easier to comprehend and accept than simpler explanations of unfortunate happenstance. They are rhetorically compelling, with their creative and flexible applications of evidence. They are also adaptable to a variety of situations (Arnold 2008; Stewart, Smith and Denton Jr. 2012). As such, they are dramatic and easily molded narratives for a variety of genres across all medias, appearing in political thrillers, murder mysteries, film noir and pulp fiction, science fiction and space operas, crime shows, horror, superhero stories, and more, for audiences of all ages. In these comics, they also offer a means to reframe a frightening and dark time in media and comics history, providing writers and artists an expressive outlet not available in congressional chambers in the 1950s.

CONCLUSION

The Code is now long gone, but its effects live on, not only in the vintage comics that still bear its stamp of approval but also in the reputation of the medium and in the business practices of the industry. A shift to direct market distribution, rather than newsstand and drugstore sales, in the 1970s "allowed publishers to disregard industry regulations on content" but also created a change in audience that impacted the industry (Nyberg 2017, 31). Casual readers were phased out as it took more and more effort, money, and deliberate intent to purchase comics from specialty stores and, now, digital subscriptions. Correspondingly, there was a decline among child readers—the very audience that had been the center of the 1950s controversy. Because the Code's guidelines, in effect until 2011, focused on making content appropriate for children, it engendered a lasting public perception of the medium as juvenile literature, even though comic book readership among children in the US is at near-historic lows. Child readership is especially low for superhero comics, which is ironic because the Code's guidelines helped to maintain superheroes as the dominant genre of the medium through its strict prohibitions on subject matter that dampened the development of crime and horror (Nyberg 1998; Tilley 2018). The Code particularly forbid any challenge to authority, making the stories about congressional misdeeds more subversive, particularly when advanced by the superheroes that the Code, inadvertently, favored. Moreover, these conspiracies captured the political pessimism of their adult creators and readers, emphasizing that, as Code historian Amy Kiste Nyberg has noted, there "is nothing inherent in the comics form that limits it to telling stories suitable only for children" (2017, 32). Comic books' expression of "corrosive cynicism" is, in fact, consistent with the news media's increasing focus on congressional scandal (Mann and Ornstein 1994). As Maren Williams, writing for the Comic Book Legal Defense Fund, noted, "Whether government-sponsored or industry-directed, as with the Comics Code Authority in the United States, censorship naturally strikes hardest at each society's most deep-seated anxieties" (2017, para. 1)—and so, too, does art, including anxieties surrounding censorship itself.

GREAT SUPERHEROIC POWERS AND GREAT PRESIDENTIAL RESPONSIBILITIES

In collaboration with DC Comics (then called National Periodical Publications), the John F. Kennedy White House launched a marketing effort in 1963 for Superman to promote Kennedy's hallmark President's Council on Physical Fitness. The result of the collaboration was a three-page story of "Superman's Mission for President Kennedy" in which the president calls upon Superman to help inspire the nation to exercise, eat better, and get stronger. The comic was in production when Kennedy was assassinated in November 1963 and was set aside until his successor, President Lyndon B. Johnson, encouraged its release as a tribute to the Kennedys (Flor 2014). The story of, and behind, "Superman's Mission for President Kennedy" is now the stuff of legend, but it was only one of many interactions between these American icons that helped to shape the image of both.

As noted in a retrospective on *BookRiot*, Superman and President Kennedy built a friendship through regular interactions (Reid 2015): in 1961, President and First Lady Jacqueline Kennedy were at the wedding reception of Superman and Lois Lane (*Superman's Girlfriend, Lois Lane* #25). A few months later, Superman presented Kennedy with a confiscated weapon of mass destruction, trusting the president to handle the power responsibly (*Superman's Pal, Jimmy Olsen* #56). Shortly after, Superman had to battle with an alien shapeshifter who had assumed Kennedy's identity (*Action Comics*, vol. 1, #283). The next year, Superman took his cousin, Supergirl, to the White House, where Kennedy officially recognized her as a hero (*Action Comics*, vol. 1, #285). In 1964, in a story clearly put into print before the president's assassination, Kennedy helped Superman by posing as his alter ego, Clark Kent, on a television show (*Action

Comics, vol. 1, #309). John F. Kennedy and Superman were now effectively one in the same, especially given that Superman himself briefly served as president just a few years earlier, if only in a dream (*Superman*, vol. 1, #122).

The 1986–87 *Watchmen* series from DC Comics featured a flashback in which the human hydrogen bomb known as Dr. Manhattan recalled "September, 1961. John Kennedy is shaking my hand, asking what it's like to be a super-hero. I tell him he should know and he nods, laughing . . ." (Moore and Gibbons 2014, 124). The funeral following "The Death of Superman" in 1993 borrowed heavily from the images of Kennedy's own interment (Alaniz 2012). Darwyn Cooke returned to the mythic Kennedy presidency in his critically acclaimed 2004 miniseries *DC: The New Frontier*, which quoted extensively from Kennedy's nomination acceptance speech at the Democratic National Convention in July 1960. In 2017, the Phantom, arguably America's first superhero, reappeared on the American market in his own mission for President Kennedy.

Though Kennedy is not the only president to be featured with, or as, a superhero, he is the embodiment of American political myth. The American presidency has been described as a "breeding ground" for myth thanks to its power and reach (Rossiter 1987, 94). As John Shelton Lawrence and Robert Jewett wrote, "The U.S. president, standing so often at center stage during historic crises, has been woven into the fabric of national mythology. Legend-making about presidents emerged as soon as the nation had presidents to ponder" (2002, 126). Kennedy has been part of American political mythology since the mid-twentieth century. His youth, charisma, and photogenic family enhanced his message of a promise for a better tomorrow. While his tragic assassination and a carefully mediated cultivation of his legacy raised him to a cultural status that extended beyond politics, Kennedy himself was strategic in crafting associations with positive political, spiritual, and artistic symbols of American identity (Felkins and Goldman 1993; Kitch 2002). Not only did Kennedy appear with Superman and engage the Man of Steel to promote the President's Council on Physical Fitness, but his daughter Caroline also had her own one-shot comic book, and several commemorative comics were released following his death, all pointing to the establishment of the Kennedy name as both political myth and pop culture icon.

THE MYTHIC AND SUPERHEROIC PRESIDENCY

The strategic alliance made between Kennedy and Superman is emblematic of what David Hoogland Noon calls "the myth of the superheroic presidency" (2016, 432). It exemplifies the presidential legend-making that developed at the end of the twentieth century, which imagined the president as a superheroic unification of "physical heroism and moral perfection" capable of single-handedly confronting and exterminating threats to America and humanity (Lawrence and Jewett 2002, 128). While this myth can be seen across assorted media platforms and genres, the focus here will be on comic books and multimedia adaptations of the traditional superhero.

Superheroes are typically seen as nationalist, acting as proxies for particular geopolitical identities, civic virtues, and community beliefs (Dittmer 2013; Deis 2013). They frequently model correct civic actions, feelings, and thoughts, suggesting behaviors for the average citizen concerned with justice (Wanzo 2009). The physique and appearance of the superhero further embodies the ideals and environment of their community (Round 2008; Devarenne 2008). Likewise, symbolic performance of the presidency helps to constitute the collective nation (Murphy 2003). In a dialectical analysis of *DC: The New Frontier*, Matt Yockey (2012) argued that the conflation of American history with comic book history aligns superheroes with a national myth, expressing a yearning for an idealized past.

This is part of what Lawrence and Jewett (2002) called the American monomyth: a narrative in which an extraordinary individual, such as a superpowered president, emerges to vanquish evil adversaries that America's ordinary civic and political institutions alone cannot defeat. The American monomyth, like American superheroes, first emerged in the national crises of the 1930s and 1940s, a time when Americans looked to the president as a savior (Nelson 2008; Lawrence and Jewett 2002). The first presidential savior was Franklin D. Roosevelt, who was also the first sitting president to appear in comic books. Among Roosevelt's early comic book cameos is in the 1942 *Action Comics* #52, in which Superman saves a future presidency from being taken over by an evil, space-age regime ("The Emperor of America"). Assorted assassination attempts on Roosevelt were also thwarted by Captain America, the Sub-Mariner, and Sgt. Fury and his Howling Commandos.

Following the Great Depression and the Second World War, the ensuing Cold War provided "exigencies that demanded strong executive responses [and] the powers of the presidency centralized. [. . .] During this period, [. . .] the presidency was the focal point of governmental activity, public identification, and national identity" (Parry-Giles and Parry-Giles 2006, 8). Jeff Smith (2009) observed, in *The Presidents We Imagine*, that the Cold War era augmented the symbolic power of the American presidency by establishing the office as Leader of the Free World. It correspondingly gave rise to a paradoxical mix of perceived weakness and idealized strength, while the growing counterculture raised questions about the comparative power of the people. Similar issues were at play for how American superheroes were being (re)imagined. Marvel (née Timely) Comics, created new heroes for the atomic age. Many of these Cold

War superheroes, such as Spider-Man, the Incredible Hulk, the Fantastic Four, and the X-Men, gained their super abilities through nuclear power, analogous to the Cold War intertwining of "bomb power" and "executive power" in the presidency (Wills 2010). The new breed of superhero was exceptionally flawed, struggling with how to use their powers responsibly and how to negotiate civic duties and familial stability. Reflecting a variety of mainstream and alternative ideologies, the same struggles and concerns were also found in popular depictions of the presidency (Costello 2009; Genter 2007; York and York 2012; York 2012; Ormrod 2014; McClelland-Nugent 2012). By the end of the Cold War, the president and the superhero, both symbols of national identity, merged, and the mythic presidency finally took on "super powers that comic books routinely assigned to other men in tights and capes" as action-adventurers (Lawrence and Jewett 2002, 128).

After the Kennedy-Superman team-ups in the early 1960s, the first explicit appearance of the superheroic presidency was the NBC animated 1967–68 television series *Super President*. The show featured the adventures of President James Norcross (aka Super President) who, with his aide Jerry Sales, championed justice by fighting evildoers. The voiceover during the show's opening credits explained,

> His power was born in a cosmic storm, every molecule charged with might. Powers that enabled him to change his molecular structure to steel, granite, or whatever the need requires. The great desire to serve his country in the cause of justice has brought James Norcross to the highest office in the land as Super President. (quoted in Collier 2018, 5)

Author Kevin Scott Collier compared Norcross to Kennedy, noting that both were youthful, promoted the space program, supported world-wide disaster relief, and were Christians (2018). Furthermore, while Kennedy teamed up with Superman, the so-called "Man of Steel," Norcross could become a man made of steel, and he fought a steel man in an episode called "Man of Steel." A twenty-five-page *Super President* comic book, which referenced the 1968 presidential election, was abandoned when Robert F. Kennedy, one of the candidates, was assassinated. Unlike John F. Kennedy's "Superman's Mission," which was published posthumously, the *Super President* comic was never released (Collier 2018).

It is perhaps not surprising that *Super President*, which took patriotism for granted and imagined America as a hero to the world, was canceled after just one season. By 1968, when its season ended, the Democratic Party had factionalized from antiwar sentiments surrounding America's lingering and deadly involvement in the Second Indo-China War in Vietnam and tensions from urban violence at home. Excessive violence in cartoons was, correspondingly, the official reason for the cancelation of *Super President* (Collier 2018). Indeed, by the time President Lyndon B. Johnson left office in 1969, the idea of a superheroic president had become farcical. "SuperLBJ" was the star of next superheroic presidency in *The Great Society Comic Book*. Published in 1966, this comic was a political satire of the Johnson administration, especially his Great Society programs.[1] Award-winning author and artist Sally Edelstein (2013) observed, "Comic books, a place where bright colors forever defeat darkness and good forever triumphed over evil was the perfect metaphor for the noble venture of LBJ's Great Society" (para. 4). The comic celebrated Johnson's social policies while presenting the quagmire of Vietnam as his downfall. Depicting SuperLBJ as a version of Superman, Vietnam was LBJ's weakness the way Kryptonite was Supe's, causing SuperLBJ to lose all his powers. A second "Great Society" comic, *Bobman and Teddy*, parodied the 1966 *Batman* television series, casting Robert F. Kennedy in the role of the Caped Crusader ("Bobman") and Ted Kennedy as his youthful sidekick ("Teddy the Wonder Boy"). Described as "irreverent satire depicting world-renown political figures as superheroes and villains," the 1966 comic depicted the Kennedys heroically defeating a host of Republican villains, while still managing to make them look absurd and bombastic (Fox 2013, para. 1).

UP IN THE SKY! A HOLLYWOOD STAR!

Following Johnson's divisive presidency, the country witnessed the criminally scandalous administration of Richard Nixon, the laughable presidency of Gerald Ford (the only president never elected to the White House), and the failed administration of Jimmy Carter. Carter's weakness as president was emphasized in a Marvel Comics *What If . . . ?* story in which Captain America was able to handily defeat both the Democratic incumbent Carter and the Republican challenger Ronald Reagan in the 1980 election. But, in reality, it was Reagan, not Captain America, who handily won the 1980 election and helped to realize the ultimate absorption of the superhero into the American monomyth.

Prior to his political career, President Reagan was an actor, known for portraying American heroes on the silver screen. The hypermasculine roles of Reagan the actor seamlessly blended into the hypermasculinity of Reagan the politician (see chapter one). The war heroes and sports legends that embodied the American monomyth on the screen were now one and the same as the American president. Furthermore, like Kennedy, Reagan harnessed the power of the comic book superhero to help advance his initiatives. In 1983, DC Comics, with sponsorship from Keebler Company, IBM Corporation, and the American Soft Drink Industry, published a three-issue series of *The New Titans* in cooperation with the president and First Lady's Drug Awareness Campaign. The White House initially wanted to use a more famous superhero, such as Superman, Batman, or Wonder Woman, but DC Comics suggested *The New Teen Titans*. Not only was it the publisher's best-selling title, but it also thought that the younger heroes would better appeal to the target audience of schoolchildren (Lifeforce Comics 2011). The books, designed to reach fourth to sixth grades, each opened with the same letter from Nancy Reagan, telling readers that they could be heroes in "one of the most important battles our nation has ever fought" (Reagan 1983, inside front cover) to combat drug use.

Indeed, Reagan's war on drugs provided the foundation for his superheroic alter ego in the satiric comic book *Reagan's Raiders* (discussed further in chapter five), but perhaps Reagan's greatest contribution to the myth of the superheroic presidency was his place in the end of the Cold War. Lawrence and Jewett argued that the super-presidency was inspired by "the United States' late-twentieth-century supremacy arising out of the Cold War victory" (2002, 128). A 1986 edition of *The Green Lantern Corps* featured Guy Gardner—a "naturally belligerent—fanatic about personal liberty"—intervening on Reagan's behalf to stop a nuclear confrontation with the Soviets (Englehart and Staton 1986, 3). Meanwhile, Marvel gave readers "a parallel dimension where the President of the United States is not Ronald Reagan—but Kyle Richmond" who oversaw a superhero team called Squadron Supreme (DeMatteis and Perlin 1982, 2)—a team whose story would eventually, via the series *Supreme Power* (2003), become entangled with the presidencies of Carter, Reagan, G. H. W. Bush, and Clinton.

In 1991, two years after the fall of the Berlin Wall marking the end of the Cold War, DC Comics imagined the 2001 presidency of Superman (*Superman Annual* #3). In it, President Superman saved the economy by having Aquaman retrieve gold lost at the bottom of the ocean. He saved the environment with solar power technology. He deterred terrorism with his own brute force. And, analogous to the de-escalating Cold War, he disarmed the world with the help of fellow superheroes. Ultimately, however, Superman put the well-being of his family ahead of the global good and, through a twist of time-travel, ensured that the idyllic Superman presidency never came to pass.

Two years later, Superman and the president again shared space in the comics. The 1993 "Funeral for a Friend" storyline followed the aftermath of Superman's death in a battle to save the Earth from a bloodthirsty monster known as Doomsday. The hero's funeral appeared in the comics almost exactly thirty years after President Kennedy was laid to rest. José Alaniz, a scholar of death and comics, observed that

> clues abound that [Kennedy's] ceremony served as the basis for the look of Superman's own funeral: the carriage (though Kennedy's body was borne by a gun

carriage, not the coach depicted in the story); the closed casket with an American flag draped over it; the eternal flame; even the massed crowds and park setting for the monument recall photographs and newsreel footage of that day. A further hint occurs after the funeral, when Lois places her engagement ring in her slain lover's coffin—recalling the same gesture made by Jacqueline Kennedy with her wedding band. (2012, 185)

And, while Superman's legend symbolically embraced the Kennedy legacy, President Bill Clinton's image embraced Superman's. Clinton, accompanied by his wife, was shown speaking at Superman's funeral, pointing to Superman as a model of civic behavior. "His powers and abilities were amazing. . . . But how much more amazing was the way he chose to use those powers! If there is one lesson in this, it is that the greatest power of all . . . is our own ability to care about and help each other" (Jurgens et al 2016, 96).

Marc DiPaolo (2011, 4491–497) argued that Superman died in 1992 to mark the end of twelve years of Republican rule, commenting on how the Republican administration had effectively killed individual freedoms in the name of the free market and national security. Moreover, DiPaolo continued, Superman's eventual resurrection in "The Reign of the Supermen" was possible because of Clinton's Democratic administration, which represented a change from the militarism and corporate excess that had been the death of Superman's spirit in the first place.

The idea that Superman, and the civic spirit he represents, shines brightest under a Democratic administration may be supported by the nostalgic return of John F. Kennedy to the superhero universe in both 2004 and 2017, during controversial Republican presidencies. Darwyn Cooke's *DC: The New Frontier* was a generations-spanning story chronicling the Silver Age of DC Comics. Cooke blended American history with comic book history to establish the Cold War origins of the Justice League of America, populated by Superman, Batman, Wonder Woman, Green Lantern, and more. Within the Cold War context, "the New Frontier" was a phrase coined by John F. Kennedy in his nomination acceptance speech at the Democratic National Convention in July 1960. Not only did Cooke allude to Kennedy's speech through the title of his book, which took place in the final year of the Dwight Eisenhower administration, but the epilogue was an extended quotation of the address, placed against a backdrop of superhero and villain vignettes. Matt Yockey interpreted the story within the utopian impulse of the superhero genre: "In his speech, Kennedy both invokes the pioneer spirit of westward expansionism and ridicules Republicans as the party of the past. Similarly, Cooke invokes the late 1950s and early 1960s as an idyllic moment in the history of the genre even as he criticizes the political and social conservatism of the period" (2012, 365).

Critics praised the book as a celebration of hope in contrast to the present, specifically the post-9/11 era of Republican President George W. Bush, and to the Cold War realities of racism, bigotry, alienation, paranoia, fascism, and nationalism (Naso 2016; Rikdad 2016; Yockey 2012). Cooke himself called it "a love letter to a bygone era or an allegorical reflection of contemporary concerns," and indicated that it was a reaction to his perception of eroding leadership and growing pessimism in American culture since the Kennedy administration (Cooke 2005, afterword; Naso 2005). Perceptions of poor leadership during the George W. Bush years were also reflected in the 2006 three-issue "President Thor" storyline in Marvel's *Ultimate Fantastic Four*. Thor, a superheroic Norse god/alien, became president in a dystopic alternate future; motivated by his populist worldview, he used alien technology to grant superpowers to six billion Americans, ultimately leading to the complete destruction of Earth.

During the early months of Republican Donald Trump's presidency in 2017, Hermes Press announced a new five-part series for *The Phantom*, "President Kennedy's Mission," inviting readers to "journey back to the swingin' 1960s" when a war with Russia was looming and President Kennedy called on his old friend Kit Walker, aka the Phantom, for help (Hermes Press n.d.). Written by Ron Goulart and illustrated by Sean Joyce, the story featured mythologized Kennedy history, espionage intrigue, and exciting space exploration, giving it, like *DC: The New Frontier*, the nostalgic patina of Cold War pop culture. But, whereas *DC: The New Frontier* linked the president to the Silver Age of comics, *The Phantom* connected Kennedy to the Golden Age of superheroes. The Phantom is arguably America's original superhero. First published by Lee Falk in February 1936, *The Phantom*'s titular character is a costumed-crime fighter based in the fictional Afrasian country of Bangalla. According to the author Kevin Patrick, "Clad in a skin-tight purple costume, his face concealed by an eye-mask and cowl, and sporting a death's head symbol on his gun-belt, the Phantom was the visual prototype for the modern superhero" (2017, 46). In "President Kennedy's Mission," Kennedy met the superhero, in his alter ego of Kit Walker, while serving in the Pacific during World War II. The comic's visuals presented the military heroism of Kennedy on equal footing with the superheroics of Walker (see figure 3.1). Both *The Phantom* and *New Frontier*, appearing during controversial Republican presidencies, offered poignant depictions of an idealized era of honor in politics by re-purposing the Kennedy myth within the utopia of the superhero genre.

The year 2017 also saw the release of a digital comic miniseries called *The Unconstitutional Actions and Adventures of the Dead Presidents*, described by *Comic Frontline* as the combination of "a love of presidential history and superhero comics [in] one epic tale" (Jay 2017, para. 2). In it, the Mayan prophesy for the end of the world in 2012 came true with a rip in the space-time continuum that

Figure 3.1. *The Phantom*'s mission for President Kennedy (Herman, Goulart, Joyce, and Molina 2017) opens with Jack Kennedy saving the crew of his PT 109 torpedo boat after it strikes a Japanese destroyer in the Solon Islands in 1943, with Kennedy leaping into action (left). A later scene (right) show the Phantom similarly leaping into action to take down criminals. The two originally meet, both as war heroes, during World War II (center). The combined visuals make Kennedy and Walker/Phantom equally super-heroic.

allowed a cosmic-powered dead Hitler to come back to conquer Earth. Thirty-eight dead presidents heeded the call to service and returned to save humanity. A select group of the presidents harnessed cosmic energy to gain superpowers based on their "historical imprints" (Garcia, Lauer, and Barna 2016, 17). For example, Kennedy gained the power of flight, the Cosmic Sword of Energy, and Cosmic Energy Blasts. Eisenhower gained flight, super strength, Golf Ball Bombs, Power Clubs, Domino Effect, and Interstate-Shield. Truman got flight, Atomic Punches, Blasts, and Explosions. Other presidents who gained powers included both Roosevelts, Grant, Lincoln, Jackson, and Washington. By 2019, only the first two of four planned issues had been released, but the book supported a Twitter feed (@theDPOTUS) that provided "pointless presidential pfacts" [*sic*] about presidents on their deathdays, such as a list of Lincoln's "epic speeches" and that Taft was the victim of "fake news" about getting stuck in a bathtub.

While the Republican presidencies of Bush and Trump triggered nostalgia for the superheroic promise of Kennedy, the myth of the superheroic presidency was fully realized under the Democratic administration of President Obama. Noon notes that "throughout the 2008 presidential campaign, Barack Obama's status as an ascendant historical figure was acknowledged across digital and print culture. Among the more playful themes that emerged, Obama was often represented as a comic book hero" (2016, 432).

After the botched and prolonged 2000 election that ushered George W. Bush in as president, the tragedy of the September 11 attacks, and the lingering wars

in Afghanistan and Iraq, America was discouraged and ready for a change. Obama's 2008 campaign was inspirational, offering voters hope. Comic book artist Alex Ross captured this in his portrait, "It's Time for a Change," unveiled at the 2008 San Diego Comic-Con International, which depicted Obama parting his jacket and shirt to reveal a spandex superhero costume, ala Clark Kent transforming himself into Superman. Artist Thierry Guetta, better known as "Mr. Brainwash," produced a street mural of Obama in the classic red and blue Superman costume. Artist Paul Richmond depicted Obama and his vice-presidential pick Joe Biden as Batman and Robin in a painting entitled "Batobama and Robiden," with opponents John McCain and Sarah Palin depicted as the villains Penguin and Catwoman. Comics scholar Adilfu Nama noted that Obama's "square jawline, captivating origin story, elegant oratory, lightning-quick intelligence, and sleek athletic profile" naturally leant itself to the superhero myth, especially given that Obama was a self-professed fan and collector of comic books (2011, 152).

During his presidency, Obama was featured with or as the hero in numerous comic books. He was endorsed by Image Comics' Savage Dragon. His inauguration was saved by Marvel's Spider-Man. He opposed, and was eventually killed by, Image's evil clone Bomb Queen. He and his daughters were saved from an evil comic book version of the Necronomicon by Dynamite's Ash. He tamed a zombie apocalypse in Antarctic's *President Evil*. He rose to power in the post-apocalyptic *Barack the Barbarian* from Devil's Due. He worked with Antarctic's *Steampunk Palin* to save the world from nuclear power. He recruited a newly revived Captain America into Marvel's Avengers. He helped rebuild an alien-ravaged Chicago in Devil's Due's *Drafted*. And he was, effectively, President Calvin Ellis, aka Superman, in DC's *Final Crisis*.

Obama was not, however, the only superheroic president on the scene during his years of service, from 2009 to 2016. The Obama years also saw the emergence of *Time Lincoln* from Antarctic Press and *Rough Riders* from AfterShock, which imagined President Abraham Lincoln as a time-traveling hero and Theodore Roosevelt as a secret government agent, respectively. It is perhaps not coincidental that both Lincoln and Roosevelt were considered progressive on race relations in their times and were reimagined as superheroic men out of time during the years of America's first Black president (see also chapter eleven). In 2011 and 2012, Marvel Comics published a monthly series, *Ultimate Comics: The Ultimates*, starring Thor and Iron Man. The thirty-issue run opened with America, and the world, facing two apocalyptic superhuman threats that resulted in the annihilation of the US government, headed by an unnamed president who looked a lot like Obama. When anarchy and chaos took over, Captain America stepped into the leadership void, becoming president of the United States. Inserting himself directly and personally into every crisis, he was a popular president because "he's out there, helping people, instead of bickering about politics" (Humphries and Tan 2012). Meanwhile, in the world of DC Comics, Batman also briefly posed, though did not officially serve, as the President of the United States in the 2012 children's comic *Batman the Brave and the Bold: President Batman*.

Comic book appearances of Trump during his 2015–2016 campaign and the years of his subsequent administration were frequently less favorable than Obama's. He did, however, appear as a superhero in the satirical *Trump's Titans* from Keenspot and the parodic *Tremendous Trump* and *My Hero MAGAdemia* from Antarctic. He was also portrayed as a misunderstood superhero in the digital comic *President Trump*. Written by Samuel McIntosh, the story featured a superpowered president doing battle with a villain/illegal immigrant named "El Chapo" who was attempting to tunnel into America. A narrative monologue on the last page reflected,

> Maybe one day every country will have the same opportunity as America. But right here, right now, even we don't hold those distant stars in our hands. Sometimes uncomfortable steps must be taken to reach our ideals. All we can do is be like they are. We must shine the best we can. (McIntosh 2017, 18)

Visually, the comic took Trump's heavyset physique and signature combed-over pompadour and turned them into the rippling muscles and long, flowing hair of a romantic hero, underscoring the president's own heroism to his admirers. A similar narrative approach was used in the 2018 *My Hero MAGAdemia*, a parody of the manga *My Hero Academia*, in which Trump, cast as Wall-Might, firmly but fairly defended his country's borders on behalf of hard-working Americans.

Given the varying degrees of superheroic associations between Democratic and Republican administrations, a four-issue run from DC Comics in 2008 is particularly notable. The series *DC Universe: Decisions* followed the Justice League as they attempted to stop serial assassination attempts on presidential candidates in the 2008 primaries. Complicating their crime-fighting efforts was an internal disagreement about whether it was ethical for superheroes to publicly support specific candidates. Ultimately, it is Superman who proclaimed that taking sides in politics would be wrong because a hero's duty is to all people, regardless of political affiliation and whoever is elected president should believe they have the full support of the superhero community in serving and protecting the public. It was, therefore, particularly noteworthy, even controversial, when in January 2020 Superman and his alter ego, Clark Kent, *endorsed* a candidate for Metropolis Mayor in *Action Comics* #1018 (see Johnston 2020).

PRESIDENTIAL PARABLES

As Noon observed, "The projection of heroic attributes onto the nation's highest political office might be understood as a crude form of wish fulfillment" (2016, 438). President Kennedy, who implored Americans to ask what they could do for their country, fearlessly called upon Superman to serve at his behest. President Obama, a marker of historicity as America's first Black president, embodied all the potential suggested by American superheroes—the possibility that the gangly teenager, the nerdy adult, or the social misfit may do great and wondrous things. In the comics' universes, presidencies of Superman, Batman, Captain America, and Thor all ushered in worlds without want or war, at least temporarily. Even the comedic webcomic-turned-book-series-turned-TV-series *Axe Cop*, about a police officer who prefers an axe to a gun, fixed the world's problems for more than one million years as *President of the World* by simply telling all "bad guys" to "poop poison and die" and threatening to "chop their heads off" (Nicolle and Nicolle 2013, 13).

Noon (2016) also suggested, however, that imagined superheroic presidents may compensate for perceived inadequacies of real presidents, a notion supported by DiPaolo's (2011) argument that superheroes may act as surrogates for poor presidential leadership, such as when Captain America beat out both Carter and Reagan for the 1980 election. The myth of the superheroic presidency embraces both these possibilities and offers a cautionary tale to Americans to be careful of what they wish for. Such is the message in the first six issues of the 2013 *Deadpool*, from Marvel, when a well-intentioned necromancer raised America's dead presidents from their graves (*Deadpool* #1). His hope was that the great leaders of America's past would be able to correct all the country's ills. Once brought back, the zombified presidents agreed that the US veered from what they envisioned during their administrations, but their solution was to kill everyone and start anew. The antihero/mercenary Deadpool is tasked with assassinating the dead presidents, but not without plenty of collateral damage. The moral of the story seems to be that the idyllic past is not always what it seems and our heroes, be they costumed crime-fighters or politicians in the Oval Office, are always flawed.

Similar warnings and tensions appear throughout the stories of superheroic presidents. Presidential superheroes particularly offer parables of excess power. "President Thor" was brought down because he wielded too much uncontrolled superpower; while he had good intentions of equalizing humanity by removing the distinction between humans and meta/superhumans, the powers he granted went unchecked and unquestioned, making the country vulnerable. In the *Ultimates*, Captain America resigned his office arguing, "America's never been perfect […] but it's always been at its best when the people are in the lead. It's time to move past the war, and the wartime president" (Humphries and Bennett 2013). His statement may be read as an indictment of the dramatic expansion, and abuse, of presidential war powers, especially under President George W. Bush (see critiques in Fletcher 2013), and, consequently, as a return of that power from the executive to the people.[2]

One timely critique of the myth of the superheroic president was presented in the CW's television series *Arrow*, based on the Green Arrow from DC Comics, a costumed crime-fighter who first appeared in comic books in 1941. The series, which premiered on October 10, 2012, followed billionaire playboy Oliver Queen (played by Stephen Amell), who, after being stranded and shanghaied in hostile lands for five years, returned home to Star City, formerly known as Starling City, to fight crime and corruption with a bow and arrow as a hooded vigilante. At the start of its fourth season, on October 14, 2015, Oliver Queen decided to run for mayor of Star City. Four months earlier, in real life, Donald Trump announced his intention to run for president, and it did not take long for viewers to draw connections between the two campaigns. Writing for Inverse.com, Eric Francisco noted, "Oliver Queen is running for mayor of Star City. He also fights crime as the Green Arrow. When the city is razed to the ground it will be his fault, a not at all subtle parable for the 2016 election" (Francisco 2015, para. 1). As a politician by day and costumed crime-fighter by night, Oliver Queen/Green Arrow was the perfect stand-in for the superheroic president. *Arrow*, however, disrupted this narrative by demonstrating that the qualities that make a good vigilante, such as a willingness to subvert the law in the name of the common good, do not necessarily make a good civic leader—and voters would be wise to remember this.[3]

The aesthetic of Oliver Queen's mayoral campaign resembled Hillary Clinton's; his slogan "UNITED" echoed her "STRONGER TOGETHER," both in pallets of blue and white (see figure 3.2). As a candidate, however, Queen was more

Figure 3.2. *Imitatio*—a mimetic tradition of an active relationship between representation and reality, or an interweaving of cultural products—is found in the Oliver Queen campaign imagery in *Arrow* (left), which echoed the 2016 Hillary Clinton campaign symbols and style (right).

like Donald Trump. Oliver Queen ran because he hoped to "return our home to greatness" (*Arrow* "The Candidate"); Trump's campaign wanted to "make America great again." Queen had no prior political experience; neither did Trump. Both made their lack of political experience a strength of their campaigns. Both Queen and Trump ran opposed by powerful women whom they accused of secret criminal activity and having immoral husbands. Queen was known in Star City as a billionaire playboy; Trump was known as multimillionaire reality star with multiple marriages (Hanna 2017). Queen was the son of the successful but corrupt CEO of Queen Consolidated, a business that dealt in everything from munitions to real estate; Trump was the son of a real estate developer. Both candidates distanced themselves from their fathers, projecting an image of individualistic, self-made men. Queen signed away his father's company and lost the nightclub he owned; Trump declared bankruptcy six times (Lee 2016a). Queen flunked out of four colleges; Trump attended two colleges as a questionable student before earning a degree that he did not value (Stripling 2016). Queen was tied to the Bratva, a powerful Russian mafia organization; Trump's presidency was accused of Russian espionage activity and collusion with the Russian government to influence the outcome of the election (Carter 2017).

Since 1840, when William Henry Harrison feminized his opponent, Martin Van Buren, masculinity has been a presidential virtue, and the twenty-first century has seen an increase in leaders "relying on the mobilization of libidinal energy" (Brock 2016, 1; Kimmel 2011). The attractiveness of hypermasculinity, both in terms of characteristics that align with a presidential "ideal" and in terms of basic libidinal appeal, has been offered as an explanation for the election of Donald Trump (Powell, Butterfield, and Jiang 2018; Brock 2016). The hypermasculine romantic hero is also standard fare in superhero comics which, from the creation of Superman, have embodied the warrior through impressive—and impossible—physiques, playing out male power fantasies (Landon 2008). The centrality of masculinity to the president, the superhero, and the superheroic presidency is captured in *Wonder Woman* #7 from November 1943. The cover proclaims "Wonder Woman for President," depicting the Amazonian giving an impassioned speech to supporters—a thousand years in the future. But the story is not really about a presidential superheroine. Instead, it features the first female US president, Arda Moore, who has established a peaceful and prosperous American matriarchy in the year 3000. The government is soon challenged by a growing men's movement working to reestablish a patriarchy and only by defeating the movement does Wonder Woman herself become president at the story's end. The narrative takes place in the far future timespan of 3000 to 3004 and in the midst of the futuristic utopia there are still gender-based power struggles. This alone suggests a pessimistic view of femininity in politics, underscored by the fact that readers never get to see Wonder Woman's presidency, ultimately leaving women out of the myth of the superheroic presidency (see also chapter eight).

Hypermasculinity is an exaggeration of stereotypical male traits, particularly physical strength, aggression, and sexuality. Trump's aggressiveness and sexuality were both key elements of his campaign, often in consort with each other, as in the now infamous tape of him asserting that women would let him grab them and kiss them because he was a star ("Transcript" 2016). Queen's impressive physique and strength was frequently showcased in *Arrow*, with actor Stephen Amell shimmying up a salmon ladder while shirtless. His sexuality was exerted through numerous love affairs and romantic partners. His aggressive nature was a major plot point and plot device throughout the series, as he negotiated the necessity of violence in the name of public safety. These two hypermasculine figures, the president and the superhero, merge in the American monomyth. The American superhero, including the mythologized president, becomes "a mere fantasmatic vehicle, representing masculinity, power, and altruism—a quality that is admired despite or because of the overt cynicism of much of the discourse on and around politics" (Brock 2016, 2). He is a man of action who, despite the questionable methods he may employ, does what needs to be done, what others will not do.

Fantasmatic men of action who exude strength and sexuality are found throughout popular culture. These characters, such as Green Arrow or Batman, often fit the so-called "Dark Triad of personality," exhibiting traits of narcissism, psychopathy, and Machiavellianism. The combination produces an antihero who believes in his superiority, acts without remorse, and believes that the end justifies the means (Jonason et al 2012). This is someone who can come across to others as a charming, confident risk-taker. Despite the undesirable elements of these personality traits, "antihero characters may be popular and real-life people who are high on the Dark Triad traits may be granted special privilege and tolerance [if] they do something positive for the group" (Jonason et al 2012, 194). Indeed, the corresponding masculine stereotypes of decisiveness, toughness, and activity are commonly considered desirable qualities for political leaders by voters who seek reassurance that someone can "do something to direct the nation's course," take action to address the problems that plague them, and indicate that their deepest dreams and ideals are attainable (Barber 1992, 6; see also Jamieson 1995; McDermott 2016). It is, therefore, unsurprising that Trump, described by press, pundits, and professionals as a narcissist, a psychopath, and a Machiavellian, was an attractive candidate to voters (Lunbeck 2017; Moran 2017; Ignatius 2016; Krugman 2017).

In other words, voters want a superhero. In 2006, journalist Matthew Yglesias described this phenomenon as the "Green Lantern Theory." In DC Comics canon, the Green Lantern Corps is an intergalactic peacekeeping force whose power is generated by rings that direct the wearer's will. Yglesias argued that "Green Lanternism" captures the popular conception of the presidency—a location through which the will of people is channeled and manifested (see Waldman 2012). *Arrow* illustrated some of the problems inherent in electing a superhero rather than a president (or mayor). The series explored complex relationships between right and wrong and between heroes and villains. The show's use of dark lighting, dark sets, and dark costuming reflected imagery commonly associated with evil rather than good. Although Arrow is subjectively better than those he fought, he did not operate according to traditional moral and civic virtues. Rather than romanticizing psychopathic and Machiavellian tendencies, *Arrow* used them to problematize heroism. During season five, after Queen became mayor of Star City, this issue was at the forefront of the character. As entertainment writer Chris E. Hayner noted, "This season has seen a massive uptick in Green Arrow's tendency to kill while seeking out vigilante justice, which as mayor would be something you'd think he would stand against" (2017, para. 5). This struggle of the law-abiding mayor/life-protecting hero versus the serial killing vigilante was at the center of a multi-episode story arc which revealed that Arrow kills not only because he thinks it necessary but because he likes it. It was a storyline that unsettled fans by stripping away the desirable decisiveness of the psychopath and left bare the antisocial, criminal aggression. Ultimately, the incompatibility of superheroing and politics was realized when Mayor Queen was impeached for his vigilantism; the season six storyline was designed to mirror the controversy surrounding President Trump's challenges to the limits of executive power when he moved to fire Justice Department employees investigating his Russian ties (Burlingame 2018).

Likewise, Image Comics' *Youngblood* series emphasized tensions between superheroism and good government. In 2009, *Youngblood* #8–9 featured cameos of Barack Obama, charging the superhero team Youngblood with sending a message to Al-Qaeda and reminding the American people "of our glorious past, this country's greatness" (Liefeld and Yackey 2009). Then, in the 2017 series reboot, the Diehard, a former cyborg superhero from the World War II era, was president of the United States at a time when America has "gotten out of the superhero business" because of the criminal activity, including assassinations and government cover-ups, involved in vigilantism (Bowers and Towe 2017). In his first hundred days, President Diehard attempted to put the trust and power back in the hands of the American people by supporting an app—called Help!—that was the superhero version of ride-sharing, allowing average citizens to request and offer, monitored and controlled, rescue services. But, just like the Uber murders that captured the public's attention in 2016, Help! had a dark side and the new president's political efforts were soon challenged by his old superhero connections.

CONCLUSION

The political spectacle with its cycle of enemies and leaders, threats and reassurances, is not unlike the structure of the superhero serial, which locks the protagonist in a pattern of facing and defeating an unceasing rotation of villains who would cause harm to society, with audiences willfully suspending their disbelief to enjoy both the descent into chaos and the return to order provided by the story. In fact, Noon (2016) has drawn a direct link between the cycle of political fantasy and disillusionment and the myth of the superheroic presidency. He argues, for example, that the multitudinous comic book depictions of Obama presented "fables of survival and redemption" in which Obama either fully restored the well-being of the nation or at least established the conditions needed for a full recovery (439–40). But, good superheroics do not necessarily make good politics. Superheroes are usually able to get things done because they can work outside the laws of physics (such as Superman who possesses "strength far beyond that of any ordinary mortal") and outside the laws of government (such as Batman who is a wanted vigilante). Politicians who work outside the system are less successful. *Arrow* demonstrated this by building tension between Green Arrow as a violent vigilante and frequent loner and his alter ego Mayor Oliver Queen as a defender of justice and a representative of the collective.

The year 2018 was arguably the year of the superhero: *Black Panther, Avengers: Infinity War, Deadpool 2, The Incredibles 2, Ant-Man & the Wasp, Venom, X-Men: Dark Phoenix,* and *Aquaman* were just a few of the major motion picture releases in the superhero genre. In the midst of "Hollywood's comic book movie renaissance" the *New York Times* asked, "When superheroes battle evil, why does Washington always lose?" (Cochrane 2018, headline), while the *Washington Post* observed, "There are no superheroes in D.C." (Flood 2018, headline). The former observed that despite themes of fighting for the public good, the "heart of American democracy is often sidelined" in the films because Washington represents history and abstract notions, more than the essence of what the country really is right now (Cochrane 2018, para. 6). The latter echoed this with deeper cynicism, remarking that in the movies, the heroes and not the government stand up for oppressed, but in real life, there are no superheroes and the government still does little for the people (Flood 2018). Such is the myth of the superheroic presidency. Like Kennedy, it envisions a new frontier where all things are possible. And, like Superman's disguise as the mild-mannered reporter Clark Kent, it usually isn't what it appears to be. Whether a superhero aids a president or is a president, the superheroic presidency depicts the complexities of Americans' democratic ideals. The public wants to believe that the president is a hero, but whether it is Captain America resigning his office because he is too powerful for it, superpowered President Trump doing unpopular things for the perceived greater good, or Deadpool assassinating admired dead presidents bent on an American genocide, superheroics are as ill-fitted to the presidency as superhero movies are to Washington, DC.

THE NIXON PREZIDENCY AND THE POLITICALLY CYNICAL COMIC BOOK

The Twenty-sixth Amendment, enfranchising over eleven million eighteen-to twenty-year-olds, was added to the US Constitution in July 1971. The following year, five burglars were arrested breaking into the Democratic National Committee headquarters at the Watergate complex in Washington, DC, which led *Washington Post* reporters Bob Woodward and Carl Bernstein to slowly uncover a series of related political crimes, conspiracies, and coverups. In 1973, President Richard Nixon took full responsibility for the "Watergate scandal," ending in his resignation in 1974. The interplay of the Voting Rights Act of 1971 and the Watergate investigation of 1972 indirectly motivated the plot of DC Comics' 1973 series *Prez: The First Teen President*.

Prez: The First Teen President took as its premise the promise of the Twenty-sixth Amendment. It was generally believed that the Voting Rights Act could have a significant impact on government, providing youths, who were active in the counterculture denouncing the "establishment," with a more effective voice in political matters. These newly enfranchised activists would be able to end "the old 'boss' type canvassing of voters," put more eighteen-to twenty-year-olds in local elected positions with grassroots impact on everything from education to city governments, and build enough voting power to decide national elections (Kubiak 1971, 322; also Brown and Brown 2004). *Prez* imagined that this would be so, foreseeing these new voters promoting youth culture from the bottom up to eventually enact a constitutional amendment to lower the age of eligibility for president, allowing a teenager named Prez Rickard to be elected to the White House.

Prez Rickard embodied the political hopes and fears of the Watergate era. Optimism for the potential of the youth movement was captured by Prez's "truth-and-love campaign" on the new Flower Party ticket and in his ability to reject the corrupt machinations of the old establishment, personified in a character named Mayor Boss Smiley (Simon and Grandenetti 2016, 29). Doubts about the practicality of the youth movement were reflected in how Prez's election "polarized the generations" and in a storyline wherein his inexperience and naivete resulted in the instigation of impeachment proceedings (Simon and Grandenetti 2016, 29). From both perspectives, *Prez: The First Teen President* captured the political climate of the Watergate-era: It is reasonable to assume that a criminal politician who is opposed to the youth movement was analogous for President Richard Nixon who committed crimes to ensure his electoral victory and aligned himself with the so-called "silent majority" that was opposed to the protest and counterculture movements of the civil rights era. Prez's impending impeachment can thus be read as analogous to negative public opinions about the presidency engendered by Watergate (see Arterton 1974; Arterton 1975; Zimmer 1979).

Subsequently called "the strangest political fiction of all time" (Reed 2007, para. 1). *Prez: The First Teen President* was abruptly canceled in 1974 after just four issues, though a fifth story appeared in the *Cancelled Comic Cavalcade* #2 of 1978. One might speculate that the "highly negative" attitudes of children toward the presidency during the height of the Watergate scandal (Arterton 1975, 478) and beyond might have limited audience interest in a comic that suggested that "the history books of tomorrow will surely tell of young men like Prez [...]—and perhaps you, too" (Simon and Grandenetti 2016, 29). Despite its short initial run, the series titular character reappeared in subsequent decades, frequently coinciding with moments of political or social turmoil, including a special paperback collection of his assorted exploits released during the polarizing 2016 presental election. He guest-starred in an issue of *Supergirl* (#10) in 1974, the same year his own series ended. He was referenced in *Animal Man* #23–24 in 1990, the year East and West Germany reunited, and the year US troops were sent to the Middle East following Iraq's invasion of Kuwait. In 1993—the first year of Bill Clinton's presidency in the aftermath of George H. W Bush's war in Iraq, the year that terrorists first bombed the World Trade Center in New York City, and the year that the US government launched a siege on the Branch Davidian cult compound in Waco, Texas—Prez Rickard was featured in "The Golden Boy" story by Neil Gaiman in *Sandman* #54. The story looked retrospectively at Prez's presidency, which succeeded Richard Nixon's, and cast Prez—who averted war in Middle East, solved the energy crisis, and advanced social justice—as a Kennedy-inspired avatar for the American Dream: young, idealistic, successful.

Two years later, in 1995, Prez reappeared in a Vertigo one-shot entitled *Smells Like Teen President*, an homage to the angst-filled grunge movement of the decade with a reference to Nirvana's 1991 hit song and teen-revolution anthem "Smells Like Teen Spirit." Grunge addressed themes of social alienation, apathy, and limitation—a reflection of the depressed, rural logging communities from which many grunge musicians originated. Apathy and alienation were key components of the comic's narrative; as one character noted, "My whole generation is so removed from and desensitized to the world around them . . ." (Brubaker and Shanower 1995). The story focused on "P. J."—a nickname for "Prez Junior"—a teenage orphan, who believed himself the illegitimate son of the now-deceased Prez, as he embarked on a journey of self-discovery. P. J. learned about the sociopolitical ills of America that killed Prez: big business and consumerism, bombs and missiles, corrupted politicians, wars, poverty, poor health care, drugs, and racial tensions. Prez's spirit imparted, "Don't let the cancer into your life. . . . Remember, live, think, and know" (Brubaker and Shanower 1995).

DC fully relaunched the *Prez* title during its DC You initiative in June 2015, the same month that Donald Trump announced his controversial presidential campaign. The new narrative was set in the year 2036, a time when society is organized by commercial technology and corporate conglomerates. This time, a teen president was possible not because the youth movement lowered the eligibility age but because a "Corporate Personhood Amendment" expanded the very definition of an individual. Nineteen-year-old Beth Ross—the star of an embarrassing viral video—was promoted as a candidate by a hacktivist group and won following a messy congressional vote. Her vice president was Preston "Prez" Rickard. Writer Mark Russell imagined this version of *Prez* as exploring the tensions between past and present, old and new. It presented what Russell saw as the conflict between the ideals and ideas of the nineteenth century, as promoted by forces like the Tea Party movement, and the needs and challenges of the twenty-first century (Rivera 2015).

In the two decades that intervened between *Smells Like Teen President* and the new *Prez*, the visage of the original Prez Rickard popped up throughout DC and Warner Bros. holdings. In 2002, a televised State of the Union address by President Rickard opened the dystopian story of *Batman: The Dark Knight Strikes Again*. Prez made two televised appearances in 2011, presiding over the opening of a time capsule in the "Triumvirate of Terror" episode of *Batman: Brave and the Bold* and as a teenage heartthrob in the "Pawn of Shadows" episode *Scooby-Doo! Mystery Incorporated*. He was referred to as somewhat disreputable by the sitting president, Calvin Ellis/Superman, in the 2012 *Action Comics* #9. And he was referenced within the 2015 *Multiversity* titles as part of DC Comics' "Convergence" event.

As Mark Russell observed, despite the relative obscurity of the 1973 comic "the idea behind 'Prez,' is very resonant" (in Rivera 2015, para. 5). Russell explained,

Figure 4.1. The bright, commercial, clock-filled town of Steadfast in *Sandman* #54. Clocks represent structure, control, and surveillance as well as the compression of past, present, and future.

The newest *Prez* opened during the election of 2036, but when its election night came to a close without a clear winner it recalled the real election night of 2000 which also produced no winner. The imagined election of 2036 was complicated when the sitting president, whose party was concerned with good Christian values, dropped out of the race because his BDSM-style personal ad became public. A group of powerful senators known as the Colonels, identifiable by lapel pins reminiscent of the KFC logo, selected an unintelligent but easily manipulated man as their new candidate. Meanwhile, teenager Beth Ross became a viral internet sensation through an online video in which she inadvertently burned her hair while cleaning the grill at the fast-food hotdog restaurant where she worked, struggling to make money to get medical treatment for her dying father. The activist group Hacker Collective Anonymous used Beth's internet infamy to exploit the public's lack of political interest by running a protest campaign for the viral "Corndog Girl." When no candidate received enough votes to win, political bartering ensued for a congressional vote, which accidentally decided the election in Beth's favor.

Beth's main adversary was Smiley Enterprise and its special interest cohorts—pharmaceuticals, weapons, telecommunications, stocks, pork barrel spending ... all marked by holograph-style icon masks (a smiley face, a bomb, a smoking dog, a pig ...). When confronted with the Beth Ross presidency,

Smiley noted, "It doesn't matter who's in charge. [...] We're not players in this game. We **are** the game" (Russell, Caldwell, and Morales 2016). Corporations dominated Beth's world and the pages of the comic books—hospitals filled with promotions, celebrity-sponsored public schools, corporatized welfare services, and human billboards—and controlled time itself: Smiley Enterprises stated, "Our product—is time. Life is made of time. And we are the world's leading manufacturer of time" (Russell, Caldwell, and Morales 2016).

Timepieces were prominent in the establishment of the Prez title, and the concept of time was a key plot point for the Prez character. Clocks had a positive connotation in the 1970s connected to Prez's small hometown and his first civic achievement as a youth. At the start of the story, the town's clocks were broken, representing the broken mechanisms of government. Prez fixed them so that newly enfranchised youths could vote, indicating the promise and potential of the youth movement. The clocks, therefore, also suggested the importance of the historical moment, indicating that the time is/was now. Prez's punctuality as president underscored the positive connotations of the clocks, hinting at the supposed maturity and reliability of American youth that motivated passage of the Twenty-sixth Amendment (Kubiak 1971). The idea of a universal "watchmaker" following Prez's death in *Sandman*, and his subsequent journey to redeem other versions of America, also reinforced the myths of the United States as a "chosen" and "millennial" nation, selected by a divine power for special purposes and responsibilities in the world (Hughes 2005).

The clocks of the 2015 series were a much more ominous symbol. With connections to corporations, time became commodified—a resource to be controlled and exploited for the financial gain of the few at the expense of the many. People themselves were now like the gears of a clock—parts of a machine. In this world, the clock is/was ticking. The time is not now, the time is almost past; it is running out. This idea of having either wasted or lost time was certainly evident in writer Mark Russell's approach to *Prez* as commentary on the failure of the youth movement. It was also apparent in the narrative itself. Beth rushed to make enough money to pay for medical services for her dying father, but she was too late. Likewise, she learned that people around the world were being killed by American activities, but she was too late to stop it. As in the original *Prez: The First Teen President*, time posed a danger.

Across all Prez stories, clocks also suggested being watched and keeping watch, in both the protective, guardianship, sense and in the voyeuristic, surveillance, sense. Fixing clocks is what put Prez on Boss Smiley's radar in *Prez: The First Teen President*. In *Smells Like Teen President*, clocks dominated the facades throughout the town of Steadfast, their faces looming over the people and visitors. In *Prez*, companies controlled their employees' use of time, even their bathroom breaks, with posted reminders that "Every Second Counts

Nixon PREZidency and the Rise of the Politically Cynical Comic Book   63

Figure 4.2. Smiling-face figures in "Prez" and *Transmetropolitan* represent corporate greed and political corruption. (Top, left-right: Simon & Grandenetti 2016, 15; Ellis, Robertson, and Ramos 2009, 26. Bottom, left-right: Gaiman, Allred, Talbot, and Buckingham 2016, 153; Russell, Caldwell, and Morales 2016, n.p.).

(and we are counting!)" (Russell, Caldwell, and Morales 2016). Even President Beth Ross's own communications room used the same technology as the NSA, allowing her to break into anyone's internet, phone, or television connection at will—which she proceeded to do in order to find people for her cabinet.

Besides the clock, the other face that dominated the pages of assorted Prez storylines is the smiley face, most prominently presented through the character of Boss Smiley. His round, grinning visage, and his yellow smiley-face logo, found in *Prez: The First Teen President*, *Sandman*, and *Prez*, was the embodiment of government and corporate corruption motivated by greed and self-interest (see figure 4.2). Indeed, the smile as a logo of corporate culture and consumerism has its real-world counterparts: The yellow smiley face was used by the Walmart company and a stylized smile is part of the Amazon.com logo. The analogy between Smiley Enterprises and such big-box retailers was made explicit in *Prez* when Boss Smiley stated, "Smiley Enterprises is the world's largest most profitable corporation. We don't make anything. People could get everything we sell somewhere else. The only difference is they wouldn't get it as quickly. As cheaply" (Russell, Caldwell, and Morales 2016).

The link between a smiley face and government corruption is found in other comics, too. The power-mad American president in the dystopian twenty-third century of the comic series *Transmetropolitan* (1997–2002), Gary Callahan, is nicknamed "the Smiler for the enormous grin he always carries as part of his public image" (Murphy 2013, 25). In a story about a journalist's crusade against the corruption of two successive US presidents, the Smiler has been compared to George W. Bush in that "increasing distrust in his administration from the people who originally supported him, is reminiscent of the decline in popularity of President Bush over his time in office" (Williams 2013, 5), but this also makes him comparable to Richard Nixon who similarly lost the trust of his own voters (Zimmer 1979). The journalist Spider Jerusalem is meanwhile branded by a triple-eyed smiley logo as a symbol of revolution.

The smiley icon rose in American pop culture prominence during the 1960s and '70s and has been occasionally associated with the psychedelic culture. It has appeared on novelty items with the words "have a nice day" and with a bleeding bullet hole through its forehead. The co-option of a counterculture symbol by the establishment for corporate ends is analogous to *Prez* writer Mark Russell's opinion about the failed youth movement when he observed, "You have the establishment and then you have the hippies revolting against the establishment, and what you end up getting are like accountants with long hair" (in Dunn 2015, para. 11). This very idea was also expressed in *Animal Man*'s encounter with Prez and the Love Syndicate of Dreamworld when the titular hero responded to a message about mindfulness and living in the present with the rejoinder, "Hippie crap. [. . .] The love generation ended up selling insurance" (Morrison 2003).

"WHO WATCHES THE WATCHMEN?"

It is important to note that both key themes/motifs of the Prez iterations involve faces—clock faces and smiley faces, joining to become a *two-faced* ideograph. This points to the cynic's impression of honesty. As rhetorician George Yoos noted,

> The cynic [. . .] may simply be calling attention to the degree that men deceive themselves about their own motives, and that they pretend to be operating on moral grounds when in fact they are only acting in self-interests. A cynic, for example, may be simply denying the honesty of most people. (1985, 59)

The corporate smiley face entreats us, like the villain Psycho-Pirate in *Animal Man*, to "smile and be happy" in the face of its deceptions and machinations. We are forced to watch the clock because the clock watches (controls) us. These same ideas were put forth through the same symbols in another post-Nixon comic series that offered a cynical look at sociopolitics: *The Watchmen*, which begged the question, alluded to throughout the Prez runs, "Who watches the Watchmen?"

Watchmen is a dystopian interpretation of recent history originally published in 1986–87 that built on political activities of the 1970s. In it, America won the war in Vietnam, Vietnam became the fifty-first state of the US, and Richard Nixon achieved four consecutive terms as president. Although the book's creative team—writer Alan Moore and artist David Gibbons—are British, the work was a nuanced commentary on America's Cold War ideologies and US national identity (Rehak 2011; Hughes 2006; Prince 2011). It was also a sophisticated consideration of the nostalgia of the superhero genre, a satire of arrogance of American foreign policy, a poetic of post-Einsteinian physics, a distanced look at social alienation and personal neuroses, a psychological consideration of modern media consumption, a Rorschach-ian personality test, and more (Bensam 2011). The focus here is those ideas captured by the book's ubiquitous use of the smiley face icon and clock faces, both of which are bloodied.

The plot focused on 1985 as the United States edged precariously close to World War III with the Soviet Union; freelance vigilantes (costumed crime-fighters) were outlawed, and most superheroes were therefore either retired or working for the government—until the murder of one of their own put them back on the streets and fighting the memories and deeds of their past. The book opened with a close-up of a yellow smiley face badge splashed with blood—remains from the costume of the murdered superhero known as the Comedian. From thereon out, the smiley face image appeared repeatedly throughout the twelve-issues/chapters of Gibbons' artwork: in the backstory of the Comedian's murder, in flashbacks of The Comedian's career, in the plugs on fire hydrants, in an image of the Galle Crater on Mars, in the view of a tunnel, in the distorted reflection in glass, in ripples of water, and on the faces of clocks—especially the Doomsday Clock that measured the country's proximity to nuclear war (Gibbons 2008).

As the emblem of the Comedian, the smiley face symbol represented the failings of American government and society. The Comedian, a government-sponsored hero, was arrogant, violent, and ironically dark, described as "the voice of hopelessness in the *Watchmen* world" (Loyd 2011, 1635). He started out with good intentions and a desire to understand the world, facing insurmountable odds, but ultimately succumbed to the insanity and evils of the world by accentuating them (Loyd 2011). Moore suggested that the smiley face was "a symbol of complete innocence" and that "putting a blood splash over the eye changes its meaning" (in Eno and Csawza 1988, para. 28); the innocence is lost and the symbol is stained, just as The Comedian's desire to make sense of the world was corrupted, and America's well-intentioned foreign policy moved the world closer to Doomsday.

As a symbol of innocence lost, the blood splattered smiley face badge was notably found in the pages of *Sandman* #54, worn by the assassin who killed Prez Rickard's fiancée. In the same story, Prez was visited by Richard Nixon, who cynically warned him that nothing he did in the White House would matter and that "the mass of voting morons" will hate him, so the only thing worth achieving was power (Gaiman, Allred, Talbot, and Buckingham 2016, 139). Both *Watchmen* and *Sandman* raised questions about the existence of a cosmic watchmaker and while they reached different conclusions, the former rejecting the idea and the latter leaving it in the realm of possibility, the very question spoke to the competing senses of urgency and futility represented by the ever-ticking clock.

At the start of *Watchmen*, the Doomsday Clock was at five minutes to midnight, indicating that nuclear war was close to being inevitable. The clock, and the time, was reflected in the stained smiley face patch, with the blood splatters marking the same position as the Doomsday Clock's minute-hand. As the twelfth and final issue of *Watchmen* opened, the clock was at midnight and dripping with blood (see figure 4.3). The imagery "echoes the shattered watch on the cover of *Time*'s Hiroshima Week issue" (Sanderson 2011, 2518), recalled in chapter VI by the human hydrogen bomb named Dr. Manhattan as "a damaged pocket-watch, stopped at the instant of the blast, face cracked . . ." (Moore and Gibbons 2014, 134). But clocks do not ever really stop; the mechanisms that run them stop, but time continues to move forward. When midnight comes, the day starts anew. As Thierry Groensteen argued, the figure of a circle, such as that of a clock or a smiley face, when used as a recurring motif carries such symbolic connotations as "eternal recommencement" (2007, 155). Thus, we get to a narrative or time loop of American politics suggesting that history does, in fact, repeat itself. At the very least, we can argue that the end of one politically cynical comic book series is not the end of political commentary; the themes will be recommenced in another title, even as time marches on.

Indeed, similarly pessimistic themes are found in another deconstructive comic series of the 1980s, Howard Chaykin's *American Flagg!* Published between 1983 and 1989, with a story set in 2031, *American Flagg!* envisioned a crisis in 1996 that ushered in a new corporate world order. It offered a vision of a politically polarized nation, unified only in its rampant commercialism, materialism, and obsession with a media-saturated, reality-TV-driven culture. Amid a deeply futuristic landscape of flying vehicles, interplanetary travel, human colonization of Mars, and advanced weaponry is a story that commented on the Cold War and the tensions of Russian communism and American capitalism, the Troubles between Ireland and Great Britain, and the Ronald Reagan

Figure 4.3. The Doomsday Clock at the start of Moore and Gibbons (2014) *Watchmen*, chapter XII.

brand of patriotism in which "*love* for the *country*" was "a devotion fed as much by history" as by nostalgia (Chaykin 2008). While Chaykin's illustrations were devoid of the round smiling faces and clock faces, his panels were nonetheless filled with circle symbols. The icon of the ruling corporate entity, Plex, was a black circle with a red star at the twelve o'clock position, a blue star at four/five o'clock, and a white star at seven/eight o'clock positions. The emblem repeatedly appeared on "vid" (TV) screens and law uniforms. It was echoed in circular satellite dishes orbiting the Earth and radar screens monitoring air traffic; in crosshairs, gun barrels, and targets; in the duplicated "o" in the onomatopoeia of machinery sound effects; in the headlights of armored vehicles; in the prominent arc of the Soviet hammer and sickle insignia; in planetary diagrams; and, in the many prominent breasts and studs of fetishistic attire of women who "exude a righteous and deadly Post-Feminist 'tude" (Yezbick 2009, 6). Again, the circle motif pointed to a narrative loop, one that underscored the comic's cyclical movement between the crisis of 1996, known as the Year of the Domino (when things fell), the current year of 2031, and the future year of 2076 (the target date for Plex's plan to sell off the remnants of the United States to reigning world superpowers).

Despite the absence of clocks, Chaykin's pages were frequently framed, shaped, or punctuated by bold digital countdowns (see figure 4.4). "As a result," Daniel F. Yezbick suggests, "the page space itself and the spatio-topical framework it supports seem to seethe or leak with chaotic, randomly subversive meanings" (2009, 11). The notation and structure of time gave a sense of both

Figure 4.4. Digital clocks or countdowns frame the visuals, and thus the story, in *American Flagg*, representing the constraints of a techno-dystopia.

urgency and external order, hinting at the techno-dystopia in which the characters existed. Chaykin's artisan style offered, according to Matthew J. Costello, "a visual portrayal of the breakdown of order that is the main theme" of the text (2012, 155). Through its imitation, or eternal recommencement, of the "mindless, rapid-fire spectacle" of the corporatized, fetishized, hyper-violent, media-saturated culture that the comic satirized, the "pseudo-spectacular page designs teach us how to navigate, sift, and critique" not only the mass communication of *American Flagg*'s world but also of our own (Yezbick 2009, 17).

"BEYOND" PREZ

Prez: The First Teen President was abruptly canceled after just four issues. Its reincarnation, *Prez*, was originally slated for two six-issue miniseries, but was suddenly canceled after the sixth issue, despite winning a Reuben Award and earning a high approval rating from readers (Manning 2016; Alverson 2016). Instead of a six-issue follow-up, writer Mark Russell concluded his *Prez* run with a twelve-page *Catwoman* 2016 election special which cameoed a young Beth Ross in a prequel-style scene that foreshadowed her 2036 presidency. But Russell was not finished with his biting commentary on politics in America. In 2016, DC Comics' launched a series of titles collectively known as Hanna-Barbera Beyond, a "new line of comics inspired by some of [Hanna-Barbera's] classic cartoons" that "offer imaginative new takes on the characters" (DCE 2016). The titles presented "new visions of the classic toons, injected with current sensibilities and aimed at the teen-plus set" but with "the heart and soul of the classic animation" for original Hanna-Barbera fans (Beedle 2016, para. 1). Dealing with themes of celebrity, consumption, corporate excess, government corruption, chemical warfare, viral epidemics, natural disaster and environmental crises, and human survival, the assorted titles—presented as one-shots, features, and runs of six, twelve, and thirty-six issues—featured classic characters like Scooby-Doo, George Jetson, Quick Draw McGraw, Atom Ant, and Jonny Quest; the titles were all poignantly political and nostalgically now (Knopf in preparation). In fact, the *Scooby Apocalypse* series and the *Wacky Raceland* series both included villains resembling President Donald Trump. Following the demise of *Prez*, Russell became the writer for two of these titles: *The Flintstones* and *Exit Stage Left: The Snagglepuss Chronicles*.

Critical Writ observed that the "politically inclined tone" of *The Flintstones* comic book was "praised for having a sense of social justice in a similar vein as *Prez*," advancing Russell's idea that "the fundamental mission of comic books [is to] identify what is wrong with the world and create characters who can set it right" (Krishef 2017, para. 1, 11–12). Of *The Flintstones*, Russel noted that the original cartoon has

> embedded commentary on consumerism. If you want a Polaroid camera, then there's a tiny bird with a chisel that has to live inside that camera, but somehow, there's never any question about whether or not subjecting that bird to a life of hellish slavery inside a camera is worth it. (quoted in Keith 2016, para. 10)

He emphasized such commentary on consumerist culture in the new comic book adaptation, showing us how the world of *The Flintstones* built civilization through the commodification and exploitation of land, natural resources, animals, people, and religion.

Alex Abad-Santos described *The Flintstones* in an interview for *Vox* as using "Bedrock's first family and Hanna-Barbera's gag-filled prehistoric vision to tell a basic truth about human nature: that a civilization's first steps to survival involves [*sic*] someone else's doom" (2017, para. 3). Through this link between civilization and destruction, paralleled to consumerism and disposability, *The Flintstones* also pointed to the fragility of human existence and experience (Brogan 2017). If Russell's *Prez* was commentary on the failure of the youth movement, *The Flintstones* could be read as commentary as how society is failing youths. Henry A. Giroux suggested that "the legacy of jaded excess" that shapes contemporary politics has created policies that impose suffering on children (2009, 1). A shrinking social welfare system and an eviscerated public education system pushes more teenagers and young adults into unemployment and prisons. Within political discourses and policies of consumerism, Giroux (2009 and 2012) argued that youth are increasingly commodified and are, thus, disposable.

A similar perspective was taken in *The Flintstones* by Russell, who believes "that one of the fundamental features of civilization is that it tends to reduce people to their economic functions" (in Abad-Santos 2017, para. 14). Russell, with artist Steve Pugh, made this case through the plight of *The Flintstones'* animal-based home goods: Rams were jackhammers. Goats were lawn mowers. Lizards were garbage disposals. Parrots were answering machines. Octopi were dishwashers. And the animal-appliances were aware of their subjugated existence. Readers found the slave labor of the animal kingdom huddling together and contemplating their existence and their doom. In a deeply emotional side story, a baby elephant-vacuum, relegated to living most of its life alone in a dark closet, befriended an armadillo-bowling ball. "Vacuum," as the elephant is named, admitted that he found comfort in "knowing that my friend Bowling Ball is on the other side of the door" (Russell, Pugh, and Chuckry 2017 #6). The inhumanity of the system was accentuated when Vacuum—essentially a child laborer—sneaked into a theater to see a movie, to experience some bit of life outside his dark closet, and was subsequently forced to clean the theater floor, ultimately dying from the filth he was force-fed. No longer fulfilling his economic function in the home, he was crammed into a trashcan, trunk draped over the edge, and left at the side of the road, leaving Bowling Ball to mourn, unheeded by the humans who used them.

Russell's other contribution to the Hanna-Barbera Beyond initiative was the *Exit Stage Left: The Snagglepuss Chronicles* (see chapter two). The story mostly took place in 1953 against the backdrop of the Cold War arms race and paranoia. The closeted-gay Southern playwright known as Snagglepuss was the toast of Broadway, rubbing elbows with the Algonquin Round Table by day and secretly meeting his Cuban refugee boyfriend, his gay best friend Huckleberry Hound, and Huck's boyfriend NYC policeman Quick Draw McGraw at the Stonewall Inn by night. Snagglepuss's success, and rumors of his personal life, made him the target of the House Committee on Un-American Activities. When powerful forces aligned to either control or purge the most influential voices in society, neither he nor his friends were safe.

Although the book focused on what it would have been like to be a gay man living in the theater scene of 1950s-era New York, and what it means to create honest and authentic art when one cannot live an honest and authentic life, the story resonated strongly with politics in the 2010s with its themes of marginalizing minorities and using fear tactics to control or eradicate targeted populations (Johnston 2018; McMillan 2017). Russell noted that Snagglepuss was

> trying to stand up for people who otherwise would be shoved under the stairs in this time of great national paranoia in the Red Scare mentality. It's very easy in a time of national catastrophe—of *perceived* national catastrophe—to throw people under the sink and forget about them. [...] He's willing to stand up for people when the rest of the country is not. (in McMillan 2017, para. 13)

The same theme was found when Russell gave the exploited laborer/animal Vacuum a voice in *The Flintstones*, and when he gave poverty-stricken teenager Beth Ross a voice in *Prez*.

If the circular form of the smiley face and the clock through "Prez" and *Watchmen* can be read as symbolizing "eternal recommencement" then the circle can be found within the narrative themes, if not the visual motifs, of *The Flintstones* and *Exit Stage Left*, as well as the other socially conscious titles within the Hanna-Barbera Beyond initiative. Mark Russell remarked,

> Somebody once said that history never repeats itself, it just rhymes an awful lot. Unfortunately, there are these themes in history—particularly American history—that never really seem to go away. Themes like marginalizing minorities and immigrants, using fear of military threats to make people go along with abuse. These themes quiet down every now and again, but they never seem to go away, so unfortunately, when you're writing about these things, they will always be timely or relevant. (in McMillan 2017, para. 16)

Indeed, the political processes and systems themselves are fraught with continuous circles of their own, such as dueling *loops* of political powerplaces that resist needed systemic changes and *spirals* of cynicism that erode citizen participation (Harich 2014; Cappella and Jamieson 1997). We turn now to the latter of these, bringing the discussion *full circle* back to the Watergate-related distrust of government to consider how these comics express sentiments of political cynicism and, in so doing, caution against being cynical.

Cynicism is often perceived as a moral failing—an attitude that undermines political and social life via its apparent hostility toward virtues of faith, hope, and charity. And yet, the cynic is often also thought to be realistic and honest, if brutally so (Vice 2011). Likewise, political cynicism has been hotly criticized as something that "saps [the public's] sense of political possibility" (Hart and Hartelius 2007, 263) and ambivalently praised as "little more than an indication of an 'interested and critical citizenry'" (de Vreese 2005, 294). In a similar vein, the media's role in contributing to political cynicism is debated. On one hand, research has suggested that the media's heavy focus on the game of politics—coverage that emphasizes politicians' motives and style rather than political issues and policies—feeds a spiral of political cynicism that damages civic engagement (Cappella and Jamieson 1997; Valentino, Beckmann, and Buhr 2001). On the other hand, there is limited empirical evidence to support a causal link between political cynicism and voter turnout, and "cynicism, when properly targeted, can redress the corruption of a political order that is widely and perhaps wisely held suspect by the public" (Bennett 2007, 280). In a political and popular culture riddled with cynicism it is difficult to determine whether the spiral starts with politicians, the press, or the public itself, or whether cynicism is the cause or the result of political challenges (Bennett 2007). But the comics discussed above suggest that political cynicism is not the enemy of political hope. Snagglepuss explained as much to HUAC, "Art is telling the world how it's killing you. How its institutions have failed you. In the end, any culture worth a damn is made by subversives because art is what tells the world it needs to change" (Russell, Feehan, Parsons, and Marzán Jr. 2018).

The cynic's discourse has been described as a process of invention "in which strategies of survival and rhetorical strategies repeatedly converge and coalesce" (Branham 1994, 336). Despite criticisms of the cynic, survival is not hostile to or disrespectful of virtues of hope or charity, nor is it dismissive of civic duty. Indeed, survival depends on these things. This is the utopic message imparted in such dystopic comic books as *Watchmen*, *Prez*, and *The Flintstones*. In the words of Vacuum, "Maybe the only meaning to life is that which we get from each other" (Russell, Pugh, and Chuckry 2017 #6). Indeed, most of these comics put the onus of bettering society on the readers, asking them to get involved whether with the political process or with humanity itself.

Prez: The First Teen President underscored the power of the vote and of grassroots initiatives when it told "the story of the most powerful man on earth. [. . .] A teenager who becomes President of the United States. It is not a true story. Not yet, but someday it may happen" (Simon and Grandenetti 2016, 8). From the Voting Rights Act of 1971, it foresaw youth candidates being elected into local offices, and then national offices, eventually gaining a majority in Congress and lowering the age requirement for president to eighteen. *Smells Like Teen President* preached the influence of the individual and made the link between the personal and political, suggesting, "The world problem is an individual problem—if the individual is at peace, has happiness, has great tolerance and an intense desire to help, then the world problem disappears" (Brubaker and

Shanower 2016, 210). *Prez* acknowledged the inequities and inequalities inherent in the American system and the helplessness that people feel because of it, but it also reminded readers that they are not powerless; at her inauguration, Beth Ross declared, "So much about this country is backwards. People with real problems don't have the money to fix them. And the people with money don't have any real problems" (Russell, Caldwell, and Morales 2016).

Exit Stage Left directed readers that "conformity and shame destroy people. And a culture that doesn't fight back is as useful as an old calendar" (Russell, Feehan, Parsons, and Marzán 2018). *Transmetropolitan*'s hero, journalist Spider Jerusalem, served as a model to readers to actively question those in power, and it indicated that political cynicism can enable civic engagement if the public is motivated by distrust to seek truth and to speak truth to power (Murphy 2013). *Watchmen* illustrated how people have two basic options when confronted with failures and grim realities: we can choose to retire from them and retreat from society and from our roles and responsibilities in the world, or we can recommit ourselves to an effort to make sense of the world (Ritchie 2011). In other words, all those circular clocks, round smiley faces, and spirals of cynicism are symbols of the ongoing quest for perfection.

CONCLUSION

The perspectives on sociopolitics offered in these assorted titles are frequently contradictory: Peace and love are desirable, but not always effective. Voting matters, but money has more say. It is necessary to know history, but life happens in the present. The individual is important, but so is the community. Survival depends on relationships, but we enter and leave the world alone. This is the juxtaposition and hyperbole of the cynic, demonstrating not only the gap between possibility and reality but also the complexities and the nuances of both which must be negotiated. As established in the introduction to this volume, comics are known to offer guidelines for desirable civic behaviors, and fictional presidencies represent a public's desires. Time and again, comics like "Prez" seem to suggest that the ideal is either illusory or doomed, while books like *Watchmen* suggest that even when we win, we lose, and *The Flintstones* show us our many failings. This is not, however, the political cynicism of hopelessness but of action. It is true that the youth movement of the 1970s did not have the sizable impact that it might have had in the devastating attitudinal wake of Nixon's Watergate scandal, but there are always more youth to mobilize—and voters aged eighteen to twenty-four are routinely pegged as potentially pivotal in election outcomes (Aloi 2004). Indeed, that is what Russell's *Prez* reboot demonstrated—what might yet happen if the youth movement succeeds in the future.

And though *Exit Stage Left* may remind readers of recent failings in the areas of diversity, inclusion, and tolerance, it is also a reminder of how far society has come since the 1950s and the days of McCarthyism.

The key message is found within the clocks that are so ubiquitous to many of the stories: Time. Change takes time. Progress, however it may be defined, takes time. And the past, present, and future of not only the country but humanity are intricately and integrally connected. The time for action is past. The time for action is now. The time for action is coming. "Who watches the watchmen?" A cynical public.

REAGAN'S RAIDERS, TRUMP'S TITANS, AND POLITICAL PARODY

A patriotic American, invincible through the miracle of science, clad in the colors of his country's flag, acts as a warrior-hero, fighting the evildoers who would corrupt the innocence of the United States. No, it's not Captain America punching Nazis in 1941, but Ronald Reagan battling terrorist cyborgs, Bolivian drug lords, and Vietnamese communists in 1986. The three-issue *Reagan's Raiders* from Solson Publications was scripted by television actor Monroe Arnold as a superhero parody and political satire, starring the fortieth president and his cabinet as superpowered global police in the Cold War (Kretsch 2016). The short-lived series is remarkable in part for its ambiguity. Journalist Frederik Strömberg (2010) and critic Ronald Kretsch (2016) both note that it is impossible to decide whether *Reagan's Raiders* was celebrating or mocking Reagan's machismo and that both supporters and detractors of Reagan could appreciate the parodic content. The series is also significant because it was revived, at least through allusion and homage, in 2017 with Keenspot's publication of *John Barron's Trump's Titans*. Like its predecessor, *Trump's Titans* was politically ambiguous, painting the superpowered Donald Trump as narcissistic and dimwitted, but also presenting his adversaries, including real-life Democratic opponents, as truly evil villains (for more, see Terror 2017). But, whereas *Reagan's Raiders* lasted but three short black-and-white issues (though was reportedly planned for at least six), and was the only comic of the Reagan era to star the president, *Trump's Titans* persisted through multiple brightly colored glossy issues, sequels issues, and a trade paperback, coexisting with more than a half-dozen other comic titles, mostly satire/parody, that star the forty-fifth president, making for one of the strongest markets of political satire comic books since the underground comix movement of the 1960s.

THE EVOLUTION OF POLITICAL CARTOONS

Political satire in comic form is most often associated with editorial/political cartoons. Editorial cartoons typically refer to "topical outbursts of image and text" that communicate attitudes or summary snapshots of situations (Worcester 2007, 223; Kemnitz 1973). These cartoons may provide political anecdotes that seek to make sense of government actions with biting partisan comment on current events, or social commentary designed to make life bearable (Press 1981; Davis 2009). They frequently operate as an inside joke, uniting a mass audience with shared culturally situated allusions while offering the audience a way to vent their frustrations with leaders or situations and making them laugh, by either reflecting the impressions of the public or making an issue salient to them (Bormann, Koester, and Bennett 1978; DeSousa and Medhurst 1982; Thibodeau 1989). They are part of the composite of political messages received by voters and constituents and have been embraced by political campaigns, "which confirms their legitimacy in the political arena of media" (Conners 2005, 480).

Political cartoons are primarily defined as "visual/verbal non-narrative commentary, typically in single-panel form, created by a staff member of a newspaper or appearing originally on the editorial pages of a newspaper" (Edwards 2001, 2149). As part of the comic strip format, they are most frequently part of the gag genre, which end with a punch line, though some, such as *Doonesbury*, fall within the serial strip genre, which may have a punch line but will also carry the story forward into future installments (Black 2010; Harvey 1994). This format for political humor is, however, in decline, along with the traditional newspaper. But, as Ilan Danjoux noted, "the apparent decline of the editorial cartoon should not be misconstrued with the erosion of the political cartoon itself" which is not, nor ever has been, bound to the newspaper (2007, 245). Larry Bush observed that "the history of cartoons has been one of artistic innovation and evolution" (2013, 72). For example, he traced the single-panel format of satirical prints to the early publication tradition of lithography, but noted that over time cartoonists established means for developing more in-depth narratives and reading experiences, such as the embedded panels used by Oliphant to provide additional commentary, the split-panel construct to sharpen contrasts or suggest the passage of time, the four-panel and serial format of the political strip as used by Garry Trudeau to provide greater explanation of issues, and a long-form cartoon used by Nick Anderson of the *Houston Chronicle*, which offers a hybrid of the single-panel satire and the four-panel strip. Collected volumes of American editorial cartoons for political purposes can be traced back to at least 1876 with Cash Thomas's *Centennial Congress Democratic House of Representatives Illustrated* and continue through the present day, both as historical collections and as contemporary humor publications.[1]

The satirical comic book may therefore be viewed as another artistic innovation of the editorial cartoon. While political messages and allegories are found in all genres of comics, from the nationalist superhero adventure to the moralist teen romance story (Duncan, Smith, and Levitz 2015), explicitly political satire and parody may be traced from early editorial lithographs to the emergence of underground comix in the 1960s. Comix were small press and self-published comic books that typically had socially relevant and/or satirical content, featuring topics such as feminism, marijuana legalization, Black Power, abortion, antiwar, and gay and lesbian issues, while frequently depicting sexual activity, violence, and drug use (Estren 2012; Rosenkranz 2003). *The Great Society Comic Book* and *Bobman and Teddy* in 1966 (see chapter three) and *The Hydrogen Bomb and Biochemical Warfare Funnies* in 1970 epitomize the blending of the traditional political cartoon content of politicians and public policy with the comic book form of stories and superheroes, ushering in the political satire comic book genre. Titles that followed vary widely in style, substance, and political orientation, but increased in number after the 1986 publication of *Reagan's Raiders*, which earned allusions in not only the 2017–19 *Trump's Titans* but also in a 2017 *President Pence* comic.

SUPERHEROES AND SUPERZEROES

Many satirical comics use superhero parody, from the Superman spoof of the *Great Society*'s SuperLBJ to the Captain America allusions in *Reagan's Raiders* and *Trump's Titans*. Superheroic identities and presidential legends are unified in the American monomyth of an extraordinary individual emerging to vanquish evil threatening the community (Lawrence and Jewett 2002; see chapter three). Both superheroes and presidents serve as symbols of the nation and models of civic duty (Dittmer 2013; Murphy 2003). The superhero as a political metaphor may, therefore, be used in satire to express praise, condemnation, or ambivalence about a politician.

Parody is intertextual and polysemic (Ceccarelli 1998; Hess 2011). It must be understood via both the subject matter of its message and the focus of its criticism (Hill 2013; Shugart 1999; Bennett 1985). In comics such as *Reagan's Raiders*, the focus of criticism was the American political milieu and the subject matter was the superhero genre. Superheroes are defined by Peter Coogan as protago-

Figure 5.1. A sample of political satire comic covers, illustrating the range of characters and parodies employed.

nists "with a universal, selfless, prosocial mission" who possess superpowers in the form of advanced technology or superior physical or mental skills, with an alternate identity that is embodied in a code name and iconic costume which typically expresses an aspect of biography, character, powers, and/or origin (2013, 257–62). This definition provides the basis for considering the messages embedded in many satirical political comics. Some of the seventy assorted issues, spanning sixty years, considered in this analysis include, in addition to *Reagan's Raiders* (1986) and *Trump's Titans* (2017–19), *The Great Society Comic Book* (1966) and *Bobman and Teddy* (1966), *Wonder Wart-Hog and the Nurds of November* (1980), *The Fanatic Four* (1994), *Political Action Comics: Major Flip Flop* (2004), "Libarro World" in *Liberality* (2006), *Barack the Barbarian* (2009) and *Sarah Palin versus the World* (2011), *President Pence* (2017), *My Hero MAG-Ademia* (2018), and *Alexandria Ocasio-Cortez and the Freshman Force* (2019) (see figure 5.1).

Parody and satire playfully distort the familiar in order to evoke expressions of amusement and disdain, using embellishments to transform imitation into caricature, or employing techniques such as irony and sarcasm to offer critical commentary (Hariman 2008; Hill 2013; Feinberg 1967). It is "the comic refunctioning of preformed linguistic or artistic material"—or repetition/imitation with a difference (Rose 1999, 52; Hess 2011). Traditional single-panel editorial cartoons refunction preformed artistic material when they use popular culture to make sense of political culture, with pop culture allusions serving as visual shorthand to connect with readers' interests, knowledge, and reality (Medhurst and DeSousa 1981). As editorial cartoonist Steve Benson explained, "In the milieu of current politics and culture and fads, we try to symbolically and instantaneously relate to our audience. [. . .] I use images that linger" (in Conners 2007, 262). Political satire comic books do the same, but with the ability to more fully engage, and develop, the story and background of the parodic object.

"The superhero's mission is to fight evil and protect the innocent; this fight is universal, prosocial, and selfless" (Coogan 2013, 264). Consistently across the satirical comics, whether the featured superheroic politicians are Republicans or Democrats, their missions put them in opposition to real-life enemies and adversaries—those of the United States itself, of the American people, of the particular politician/administration, or of the political party. *Reagan's Raiders*, for example, was firmly established within the Cold War contexts of the good guys versus the evil empire, and Reagan lead missions against terrorist groups and drug cartels with Russian ties. SuperLBJ in *The Great Society Comic Book* fought the quagmire of Vietnam politics; Bobby and Ted Kennedy as *Bobman and Teddy* fought Hubert Humphrey; *Wonder Wart-Hog* fought corporate corruption; *Reagan's Raiders* fought communists; the Clintons fought Rush Limbaugh in *The Fanatic Four* and Bob Dole in *Socialism Trek*; John Kerry and John

Edwards as *Major Flip Flop* and Leftwing the Wonder Boy team up with Michael Moore to fight George W. Bush, Dick Cheney, and Kerry's own voting record; *Trump's Titans* fought Hillary Clinton, George Soros, Facebook, the mainstream media, and public opinion; Wall Might, *My Hero MAGAdemia*'s stand-in for Trump, fought illegally immigrating Mexicans; and, a retired Obama, as *Barack Panther*, fought Dick Cheney, Donald Trump, and Kanye West. In each instance, the heroes represent a version of right or good and their opponents an idea of wrong or evil.

The stories that were clearly critical of their political target framed these missions as absurd, ego-driven, wrought with inconsistencies, and/or doomed to failure. For example, in Capital Capers' conservatively oriented *Socialism Trek*, a parody of the science-fiction franchise *Star Trek*, Bill and Hillary Clinton "are no longer aboard the USS-Free Enterprise" but "are now on our new ship the USS-R" with a mission "to spread free, universal health care for everyone" (Loise and Barrington 1994). Hillary planned to pay for the health care through "a sin tax" on cigarettes, though Bill argued that cigarettes caused more people to *need* health care "meaning our mission is useless" (Loise and Barrington 1994). John Kerry's battle for the presidency in 2004 was hampered by his own ego; as Major Flip Flop—a loose parody of Batman as the secret alter ego of a multimillionaire—he frequently interrupted his own political crime fighting to get his hair done by an elite stylist. The *X-Presidents*, a parody of Marvel's mutant X-Men first released as animated shorts on *Saturday Night Live*, were frequently shown to be hypocritical, getting caught up in orgies and acts of deviance while trying to fight for morality battling people from "a world where children are brought up without religion or values" (Smigel and McKay 2000, 61).

Stories that use superhero parody to *praise* their political target, on the other hand, emphasized the heroes' missions as righteous by presenting them in simplistic terms and by exaggerating the villainy of opponents. For example, *My Hero MAGAdemia*—a parody of the manga *My Hero Academia*—described Trump supporters as people who "gained extraordinary abilities, such as blue-collar trade skills, rational thought and masculinity" and were unfairly "labeled 'deplorables' by the elites and hunted down by the swamp creatures." Opponents of Trump were described as "crazed and confused to the point where they could no longer identify their own genders or spell their own pronouns." The Trump immigration policy and ideal of a southern border wall was presented as a basic three-step process: "Step one . . . Learn a Skill!! Step two: Learn English! And step three: Wait . . . Your . . . Turn!" (Lim, Pellegrini, and Smith 2018). The horror-satire series *President Evil* made the superheroic presidency and American monomyth manifest by frequently depicting Obama literally standing alone against hordes of zombies. As Marc DiPaolo noted,

President Evil depicts Barack Obama as a superhero figure who is the only man standing between the American people and Armageddon. It also depicts as evil-to-the-core the leadership of the Republican Party, and its corporate sponsors, which will do everything in its power, legal and illegal, to humiliate Obama, reclaim the government, and destroy democracy. (2011, 6685–687)

The satire of *President Evil* (a parody of the *Resident Evil* video game franchise) was found in the undead and militaristic wordplay B*arot* Obama, John Mc*Pain*, Sarah Pala*din*, Dick *Chainsaw*, and in moments such as a zombified George W. Bush eating his own brain. *Wonder Wart Hog and the Nurds of November* presented a suffering citizen as the story's hero, standing alone against government failure, corporate greed, and public selfishness. His mission was both righteous in its opposition to true villainy and flawed in its naïve belief that the will of the people would prevail (it was undermined by the Electoral College) and that the people would choose wisely (they elect surprisingly not-dead Hitler in the midst of a New Year's hangover).

Comics that are more ambivalent use something of a blended approach, presenting missions that are virtuous but motivated by selfishness or bungled by incompetence. The first issue of *Trump's Titans* featured the superpowered administration facing off against the Global Tyranny Organization backed by a demonic Hillary Clinton and a diabolical George Soros. The villainous Clinton and Soros were depicted as felonious and malicious, using deception, violence, and brainwashing in their efforts to undermine and overthrow Trump. Soros was visually represented as a variation of Darth Sidious from *Star Wars*, a charismatic leader who uses Machiavellian manipulation to rise to power to transform his government from a republic into an empire. Trump's battle to defeat such a nemesis accordingly appeared to be in line with the standard superheroic mission of fighting evil and injustice. The mission, however, was not prosocial insofar as its primary objective was the *personal* gain of Trump. He was, first and foremost, concerned with maintaining his own power and dominance; secondly, he was concerned with achieving and maintaining America's dominance in the global theater—but primarily for the purpose of simply *having* dominance.

"Powers—or superpowers, to emphasize the exaggeration inherent in the superhero genre—are often put forward as the central, defining element of the superhero; they put the super in superhero" (Coogan 2013, 283). They may be supernatural abilities, mystical talents, above-average physical or mental prowess, or enhancements via advanced technology. Whatever the source of the powers, they are about creating and preserving a better world through an alternate version of humanity—one that is speedier, stronger, smarter, and selfless (Brooker 2013). In the political satire superhero and genre parody comics, politicians and average citizens are enhanced or made more powerful by virtue of extraordinary strength, steampower and military technology, scientific advancements, radioactivity, excessive wealth, psychic foresight, genius intellect and strategic skills, time travel, the abilities of flight, invisibility, elasticity, pyrokinesis, and invincibility, along with some more unusual powers such as vomiting poison, talking to birds, making trees explode, and holding multiple contradictory opinions.

The comics that present positive views of their political targets often connect the heroes' powers to a sense of their innate goodness or to the perceived righteousness of their political cause. *My Hero MAGAdemia*'s Wall-Might [Trump] was endowed by "the E Pluribus Unum so that he could become America's mightiest hero" (Lim, Pellegrini, and Smith 2018); in other words, he was given the power of the people, the many, to rise as the one leader. In the steampunk-satire series *Time Lincoln*, from Antarctic Press, Abraham Lincoln was, at the moment of his assassination, given the ability to travel through time, marking him as a man ahead of his time; his natural physical prowess as a wrestler was augmented by a mechanical shoulder-to-elbow bracer and by brass gauntlets. In the same series, Martin Luther King Jr. possessed the power of will—like DC's Green Lantern's ability to harness and manifest willpower—and was able to exert "his will against carnage and violence" (Perry 2014). *Barack Panther*, a parody of Marvel's Black Panther, saw Obama embrace his African heritage to become "the protector of the innocent, the guardian of righteousness" (Shannon and Denham 2018). SuperLBJ in *The Great Society* became a champion for the American way whose superpowers were granted as a necessity given the enormous challenges of his day. Interestingly, *The Great Society Comic Book*, while partially favorable to Johnson, also reflected his weaknesses as part of his superpowers; he was undone by his involvement in Vietnam, with the war depicted as his version of Superman's Kryptonite—the one thing capable of harming the champion of good.

Satire that is critical of its political target often gives the main characters' powers premised in or related to their foibles. *Major Flip Flop*, aka John Kerry, for example, had "uncanny flip flop abilities," described as "the amazing power to be on both sides of any issue at the same time" (Todd and Mott 2004, 2 and 1). The *X-Presidents* were made extraordinary through a "hurricane-powered dose of radiation while appearing at a celebrity golf tournament" (Smigel and McKay 2000, 1). *The Fanatic Four*, a parody of Marvel's *Fantastic Four*, endowed Bill Clinton with a body of rubber causing him to "think of how popular I'll be with the laaadiees" (Barrington and Loise 1994), an allusion to his numerous alleged affairs. Hillary Clinton, meanwhile, became invisible, permitting her to undermine her husband, a nod to her reputation of being the head of the Clinton household. And the Clinton-era attorney general, Janet Reno, got skin formed of rocks, as a manifestation of her anger and temperament. The

Tremendous Trump, a parody of Marvel's *Incredible Hulk*, ate a radioactive bag of "CheezToes" snacks that gave him extraordinary size and strength when he got "hangry," transforming him into a hulking, simple minded, orange, rage and greed-fueled, monster (Perez, Dunn, and Galvan 2017, 3 and 10). "Libarro World" created conservative doppelgangers of high-profile liberals based on each politician's weakness: John Kerry became a hawkish military hero; Hillary Clinton changed into an anti-feminist; Howard Dean was transformed into a placid genius; and, Ted Kennedy converted to a distinguished teetotaler. *President Pence* was granted the power of White Male Privilege, "the only power that matters in this world—right next to military might, of course" (Perez and Dunn 2017).

The more ambivalent stories seemingly turn politicians' potential weaknesses into their strengths. In *Reagan's Raiders*, age became an asset rather than a liability. Reagan and his administration, in their determination to end global terrorism, submitted themselves to military research as "Project Alpha-Soldier," which was proven safer and more effective on older men than on younger. Through this process, Reagan and his cabinet underwent a temporary molecular transformation that gave them enhanced, and youthful, strength, speed, agility, and endurance, which partnered effectively with the wisdom and experience of their advanced years (Arnold and Buckler 1986). *Trump's Titans* likewise made hubris a quality. Genetic research led by Trump's uncle John at MIT was reserved to turn the president and his cronies into superheroes. Unused by previous presidents because the responsibility of the power was too great, Trump unleashed the technology to become the greatest president in history, getting "*all* powers that exist" while his team of Mike Pence, Steve Bannon, and Jared Kushner got the power to make trees explode, to vomit poison acid, and to talk to birds, respectively (Barron and Remulac 2017). Thus, Reagan's advanced age and Trump's ego were translated into superpowers, though it is unclear whether these stories celebrated the presidents as a force of American patriotism, and for rising above their naysayers, or whether the comics mocked them as a farce of American nationalism, and for being too flawed to be politically effective.

Since Superman first appeared in fitted clothing that showcased his muscles, "S" emblazoned on his chest, cape billowing behind him, the dramatic, primary-colored costume has been an essential and easily recognized part of the superhero formula and its appeal (Brownie and Graydon 2015). The costume helps to tell the superhero story by suggesting something of the superhero's mission, powers, origin, or personality (Coogan 2013). *Reagan's Raiders* and *Trump's Titans* were both wrapped in variations of the American flag: red and white stripes, blue fields, white or golden eagles and stars. (The eagle of *Trump's Titans*, may, however, have symbolized Nazi Germany as much as the United States, given that the comic's title font replicates the SS emblem of the Third Reich;

Figure 5.2. The S's in "Trump'**s** Titan**s**" (top left) echo the shape of the S's in the Third Reich's SS insignia (top right), and the eagle on Trump's superhero costume (bottom left) shares a similar shape with the eagle used in Nazi iconography (bottom right).

see figure 5.2.) SuperLBJ wore an inversion of Superman's classic costume, with white briefs over a red leotard with a blue cape. Wall-Might of *My Hero MAGAdemia* wore a flag tie with a dark suit. *Tremendous Trump* and Antarctic's satire of California Governor Arnold Schwarzenegger, *The Governator*, both wore the rags of the suits that their bodies—and perhaps also their personalities—grew too large to hold, while *President Evil*'s Barot Obama was found in a suit tattered from fighting zombie mobs. *Steampunk Palin*, starring former Republican vice-presidential nominee and Alaska Governor Sarah Palin, and *Time Lincoln* feature their protagonists clothed in Victorian garb, accented with brass goggles, gauntlets, and guns. *Barack Panther* is costumed in a black leotard with a cat mask, while his daughters wear African dresses. *President Pence* is found alternately in spandex and cape resembling Marvel's Shazam or the chest harness and briefs of Mattel's He-Man. The crew in *Socialism Trek* wears uniforms reminiscent of those on *Star Trek: The Next Generation*, and *The Fanatic Four* wear blue leotards resembling those of their Marvel counterpart and inspiration, *The Fantastic Four*.

In terms of costuming, there is little to distinguish satires that praise their main characters and those that criticize them. The costume is a marker of the superhero genre and is thus a logical component of a superhero parody (Coogan 2013). The use of the flag in a number of the satires is consistent with the costuming in actual superhero comics wherein the heroes are visually linked with the people they serve and with ideas of nationalism (Dittmer 2013);

Figure 5.3. Tattered suits and partial nudity of politicians in superhero parodies is common, suggesting raw masculinity, larger-than-life qualities, and being metaphorically or symbolically shredded by the demands of the office.

Captain America, Captain Britain, Captain Canuck, and the Red Guardian, for example, all wear emblems of their nations. Such visualization is also fitting in representing the origin and situation of a president in service to, or in power because of, a country. The steampunk trappings of *Steampunk Palin* and *Time Lincoln* restrain and mechanize their bodies while giving them weight and bulk, expressing formidable power and presence of the politicians who wear the gear (Sundén 2015; Sundén 2013; Brownie and Graydon 2015). Similarly, the tattered suits of *Tremendous Trump*, *The Governator*, and *President Evil* speak to physical and symbolic size of the men, and to the challenges of being metaphorically torn apart by the press and public opinion (see figure 5.3). The partial nudity of these figures may also be read, within the superhero genre, as indicative of what Barbara Brownie and Danny Graydon called "an intoxicating demonstration of personal and ideological confidence" (2015, 1)—a demonstration they are persons who are positive about themselves, what they stand for, and what they can do. It is part of the hypermasculinity of both the presidency and the superhero genre (see chapters one, three, and eight).

Satire depends on the audience devoting sufficient intellectual and emotional engagement to understand the message—rejecting its literal meaning, recognizing its incongruities, and seeking alternative interpretations (Booth 1974; Burke 1945). Parody works best when its content resembles the thing it ridicules and criticizes, so long as the audience is knowledgeable about the object of the parody (Hess 2011; Shugart 1999; Bennett 1985). But, satire's resemblance to the object of its derision is both a persuasive strength and weakness. The familiarity of its form, or its cushion of unthreatening humor, may make controversial content more palatable to some audiences, thus encouraging audiences to consider new ideas (Meyer 2000; Nabi, Moyer-Gusé and Byrne 2007; Black 2009; Knopf 2017); as rhetorical theorist Kenneth Burke explained, the comedic form produces "maximum consciousness" allowing people to be more charitable in their assessments of flaws and foibles (1984, 4). At the same time, however, satire's similarity with preconceived attitudes may also serve to only reinforce those attitudes (Bebber 2014; LaMarre, Landreville, and Beam 2009; Vidmar and Rokeach 1974). When the meaning is subtle or even ambiguous, interpretation is likely to be guided by preexisting beliefs, which then may be bolstered rather than challenged (Zillman and Cantor 1972; Podlas 2013). Such is the case with comics like *Reagan's Raiders* and *Trump's Titans*, which have been described as ideologically ambiguous and flawed (Kretsch 2016; Terror 2017).

Bleeding Cool columnist Jude Terror noted that *Trump's Titans* took no sides. It depicted Trump's behavior as "outlandish and despicable (though arguably hardly more so than it is in real life), but there's no consequences; no comeuppance," and so can be read either as a criticism of his actions or as a perpetuation of his ideologies (2017, para. 10). It is not, for example, clear whether the Schutzstaffel styling in the title or Third Reich iconicity in the costuming was an indictment or an endorsement of Nazi ideology. But even a story like *Tremendous Trump*, in which Trump was more clearly depicted as grotesquely fat, stupid, arrogant, gluttonous, impulsive, and angry, and was also positioned in opposition to truth and justice, the parody complicated the message, opening it to multiple interpretations.

How one reads *Tremendous Trump* may depend on how one reads not only Trump, himself—who he is and what he represents—but also how one reads the source text of Marvel's *Incredible Hulk*. Hulk allusions appear multiple times in the Trump parodies, making it a particularly apt example for considering the polysemic nature of satire (see figure 5.4). The story of the Incredible Hulk is the story of a science prodigy, Bruce Banner. Recruited as a teenager to develop weapons systems for the US Army, Banner's experiments with atomic weaponry exposed him to gamma radiation giving him excessive size and strength whenever he gets angry, and the angrier he gets, the stronger he is (Dougall 2014b). First appearing in Marvel Comics' *Incredible Hulk* #1 in 1962, his story has been adapted across media formats. A psychological review of the 2008 film *The Incredible Hulk* noted that even though Banner attempts to control his anger, the emotion is accepted as "a sign of manliness, of readiness to fight," making anger something to be proud of, so long as it can be put to good purpose (Scheff 2008, para. 8). *Tremendous Trump*'s parody of the Hulk offered commentary on Trump's personality and temperament, suggesting that Trump has tenuous control over emotions of anger and that his manliness or toughness is rooted in that anger. Whether this is seen as something monstrous or powerful depends on

Figure 5.4. Hulk-based Trump parodies. Top left: *The Incredible Hulk* #1 (Marvel Comics, 1962) and *The Tremendous Trump* #1 (Antarctic Press, 2017). Top right: *Marvel Treasury Edition* #5 (Marvel Comics, 1975) and *The Unquotable Trump* (Drawn & Quarterly, 2017). Bottom left: *The Sensational She-Hulk* (Marvel Comics, 1989) and *The Tremendous Trump She-Trump* (Antarctic Press, 2018). Bottom right: *The Incredible Hulk* #206 (Marvel Comics, 1976), page 26 in *The Unquotable Trump* (Drawn & Quarterly, 2017), *Tremendous Trump: A Man-Child Covfefe* (Antarctic Press, 2017).

how one perceives the purposes to which the anger is directed. The connection between atomic power and the Hulk character is also significant. The original Hulk is exposed to radiation in a quest for new nuclear weapons, which is what gives him superpowers; the real Trump also called for the development of new nuclear weapons, and the Hulk allusion in *Tremendous Trump* can therefore be read as either a cautionary tale of nuclear dangers or as a suggestion about the desirability of nuclear strength.

Parodies of Captain America are also worthy of a closer look, given its use in both *Reagan's Raiders* and *Trump's Titans*. Introduced in 1941 as a response to Hitler's reign in Europe, Captain America is the super alter ego of Steve Rogers. Upon attempting to enlist in the Army, Rogers was classified as "4F," unqualified for military service, because of physical frailty. Eager to do his patriotic service, he subsequently agreed to act as a test subject for a "Super-Soldier Serum" being developed to create a battalion of supreme fighting men. The serum caused Rogers to double in size, giving him above-average strength and nearly immortal resilience (Dougall 2014a). Since his original appearance, punching Hitler in the jaw on the cover of *Captain America* #1, Captain America has played a role in the creation of a common identity, literally embodying American nationalism and connecting to political projects of domestic order and international relations. Although it is science that gives Rogers his superior abilities, it is his personal sense of duty, his innate goodness, and his own hard work that makes him Captain America—"an extension of the Horatio Alger story into the world of superheroes" (Dittmer 2005, 629).

The polyvalent nature of *Reagan's Raiders* and *Trump's Titans* presents at least two possible interpretations of the Captain America allusions: Reagan and Trump each as a renewal of the American spirit, or Reagan and Trump as corruptions of the American identity. The latter is more likely in *Trump's Titans* given the titular character disavows responsibility and is fixated on acquiring power: In the inaugural *Trump's Titans* issue, former President Obama guards the super serum in a secret laboratory deep beneath the White House, warning Trump, in an echo of Spider-Man's moral compass, "With great power comes great responsibility" (Barron and Remulac 2017). Trump responded by punching Obama in the jaw, casting Obama as Hitler to Trump's Captain America. Reading *Trump's Titans* as a corruption of American idealism is enabled by a 2016 Marvel storyline in which Captain America was introduced as a longtime double agent and Nazi-sympathizer, a story that resonated with Trump's real-life failure to condemn White supremacists who demonstrated in Charlottesville, Virginia, in 2017 (see Thrush and Haberman 2017).

Other satirical political graphic narratives more closely resemble children's books than genre comics. There are coloring books, such as *Going Rouge: The Sarah Palin Rogue Coloring & Activity Book* (2009, TBTM Media) and *Trump vs. Clinton Adult Coloring Book* (2016, Antarctic Press); parodies of children's classics, such as *How the Trump Stole Christmas* (2017, Antarctic Press) and *The Three Little Pigs Buy the White House* (2004, Thomas Dunne Books); storybooks, such as *Thump: The First Bundred Days* (2017, Post Hill Press); and alphabet books, such as *Goldwater Made Simple from A to Z with BMG* (1964, Rodney). The use of a children's book for parody offers a "format easily recognized and understood by the general public" guaranteeing "access to a large and diverse popular culture audience" (Gring-Pemble and Watson 2006, 136). In turn, this also opens the text to varying interpretations. One may choose, for example, to interpret the childish, simplified vision of particular politicians as an insult to the intelligence of the subjects or supporters or as an insult to the intelligence of their detractors. The coloring book format further enables multiple interpretations by inviting readers to finish the images for themselves, allowing pictures to be completed in ways that can entirely change any original or intended message to ones more aligned with individuals' preexisting beliefs.

Not all political satire comics use parody. Another subset of the genre is less fanciful, relying more on selected aspects of public record to make an argument against a political figure, or, in the case of the pro-life *I Know That We're a*

Throw-Away Society . . . But this is Ridiculous (1989, Freedomlight Publications) by Dick Hafer, a political idea or ideology. These comics are satirical biographies, drawing both from the spirit of satire, as "a hard-knuckled critique of power" that "exposes some aspect of reality to ridicule in the form of aesthetic expression" and passes judgment on perceived wrong-doing, and on the format of the campaign comic, which engages in strategic political communication (Jones 2010, 83, 238; Brantner and Lobinger 2004). These comics are largely biographical and may include notes or bibliographies indicating the source material for the content presented. They exist as criticisms of Republican politicians, such as *Great Morons in History featuring Dan Quayle* (1992, Revolutionary Comics) and *Read My Lips: The Unofficial Cartoon Biography of George Bush*, and as criticisms of Democratic politicians, including *Shafted! Bill and Hillary's Excellent Adventure* and *Clinton Cash: A Graphic Novel*.

While traditional comedy tends to be thought of as escapist and laugh-inducing, satire engages with reality and is not always "ha-ha" funny (Thompson 2009). Indeed, a number of political satire comics offer rather bleak stories. Dick Hafer's *Shafted! Bill and Hillary's Excellent Adventure* (1993, A.K.A., Inc.) expressed shock and dismay at the election of Bill Clinton as president of the United States following years of Clinton's unethical behaviors: dishonestly avoiding the draft during the war in Vietnam; doing business with enemies of the United States; records of incongruity and hypocrisy between public statements and political action—claims of which were mostly footnoted throughout the book with dates, page numbers, and names of major newspapers. And, Hafer's *Every Family Has One* (1992, Books, Inc.) reminded readers of Ted Kennedy's well-publicized car crash at Chappaquiddick that killed a young woman. Likewise, *Clinton Cash*, a graphic novel adaptation of the 2015 biography by Peter Schweizer, told a story of financial corruption by the Clintons that began during the end of the Clinton presidency and continued through Hillary Clinton's time as the secretary of state. Neither story is funny. The satirical element is found through the books' juxtaposition of the visual-verbal elements of graphic narratives. In *Shafted!*, Hafer presented a coma patient awakening after twenty years to Clinton's election, shocked because he knew Clinton in his days as an antiwar protestor, draft dodger, and college dropout. Humor was found in the narrator's disheveled appearance and disoriented situation; in visual depictions of a young Clinton as a bearded, buck-toothed, hippy; and in one-liner quips, as when the coma patient asked an old friend if he knew "Bill's wife over the years?" and the patient's doctor interjected, "You mean Madam President?" (Hafer 1993, 15). *Clinton Cash* made use of exaggeration and interpretation in the visuals to add sarcasm and irony to its biographical text. For example, as narration revealed that "both Clintons offered guarantees" to Obama that there would be no conflicts of interest between US foreign policy and the work of the Clinton Foundation, the visual perspective changed to show both Clintons standing with the fingers crossed behind their back—an indicator of deceit (Dixon and Smith 2016). A visual motif of the comic is money raining down around the Clintons, suggesting greed, dishonesty, and/or hypocrisy, depending on how the image was juxtaposed with the verbal content.

A similar approach to humor was found in *Read My Lips*. Narration boxes throughout the panels provided information about the life of George H. W. Bush, while visual interpretations and imagined dialogue provided commentary about Bush. For example, one panel explained that, as president, "one of the first things Bush started was an open door policy where anyone could see the president anytime." The accompanying visual was of Bush peeking around a bathroom stall, bare knees sticking out, exclaiming, "Not anytime, for gosh sakes!" (Tolbert, Grahame, and Braun 1992, 46). The visual provided a cheap laugh at catching the president on the toilet along with a suggestion that Bush's initiatives might have been frivolous or poorly planned.

Great Morons in History took a slightly different approach, one that the creators explicated as part of the story itself. In the book's opening pages, the writer (visually represented as a devil) and the artist (visually represented as an angel) explained a problem they faced with making a satirical biography of Vice President Dan Quayle was that "most of Danny Boy's big gaffes have been in speeches, and there are videos that do a better job of milking those than we ever could! Besides, speeches are so hard to draw, and boring!" (Kieffer and Paradise 1992, 2).

Instead, the book used dialogue between the creators to bring up Quayle's gaffes using the good/evil interplay between them to ironically suggest fair treatment of the vice president. It also featured top ten lists in the style of comedian David Letterman on *The Late Show*, along with an interpreted and exaggerated biography, an interactive maze, and a superhero-type origin story. The bulk of the gags focused on Quayle's intelligence and charm—or lack thereof.

Another creator who used an innovative method to political satire, blending realism with fantasy, truth with fiction, and fact with interpretation, was Steven Weissman in his graphic narratives about the two terms of Obama: the 2012 *Barack Hussein Obama* and the 2016 *Looking for America's Dog*. The works were described by Fantagraphics as surrealist and experimental combinations of metaphysical and political realities. Presented with a limited color palette, the works were as much commentary on American society as they were about the Obama presidency. The novels raised questions about how the people perceive Obama, how politicians wield power, and what the public expects of its leaders. The uses of satiric humor were varied. Weissman used discordance, as when he depicted Obama turning into a parakeet; juxtaposition, shown by alternating between references to Obama's incredible power and his participation in average activities like going to the movies; verbal humor, particularly through techniques like bombast or sarcasm, such as found in a scene wherein Obama dismisses his daughters from a meeting by telling them, "If I wanna know what's going on with the Jonas Bros, I'll give you guys a call" (Weissman 2012); and visual gags, such as illustrating Hillary Clinton with bulging veins and bugged, bloodshot eyes.

POSSIBILITIES AND PITFALLS OF PARODIES

In 1981, Martin Medhurst and Michael DeSousa identified a taxonomy of graphic discourse useful for understanding the workings of political cartoons. Part of this taxonomy included the four elements of rhetorical invention: *political commonplaces*, the depictions of, or connections to, campaigns, governance, current events, and the political process, which are the basis of political cartoons and include such things as preparing for and participating in debates, campaign traditions such as shaking hands and kissing babies, responding to specific issues of the moment, nominating conventions, the state of the economy, issues of national defense and international relations, polling, and voting; *traits of the featured characters*, physical or psychological exaggerations of broadly recognized and agreed-upon characteristics, such as honesty or intelligence, that are represented as symbols of image or text; *idiosyncratic situational factors*, the situational themes outside the realm of political commonplaces, such as natural disasters and high-profile crimes, or events that have little relevance beyond their immediate moment that give context to the political scene; and *literary/cultural allusions*, the often ephemeral references to literature, music, film, television, comic books, celebrities, and holidays, which often make use of well-known historical or literary figures, ideographs like the Iwo Jima flag-raising, sports and games (especially horse races or boxing matches), children's literature, brand names, advertising, and films, all of which help artists to explain their ideas quickly (Medhurst and DeSousa 1981; Conners 2005; Edwards and Winkler 1997).

The rhetorical elements of a political cartoon provide a useful structure to compare and contrast political satire comics. Satirical political biographies differ from political parodies, but both share these four traits with traditional political cartoons. Political parodies tend to focus on the traits of the featured characters (e.g., physical appearances like thick ankles for Hillary Clinton; wardrobe, such as Trump's long tie; speaking styles like Reagan's use of "well" to begin thoughts; family relationships; and reputation, such as Bill Clinton's womanizing), idiosyncratic situational factors (e.g., the popularity of fidget spinners that framed *Trump's Titans vs. Fidget Spinner Force*), and literary/cultural allusions (e.g., Captain America or the Incredible Hulk, as discussed above). Satirical biographies, by contrast, focus more on historical and popular records of people and events, relying on political commonplaces for the content and as the organizing factor for any traits and situational factors included. For example, two satirical comics, *Presidential Affairs* (2017, Squash Comics) and *Monica's Story* (1999, Alternative Comics), exposed the extramarital affairs, sexual harassment, and sexual assault cases of Bill Clinton, particularly his involvement with White House intern Monica Lewinsky. In both comics, Clinton's physical actions (groping and leering), his reputation (of being a "ladies' man" or womanizer), and his wardrobe (specifically neckties gifted him by Lewinsky) were key personal traits emphasized in the story, but they were traits that were directly connected to the political commonplaces of presidential business in the West Wing of the White House, his 1996 re-election campaign, and media interviews.

Despite the shared taxonomy of graphic discourse, political satire comics may be failing to achieve the relevance and impact their single-paneled predecessors communicate. Political cartoons have long been recognized for their ability to offer new visions of campaigns or candidates, highlighting and clarifying values and images (Morrison 1969). Within traditional political communication channels, they are a uniquely visual form of communication for orienting social issues, both offering and triggering deep reflection (Abraham 2009). And, as comics creator Patrick Chappatte noted of the declining political cartoon industry, "In the insane world we live in, the art of visual commentary is needed more than ever. And so is humor" (quoted in Cavna 2019, para. 14). But, in their efforts to develop full narratives, political satire comics seem to lose some of the immediacy and contextualization that allows editorial cartoons to clearly reframe events and ideologies for consideration. *Reagan's Raiders*, for example, reframed the Reagan administration into superheroes, allowing them to serve their country outside the confines of the presidential office and the law itself, but there was no exploration of what such limitless presidential power would mean for the country or the world, or even what it meant in the context of the Cold War or the War on the Drugs. (And, as discussed in chapter three, good superheroes are not necessarily good presidents.) Similarly, *Trump's Titans* and the *Tremendous Trump* drew attention to the hubris of the Trump administration, but they offered no insight as to what that hubris might mean to the American people. In other instances, the simplification of complex ideas for narrative purposes obfuscates rather than clarifies the issues at stake, as when communism is represented via evil cyborgs rather than as a nuanced political philosophy (*Reagan's Raiders*) and when an immigration policy is depicted as a wall of children's blocks (*Thump*).

Two exceptions to such satirical vagueness are R. Sikoryak's *Unquotable Trump* and DM Higgins's *Pres. Supervillain*. Both attempted to blend the aesthetic of comic books with the impact of editorial cartoons by reframing actual quotes of Donald Trump with the imagery from famous comics. Sikoryak's work reimagined classic comic book covers using Trump and his words. In so doing, it cast Trump as the villain in opposition to many long beloved American icons: an image of Trump as the villainous Joker threatening the heroic Batman, while boasting about being able to shoot someone and maintain support, framed the politician as an evil madman, for example. Higgins did similar work by editing Trump quotes into the speech bubbles of old Captain America comics, casting Trump as the Nazi villain Red Skull. While these efforts very deliberately tried to reframe current political events, their complete reliance on popular culture allusions, devoid of political commonplaces and limited on personal traits, restricted their rhetorical possibilities and audience reach—though less so for *Pres. Supervillain*, which frequently pointed readers to the news source material for the reworked images.

Another satirical comic that was less ambiguous in its criticism was the 2020 *Bronx Heroes in Trumpland*. The graphic novel, by Ray Felix, Tom Sciacca, and Tom Ahearn, opened with three forewords that focus on the political moment, the use of parody and satire as political criticism and its place in the history of alternative comic books, and the power of people in social movements. On the first page, Donald Trump, who was subsequently cast as a supervillain in the piece, was described as "a monstrous infestation intent on corrupting our political landscape for his own personal profit" (Sodaro 2020, 9). This was not a story written to simply mock the president or make fun of the superhero genre but was instead written to be both a catharsis and a rallying call for those who were horrified by Trump's rise to power and his administration.

CONCLUSION

Political superhero parodies often do little more than turn politicians' strengths and weaknesses into predictable plot devices and forgettable gag humor. They are as likely to ridicule the superhero genre as they are American politics. Satirical biographies are stronger in their ability to convey information and ideas relevant to public discourse, but their tendency toward the presentation rather than interpretation of facts also limits their ability to poignantly, poetically, or playfully, orient political issues. Moreover, the acquisition of most political satire comics requires motivation and commitment, via the act of purchasing, suggesting that even a compelling story like *Presidential Affairs* or an engaging satire like *Looking for America's Dog* will find their way predominantly to the hands of readers already sympathetic to their message.

THE FALL OF THE TOWERS AND THE RISE OF POLITICAL COMICS JOURNALISM

On September 11, 2001, more than a dozen terrorists hijacked commercial airplanes and flew them into the World Trade Center and the Pentagon, with one plane crashing into a Pennsylvania field, killing nearly 3,000 people and injuring about 6,000 more. In order to understand how such an egregious act of terrorism was possible, a bipartisan congressional committee was assembled. The so-called 9/11 Commission traced the path of the terrorists, reviewed the responses to their actions, and examined the (in)effectiveness of those responses in an effort to better prepare the US for future attacks. After nearly three years of gathering evidence, the commission released *The 9/11 Report* to the public. The 585-page document sold more than one million copies, but it was considered too overwhelming and tedious for the average American to process (9/11 Commission 2004; Goldstein 2006). Sid Jacobson and Ernie Colón collaborated to address the accessibility problem and created *The 9/11 Report: A Graphic Adaptation*, a 130-page, digest-sized graphic novel that interpreted the essential facts of the original 9/11 report with images in order to transform it into a visually engaging story (Goldstein 2006; Culturebox 2006).

As Sonia Baelo-Allué wrote, "The 9/11 terrorist attack on the United States can be considered a cultural trauma and an *intermedia phenomenon*" (2011, 184: emphasis added). Reportage of the attacks seemingly blended the conventions of journalism and fiction, offering unique coverage that engaged multivocality, point-of-view, interior monologue, and plot/narrative structure. *The 9/11 Report* was no exception, engaging literary style and bringing together two distinct, interrelated stories: that of the Islamic fundamentalists and that of the US government. The graphic adaptation added to this by using "the agile and colorful style of superhero comics," such as illustrated onomatopoeia and an array of visual devices, including silhouettes, cinematic close-ups, splash pages, graphic timelines, and a restrained palette (Baelo-Allué 2011, 185; Worcester 2011). A-J Aronstein noted that the commission's report alongside its graphic novel adaptation "are proof that an event like 9/11 can actually produce new artistic forms. The effort to describe and understand—to probe and render aesthetically—gives rise to new ways of thinking about the world" (2011, para. 16). And, indeed, the comics medium responded uniquely to the terror and aftermath of 9/11, diegetically rebuilding and destroying the towers again and again (see discussion in Wilde 2019).

The 9/11 Report: A Graphic Adaptation did, arguably, give rise to a new subgenre of comics: the graphic government report, with such succeeding publications as *The Torture Report: A Graphic Adaptation* (also by Jacobson and Colón) and the *Mueller Report Graphic Novel* by Barbara Slate. Its art form, however, was not particularly new. In part, it can be understood as an application of comics journalism. Comics journalism, also called graphic reportage or comix reportage, is serious nonfiction that blends visual storytelling with reporting of current events. It first began appearing as a distinct genre in the mid-1990s, had its own regular news publication, *Symbolia*, by 2012, and was mainstreamed in such outlets as *Harper's* and the *New Yorker* by 2015 (Haber 2012; Asselin 2015). The narrative structure of comics journalism is not unlike that of standard news reporting and draws on the same devices, such as conducting interviews, incorporating personal and source observations, and selecting and using quotes accurately. The visual component of the comics helps to focus readers' attention on certain aspects of the stories, often in a style reminiscent of a print photograph or broadcast screen (Nyberg 2006; Nyberg 2012; Williams 2005; Davies 2017; Sacco 2013). Both standard print journalism and comics journalism use the inverted pyramid structure of prioritizing the most important information or details (Nelson 2018). Graphic reportage is an example of hybridization that traverses and blends styles of journalism, art, and literature as a new way to meaningfully engage audiences (Gutiérrez, Rodríguez and Guereñu 2018; Haber 2012).

Blake Nelson's guide for making comics journalism includes such tips as writing "a traditional print article first" (2018, 20) while also noting that narrative moments are preferable and that any missing details should be either omitted or abstracted—techniques not as common to more traditional print journalism, which stresses facts rather than narrative, verification rather than abstraction, and truth above all else (Kovach and Rosentiel 2001). Nelson's (2018) visual tips include a suggestion to request and take reference photos and to ask visual questions as part of the research process; he reminds creators that, in comics, space and time are conflated, and that readers may be more likely to empathize with sources/people drawn more abstractly than those drawn more realistically. Comics journalist Joe Sacco (2013), however, emphasizes the need for accuracy in drawings and indicates that facial expressions should be true-to-life or neutral. Additionally, it is suggested that the tone of the art should match the tone of the story.

ILLUSTRATING GOVERNMENT

Graphic reportage not only provides the content of more traditional journalism but it also "enables a different kind of literacy" with visual stories about the impact and context of events (Koenig 2013, para. 40). Jörn Ahrens observed that "the aesthetic approach of the comics medium is able to cover the present, past, and the imaginary likewise" (2019, 1). Perhaps because of the potential of the genre to explain abstract ideas, to establish a mood for the story, to create empathy between subjects or sources and audiences, and to help readers make connections between their lives and those of others, much of comics journalism has dealt with humanitarian and environmental crises, including war, immigration, refugees and migrants, civil rights, violence, crime, mental illness, health care, housing, food safety, and climate change (Kaneya 2014; Tornoe 2013; Haber 2012; Walker 2010). The more bureaucratic affairs of government and electoral politics, nonetheless, have made their way into the genre since the 2006 publication of *The 9/11 Report: A Graphic Adaptation*. Jacobson and Colón followed up their best-selling success of the graphic 9/11 report with *The Torture Report: A Graphic Adaptation* (2017, Nation Books), a visual interpretation of the 500-plus-page report from the Senate Intelligence Committee in 2014 that exposed and denounced the Central Intelligence Agency's use of "enhanced interrogation techniques" during the George W. Bush presidency. The graphic adaptation was described as powerful, disturbing, and haunting, with the text made more unsettling by abundant, but not gruesome, illustrations of torture (Books 2017; Castaneda 2017). Colón teamed up with author Dan Mishkin and illustrator Jerzy Drozd to produce *The Warren Commission Report: A Graphic Investigation into the Kennedy Assassination* (2014, Abrams Comicarts). As described in *PopMatters*, the volume used "the graphic format to present, in effect, a nonfiction essay, contextualizing and summarizing complicated, highly charged, controversial historic events" (Carter 2015, para. 2) in a way that was comprehensive without being overwhelming and that paid aesthetic homage to an event ingrained in the visual culture of public memory.

Illustrator Barbara Slate crafted the *Mueller Report Graphic Novel* in 2019. As she wrote, she shared the research, writing, creative, and production processes with fans on social media.[1] Slate, writer for numerous mainstream comic book publishers and creator of the feminist cartoon character Ms. Liz for *Cosmopolitan* and NBC's *Today* in 1976, posted the first page of the *Mueller Report Graphic Novel* on Facebook and Twitter on April 21, 2019, just three days after the redacted report was released to the public. Receiving a fast, large, and enthusiastic response, she continued to share a page a day, along with blogs and photos of the process, leading up to a published release special in two volumes, the first of which was available in summer 2019 (Slate 2019). *Comics Beat* described the work as "something that is half-public service, half-wild ride, both crucial and rollicking," transforming the report into a narrative that readers can follow by untangling a convoluted assortment of actions, actors, and organizations (Seven 2019, para. 9). The following June, comics publisher IDW announced its own graphic adaptation of the 448-page Mueller Report, written by Steven Duin and illustrated by *MAD Magazine* and *New Yorker* cartoonist Shannon Wheeler. The book's editor, Justin Eisinger, indicated that by turning the substantial report into "lighter reading" more people would be informed about Mueller's findings in "the most important law enforcement document created in our lifetime" (quoted in Lou 2019, para. 5). Considerably longer than Slate's twenty-plus-page volume, IDW's 220-page graphic novel was released in late summer 2020. Additionally, the *Washington Post* published *The Mueller Report Illustrated: The Obstruction Investigation* in 2019, with text and analysis by Rosalind S. Helderman accompanied by comic-style illustrations from Jan Feindt. And, *Insider* hired creators from DC and Marvel Comics, Anthony Del Col and Josh Adams to tell the story of Trump's impeachment in a February 2020 webcomic.

Writers Michael Hoerger and Mia Partlow with artist Nate Powell took a historical approach to providing a graphic account of government affairs with their 2010, zine-styled, *Edible Secrets: A Food Tour of Classified U.S. History*; based on over 500,000 declassified memos, debriefings, and transcripts, the book explored assassination plots, Black Panther arrests, Reagonomics, communism, and more, all through the lens of food development and use (Microcosm 2010). Another creative and historical piece of graphic reportage released in 2010, from author Mike de Seve and illustrator Daniel Burwen, was *Operation Ajax: The Story of the CIA Coup that Remade the Middle East* (2015, Verso). Despite being classified as historical fiction, the graphic novel was inspired by the investigative journalism of Stephen Kinzer's book *All the Shah's Men: An American Coup and the Roots of Middle East Terror* (2003, John Wiley & Sons). In 2012, *Operation Ajax* was transformed into an interactive media experience via an Apple app called *CIA: Operation Ajax*. Incorporating music, sound effects, and 3-D rendering, the interactive version of the graphic novel used deliberate pacing and opportunities for immersive experiences that allowed readers to access supplemental materials, such as actual CIA documents.

Graphic reportage of campaign politics has also appeared from time to time. Comic book biographies of presidential candidates, from such publishers as IDW and BOOM, were particularly popular in 2008 and 2012 (see chapter one). The 2008 election also saw the publication of *08: A Graphic Diary of the Campaign Trail* by Michael Crowley, a senior editor at the *New Republic*, and Dan Goldman. *Publisher's Weekly* (2008/2009) called the 160-page graphic novel "a brief and breezy graphic account" of "the longest presidential campaign in American history" leading up to the November 2008 contest between Republican John McCain and Democrat Barack Obama. The story was told from the perspective of a veteran political reporter, primarily providing a cynical, illustrated, timeline of the campaign.

In 2012, the electronic comics journalism magazine *Symbolia* ran pieces on the history of third-party politics in the United States and little, or lesser, known outsider and radical political candidates, such as John Russell, an activist Democrat who ran for Congress against Republican incumbent Gus Bilirakis in Florida's Twelfth District. *The Guardian*, meanwhile, featured an animated graphic novel entitled *America: Elect!*, which offered a retrospective look at the 2012 re-election of Barack Obama as president, summarizing what it described as "a long—really long—campaign, one full of twists and turns, gaffes and memes" (Adams and McCann 2012, para. 1). Sarah Glidden (2016) explored the campaign of Jill Stein and third-party politics in a biographical comic for *The Nib*, a daily comics publication that features comics form coverage of world issues and events, including political cartoons, journalism, essays, and memoir. In the aftermath of the controversial 2016 election, Andy Warner (2017) published a comic on *The Nib* about the gutting of the Voting Rights Act, Donald Trump, and the impact of Jeff Sessions's leadership in the Department of Justice. Also, Margreet de Heer (2017) produced a long comic strip, entitled "Not Our President," which factually focused on the history and characteristics of democracy. As the 2020 election heated up and the coronavirus/COVID-19 pandemic changed life around the world, *The Nib* released *Epidemic* by Niki Smith. When Vice President Mike Pence was put in charge of the White House's coronavirus response, Smith's work was designed to expose Pence's inadequate handling of the AIDS epidemic when he was governor of Indiana.

The media itself, the other side of the political coin opposite the government, has also been the topic, or target, of some comics journalism enterprises: The 2011 book written by journalist Brooke Gladstone and illustrated by Josh Neufeld, *The Influencing Machine* was heralded as "a media manifesto" (Cooke 2012, para. 2) that argued, with historical context, that "we get the media we deserve: it doesn't control us so much as pander to us" (Cooke 2012, para. 3). Erin Polgreen and Joyce Rice, cofounders of *Symbolia Magazine*, took this message further in their 2014 call-to-action comic, "The Power of Storytelling (A

Cautionary Tale)" in *YES! Magazine*, to suggest that it is up to the people to control the story and to be heard above the din of corporate media. In 2017, Josh Neufeld, a "Brooklyn-based cartoonist known for his nonfiction narratives of political and social upheaval, told through voices of witnesses," produced "The Trump Russia-Memos"—a comics-style "account of the so-called 'dossier' that had the media world buzzing"—for the *Columbia Journalism Review* (Neufeld 2017). The five-page comic explored the meaning of journalism in the twenty-first century by looking at a moment when, digital entertainment and news company, *BuzzFeed* posted an unverified exposé of the president and made journalists themselves the subject of the news.

BLACK AND WHITE AND RE(A)D ALL OVER

In *ImageTexT*'s 2019 special issue on "Graphic Realities: Comics as Documentary, History, and Journalism," Nina Mickwitz noted, "Witnessing and first-person accounts feature prominently in the current generation of non-fiction comics" (2019, 5). Prominent in such accounts is the work of writer and artist Joe Sacco, whose portfolio includes *Palestine* (1993), *Safe Area Gorazde* (2000), *The Fixer: A Story from Sarajevo* (2004), *War's End: Profiles from Bosnia, 1995–96* (2005), and *Footnotes in Gaza* (2009), among others. Although some creators believe comics journalism requires some effort at objectivity or balanced reporting, Sacco "frames the form of comics journalism as a counterpoint to this traditional concept of objectivity" (Macdonald 2015, 54; Davies 2017). He draws himself into his stories, thus acknowledging the way his experiences, social position, and values influence his understanding of events (Sacco 2013; Macdonald 2015). As Tristam Walker observed, Sacco's "graphic representation of himself shows his interaction with his new environment and becomes our connection to worlds shaped by war and occupation and distorted by the rapid frames of twenty-four-hour rolling news" (2010, 75–76). Such self-reference also helps to make the process of reporting—of journalistic interpretation—transparent, whereas traditional journalistic objectivity attempts to erase traces of the journalist (Sacco 2013; Macdonald 2015). In this way, comics journalism enters activism, offering "an artistic representation documenting a real event" taking advantage of the medium's opportunities to explain concepts as well as events (in Davies 2017, 7; see also Gutiérrez, Rodríguez and Guereñu 2018).

Each of the above-mentioned graphic adaptations of government reports and the comics journalism of political media and campaigns approach authorship, interpretation, subjectivity, transparency, or activism in different ways. Jacobson and Colón in their versions of *The 9/11 Report* and *The Torture Report* are completely absent from their work. Accuracy in their adaptation was visible

Figure 6.1. Jacobson and Colón (2006) ensure that recommendations by and from the 9/11 Commission are clearly that, and not their own, by using an image of the original published report as a "speaker" in their graphic adaptation.

to anyone who chooses to read both the original reports and the graphic adaptations of them. In *The 9/11 Report*, they, in fact, emphasized that the recommendations made for emergency preparedness and counterterrorism measures are those of the 9/11 Commission, and not their own, by inserting an image of the original report into their adaptation (see figure 6.1).

Brooke Gladstone, a media celebrity in her own right as the co-host of NPR's *On the Media*, was drawn prominently into *The Influencing Machine*. From the

Figure 6.2. In the bottom image, de Heer (2017) establishes her voice in the comic. In the top image, she establishes her place in the subject matter near the head of the marchers.

center of the front cover to the center of the last panel, her likeness appeared approximately 250 times. As the narrator, these appearances included Gladstone in her radio booth and as a talking head, as well as such imagery as Gladstone as a dog, a bird, an abstraction, a newsboy, the Statue of Liberty, oracles in a tarot deck, and reflections in her own glasses. Such imagery underscored that it was Gladstone's voice the reader encountered. Her repeated appearances also highlighted Gladstone's own social position in relation to the ideas and events discussed: her position as a woman in a patriarchal history and male-dominated industry, and her role within the very media enterprise she critiqued. Her illustrator, Josh Neufeld, made a similar cameo in his *Columbia Journalism Review* comic of "The Trump-Russia Memos," appearing in the last panel of the five-page work to observe that "the media isn't the exclusive club it used to be. In some sense, we're all the media now" (Neufeld 2017, 93). De Heer also made brief cameo appearances in "Not Our President," establishing herself as the author in the opening and then reorienting the reader to her voice near the end. She also appeared in a crowd of protestors in the title artwork, if you look for her, establishing her role as citizen within the comic's subject of democracy (see figure 6.2). Polgreen and Rice, by contrast, left themselves entirely out of their activist comic, "The Power of Storytelling," though they provided a separate cartoon visual of them working together as part of their creator biography at the end; notably, this black-and-white visual was quite distinct from their graphic report, distanced by space from the full-color narrative panels.

Glidden seemingly appeared in her graphic reportage on Jill Stein; at the very least, some female journalist made repeated appearances throughout the panels, giving the comic the feel of watching a televised news interview. A similar aesthetic was achieved by Warner in his Voting Rights Act comic by making the political correspondent Ari Berman, author of *Give Us the Ballot: The Modern Struggle for Voting Rights in America*, the narrator. Berman was introduced in the third panel and reappears throughout the comic, usually framed

Figure 6.3. Warner's (2017) use of political correspondent Ari Berman, frequently appearing as an inset-narrator, gives his comic about the Voting Rights Act the feel of a televised news exposé.

by insets which emphasize his role as the storyteller (see figure 6.3). Crowley and Goldman preferred to insert fictional reporters—Harlan Jessop and Jason Newbury—into their *08* campaign trail account, though either was rarely seen through most of the graphic diary so it read more like a multi-biographical account of the candidates themselves than like the story of a reporter following the campaign.

One of Gladstone's appearances in *The Influencing Machine* notably happened outside the traditional confines of book content, with a full-body image at the top of the copyright page proclaiming, "Most of the words spoken herein by actual people are drawn from historical documents, transcripts, or interviews. [. . .] Great care was taken to ensure that no remark was taken out of context" (Gladstone and Neufeld 2011, front matter).

This spoke to not only the importance of accuracy, even in interpretational journalism, but also to the process of representation. Barbara Slate's *Mueller Report Graphic Novel* emphasized her role in interpreting and representing the report via her social media presence. The first pages of the graphic novel appeared on Slate's Facebook page for her book "You Can Do a Graphic Novel." As the Mueller novel developed further, she created a separate Facebook account just for the work, releasing more pages as she completed them and sharing photos of her workspace and updates about the revising and editing process. While Slate did not insert herself into the *Mueller Report* any more than Jacobson and Colón inserted themselves into the *9/11 Report* or the *Torture Report*, she made her role in the adaptation of the report very transparent. For example, on June 20, 2019, she described her writing method as one in which she went through the original report, highlighted sections in pink for the narration, sections in blue for dialogue, and sections in pencil that she wanted to revisit. This explanation was accompanied with a photograph of such work-in-progress.

Edible Secrets relied on declassified documents to establish the work's authenticity, though the somewhat cynical and bemused voices of the writers were readily apparent, even if their images were not. For example, the book provided an historical account for how communist spies Julius and Ethel Rosenberg used a box of Jell-O to communicate within their network. The documented history was also accompanied by critical commentary on the US government's handling of the Red Scare, which included a "DIY Evidence" page with a Jell-O box cutout that encouraged readers to "follow the government's lead and fabricate your own evidence. Show the defense who's boss by parading these two box halves up and down the jury box" (Hoerger, Partlow and Powell 2010, 43).

Shorter pieces of political graphic reportage, such as found in the online periodicals of *Symbolia* and the *Guardian* offered the most traditionally objective journalistic feel because both the creators and the narrators were largely absent from the stories with little obvious commentary. The *Guardian*'s "America Elect!" animated graphic novel about the 2012 presidential election, for example, was written in short declarative statements that create a detached or dispassionate tone. For example, the middle portion of the comic read as follows:

> As Hurricane Isaac threatens to overshadow the Republican conventions, Romney struggles to win over independent voters.
> A damning secret video appears.
> Romney arrives at the first presidential debate in Denver harried by critics questioning his abilities.
> But Romney dramatically turns the tables, stunning pundits and an ill-prepared Obama with a forceful debate performance that jettisons his rightward shift (Adams and McCann 2012)

Set against mostly black-and-white images, the abrupt writing style created the feel of an event timeline published in a print newspaper—even though small visual touches, such as a triumphant red elephant moving across a storm-battered landscape, might have influenced reader interpretation of the campaign moments.

Returning to the guidelines or advice offered by Nelson (2018) and Sacco (2013) on the depictions of sources in graphic reportage, we shift now from representations of the creators of comics journalism to the representations of their subjects. Nelson believes that readers might empathize more with sources that appeared more abstract than realistic and Sacco argues for accuracy and true-to-life illustrations for the same effect. Representations of politicians, government officials, and other specific, high-profile people, across the assorted titles, are almost always true-to-life and realistic. In Jacobson and Colón's *9/11*

Figure 6.4. The rendering of Osama bin Laden in *The 9/11 Report: A Graphic Adaptation* (top, left) mirrors an Associated Press photograph (top, right), which ran in the *Los Angeles Times* among other news outlets. And, an illustration in *08: A Graphic Diary of the Campaign Trail* of Hillary Clinton meeting "a black Elvis on the trail" (bottom, left) is seemingly based on an uncredited photo featured on the humor site *Buffet o'Blog* and in a *Daily Mail* article (bottom, right).

Report, for example, many images appear faithfully recreated from widely and repeatedly circulated stock news images. Likewise, *The Warren Commission Report* was praised for its "excellent use throughout of echoes and representations of familiar photographs and newsreel imagery" (Carter 2015, para. 3). *08* featured a dramatic, stark-contrast, black-and-white artistic style that gave the book a gritty, newsprint aesthetic; it, too, often accurately recreated images found in campaign news coverage—though they were more likely to be offbeat or unflattering reference photos, such as a blog's snapshot of Hillary Clinton with a Black Elvis impersonator. Such artistic choices in *08* underscored its cynical interpretation of the election (see figure 6.4).

Slate's *Mueller Report* used "a new drawing style, developed for a graphic memoir [. . .] very different from the more mainstream comic book styles [she] used for DC and Marvel." She found drawing the characters (people) to be both interesting and challenging but noted, "Luckily most of them are right out of central casting," suggesting that they fit into standard archetypes and stereotypes used in cartoon art (quoted in Bussel 2019a, para. 7; for cartooning stereotypes, see Eisner 2008). *Edible Secrets*, consistent with its zine style, used a combination of realistic illustrations and actual photographs, all in grayscale, which added to the book's performance as an archival presentation of declassified documentation. *Operation Ajax* engaged a more typical comic book style, with detailed, action-oriented illustrations. While the book was in full-color, many panels used a limited palette; the colors thus operated hermeneutically to shape reader interpretation; varieties of muted browns, for example, reflected the dessert landscape of Iran and the barren existence of its countrymen, in sharp contrast to the garish reds, whites, and blues used for an entitled England and brash United States. Color also shaped the interpretation of events in *The Warren Commission Report*; the alleged assassin, Lee Harvey Oswald, for example, was depicted in black-and-white amidst an otherwise color-inked world, visually capturing the mystery surrounding his biography and involvement in an assassination plot. And a solid black background set a somber, deadly tone in Smith's criticism of Mike Pence's handling of AIDS in "Epidemic."

More cartoonish graphics were found in the graphic reports that were more clearly offering political commentary or levity, not unlike *08*'s cynical use of absurd imagery. Neufeld's "The Trump-Russia Memos" about Trump's alleged Russia collusion, for example, was illustrated in blue-scale, with all people depicted in shades of blue and black (Neufeld used the same color-palette in *The Influencing Machine*), except for Donald Trump, whose likeness was accented with a very bright yellow head of hair. Bright yellow accents were similarly found throughout the otherwise black-and-white pages of the *Washington Post*'s illustrated Mueller Report. While the *Post* tended toward realism that resembled photocopied photographs, Slate's version of the *Mueller Report* was drawn in a more simplified style with few details. Arguably the most simplistic face in her entire work was that of Trump, whose eyes were simply dots beneath wide slashes of eyebrows, his nose, when present, a mere curved dash, his mouth either a flattened arc or a gaping "o" encircled by pursed lips (a feature also emphasized by political cartoonists Clay Jones and Dave Granlund). The shock of yellow hair, prominent eyebrows, and thin-lipped smile were also found in Warner's "The Voting Rights Act Was Gutted."

The particulars of Trump's depictions are significant because so much has been written about cartoonists' struggles in illustrating him. An October 2016 *Vanity Fair* video featured four cartoonists caricaturing Trump, poking fun at his girth, his hair, his "ratlike" nose, his "sphincter muscle" of a mouth, his small facial features, and his greedy, disdainful personality (Politics 2016). In December of 2017, *Politico* took stock of Trump's first year as president in political cartoons to see how the best political cartoonists in the nation were choosing to caricaturize him. Artist Kevin Kallaugher commented that "drawing Donald Trump is a little bit harder than most people think" because "he came into office as a fully formed cartoon character" (quoted in Wuerker 2017). Kallaugher, and others, noted Trump's orange skin, lumpy build, frumpy suits, exceptionally long red ties, prominent eyebrows, sunken eyes, pursed mouth and overbite, and angry expressions lurking below a billow of yellow hair—the same features that non-caricature cartoons seemed to use in representing Trump. Four months later, the *Atlantic*'s Sarah Boxer (2016) asked, despite all these ready-made cartoon features, "Why is Donald Trump so hard to caricature?" She argued that none of these defining characteristics were proving indelible. The impulse to lampoon his weight seemed unsophisticated. Emphasizing his crassness simultaneously amplified it. Depicting him as childish made him seem more innocent. Mocking his speech just gave him more media space, though, on that point, Mark Peters (2017) has called using Trump's words against him in cartoons is using "comics as interpretive journalism." Ultimately, *Newsweek* proclaimed that Trump's defining feature for cartoonists was his "overcompensatingly" long ties that, according to cartoonist Pat Bagley, indicated Trump was not normal (Perez 2017).

Abstractions for the purpose of identification or, as with Trump's tie, for disidentification and distance are also found throughout the works. *Insider*'s account of Trump's impeachment, by Adams and Del Col, introduced the key players as Russian nesting dolls, with Trump as the largest figure, capable of holding within his girth the figures of attorney Rudy Giuliani, Speaker of the House Nancy Pelosi, and Ukrainian President Volodymyr Zelensky.

The activist message in "The Power of Storytelling," which encouraged readers to make their own voices heard and to tell their own stories, was underscored by a somewhat generic cast of diverse characters. Nondescript features allowed readers to place themselves in the narrative, to achieve closure—what Scott McCloud defines as the "phenomenon of observing the parts but perceiving the whole"—by mentally completing the gaps in the images with specifics from their own lives (1993, 63). In *The 9/11 Report*, several aliased FBI agents and analysts were made sympathetically human by being depicted as people with visual specificity. Although they were not recognizable as *particular* individuals, they were recognizable as ordinary human beings, as people readers *might* know; this humanized their efforts and their failures, in the 9/11 disaster (for example, see images of "John," "Dave," and "Jane" in Jacobson and Colón 2006, 81–82). Conversely, in *The Torture Report* interrogators were frequently depicted as dark black silhouettes, removing both their identity *and* their humanity, while the tortured detainees were depicted with considerable anatomical and expressive detail, emphasizing the contortions and anguishes of their bodies and minds. It is also worth noting that Colón's artwork in *The 9/11 Report* was done in full color, while the art in *The Torture Report* was grayscale and black-and-white. The colorless art in the latter work downplayed the goriness of the torture scenes—hinting at, rather than exhibiting, blood—while enhancing the serious and somber mood and dark drama of the issue.

TRUTH OR POLITICS?

Political pundit John Calvin "Cal" Thomas reportedly once said, "One of the reasons people hate politics is that truth is rarely a politician's objective. Election and power are." The tension between truth and politics, and thus the tension between journalists and politicians, is visible throughout the examples of graphic government reportage and comics political journalism examined here. Historically, the press has been skeptical of, even adversarial to, political powers, though such reporting has been in decline since the media was, first, managed by the government during Operation Desert Shield/Storm in the early 1990s and, then, dutifully reported in White House press releases in the wake of 9/11 (see Sabato 2000; Bennett and Paletz 1994; Iyengar 2016). It is, therefore, consistent with the journalistic genre that these graphic accounts paint a largely unflattering picture of the government and related political enterprises. However, because of tensions that exist between "the combination of factual claims and fictive form," as in new journalism and fabulations—which we might extend to encompass graphic interpretations and reinterpretations of nonfiction—it is, at times, difficult to distinguish between the narration of the work and the voice of the graphic content creators (Hellman 1979, 17).

In the cases of *The 9/11 Report*, *The Torture Report*, and the *Mueller Report*, the comics creators were re-presenting government documents in visual and accessible ways for public consumption. Subjectivity was shaped not by content so much as by representational choices, such as the expression on George W. Bush's or Dick Cheney's face, how much to humanize tortured prisoners, and how to handle redacted content. Even objective analyses of the original reports themselves, however, indicate that there is no good way to frame government and political actions from these reports. The American Civil Liberties Union, for example, stated of the original *9/11 Commission Report* that it "exhaustively *details the failures* of the intelligence agencies [. . .] and proposes major structural changes to address those failures," and that "the failure to 'connect the dots' to prevent the terrorist attacks of 9/11 must *rank among the worst intelligence failures* in American history" (Edgar n.d., para. 1–2: emphasis added). The *New York Times* identified seven key points from the CIA torture report, each one focused on uses of deception and coercion by government officials, from the agency not reporting the full extent or brutality of interrogation techniques and misleading Congress about the effectiveness of the techniques to it leaking classified, and falsified, information to journalists in order to positively influence public perception and support of enhanced interrogation techniques (Ashkenas, Fairfield, Keller, and Volpe 2014). Bloomberg News similarly highlighted the top takeaways from the Mueller Report, a 408-page document summarizing the investigation into Russian interference in the 2016 election and possible obstructions of justice. These takeaways included at least ten instances of possible obstruction of justice by Trump, who provided inadequate answers to questions about his activities, and an assortment of examples of internal disagreements and tensions within the federal government, such as what warranted criminal intent and sufficient evidence (Dennis, Strohm, and McLaughlin 2019). Therefore, even when exercising as much neutrality as humanly possible, the work of Jacobson, Colón, and Slate could not help but present an unflattering and critical account of government actions and political actors. Indeed, the text-heavy presentation of *The Torture Report*, with "detailed text overflowing on every page, which closely follows the original report," allowed the findings to speak mostly for themselves with little interpretation from the creative team (Castaneda 2017, para. 8). The notable exception to this is *Edible Secrets*, which was likewise premised on copious amounts of government documents, but also provided clear commentary on the events described in addition to its graphic adaptation of the documents themselves.

Campaign comics, by the competitive and partisan nature of campaigns themselves, may naturally lend themselves to more creator subjectivity and persuasive intent. Crowley and Goldman's *08* campaign trail diary, the *Guardian*'s interactive "America: Elect!" graphic novel on the 2012 campaign, *Symbolia Magazine*'s 2013 feature on "Third Party Politics in the United States," Glidden's 2016 biography of third-party candidate Jill Stein, and even de Heer's and Warner's 2017 comics about the fallout and effects of the 2016 election were each ostensibly motivated by ideology. These underlying ideologies may or may not have been partisan, but they all suggested ideas about the political process and democracy.

According to its own promotional description, *08* took "its cue from campaign classics like *Fear and Loathing: On the Campaign Trail '72* and *The Making of the President* series" to bring "politico journalism into the graphic novel form" (Crowley and Goldman 2009, back cover). These classic books provided both an insider view of political campaigns and a critique of campaign journalism. In *Fear and Loathing: On the Campaign Trail '72*, author Hunter S. Thompson observed,

> There's an excitement and pace to the presidential campaign that definitely keeps you wired. It's a grueling trip, but that insane kind of zipping from place to place ... [...] It's frantic, kind of chasing after the Golden Fleece, and probably a lot more fun if you don't win or if you have no real stake in it ... (2012/1972, 469)

08 attempts to similarly capture "the excitement, drama and suspense" of what its summary calls "the most historic election of our time" (Sobowale 2009, para. 1; Crowley and Goldman 2009, back cover). Thompson's work was also shaped by his hatred of Richard Nixon, which began during Nixon's term as Eisenhower's vice president and was intensified through Nixon's support of Barry Goldwater's 1964 campaign, which expressed, to Thompson, a dangerous, even apocalyptic ideology (Denevi 2017). Crowley and Goldman's invocation of Thompson's work, therefore, suggests a similar partisanship, underscored by sharp criticism of George W. Bush's unscrupulous campaign tactics in the 2000 primaries as they set the stage of John McCain's 2008 run.

Nonetheless, *08* seemed to be more about recording and reporting the historicity of the campaign than about offering partisan commentary on it. Whereas Thompson's work linked observation to perception, often in deeply personal and psychological ways, despite a fictive narrator (Hellman 1979), Crowley and Goldman tended to reflect a more general malaise of ill-defined discontent and vague hope connected to candidates, as if trying to capture the overall mood of the entire electorate. As one review noted, *08* managed to cover every candidate, from the fringe to the center, and the various issues that emerged during the campaign, but offered little new information or insight for those that followed the race through other media, making the book more a campaign keepsake than a provocative viewpoint (Sobowale 2009).

"America: Elect!," from the *Guardian*, achieved a similar purpose in its shorter, but animated, retrospective of the 2012 campaign, focusing on how Republican Mitt Romney returned from his 2008 primary defeat to be a viable candidate who lagged behind an incumbent president by a mere single percentage point in pre-election polls. Given that the *Guardian* is foundationally a British newspaper, the primary function of their graphic report seemed to be explaining the "twists and turns" of the 2012 election to non-American audiences (Adams and McCann 2012, para. 1).

The 2016 comic coverage of a Jill Stein campaign stop in Anacortes, Washington, provided a neutral report of Stein's activities at the event, which in turn offered a favorable look at political activism, the Green Party, and Stein's platform, especially by quoting attendees who responded positively to Stein's campaign speech at the event. Simultaneously, by explaining the challenges facing third-party candidates in US politics, author/artist Glidden (2016) took a poke at Donald Trump, humorously juxtaposing him with Abraham Lincoln: a stovepipe hat was perched atop Trump's yellow quaff, a speech balloon proclaiming, "Four score and seven yuge deals ago!" In addition to covering a Stein speech in Washington about her Green New Deal, Glidden included an interview with the candidate at her home in Massachusetts. The interview traced Stein's emergence into politics, from her exposure to radicalism while a medical student at Harvard University to her emerging environmentalism in the 1980s, a near-death health crisis that prompted her to join the advocacy group Physicians for Social Responsibility in the 1990s, which ultimately led to being the Green Party candidate for Massachusetts governor in 2002 and presidential candidate in 2012.

Symbolia Magazine's 2013 feature on third-party history and outsider candidates served the function of opening public dialogue and giving media exposure to lesser-heard political voices. "Third Party Politics in the United States" was a two-part series to examine independent politics in the United States, recognizing that "independent candidates have led, shared, and even popularized ideas outside the political mainstream" (Beyerstein and Rice 2013). Likewise, Glidden's graphic reporting of Jill Stein's 2016 campaign advocated as much for a reformation of the political system that would make third-party candidates more viable as it did for Stein's campaign. The closing three panels of the comic discussed how Glidden's progressive friends liked Stein's ideas but did not want to vote for a candidate who might lose. Glidden (2016) concluded by observing, "Maybe if we had a system that allowed smaller parties and other voices to participate more fully, we wouldn't have gotten" to a point where many people were voting against the candidate they most feared instead of for the candidate they most supported. Warner and de Heer's post-2016 election comics likewise shared the ideal of improving the political process through voting rights and more representational democracy. Improving the process and giving voice to the voiceless was also at the heart of the media-focused comics, which complementarily suggested, "We get the media we deserve (Gladstone and Neufeld 2011, 156), "The Internet *is* the biggest equalizer that ever existed" (Polgreen and Rice 2014), and, "In some sense, we're all the media now" (Neufeld 2017, 93).

Since the 1990s, the number of staff political cartoonists in North American papers decreased from hundreds to dozens, with even veteran and Pulitzer Prize-winning cartoonists losing their jobs. Many of these artists "generally work in traditional political cartoon formats of one or two panels" while Pulitzer Prizes have increasingly recognized longer-form work with more narrative commentary (Cavna 2019, para. 8). In fact, in 2018, the Pulitzer Board honored the nonfiction graphic novel series "Welcome to the New World" by journalist Jake Halpern and illustrator Michael Sloan. A twenty-part series for the *New York Times*, "Welcome to the New World" was based on interviews Halpern conducted throughout 2016 with two Syrian refugee families who sought sanctuary from the devastating war and humanitarian crisis in Syria. Neither Halpern nor Sloan had done comics before and were pessimistic about the endeavor given the *New York Times*' poor track record with cartoons (Ayres 2018). The support for, and success of, the project speaks to the power of comics journalism—especially at a time when traditional political cartoons are losing their footing. The *New York Times* first experimented with comics journalism in 2016 with its graphical "Inside Death Row" series by Patrick Chappatte and Anne-Frederique Widmann. The *New York Times* editorial page editor James Bennet believes that such "illustrated" or "long-form visual journalism expresses 'nuance, complexity and strong voice from a diversity of viewpoints'" across media platforms (quoted in Cavna 2019, para. 12).

This is what graphic reportage offers that other forms of politico journalism and government documentation do not, and often cannot, provide: multimodal, multivocal, multiplatform accessibility. As noted in the previous chapter, the decline of the traditional format of political cartooning, which coincides with the decline of the traditional newspaper, does not necessarily mean the decline of political cartooning in general (Danjoux 2007). As Larry Bush demonstrated, "The history of cartoons has been one of artistic innovation and evolution" (2013, 72). The scrollwork animation of "America: Elect!" and the interactive app-based platform of *Operation Ajax* both epitomize how narrative political comics can engage audiences in ways not available to the single-panel political cartoon. While the mid-length "America: Elect!" might capture readers the same as a traditional comic strip, its animation, triggered by the reader moving through the narrative, gives audiences more control in the media experience. *Operation Ajax* takes that further, blending the experience of reading a comic book with that of reading online news articles by providing readers the opportunity to dig deeper, or not, while also appealing to a multi-sensory experience through animation and sound.

Even without such digital bells and whistles, long-form visual journalism engages audiences differently. The structure of comics encourages audience involvement in ways that are unique from other media, adding to the particularly persuasive power of the comic outlet (see, for example, McCloud 1993; Wolk 2007). In McLuhan's (1964) terms, comics are a cool medium: they are low resolution with gaps in imagery and text, mandating that the audience not only pay closer attention but also mentally fill in the blanks. This encourages closer readings and effectively makes the attentive audience part of the story; comics, compared to un-illustrated texts, encourage slower reading (Marshall 2012). These narratives, thereby, engender critical thinking and memory capabilities in audiences, thus triggering deeper understanding of issues and peoples.

Reading a comic requires overcoming the gaps: the gutter space between images, the static illustrations that represent motion, the iconography that suggests mood and other non-visual sensations, and so on. As McCloud (1993) writes:

> We all live in a state of *profound isolation*. No other human being can ever know what it's like to be you from the inside. And no amount of *reaching out* to *others* can ever make them feel exactly what you feel. All media of communication are a *by-product* of our sad *inability* to communicate *directly* from *mind to mind*. Sad, of

course, because nearly all problems in human history *stem* from that inability. Each medium [...] serves as a bridge *between* minds. Media convert thoughts into forms that can transverse the *physical world* and be *re*-converted by one or more senses *back* into thoughts. (1993, 194–95)

Comics journalism, with its humanitarian leanings and activist-bent, is also about overcoming gaps—particularly the spaces between "me" and "we," "us" and "them," "here" and "there," and between language and action.

CONCLUSION

In 2012, the Toronto-based *Ad Astra Comix* blog observed that it was started as a place to talk about political comics, but that the project was challenging because "political comics don't present themselves as a huge swath of the graphic novel market—you have to hunt for them"; creating, let alone finding, "a good political comic book is *very hard*" (NMG 2012, para. 2). But, the blog, as in the comics it covers, recognized that political comics and comix reportage provide means to make people who might otherwise not encounter certain sources, aware of important information, ideas, and events (Mackay 2016). Indeed, the potential of the medium and genre was acknowledged by cooperation between *Ad Astra Comix*, whose tagline is "the panel is political," and the academic International Studies Association in 2014; as ISA launched the *Journal of Narrative Politics*, whose aim is to encourage lesser-heard voices and to recognize the expression of narrative as a mode of knowing, *Ad Astra Comix* promoted its work with the Graphic History Collective, a group of activists, creators, and researchers who produce alternative, or people's, histories in accessible formats to enable understanding of the historical roots of contemporary social issues (Guinilling 2014).

Returning to the literature of 9/11, critic A-J Aronstein suggested that "an event like 9/11 can actually produce new artistic forms" when an "effort to describe and understand [...] gives rise to new ways of thinking about the world" (2011, para. 16). The existence of *Ad Astra Comix*, the ISA's *Journal of Narrative Politics*, the Graphic History Collective, the short-lived but innovative *Symbolia Magazine*, the *CIA: Operation Ajax* interactive app/graphic novel, and the end of political cartoons appearing in the *New York Times*, as well as the creation of *The 9/11 Report: A Graphic Adaptation*, indicates that it does not take something as dramatic as a deadly terrorist attack to give rise to new ways of thinking and talking about the world. In fact, it is simply the desire to describe, to understand, to relate, and to connect that produces new, improved, or repurposed modes of communication.

COMIC BOOK VERSIONS OF PRESIDENTIAL CAMPAIGNS

The 2004 US presidential election raised numerous concerns about various aspects of the voting process, including registration, access, accuracy, and fraud. Several states were at the center of concerns, including Nevada, Oregon, Florida, Michigan, and Ohio. Voter suppression was the main concern of Ohio. In response, author Sheri Leigh Myers and artist Sophie Goldstein produced the 2006 graphic novel *Cheated!*, from Wake Up and Save Your Country. The comic tells "the stories of the men and women who fought for their most basic and sacred right: the right to vote" in hopes that "may we not be cheated again" (Myers and Goldstein 2006, back cover). Those hopes, however, were dashed with the 2013 *Shelby County v. Holder* decision that invalidated protections provided by the Voting Rights Act, leaving communities even more vulnerable to disenfranchisement (Newkirk II 2018).

This chapter explores comic books and graphic novels, both nonfiction and fiction, for how they represent voting, civic engagement, and the process of American elections. Janice Hocker Rushing (1986) suggests that myth provides an underlying structure to public discourse, shaping the people's sense of identity, which guides a community's moral vision. Popular culture narratives are instrumental in crafting those myths and public narratives (e.g., Gunn 2008; Ott 2010). Liesbet Van Zoonen (2005) identified two common, often interweaving narrative types found in political fiction which are relevant to public perceptions of political and electoral processes: the Quest, wherein an honest and virtuous politician works to overcome obstacles in pursuit of their political ideals, and the Conspiracy, in which shadowy or ambiguous self-interested parties frustrate the democratic process for their own purposes. "While quest and conspiracy narratives both include clearly defined individual protagonists and antagonists, two other narratives are driven by collective processes often beyond the control of the individual"; these narratives have a "dark and light variety, with the former usually telling how the inexplicable workings of the system or 'machine' frustrate the ideals of individual politicians [the 'bureaucracy' narrative] and the latter portraying a community of candidates and support staff in their everyday interactions, failures and victories [the 'soap' narrative]" (Van Zoonen and Wring 2012, 266–67).

Cheated! may not be political fiction, but its narrative is one that epitomizes both the quests and conspiracies of democracy. In it, a group of civic-minded citizens, supported by virtuous politicians, faced insurmountable odds, in the form of financial challenges, public opinion, and power inequities, to defend the democratic ideal of a government of the people as it is manifested through voting. Simultaneously, by exposing government corruption and campaign manipulation and propaganda, the graphic novel highlighted the realities of conspiracy. In addition to dramatizing the testimony and experiences of those who were denied their vote and those who fought for the sacredness of every vote, *Cheated!* made multiple calls to readers to support election protection. Two pages following the story provided additional information to readers on how to "Get Involved, Protect Your Vote!!!" and to "Get Informed & Stay Informed!!!"—directing people to the Election Defense Alliance and Black Box Voting, in addition to a variety of independent sources covering the 2004 voting scandals, with further resources found in the book's references. While *Cheated!* was specifically situated in the events of 2004, its support of voting as a civic right and responsibility continued a sequential art tradition that was established five decades earlier.

GOOD GOVERNMENT COMICS

The same decade that saw a boon of campaign comics, the 1950s (see chapter one), also saw the emergence of "good government" comic books that emphasized the importance of voting (see Yoe 2020). Around 1950, the Armed Forces Information and Education Division of the Office of the Secretary of Defense published *Strong for the People*, a comic outlining how the government works and admonishing readers in the armed forces that "your job as a *serviceman* is to defend democracy. Your job as a *citizen* is to practice it. [. . .] Voting is an important *duty!*"[1] In 1952, Harvey Comics (known for *Casper the Friendly Ghost* and *Richie Rich*) published *Your Vote is Vital*, which offered guidelines on how to register, select a candidate, and vote (Kremer and Avison 1952). The US government released three voting comics in 1960 (Persoff 2012): *The Next Four Years* suggested that the preamble to the Constitution is a good guideline for choosing a president; *If Your Kids Could Vote* reasoned that children's interests, like good schools and good parks, were in everyone's best interests; and, *The Man Who Stole Your Vote* argued that not voting would let another vote count twice. The National Association for the Advancement of Colored People published *The Street Where You Live* in 1960, encouraging African Americans to register to vote in order to improve their communities. The NAACP reinforced this theme in a 1964 comic book *The Future Rests in Your Hands*, stressing the importance of multiple forms of civic engagement: voting, education, and employment. In 2008, Voto Latino, Change to Win, and the Rainbow/PUSH Coalition teamed with Greg Palast, Robert Kennedy Jr., and TopShelf Productions to publish *Steal Back Your Vote*, a magazine of comics and brief articles geared toward exposing voter suppression.

A children's comic in 1964 offered similar civics lessons. *Alvin for President*, based on Ross Bagdasarian's characters Alvin and the Chipmunks, entertainingly explained that the government consists "of a valuable system of *controls* that will help large and diverse groups of *people* to live amicably side by side" and that such a body requires a highly qualified leader that "all the citizens of the country should share in selecting" (unknown 1964, "Clyde Crash Cup"). Through a short-lived presidential run by Alvin, the book's pun- and alliteration-filled pages explained functions of the government, the purpose of the presidency, and the elements of campaigns, before celebrating the unnamed "serious, dedicated statesman" running for office that year (unknown 1964, "The Big Night"). Other classic cartoon characters who got into politics over the years included Bullwinkle the Moose, twice in 1988, once by accidentally saving President Ronald Reagan from a Russian assassination attempt and again as a successful presidential candidate himself; Looney Tunes' Daffy Duck in 1997, as part of an effort to outlaw rabbits; and Disney's Darkwing Duck and Launchpad McQuack in 2011, each running for mayor of St. Canard to save the city from crime.

In 2004, Antarctic Press did its own "insulting, sarcastic, and politically incorrect" take on the good government comic. *You Can Vote!* assumed its audience was sick of hearing about the election, hated all the candidates, and was tired of the system, but still emphasized the importance of voting (Dlin and Kilpatrick 2004). The book offered historical context and relevant facts about voting and elections, interspersed with tongue-in-cheek sarcasm. These elements were combined into a playable game in which players needed to earn 270 "electoral votes" to win.

With the historic election of President Barack Obama in 2008, a self-professed comic book fan, *The Amazing Spider-Man Election Day* took a brief foray into good government themes with a plot set amid New York City's mayoral election. The story began thirty-six hours before the polls opened, with readers

Figure 7.1. An excerpted scene from the 2016 *Ms. Marvel* #13 (left) alludes to Eugène Delacroix's painting "Liberty Leading the People" (right), which commemorated France's July Revolution of 1830.

witnessing a crime-in-progress by supervillains Boomerang and Shocker. As the two prepared to cause trouble, they discussed the relative virtues and necessity of voting in the upcoming election. Shocker was disinterested, being a supervillain who had not kept up on current events. Boomerang sought to convince him that even though he might be a supervillain, his secret identity/alter ego still had a right and a responsibility to vote: "Where's your sense of civic duty?" Boomerang asked. "Dude, thousands of men and women are dying in Iraq and Afghanistan right now to preserve *democracy*. You don't vote, it's like you're telling them everything they're sacrificing doesn't matter." Shocker acquiesced to vote for whichever candidate was "softer on crime" (Guggenheim, Romita Jr., and Kitson 2010). The 2008 election also saw *Pirates vs. Ninjas: Debate in 08* that offered a farcical look at campaign rhetoric and media coverage.

Eight years later, as Obama's second term drew to a close, comic books again worked to get out the vote. Kamala Khan, aka Marvel's teenage American Muslim superhero Ms. Marvel, urged voters to go to the polls in *Ms. Marvel* #13. The story focused on Kamala's effort to get out the vote in her Jersey City neighborhood by going door to door and disabusing people of their misguided ideas about voting.[2] One splash page featured Ms. Marvel hoisting a flag to lead a group of minority voters "to the polls," a visual allusion to the French painting of "Liberty Leading the People," which likewise depicted a mixture of social classes as revolutionaries (Wilson, Andolfo, Herring, and Caramagna 2016) (see figure 7.1).

Ms. Marvel was not alone in her crusade. Many comic book titles capitalized on the 2016 election, bringing attention to the process even if not directly promoting involvement in it. November 2, 2016, saw the release of several election specials (see figure 7.2.): *Faith* #5 featured Democratic candidate Hillary Clinton. *Catwoman Election Night* saw the return of *Prez* Beth Ross (see chapters four and eight). The cover of *Bitch Planet* #9 proclaimed "VOTE." Similarly, the cover of *The Flintstones* #5 declared "Bedrock the Vote," offering a storyline with both a mayoral and middle school class president election and reminding readers, "Your vote counts whether you know what you're doing or not!" (Russell and Pugh 2017).

In the months leading up to the 2016 election, *Army of Darkness* ran *Ash for President*. *Peanuts*' Snoopy ran for class president. Princess Bubblegum became President when the land of Ooo held its first election in *Adventure Time: President Bubblegum*. In *My Little Pony: Friendship is Magic* #46–47, Ponyville also had its first election, seemingly inspired by the 2016 presidential campaigns of former Secretary of State Hillary Clinton and real estate mogul Donald Trump. American Mythology Productions released *The Three Stooges: Red White and Stooge*, which not only embroiled the classic comedic trio in the political scene but also allowed readers to vote for the Stooge they most wanted to see in the White House; Curly won. *Citizen Jack* and *Vote Loki* were both 2015/2016 limited-run series that used the presidential election for their plot settings and motivations. And, the 2015–18 digital miniseries *Campaigners* imagined the heroism of one teenage girl trying to change a system in a dystopian future where presidential debates had been replaced by deathmatches.

By October of 2019, comics were already gearing up for the 2020 presidential election when Dark Horse released the first issue of *The Mask: I Pledge Allegiance to the Mask* miniseries, in which "bizarre Tex Avery-style killings [were] on a collision course with a bizarre political campaign where a homicidal maniac wants to 'Make America Green Again'!" (quoted in Welch 2019, para. 2). In December 2019, Image Comics published the first issue of *Killadelphia*, which blended presidential history and urban politics with Gothic horror in what *Comics Beat* described as "a comic about cops, corruption, poverty, and vampires [that] promise a kind of horror that's grounded in reality" (Denis 2019, para. 1). December 2019 also saw the introduction of Frank Miller and Rafael Grampá's *Dark Knight Returns: The Golden Child*, which offered unabashedly critical political commentary by featuring supervillains Darkside and the Joker aligning with Trump re-election efforts. In February 2020, as the Democratic primaries were slowly winnowing down the number of viable presidential candidates to face Donald Trump in the general election, Arsenal Pulp Press

Figure 7.2. The election of 2016 inspired many politically themed comic series and stories, and repeated comic book calls to get out the vote, as seen in this collection of political and election-special covers.

announced the forthcoming release of *Bronx Heroes in Trumpland*—a comedic comic that revived obscure superheroes from 1977 and 1993 to succeed "where Mueller, Hillary Clinton and the US Congress failed" by finally defeating Donald Trump. Meanwhile, Marvel's 2020 *Gwen Stacy* was running for student body president at her high school.

While some comics, such as Bullwinkle and the Three Stooges, exemplified the Quest narrative by highlighting the importance and ability of a concerned citizen wanting to make a difference, others, such as *Catwoman* and *The Golden Child* featured Conspiracies, with criminal elements and shady backroom dealings that were trying to influence elections for selfish, power-hungry, ends. Others blended these, to show that the earnest intentions of good citizens were the only solution to political corruption. These themes, and more, are discussed below.

CHEATERS AND CHEATING

The 1973 short-lived comic series *Prez: First Teen President* from DC Comics (see chapter four) pit its titular hero against corrupt politicians who attempted to thwart the political system. Nineteen-year-old Senator Prez Rickard ran on the youth-based Flower Party ticket "to win the presidency after a truth-and-love campaign which polarized the generations" (Simon and Grandenetti 2016, 29). Prez gained his first political office not through love, however, but through the machinations of a crooked mayor, the criminal Boss Smiley, who used Prez to ensure the youth vote would not interfere with his profit-driven, anti-environmental policies. Likewise, the 2015 relaunch of *Prez*, featuring nineteen-year-old President Beth Ross, opened with an election that was beleaguered by sexual scandal, secret cabals in the Senate, and computer hacking. While Prez Rickard eventually won the White House by campaigning on a platform of truth, Beth Ross won by accident because she was the least offensive candidate to appear on the ballot. A young Beth even made a prequel cameo appearance in the 2016 *Catwoman: Election Night Special*, which similarly featured a campaign with little choice in candidates. Although Catwoman cynically observed, "Only in Gotham could the choice for mayor be between a convicted felon and a cold-blooded killer" (Finch and Davis 2017), Beth optimistically predicted that she could someday fix the electoral system as president.

While the United States celebrated its bicentennial in 1976, Marvel Comics' Howard the Duck—an alien, anthropomorphic duck—ran for president. The *Howard the Duck* series was generally comprised of social satires and genre parodies. Early in Howard's earthly adventures (issues #7–9), he and his human friend, model Beverly Switzler, got jobs at the presidential nominating convention for the "All-Night Party." When the party couldn't decide what its platform should be, Howard offered some common-sense advice and ultimately earned the nomination and their presidential candidate. His candidacy quickly gathered steam thanks to Howard's unique appearance, amplified by a theatrical campaign. Howard earned enough traction to earn the diegetic attention of respected newsman Walter Cronkite and his political opponents for the office, President Gerald Ford and Governor Jimmy Carter.

The story of Howard's campaign highlighted a certain cynicism about American electoral politics, suggesting that "today's candidate doesn't think [. . .] he *recites*—nice, safe, pre-tested bromidic bombasts" (Gerber and Colon 1976, 11). An ad agency manufactured "wild-eyed political promises" without Howard's input or knowledge (Gerber and Colon 1976, 6). "Expert *equivocateurs*" compiled a book of "every *syllable* Howard will utter within earshot of a reporter" until the election (Gerber and Colon 1976, 11). Howard was given a makeover to look "distinguished. Subtle. [With] razor-sharp lines—yet tastefully understated" (Gerber and Colon 1976, 11). And yet, amidst the apparent hucksterism of campaign rhetoric, Howard's own honesty and his campaign's populist appeal hinted at optimism for democracy and the power of the people. But the story did not merely present a Quest narrative of an honest politician fighting for his political ideas. It also offered a Conspiracy narrative of a shadowy figure thwarting the process. In a plot twist eerily prescient of clandestine Russian-influence in the 2016 presidential election, Howard's 1976 campaign was sabotaged by a foreign agent—the Beaver, a French-Canadian who hated the United States.[3] While the Central Intelligence Agency was aware of the unethical and illegal interference, it chose to not get involved because it wanted Howard to lose. In the end, justice was served, but Howard—an honest politician—was turned off from politics for good.

As the election between President George H. W. Bush and Governor Bill Clinton heated up in 1992, DC Comics featured one of their own personalities making a bid for president: Etrigan the Demon. Summoned from Hell by Merlin, Etrigan is bound to a human named Jason Blood, making him a reluctant, unpredictable ally with the forces of good. In the four-part "Political Asylum" story arc, Etrigan was summoned inadvertently by a political strategist who programmed a computer to find the ideal conservative candidate. The "model candidate" was a "fiscal conservative" with a "drastic economic recovery plan." He was "tall and well built" with a "commanding physical presence" and a "winning smile," "warm eyes," a "deep speaking voice," and "firm handshake." He gave "straight answers" and promised "simple answers to complex problems," and he couldn't "be bullied by special interest groups" (McDuffie, Semeiks, and Smith 1992 #26, 4). Fitting the description, Etrigan appeared to be the means to a multimillionaire's quest for smaller government and "total power" and was persuaded to run for president (McDuffie, Semeiks, and Smith 1992 #26, 12).

Etrigan was placed in opposition to real-life incumbent President George H. W. Bush for the Republican nomination (*The Demon* even made jokes at the expense of Vice President Dan Quayle's reputation for stupidity) and his platform was aligned with conservative Pat Buchanan and Ku Klux Klansman David Duke, despite charges from the diegetic Bush campaign that Etrigan was "a demon, an affront to the very god we all worship. And worst of all, he's a *liberal*" (McDuffie, Semeiks, and Smith 1992 #28, 16). Meanwhile, Etrigan touted his accomplishments as governor of Hell, which included, "*No* new taxes . . . and *no* prisoner furlough program" (McDuffie, Semeiks, and Smith 1992 #28, 17). Thus, Etrigan satirized the real campaign of 1992: the 1992 Republican primaries featured competition among President George H. W. Bush, paleoconservative politician Pat Buchanan, and former KKK Grand Wizard David Duke. Etrigan's campaign ad, emphasizing "no new taxes" in Hell, was an echo of a Buchanan ad attacking Bush's broken 1988 campaign promise to "read my lips, no new taxes." Etrigan's opposition to prison furloughs similarly mirrored Republican attacks on 1988 Democratic candidate Governor Michael Dukakis's furlough program in Massachusetts. Likewise, the diegetic Bush ad opposing Etrigan was a continuation of the real 1988 election's aggressive assault on liberalism (see Garry 1992). Furthermore, Etrigan, like real 1992 Democratic candidate Bill Clinton, appeared on MTV.

The "Political Asylum" storyline also managed to frame the campaign and election process in a way that surpassed 1992 to resonate decades later. The Demon announced his candidacy at "an unemployment office in recession-plagued Detroit," citing "both disappointment with current policies and a 'desire for immense personal power' as his motivations" while vehemently denying "reports that his campaign is an elaborate hoax" (McDuffie, Semeiks, and Smith 1992 #27, 2). He launched himself to celebrity status by publishing a book called "America Rules! A New Vision for America's Future." Rising to the top of the best-seller list, Etrigan's manifesto called for an increase in the military-industrial complex and world domination in order to erase the deficit. Decades later, back in the real political realm, the Republican primaries of 2015–16 saw a public that was dubious as to the seriousness, or at least the viability, of Donald Trump's campaign, and Trump, like Etrigan before him, had to disprove the belief that his campaign was a joke (Reeve 2015). Also like Etrigan, Trump presented his political positions in a book, *The America We Deserve* (2000, Renaissance Books)—a title not unlike Etrigan's *A New Vision for America's Future* (McDuffie, Semeiks, and Smith 1992 #27, 8; see figure 7.3). Of Etrigan, a news report stated, "Little. Yellow. Different. These are the words being used to describe the most controversial of presidential candidates" (McDuffie, Semeiks, and Smith 1992 #27, 6). Trump was comparably said to "look a little orange," described as "different—not just because he is obnoxious, tacky and vulgar [but]

Figure 7.3. Etrigan the Demon's 1992 campaign included an election platform book (left: *The Demon* #27, 6), prescient of Donald Trump's 2000-election book (right).

because of what he believes" and was considered potentially "too controversial for election 2016" (Boyer 2016, para. 1; Zakaria 2016, para. 3; Suson 2015).

Etrigan wore a button with the words "Demon 1st," calling to mind the slogan "America First," used by Trump to describe his foreign policy (Dunn 2016); another Etrigan button proclaimed, "Take Back America—and give it to me," much like Trump proclaimed, "We're going to take the country back" (McDuffie, Semeiks, and Smith 1992 #27, 1; *Fox & Friends* 2015, para. 3). In Etrigan's campaign ad, he was called the candidate with "the will to make us great again" which was not unlike Trump's slogan of "Make America Great Again" (McDuffie, Semeiks, and Smith 1992 #28, 17). Etrigan's followers wanted to "throw all those bums in Washington out on their butts," just as Trump's campaign refrain was "drain the swamp" (McDuffie, Semeiks, and Smith 1992 #27, 7; Kelly 2016). A pundit observed of Etrigan's platform, "It sounds like you intend to force the rest of the world to pay for America's inflated lifestyle" (McDuffie, Semeiks, and Smith 1992 #27, 12). Trump's rhetoric similarly suggested that other countries pay for American policies, such as Mexico paying for a US border wall (Thiessen 2017). The pundit also asked Etrigan, "Isn't your plan too simple?" (McDuffie, Semeiks, and Smith 1992 #27, 12). Simplicity was a significant factor in the appeal of Trump's rhetoric, which made politics seem "straightforward" for people without the time or inclination for research or consideration of the complex nuances in perceived problems (Goldhill 2017, para. 11).

The uncanny similarities between the fictional yellow candidate of 1992 and the real orange candidate of 2016 point to the ability of the *The Demon*'s creative team to recognize, distill, and represent the history and hyperbole, symbols and slogans, trends and tropes, culture and coverage of presidential politics. The story acknowledged a certain cyclical predictability in both campaign messages and voter response. They argued, as did the good government comics of earlier decades, that democracy's greatest strength is the power of the people, but its greatest weakness is an apathetic electorate. As Superman tried to explain to Etrigan's supporters, "As for Etrigan, his appeal is aimed at what is lowest in each of us," Superman stated at a press conference. "I can save you from super criminals—Sometimes I can save you from natural disasters." But, Superman warns, "What I cannot do is save you from *yourselves*." Despite this bleak look at the American electorate, Superman suggested hope for American democracy by asserting, "Only **you** possess that power" (McDuffie, Semeiks, and Smith 1992 #29, 10). When Etrigan's own campaign manager decided to send the Demon back to Hell for the good of the country, she observed, "One woman, one vote," reaffirming an underlying faith in the power of the people and the vote (McDuffie, Semeiks, and Smith 1992 #29, 21).

The 2010s saw a new wave of political skepticism as America transitioned from the terror war years of George W. Bush (2000–2008) to the culture war years that gave rise to Donald Trump (2008–2017). WildStorm's 2010 *Sparta U.S.A.* captured the pessimistic worldview. As described by the publisher, "There's never been a more American town than Sparta. In Sparta they believe in life, liberty and the pursuit of happiness through treachery, blackmail and murder—just like the Maestro taught them as he learned it from the U.S. President."

Similar themes appeared in Vertigo's 2012–13 political science fiction series *Saucer Country*, which built a narrative premised on the events of the 2008 and 2012 elections that would later resonate with themes of 2016.

Written by Paul Cornell and drawn by Ryan Kelly, *Saucer Country* featured a fictional governor of New Mexico, Arcadia Alvarado, as she negotiated the emotional toll of a presidential bid and the mental toll of an alien abduction. *Saucer Country* picked up the threads of anti-immigration sentiment that became a hallmark issue in the 2016 election. Published during the years that ushered in the era of border walls and immigration bans, *Saucer Country* used the possibility of invasion by extraterrestrial aliens to offer meta-commentary on the rhetoric surrounding both legal and illegal immigration. Alvarado's campaign speech declared, "People talk about guarding the border, they talk about not letting in 'aliens'—but let's say it out loud— Americans **are** aliens" (Cornell and Kelly 2012). The series employed a typical combination of Quest and Conspiracy narratives to present an earnest, Mexican American woman facing off against both seen and unseen opposition from old, white-haired and gray-skinned, men, optimistically promising that truth and justice would prevail in the end (see chapter eight).

POLITICAL HORROR SHOWS

At an October 2015 Republican primary debate, CNBC moderator John Harwood asked,

> Mr. Trump, you've done very well in this campaign so far by promising to build a wall and make another country pay for it, send 11 million people out of the country, cut taxes $10 trillion without increasing the deficit, and make Americans better off because your greatness would replace the stupidity and incompetence of others. Let's be honest. Is this a comic-book version of a presidential campaign? (quoted in LoGiurato and Campbell 2015, para. 3–4)

The crux of Harwood's question was the infeasibility of Trump's proposals. Harwood might, however, also have taken inspiration from the burgeoning comic book presidential campaigns across genres and publishers of the 2015–16 election cycle.

As the primaries began to take shape in mid-2015, Image Comics introduced the six-issue miniseries *Citizen Jack*, "a comedy-horror for people who hate politics" (Arrant 2015, para. 4). Of the series, Harwood might have asked, "Is this a comic book version of the Trump campaign?" The series followed the unlikely presidential campaign of populist, dark horse candidate Jack Northworthy. Originally scheduled for March 2015, the release of *Citizen Jack* was pushed back to November 2015. In the intervening months, Donald Trump announced his controversial candidacy, prompting reader comparisons of Northworthy to Trump. Both were businessmen with questionable practices and a history of financial setbacks. Both had very public divorces and were dogged by sexual scandals. Both were heavyset with long, side-swept, hair. Both made outrageous statements on the campaign trail and promised to clear Washington of political insiders. Both seemed unelectable. Trump famously stated, "I could stand in the middle of 5th Avenue and shoot somebody and I wouldn't lose voters" (quoted in Cupp 2016, para. 1). Northworthy attacked a would-be assassin, was framed for the murder of his opponent, killed his own father, and *gained voters* because the people responded favorably to "a man of action" and partisanship superseded justice.

The similarities continued well beyond the end of both the series and the 2016 campaign, making *Citizen Jack* not only up to date but ahead of its time. In the February 2016 issue, Northworthy attacked a member of the press (Humphries et al 2016 #4). In 2018, Trump supported the physical assault of a *Guardian* reporter by Congressman Greg Gianforte (Pilkington 2018). In the April 2016 issue, a political pundit said of Northworthy, "The things he says are *ignorant* and *hateful* lies, not *political opinions* worthy of debate! To pretend otherwise is to make extremist values seem *normal* in this country!" (Humphries et al 2016 #5). By June 2018, Trump's supporters would similarly be accused of being ignorant and hateful believers of lies (Paleologos 2018).

Northworthy was a drunken and dishonest snowblower salesman from Minnesota (suggesting that his campaign was a "snow job"—a deception). Facing economic hardships after being impeached as mayor, he decided to run for president because "political elites are killing this country" (Humphries et al 2015 #1). His campaign was directed by a twelve-foot satanic demon named Marlinspike (see figure 7.4). Marlinspike was a purple demon—a combination of the Republican-red and Democrat-blue tones that dominated the artwork, and the color of autocratic royalty. He shared his name with a nautical instrument; a marline spike is a pointed iron implement used in separating the strands of splicing for marine rope work; in other words, he was a divider, not a uniter. He was described as a fallen angel. In Judeo-Christian traditions, this kind of demon is likely to be both malicious and mischievous. Historically, demonic personifications have allowed people to characterize and specify otherwise indescribable evil, permitting them to give name to the causes of their suffering (Delbanco 1995; O'Leary 1994; Russell 1977). The demon Marlinspike was, therefore, political catharsis for the American people—a way to conceptualize their frustrations in a figure to blame for the country's ills. His purple color visually represented partisan politics and unchecked authority. His name suggested the separations or divisions within the American electorate. His demonic origins pointed to unredeemable offenses of the political process and government rule. This demonic personification was, however, also an externalization of the failures of the American people themselves. Although Marlinspike gave a culpable shape to collective political anxieties, his machinations required human complicity; Satan may offer temptation, but it is people themselves who choose to sin. Thus, when voters in 2016 simply viewed their decision at the polls as one of choosing "the lesser of two evils"—as proclaimed in headlines from *CNN*, the *Washington Post*, and other outlets—the fact remained that voters knowingly chose evil (e.g., Long 2016; Rieder 2016; Illing 2016).

At the end of the series, Northworthy said, "We're all trapped in a hell of our own making. And there is no escape" (Humphries et al 2016 #6). Indeed, *Citizen Jack* did not offer a glimmer of hope in the power of people in the way

Figure 7.4. *Citizen Jack* depicted the corrupted political campaign of Jack Northworthy, an egotistical salesman under the control a mischievous, autocratic demon named Marlinspike, seen here in *Citizen Jack* #6.

that Etrigan did. In fact, it suggested that the people are the ones to blame for any political mess there may be. It mocked the hyperbolic rhetoric of campaigns and media with such fear-mongering news headlines as "Terrorist cells buying marijuana with food stamps—*in your back yard*!" and extreme political accusations like "we are dangerously close to four years of [a] feminist sharia agenda in the White House" (Humphries et al 2015 #1). And it further indicated that the public buys into this spectacle: the narrative was driven by a presumed loss of rational discourse in American politics. Northworthy condemned "intellectual elites" (Humphries et al 2015 #2). He proclaimed, "This isn't an election, America! *It's a war!*" (Humphries et al 2015 #2). The story dismissed not only candidates' violence as inconsequential to voting decisions, but also asserted that candidates' criminal activities, including embezzlement, campaign fraud, and corporate corruption, aren't anything that "America *gives a shit about!*" (Humphries et al 2016 #5). And, at the end of the series, a candidate who admittedly had no political knowledge, was implicated in at least two murders, advocated for the death of children, and had sexual orgies in front of his own campaign team won the election and gained the White House. Meanwhile, at the end of the real 2016 campaign, a candidate who admittedly had no political experience, advocated for violence, mocked those with disabilities, women, and people of color, and had publicly attested to a history of sexual assault also won the election and became the president of the United States.

Demonic forces were also at work in the *Army of Darkness: Election Special*, which similarly showcased a campaign being manipulated by supernatural evil. The *Army of Darkness* (*AoD*) comics series is premised on the *Army of Darkness* film, which was part of the *Evil Dead* cinematic and television series. All are billed as comedy-horrors. The main protagonist is Ash Williams, who fate has chosen to protect the world from supernatural evil. In "Election Special," Ash was warned by the Necronomicon that the US presidential election would usher in "the end of all things" through an agent of the Great Darkness, who also happened to be a presidential candidate, declaring that through the election, "The people will bring darkness. . . . upon themselves" (Serrano and Galindo 2016). The comic suggested that both the candidates and the media will "say anything they want" and that people "prefer the lie over the truth" (Serrano and Galindo 2016), though it also retained a belief that people would be smarter than that.

In addition to its condemnation of the political spectacle in general, *AoD* also offered direct criticism of the 2016 election. Just as in the real world, it presented "an election too close to call" (Serrano and Galindo 2016). Its candidates were a blonde Valerie Sexton, which almost rhymes with Hillary Clinton, and a bald, aged Brock Anders, which sounds a bit like Bernie Sanders. Both Sexton and Clinton were linked to the Illuminati, and both the Anders and Sanders campaigns were credited to social media hype (Dmitry 2016; Auerbach 2016). The comic further described the "psychic impressions" of the Democratic rallies as having a sense of "optimism and ambition," while the Republican rallies emanated "entitlement" (Serrano and Galindo 2016).

The book's presentation of Donald Trump was made through the "Patriot Party," seemingly based on the Tea Party, given that both used the slogan "Don't Tread On Me." *AoD*'s red-hat-wearing candidate was supposed to, like Trump, "make our country great again" (Serrano and Galindo 2016)—until he was killed by a demon. In turn, Ash killed the demonic assassin and subsequently became the Patriot Party candidate. In yet another allusion to Trump's boast about being able to shoot someone and not lose voters, the media reported, "When asked about how he became the Patriot Party candidate, Williams simply responded, 'I shot a guy.' . . . He rose 10 points in the following poll" (Serrano and Galindo 2016). In *AoD*, both major party candidates were agents of darkness, thus the election truly was a choice of two evils—though good prevailed in the end. Ash killed the demons and, by default, was elected president. Ash, with a simple message of "Stop Talking. Start Doing," represented the public's desire for a man of action in the White House (Serrano and Galindo 2016).

Marvel Comics also put forth a campaign of villainy with a candidate called "the Lesser Evil" in its four-issue miniseries *Vote Loki*. The titular character, Loki Laufeyson, has been a recurring Marvel villain and occasional antihero since 1949. He is the adoptive son of the Norse god Odin, brother to the superhero Thor, and an alien from the planet Asgard. He is described as the God of Mischief, the God of Chaos, the God of Evil, and the God of Stories. Loki's run for the presidency, against an unnamed blonde female Democratic candidate and an unnamed red-tie-wearing male candidate, focused attention on political cynicism, political disengagement, and the public's sentiment that there were no good candidates in the 2016 election (Balz and Guskin 2016). As proclaimed by the terrorist cell HYDRA while attempting an attack on a presidential debate in issue #1, "America, your choice is false! No matter your President, this country will soon be *ash* [. . .]!" (Hastings, Foss, and Chuckry 2016 #1).[4]

Scenes depicted citizens watching the news, viewing debates, and attending rallies, making politically sardonic comments, such as "They were *both* lying through their *teeth* up there! Why vote for either?!" (Hastings, Foss, and Chuckry 2016 #1), "I've never voted before, because I think politicians are all the same, you know, like Democrat. Republican. It's all just about the money," and "Our government can either be one of *two* things! Corrupt, or incompetent!" (Hastings, Foss, and Chuckry 2016 #4). Loki's campaign played on their frustrations by acknowledging the validity of their doubts. His platform was simple: "If I were your President, I'd have the guts to lie right to your face. And you'd love it," which was succinctly captured in his slogan of "BEL*IE*VE" (Hastings, Foss, and Chuckry 2016 #1, cover). (See cover in figure 7.2.)

Loki's campaign messages were two faceted: The first was that "the other two candidates are bad" (Hastings, Foss, and Chuckry 2016 #4). A year ahead of the real 2016 election, the Pew Research Center (2015) reported the Americans' trust in the government was among its lowest levels of the past fifty years. *Vote Loki* reflected such cynicism. He told his prospective voters, "These candidates dance around questions like they're hot irons. They make up half-positions based on whatever people *want* to hear, and they clearly stand in contrast to their *true* history. And then once they take office, they do whatever they want anyway, as *quiiiietly* as possible" (Hastings, Foss, and Chuckry 2016 #1).

Such a sentiment seemed to represent the 74 percent of Americans who believe that most elected officials put their own interests ahead of those of the country (Pew 2015).

The second facet of Loki's campaign was besting the mainstream media and winning the image war. Each time he successfully spun a negative news story to his favor, his supporters would celebrate how "he does not let the media rule him like all those others" (Hastings, McCaffrey, and Chuckry 2016). But this meant that his was a campaign of style over substance. As the election drew near, Loki himself was forced to admit, "I've been working *so hard* to *fight* your *terrified media* that I've hardly had a moment to sit down and give [the issues] the *respect* [they] deserve" (Hastings, Foss, and Chuckry 2016 #4). Similar public and political tensions surrounding the media were foregrounded during the 2016 election through Trump's repeated blunt, and often successful, criticisms about mainstream news (Shafer 2016). The "inaccuracies, melodrama, bias, [and] outrage" showcased by journalists left America particularly wary of, and weary with, the press (Harper 2016, para. 1).

Vote Loki tended toward a pessimistic view of the American electorate. Citizens were depicted as disengaged and reactionary. Loki observed, "Voters just decide which story they believe. Facts and studies can be presented for either side, but if you *believe* the story, then information that disproves it only hardens your beliefs" (Hastings, Foss, and Chuckry 2016 #1). The final issue, dated November 2016, even depicted election-based riots weeks before real-life, occasionally violent post-election protests swept the country (Mele and Correal 2016). But while the book did not hold out much confidence for the American political system, it did offer a more optimistic view of the individual American. As the miniseries ended, Loki explained, "Sometimes the best thing you can do . . . is to affect change on a smaller, more individual level. Maybe one shouldn't put all their *values, hopes,* and *ideals* into *one big thing* that couldn't possibly be everything you wanted in it" (Hastings, Foss, and Chuckry 2016 #4).

Like the argument that "the personal is political," Loki's suggestion pointed to the connections between personal experiences and larger political implications.

Four years later, as the primaries for the 2020 election got underway, comics revisited and revived these same demonic themes. The four-issue *I Pledge Allegiance to the Mask* told the tale of a presidential candidate who won the White House by harnessing the power of a mystical mask. The mask removed all inhibitions, both legal and moral, from its wearer, who was also granted supernatural abilities. Thus, the candidate is prone to not only killing off his competition, but to telling the public that anyone who disagrees with or dislikes him are traitors, whiners, or wimps (echoing Trump's charges that his detractors are "losers" or are "sad"). Murder and mayhem marked the campaign and the new president's first weeks in office. The reign of terror ended when the president committed suicide and the White House exploded. In the final scene of the book, the mask was seen affixed to the Statue of Liberty, telling the readers that the political horrors that ensued were not because of its influence but because of the American people: "The truth is, you don't need me. You never did. Because the truth is . . . you *are* me" (Cantwell and Reynolds 2020).

Image Comics' *Killadelphia*, set during a Philadelphia mayoral election, imagined the dark lengths a president would go to in order to secure his place in history. The story suggested that Philadelphia's high murder rate was caused, in part, by a nest of vampires led by an undead President John Adams, who believed his greatness was eclipsed by that of George Washington and Alexander Hamilton. Through death and undeath, Adams hoped to create a new society that "would be a balance of the underprivileged and the elite" (Barnes, Alexander, and NCT 2020). The story was reminiscent of the "true" legend of the vampire who served President Andrew Johnson after the Civil War (see Schneck 2005) and it relied on symbolism of vampires as cruel and manipulative autocrats (Nelson 2005), placing issues of race and class at the center of decisions about who would live and who would die.[5]

These evil politician comics presented predominantly dark varieties of the Conspiracy narrative, with shadowy self-interests frustrating the democratic process. That all five comics made gods and demons[6] their agents of conspiracies suggests that the political process is beyond the control of average citizens, thus relieving audiences of responsibility rather than motivating them to take action against such corruption (see Knopf 2020a). Among these comics, *AoD* was the only one that indicated that the general public is, or at least can be, smart enough to see through the lies, and only *Vote Loki* provided any direction for civic action.

CONCLUSION

Voting has long been heralded as the epitome of American civic activity—a duty and responsibility, a right and privilege. A government, as Abraham Lincoln said, "*of* the people, *by* the people, and *for* the people" is a fundamental part of the American identity and mythology outlined in the Declaration of Independence and established in the United States Constitution: voting is a means to pursuing life, liberty, and happiness. If, and when, the *quest* for life, liberty, and happiness is challenged by self-interested *conspiracies*, it is the obligation of the people to rise up and unite at the ballot box in the interests of the common welfare. From the 1952 *Your Vote is Vital* to the 2008 *Spider-Man Election Day*, this is the message perpetuated in comics. Democracy depends on the people. Implicit in such messages is an acknowledgment that without the power of the people, corruption and malevolence likely will prevail. Indeed, this is the message implied by the titles of *The Man Who Stole Your Vote* and *Cheated!* Following the widespread voter suppression during the 2004 presidential election, the comics increasingly focused on conspiracy narratives of American democracy, from alien cover-ups and campaign sabotage in *Saucer Country* to the reigns of demons and chaos in *Citizen Jack* and *I Pledge Allegiance to the Mask*. The agency of the honest and virtuous individual, while still lauded, was less effective against inhuman, literally and figuratively, political machines and machinations.

At one level, the bleak election stories that seemed to dominate politically themed comic books of the 2010s can be read as an indictment of the process that simply feeds public antipathy and apathy. What is the purpose of voting in a system that does not support the people, or for candidates who offer no true, let alone, good choice? But, at another level, these comics indicate that same problem is the very reason that citizens *should* concern themselves with politics. The stories do not just criticize the corruption of politicians, but they also criticize the public that has enabled them, through its preference for easy answers, its attraction to the sensational, its desire for personal rather than communal welfare, and its ignorance of what was happening until it was too late.

Many of the comics discussed here demonstrate a sense that voters are tired of campaign rhetoric and political talk and that they want a candidate of action rather than talk. This points to voters' real experiences of "campaign fatigue": of being sick of the advertisements, of feeling confined by outdated parties, and of feeling frustrated by an ever-changing array of issues that are discussed but not resolved (for example, O'Brien 2018). But it is also a call to action for readers/voters—a reminder to not just complain about politics but to *do* something about them, to serve and help others, and, of course, to vote.

THE DIFFERENCE BETWEEN A SUPERHERO AND A FEMALE POLITICIAN IS A CAPE

The 2008 election arguably changed the political landscape for women in American politics. This was the year when a woman, Hillary Clinton, won a state presidential primary for the first time in US history. And it was the year that a woman, Sarah Palin, was the vice-presidential nominee on a major party ticket for only the second time in the nation's history; Palin "concluded her appearance in a national debate by reaching for her newborn baby. [. . .] [and that] maternal reach was a roaring first in presidential politics" (Traister 2010, 2–3). Women ran for seats in the House of Representatives in 163 districts that year (Ingold et al 2018). Women voters emerged as a deciding force in 2008, not only voting as a more cohesive block than men, but also tripling their amount of campaign donations compared to the 2000 election (Menin 2009). Palin and Clinton both ran against a self-described comic book fan who would earn the distinction of being the president who "has probably appeared in more comics than any other politician" (Arts 2019, para. 6). It is, therefore, not surprising that the election inspired the *Female Force* comic book line (see chapter one) and what *BuzzFeed* and the *Atlantic* described as "an entire cottage industry of Palin-infused comic books" (Hudson 2011, para 2).

Both comics and politics have traditionally been male-dominated arenas. American politics marshal masculine metaphors of horse races and boxing matches (Iyengar 2016); both the media and voters preference masculine traits, such as reason, over feminine traits, such as intuition, and masculine issues, like international security, over feminine issues, like social security (see, for example, Falk 2008; Carroll 1994; Stäheli 2003). The president's masculinity has long been equated with his ability to lead (Kimmel 2011). This phenomenon influences not only how people vote but also who runs. Women have historically been deterred from seeking political office because the demands of the job are put in opposition to the roles as wives and mothers (Menin 2009).

Similarly, the genre of the superhero has been a male-dominated power fantasy embodied by hypermasculine physicality (Gateward and Jennings 2015; Landon 2008). Superheroics are accordingly defined in traditionally masculine terms (Baker and Raney 2007). "Certainly, women can be heroes, but they are very rarely *obligated* to be heroes" (Berlatsky 2015, loc. 1372). Male domination has consequently carried over into comic book fandom, where the media mostly frame a large and growing group of women fans as star-struck teens, exhibitionists, or the girlfriends of male fans (Jenkins 2013). Beyond such stereotypes, female comic fans are often invisible, with fandom labels like "geek" and "nerd" often coded as male unless specifically modified as female (Scott 2013; Busse 2013; Anderegg 2007), just as the term "superhero" is usually coded as male unless modified as "female superhero" or feminized as "superheroine."

SUPERMOMS AND HOCKEY MOMS

The combination of the masculine fields of politics and comics presents a variety of challenges and opportunities for female figures in politically themed graphic narratives. In both politics and comics, women's ability to broaden representation is shaped, positively and negatively, by the biases and stereotypes of their male-dominated environments. These gender role expectations put women in "double binds"—conflicts between social norms that limit women's options of action and communication, and undermine their power (Jamieson 1995). One example that is particularly relevant to the female politician *and* the female superhero is found in the construct of the "supermom."

As a product of second-wave feminist ideas about the boundless capabilities of women, motherhood has been inextricably linked to superheroism. The "supermom" is a woman who is seemingly successful in both the public and private spheres (D'Amore 2012). Motherhood is, however, contested in contemporary discourse with cultural schemas that view maternal and career identities as competing. Selfish/selfless messages simultaneously support women for forsaking non-maternal identities as being good, self-sacrificing mothers but criticize them for being weak women, and success/failure messages suggest that work-family tensions are a precursor to failure in both realms (Johnston and Swanson 2003). Superhero comics highlight these double binds as "a genre obsessed with perpetuating a fantasy of hegemonic masculinity the options for maternal roles are clearly limited" (Brown 2011b, 81). Treatment of motherhood in superhero stories highlights the genre's conflicting messages about womanhood, with maternal desires often portrayed as destructive, forcing superhuman mothers to choose between heroics and maternity (Brown 2011b; Stuller 2010). In a genre dedicated to the preservation of boundaries—good and evil, right and wrong— the pregnant or maternal body defies boundaries: it expands beyond the sleek proportions of a superhero physique, collapsing distinctions of inside/outside and self/other (Brown 2011b). That blurred private/public boundary is likewise problematic for the female politicians. Motherhood and political authority are often viewed by voters as antithetical (Witt, Paget, and Matthews 1995). Motherhood, a feminine ideal, suggests professional inexperience and sexuality, which in turn carries a fear of "PMS going nuclear" (Carmon 2015, para. 6). Additionally, as Palin's 2008 vice-presidential nomination demonstrated, there is an underlying assumption that a woman cannot effectively be both a mother and a leader. *Glamour* noted that major news networks implied that simply by campaigning Palin was neglecting, even harming, her children (Carpenter 2008).

Journalists tend to discuss female politicians in intimate terms, with details about their appearance and domesticity (Devere and Davies 2006; Devitt 2002; Burke and Mazzarella 2008). Therefore, political women may find it necessary to use such intimacies as justification for public activities. Militant motherhood, a strategy employed in the American labor movement by such leaders as Mary Harris "Mother" Jones, is "defined as women's use of maternal responsibilities to justify engagement beyond the domestic sphere," a kind of symbolic motherhood in which women activists use their assumed maternal roles to bolster their ethos in the public sphere (Mooney 2007, 975; Tonn 1996). Matronly knowledge is likewise a rhetorical position adopted by contemporary female politicians, especially on the political right, in an effort to reconcile the gender tensions between the public and private spheres (Dow and Tonn 1993; Scholwater 2012). Indeed, Palin introduced herself to the nation by explaining, "I was just your average hockey mom and signed up for the PTA. [. . .] You know, they say the difference between a hockey mom and a pit bull? Lipstick" (Palin 2008, para. 26–27).

The following discussion of real, fictionalized, and fictional female politicians, as well as political wives and daughters, in comic books further explores such tensions. The discussion is shaped by Karrin Vasby Anderson and Kristina Horn Sheeler's (2005) description of the four metaphoric clusters most commonly associated with women in politics: the Pioneer, a groundbreaker; the Puppet, a passive extension of a male politician; the Hostess/Beauty Queen, a decorative and complementary aid to men; and the Unruly Woman, disruptive and/or unfeminine. These metaphors, which belittle women's political contributions, share some commonalities with four pervasive, and contradictory, images of American womanhood: the matron, a loving and attentive mother; the siren, a seducer of men; the ingénue, innocent and youthful; and the professional, a force to be reckoned with in the workplace (Hahn 2003).

Figure 8.1. Thomas Nast's depiction of reformer and would-be president Victoria Woodhull for *Harper's Weekly* cast her as evil in her departure from social norms and proprieties of the nineteenth century.

To better understand the proliferation of Palin comics in 2008, and the subsequent Palin and Clinton-inspired comics of 2012 and 2016, we begin with the first woman to run for president. *Smithsonian Magazine* reminded readers during the 2016 election, "Over the centuries, more than 200 women have sought the country's highest office, to varying degrees of success. And leading the way for all of them was Victoria Claflin Woodhull: a nineteenth-century women's rights activist and business owner" (Lewis 2016, para. 1). Woodhull, a spiritualist, broker, and printer, announced her candidacy through a letter to the *New York Herald* in April 1870, saying, "I am quite well aware that in assuming this position I shall evoke more ridicule than enthusiasm at the outset. But this is an epoch of sudden changes and startling surprises. What may appear absurd today will assume a serious aspect to-morrow" (quoted in Lewis 2016, para. 5). Two years later, she was officially nominated as the presidential candidate for the Equal Rights Party and was subsequently mocked in the press. As an advocate of "free love," a belief that women should be free to choose if and who they wanted to marry and divorce, she was reviled by renown political cartoonist Thomas Nast, who suggested in a cartoon for *Harper's Weekly* that Woodhull was either the devil or his wife (see figure 8.1).

Nast's cartoon used, and arguably even helped to establish, the metaphoric cluster of the Unruly Woman. These metaphors demonstrate "how some political women simply, do not measure up in the poise and appearance category" and they emphasize disruption of traditional attractiveness and family structure dynamics, demonstrating how a woman running for masculine office is "unfitting, disorienting," laughable, or unlikely (Anderson and Sheeler 2005, 27). Kathleen Rowe (1995) argues that the Unruly Woman is one who defies, and may redefine, gender norms. She is a woman who creates disorder by not being subservient or inferior to men, is excessive in appearance or behavior, can recognize her own foibles, and is marginal or taboo. Nast's cartoon emphasized the former and latter of these characteristics by suggesting that Woodhull upset the moral order. The comics of the 2008 election also contributed to the Unruly Woman metaphors in the media coverage of the campaign through such titles as *Going Rouge: The Sarah Palin Rogue Coloring & Activity Book* (2009, TBTM Media), *Sarah Palin: Rogue Warrior* (2010, Antarctic), and the "Scott Pilgrim"-inspired *Sarah Palin versus the World* (2011, Antarctic). Because Palin did not follow the script of the John McCain campaign, she was labeled a "rogue" by the camp and the media—though at least some feminist scholars have suggested that her rogue affect was not authentic because it did not disrupt rigidly defined gender norms (e.g., Jolles 2012).

Jumping ahead nearly sixty years after Woodhull's 1872 campaign, we arrive at possibly the first woman to run for president *in comics*: one of illustrator Nell Brinkley's flapper heroines, known as "Brinkley Girls," in a series called *Dimples' Day Dreams* in 1928, just eight years after women gained suffrage. While the campaign was only a fantasy, it was a pivotal moment. Brinkley was considered the "Queen of Comics" during her nearly four-decade career doing illustrations for major newspapers and magazines, and her iconic Brinkley Girl was popular not only in comics but also theater, film, song, poetry, and commercials (see Robbins 2009). The Brinkley Girl first gained her fame in a nationally syndicated illustration entitled "The Three Graces," in which three young, attractive, patriotic women celebrated suffrage, preparedness, and Americanism (Robbins 2001b). Consistent with the metaphoric cluster of the Hostess/Beauty Queen, it was the loveliness of the Brinkley Girl that made her suffrage support acceptable; the Hostess/Beauty Queen in politics is a "sometimes giddy, attractive, social" creature whose femininity stays within the confines of traditional domestic roles (Anderson and Sheeler 2005, 20). Dimples imagines

Figure 8.2. Betty Boop's presidential run in 1932 lampooned President Hoover and visually suggested that a woman needed to be masculine in politics, as depicted in this screenshot.

being a politician, "orating for the peepul—(with liberal Lincoln) quotes," being elected mayor, governor, or "even President," and wearing a smart black pantsuit, adorned with feathers, and dainty high heels at her inauguration (in Robbins 2001b, 110). Moreover, her dream of a presidential bid seems to have inspired Wonder Woman's own fantastic, futuristic campaign in 1943—at least aesthetically, as noted by Wonder Woman artist and comics herstorian Trina Robbins (2016)—though Wonder Woman creator William Moulton Marston believed it would be the year 3000, rather than 1928, before a woman president would be a viable proposition.

Dimples was not the only flapper to run for president. In 1932, Betty Boop ran for president in a Max Fleischer animated short from Paramount Pictures. Betty's opening number, performed for a large adoring crowd, began with her singing in her trademark childish soprano, wearing her usual short, fitted jazz dress. As she explained how things would be "if you send me to Washington," she covered her dress with a suit and tie and her curls with a top hat. Her voice dropped to a masculine baritone, and her round baby face, with its big eyes and button nose, morphed to feature jowls, hooded eyes, and thin lips in a caricature of President Herbert Hoover (see figure 8.2). More than a vaudevillian spoof, the transformation underscored the presidency as decidedly masculine and reiterated the need for women to manage their femininity in order to demonstrate suitability for office. The short was reimagined in 1948 as a *Popeye the Sailor* segment, "Olive Oyl for President";[1] after Popeye told Olive that women weren't running for president "because they're too busy running for husbands," she imagined what it would be like if she became president. (Popeye himself ran for president in a 1956 cartoon.)

Artist Virginia Huget, creator of multiple comic strips starring women including "Peggy Lux" for the Lux Soap company, ran "Peggy Lux for President" in soap ads in the mid-1930s with a campaign slogan of "Down with Runs." While campaigning, Peggy saved a lonely woman from spinsterhood, as well as a runaway housewife in a loveless marriage, both at the brink of suicide, by advising them to fight perspiration odor in their lingerie and underwear by using Lux.[2] In another installment, Peggy's opponents, Alkali Ike and Cake-Soap Rubbing, conceded defeat; Peggy was left to fight a war in the country of Runfobia, where men and women battled with each other because women's ruined silk stockings were too costly for men (reprinted in Robbins 2001a, 30). Lux exemplified the Hostess/Beauty Queen. Her primary concern was with the domestic sphere and the duty of washing clothes. She was dedicated to maintaining attractive femininity through controlling odor and ruined stockings. She was devoted to saving male-female relations, especially marriages, by ensuring that other women appropriately attended to domestic and intimate matters in ways that appeased men.

Lux's wartime presidency further highlighted a particular dynamic of gender in Western public discourse: Western citizenship is closely associated with heterosexual male privilege and American language thus presents a gendered binary of discourse that assumes male rationality/female emotionality, male activity/female passivity, male toughness/female softness, and so on. Metaphors within that discourse system perpetuate gender roles and expectations by casting males as producers, warriors, and sexual aggressors, and women as consumers, dependents, and sexually submissive. In eco-politics, this is seen through norms of men as workers and women as shoppers, with men earning an income outside the home and women earning a keep in the home through marriage, childrearing, and sex. Politically, this continues through men as lawmakers and women as law-followers, men as politicians and women as voters (Hahn 2003).

"Peggy Lux for President" fit within this schema in several ways. First, the Runfobia War started because "the men say runs keep them broke" and they refuse to buy the women any more silk stockings (in Robbins 2001a, 30). This reinforced the idea of women as dependent and as consumers, and men as workers. Second, in this war, both men and women wore military uniforms (with the women outfitted to resemble nutcracker soldiers and the men to resemble French legionnaires), but only the men carried guns. This perpetuated the idea of men as warriors. Third, the war ended after Peggy convinced the women to change their laundry habits and then "slips into the men's camp to tell them the women have reformed" (in Robbins 2001a, 30). This cast women as submissive, which was emphasized when Peggy was captured as a spy, bound, and held at gunpoint by the men.

Another female president faced a battle of the sexes in the November 1943 *Wonder Woman* #7 (see chapter four). Gazing into the future from Paradise Island in 1943, Wonder Woman and her mother, Hippolyta, saw the United

States in the year 3000. They, with their readers, witnessed the future country under matriarchal rule with the first woman president, Arda Moore, who believed, "'Woman' is a prouder title than President!" (Moulton 1943, 5A). They saw a world in which women controlled their own bodies, at least with regards to clothes. They saw a peaceful and prosperous, but politically contentious, nation. Moore ended political corruption and made public service profit-free, which upset Senator Heeman (read: he-man), who asserted "women are feather brained idealists" (Moulton 1943, 6A). Moore imprisoned opposition political leader Grafton Patronage (read: graft and patronage), who launched an assassination plot against her claiming women to be "dumb" (Moulton 1943, 7A). And Moore was openly opposed by Professor Manly, leader of the Man's Party, who ran Moore's own military aide, Steve Trevor, for president against her in the 3004 election. When Moore dropped out of the race, Wonder Woman, as Diana Prince, and her sidekick, Etta Candy, became the presidential and vice-presidential nominees of the Woman's Party. The Man's Party used violence and illegal guns to hijack the voting to ensure it won. Through some dramatic derring-do, Wonder Woman saved everyone from Manly's machinations and was sworn in, "after many years of faithful service to her country," as the duly elected president of the United States (Moulton 1943, 13B).

The matriarchal presidencies of Wonder Woman were consistent with the beliefs of her creator, William Moulton Marston, in emancipation of, and through, females, echoed by Hippolyta's observation of the future female president, "All men are much happier when their strong aggressive natures are controlled by a wise and loving woman" (Moulton 1943, 13B). In 1941, Marston introduced Wonder Woman based on his theory that a close understanding of the binary emotions of dominance-submission could open the way for human liberation (Bunn 1997; Berlatsky 2015). Marston felt that the American patriarchal system was motivated by aggression, causing war, greed, and general strife. He believed that things would improve if men chose to surrender to the "loving authority" of women. His *Wonder Woman* comics, as a result, were filled with bondage imagery meant as a metaphor for such willing submission. Despite Marston's belief in women's superiority, the bondage imagery—which is plentiful in the "Wonder Woman for President" stories—complicated his feminist messages. Some read it "feminism as fetish," representing deeper metaphors of economic, political, and social bindings of women, with Wonder Woman proving that strength and victory were possible despite such restraints (Lepore 2015, 4993; see also Berlatsky 2015; Emad 2006; Hanley 2014). Wonder Woman's questionable place as a female role model was a matter of international debate in 2016 when she was appointed, then quickly dismissed, as a United Nations honorary ambassador for women and girls, with her skimpy costume, violent tendencies, and American motif cited as being inappropriate (Roberts 2016).

The female presidency of Wonder Woman primarily fit within the Hostess/Beauty Queen metaphoric clusters with only a limited element of being an Unruly Woman. Senator Heeman accused her, "You've stopped us men from making money out of public office," implying that she reversed the role of producers and consumers (Moulton 1943, 6A). Steve Trevor suggested that the matriarchy emasculated men and argued that a male president would "put more strength into the government" (Moulton 1943, 2B). But those were the only visible disruptions to the traditional gender-binary. Both Moore and Prince in their political capacities dressed in slinky evening gowns; as Hippolyta noted, "When women control their own styles they're bound to be picturesque and alluring!" (Moulton 1942, 3A). Moore's federal prison was more of a hotel—there were no locks, bars, or restraints, and its occupants were made comfortable—showing the hospitality of women. On the campaign trail, "Diana's able speeches and Etta's humor appeal equally to men and women" (Moulton 1943, 4B). Wonder Woman successfully blended the maternal ideal with a philosophy of love, the seductive ideal through revealing clothing, the innocent ideal through a dedication to justice, and the professional image as a fighter. She was the perfect woman according to hegemonic norms, making her the perfect political hostess, staying confined to a prescribed gender order.

The complicated feminism and mixed political metaphors of Wonder Woman continued into more recent political comic book representations. In 2019, freshman Congressperson Alexandria Ocasio-Cortez, known affectionately to supporters as AOC, became a comic book superhero in a special commemorative issue, *Alexandria Ocasio-Cortez and the Freshman Force*, which featured "an anthology of short stories as the Congresswoman takes on the GOP in heroic, satirical adventures" from Devil's Due Publishing (Stone 2019, para. 2). The book was inspired by one of AOC's tweets in which she quoted the graphic novel *Watchmen* by Alan Moore. A portion of the book's proceeds benefitted RAICES, a nonprofit serving immigrant children, families, and refugees, and the USO, which supports military service members and their families. While the comic was not endorsed by either charity or by AOC, Ocasio-Cortez told *TMZ* that she was honored and humbled by the publication (Bussel 2019b; Cronin 2019).[3]

The comic came in at least seventeen variant covers, including twelve collectible covers, offering different color combinations, poses, and costumes of the controversial Representative (Fox 2019; see figure 8.3). One of these variants was called the "Washington Warrior Collector Variant" and featured AOC in a costume reminiscent of Wonder Woman's in the 2017 film with Gal Gadot: molded leather bustier, Roman skirt, knee-high boots, gauntlets, and tiara. Another variant by artist Carla Cogen—planned in a small run of 250 copies exclusively for a New York comic shop, the Collector Cave, a Bronx store in Ocasio-Cortez's district—featured AOC in Wonder Woman's iconic red, white,

Figure 8.3. The Devil's Due *Alexandria Ocasio-Cortez and the Freshman Force* came in many collectible variant covers with pop culture allusions, the most notable and controversial being of Wonder Woman.

and star-spangled-blue leotard and red boots. Done as a portrait rather than a cartoon, which protected the Washington Warrior image as satire under First Amendment laws, the publisher received a cease-and-desist letter from Wonder Woman-owner DC Comics, making the cover an even more coveted collector's item (Johnston 2019; Brueck 2019).

Other pop culture allusions used in the variant covers—which included Spider-Man (specifically the Barack Obama cover from 2009), Captain America, Supergirl, Batman, *The Right Stuff*, Mad Max, *Hamilton*, and Super Mario Bros.—did not gain the attention, or seemingly the popularity, of the Wonder Woman-inspired covers, including the special "Cease & DCist Edition," in which Devil's Due parodied *MAD Magazine* and DC Comics' characters Supergirl, Batman, and the Green Lantern, to strike back at DC Comics (Aguilar 2019). The controversy of the Wonder Woman cover may be attributed in part to the complicated place of Wonder Woman in American gender politics. As Elizabeth Coody (2019) argues, Wonder Woman is an "empty" icon: she means many different things to many different people, and those meanings have changed as society has changed. Popular in the 1940s, her cultural status waned in the 1950s as women returned to the kitchen from the wartime workforces. But, by 1972, as women's liberation came to the fore, she became the cover girl for *Ms.* under the headline "Wonder Woman for President"—the same year that Shirley Chisholm, the first Black woman elected to Congress, really *was* running for president. As Vanessa Garcia contemplates:

> A woman did not win the presidency, but women had made it into the workforce, full force.
> Perhaps Wonder Woman had something to do with that. She was both recording the successes of women and also attempting to push them further. But, perhaps too, she was also part of the problem. [...]
> [Women] were working outside the home while also continuing to carry the brunt of childcare. Oh, and they still had to look hot while they did it. Let's not forget that the Wonder Woman of the '70s was, after all, played by Lynda Carter, crowned Ms. World America, 1972. (2017, para. 15–17)

By 2012, the *Atlantic* noted that "women still can't have it all" (Slaughter 2012)—as exhibited by Clinton's losses in 2008 and again 2016.

And again, Wonder Woman loomed large on the pop culture scene. "But will she prevail this time," asked Garcia (2017, para. 19)?

> At first, it's easy to think: Yes! Because this time the director, Jenkins, is a woman, wary of the easy pitfalls that could plague Wonder Woman. [...]
> Still Gal Gadot, the actress and model who plays Wonder Woman, is a beauty pageant winner like Carter before her: Miss Israel, 2004. Gadot also studied law and

was in the Israeli army for two years, so she's not all veneer, but what if Jenkins had cast someone, like Serena Williams, whose body exuded power? [...]

Perhaps the answer is that women like Serena Williams are considered "too unruly ... too strong ... too masculine, too rude, too fashionable, too black," as Anne Helen Petersen writes in *Too Fat, Too Slutty, Too Loud: The Rise and Reign of the Unruly Woman*. And yet the "unruly woman" is exactly what we need if Wonder Woman is to work any wonder at all [...]. (Garcia 2017, para. 20–22)

It is significant that the performer who played *Wonder Woman* on television in the 1970s, beauty queen Lynda Carter, was newly cast as President Olivia Marsdin[4] on the CW series *Supergirl* at this same time, reinforcing cultural and political preferences for feminine women who are not too unruly. Even so, Marsdin's character exemplified cultural suspicions of even proper female politicians. It was revealed in 2017 that Marsdin was not human but of the Durlan alien race, reptilian shape-shifters from a planet irradiated by a nuclear war (Moore 2017). In the real world, twelve million Americans, 4 percent of the population, are actually convinced that the United States government is run by reptilians, or lizard people from another planet, with Hillary Clinton believed to be among the ranks of the reptilian elite (Bump 2013; *TIME* 2008).

STRANGE VISITORS FROM ANOTHER PLANET

The Clinton-alien connections are also found in Vertigo's 2012–13 miniseries *Saucer Country* and its 2017 sequel from IDW, *Saucer State*, by Paul Cornell and Ryan Kelly. The series (see chapter seven) followed the leading Democratic candidate for president of the United States, New Mexico Governor Arcadia Alvarado, while she managed a presidential bid interrupted by an alien abduction and a presidential term marked by a pending alien invasion. While the original *Saucer Country* run offered somewhat general critical commentary on US politics, with a conveniently timed initial release of the week following Super Tuesday during the 2012 primaries, the sequel, *Saucer State*, was specifically designed to comment on the 2016 presidential contest (Young 2012; Cornell 2017).

Aliens in the *Saucer* series marked Alvarado, a Latina in the predominantly White, male political realm, as an outsider, as unruly (Knopf 2020b).[5] Culture "routinely defines women as different, as the Other—as aliens" (Barr 1993, 64). Erika Falk likewise notes that media coverage of women's political campaigns has historically argued that "women are unnatural in politics" (2008, 30). And there were strong correlations between the fictional campaign of Arcadia Alvarado and the real campaigns of Hillary Clinton. In a *Saucer Country* campaign speech, Alvarado remarked,

The campaign's tiring America out, it's tiring me out. I've been in flat shoes the last three days. And you know what—? The president's camp tried to use *that* against me, too. "Do you want a woman in the White House who *tires* so easily?" One blogger called me "unfeminine." (Cornell and Kelly 2013)

This echoed the highly publicized moment from the 2008 campaign when a tired Clinton got teary-eyed talking to a prospective voter who asked her "how she does it" (Goldenberg and Adams 2008, para. 1).

As Kelly Wilz notes, "the 2008 election brought both subtly gendered criticisms and overtly sexist treatment of Hillary Clinton and Sarah Palin, forms of bias that [were] alive and well in the 2016 campaign cycle. Whether it be Secretary Clinton's 'yelling' or Carly Fiorina's wrinkles," female politicians were held to different standards than their male counterparts (2016, 357). It is, therefore, more than coincidental that 2016 saw the start of the "President Bitch" story arc in *Bitch Planet*—a dystopian series from Image Comics in which "non-compliant," unfeminine, un-submissive, and unruly women were separated from society and incarcerated.

Clinton, considered by many to be a "bitch" herself, was unsurprisingly framed as an Unruly Woman in her comic book appearances (Anderson 1999). The satirical *Socialism Trek* and *Fanatic* from Capital Capers in 1994 presented First Lady Clinton as a pushy, critical nag. Likewise, the cover of *Shafted: Bill and Hillary's Excellent Adventure* (1993) depicted Clinton riding on her husband's back as if he were a horse. *Major Flip Flop* (2004) and *Trump's Titans* (2017) cast candidate Clinton as a shadowy villain, a figure obsessed with gaining the presidency who allied herself with dark forces and unethical means in her efforts to win (see chapter five). Such obsession was also suggested in *President Evil: Make America (Taste) Great Again* (2016) when Clinton attempted to leverage the contained Zlu-2 zombie virus to take the presidency back from Donald Trump after his election. This unruly, ruthless nature was at the heart of the 2016 graphic novel *Clinton Cash*, which detailed allegations of Clinton's misuse of power for personal profit.

Even when endorsed by comics, as she was by gracing the cover of the Election 2016 Special issue of Valiant's *Faith* #5, Clinton's unruliness was evident. Faith, first introduced into the DC Universe in 1992, is a plus-size superhero, nicknamed by her teammates as "the Fat Lady" because "it's not over until the fat lady sings." Faith is perhaps most notable as a hero because she is fat (see Tongco 2016; Dodson 2016; Mazziotta 2015; Paoletta 2015). As an NPR headline proclaimed, "*Faith* makes fat a force to reckon with" (Lehoczky 2016). She is the "too fat" of Petersen's (2017) *Too Fat, Too Slutty, Too Loud: The Rise and Reign of the Unruly Woman*. And on issue #5, she is dwarfed by a broadly smiling Hillary Clinton, calling to mind Clinton's "too loud" cackle. As Elaine K. Miller (2009) noted of 2008 political cartoons, Clinton was often identified visually by her laugh; with her head thrown back and mouth agape, she was presented as being too brash and too much.

Despite being crowned Miss Wasilla in 1984 and being dismissed as a political rogue in 2008, Palin's comic book appearances tended mostly toward the metaphoric cluster of the Pioneer, rather than of the Beauty Queen or the Unruly Woman. The differences between Clinton and Palin found in cartoon representations echoed ideological "differences in their personas as symbolic women" (Edwards and McDonald II 2010, 326). The Pioneer is "someone who is a trailblazer or groundbreaker," who is determined, practical, and hardworking, with a "pioneering spirit" that appeals to common folks (Anderson and Sheeler 2005, 14–15). But the Pioneer metaphor also implies that, as a "first," the female politician is a novelty, lacking the credibility of history and precedent for achievements (Falk 2008).

Thanks to Palin's home of Alaska, her hunting pastime, and her colloquial speech patterns, the metaphor was a natural fit. The cover of *Going Rouge: The Sarah Palin Rogue Coloring & Activity Book* depicted a larger-than-life Palin lounging on top of the White House, dressed in a cowboy hat, fringed shirt, and fur-lined boots, a six-shooter in hand and a bandoleer draped across her cleavage. The costuming, beyond its sexualization, elicited ideas of the American Wild West and pioneers of the Old West. On the first page of Antarctic Press's *Sarah Palin Rogue Warrior* (Dlin and Wight 2010), Ben Dunn reimagined Palin as Wonder Woman, America's first female superhero, introducing her as Wonder Palin "from the wilds of Alaska" (1), suggesting ideas of the frontier. Imagery of the rugged individual was used throughout the same volume, in Brian Denham's "Rogue Warrior" pinup art (16–17), with a bikini-clad Palin wearing a trapper's hat and hoisting a semi-automatic rifle; in Ben Dunn's story "Open Season" (9–15), with a hunting Palin camouflaged in polar bear skin; in Rod Espinosa's "Bear Hunter" (18) pinup art, with a gun-toting Palin in Victorian lingerie and polar bear skin cape; and in Chris Allen's "Hunters at Hooters" pinup (25), which flipped the script on Palin, whose head is mounted as a trophy on the wall above a bar populated with anthropomorphic animals. A similar motif was found on a variant cover of *Barack the Barbarian* #1, on which the character "Red Sarah, the fighting queen of the north," posed seductively in a fur bikini and wolf-skin cloak.

The steampunk aesthetic seen in the Victorian lingerie of the "Bear Hunter" pinup was expanded on in another Antarctic title, *Steampunk Palin*, a satirical comic about an effort to convert the world from oil and nuclear power to steam. In the story, Palin, McCain, and Obama (alias "Robama") have, through assorted circumstances, been transformed into steam-powered cyborgs and must work together to fight the evil Big Oil and Nuke run by a corrupted Al Gore (aka Professor Greenhouse). Before setting out into the wasteland, or wilderness, of the country, they covered their mechanized bodies with the only available clothing they could find—Victorian costumes left over from a theater production (Felker and Dunn 2010). Steampunk is both a genre and aesthetic premised on reimagined Victoriana that offers a semi-critical consideration of historical legacy in light of contemporary attitudes (e.g., Good 2010; Raz 2011; Hantke 1999; Cherry and Mellins 2011). Thus, a steampunked Palin becomes a figure from an idealized past leading the way to a nostalgic future.

These figures of the Unruly Woman, exemplified by Clinton, and the Pioneer, epitomized by Palin, merged in Mark Russell's 2015 reboot of DC's *Prez* (see chapters four and seven). The original *Prez* in 1973 reinforced the office of the president as decidedly masculine, declaring, "The history books of tomorrow will surely tell of young men like Prez" (Simon and Grandenetti 2016, 29). In 2015, however, the new teenage president was a young woman: Beth Ross. At her inauguration, Ross embodied the Pioneer and the status of being unprecedented, proclaiming, "I may not know what I'm doing, but so what? Everything started with someone who didn't know what they were doing" (Russell, Caldwell, and Morales 2016). Her vice president and political mentor advised her that because she was not a politician, she could be the *first* president to do things like fill a cabinet with truly smart people. This made her not only a novelty but also disruptive to the masculine tradition of presidential politics as usual.

The new *Prez* series nonetheless offered some direct challenges to the patriarchy. Ross's favorite band was called "Trans Vaginal Mesh" (Russell, Caldwell, and Morales 2016)—a name that operated as insidious product placement in her corporatized world and as a queered feminist statement of transgendered or nonbinary womanhood. She actively resented the male domination of government and addressed the condescending double standards of gender. When a senator greeted her with the words, "Why, what a lovely young woman," she replied, "Thanks! You're an acceptable-looking older man" (Russell, Caldwell, and Morales 2016). Gender roles were further tested by Ross's robotic bodyguard. Built in a secret laboratory as "War Beast," the robot escaped and sought sanctuary at a church. In therapy, War Beast revealed that it is looking for redemption as "Tina" and joined an LGBTQ/R(obot) support group to start a new life (Russell, Caldwell and Morales 2016). Despite the effort to represent LGBTQAIPD[6] issues, it should be noted that the comic's linking of violence and masculinity in War Beast, versus peace and femininity in Tina, reinforced, rather than disrupted, gender typing. Additionally, a transgender robot dehumanized the LGBTQAIPD community.

Another series that made some attempt at foregrounding gendered issues in campaigning is the 2019 *Archie: The Married Life—10th Anniversary*. When mayor-turned-congressperson "Moose" Mason ran for re-election, he was challenged by Cheryl Blossom, who remembered Moose's youthful reputation for being a bully and exploited his abusive past for her own gain. The story raised the specter of #MeToo, underscoring the influence of social media in the making and breaking of political reputations.

FEMALES OF THE FIRST FAMILIES

The wives and daughters of male politicians are similarly confined by gender norms, expected to "represent what we pretend is a single universally accepted ideal for US womanhood" (Campbell 1996, 191). Lisa M. Burns writes, "Over the years first ladies have performed a variety of public and private roles from hostess, escort, and volunteer to advisor and policy maker. Because this is a gendered role, there are social norms and expectations associated with its performance," conforming to standards of femininity especially within the domestic sphere and family structure (2008, 3). The media most often frames discussions of First Ladies of the United States (FLOTUS) according to: gender, placing them in the double-bind of ideal womanhood and liberated womanhood; personification, summarily placing them in the history and traditions of the FLOTUS institution; and/or, iconicity, comparing each FLOTUS to those before. The FLOTUS image has evolved across several different roles that reflected their historical moment: the Public Woman, a model of American womanhood and proper public activity; the Political Celebrity, imbuing domesticity with political significance; the Political Activist, reflecting the contestation surrounding women's liberation; and the Political Interloper, concerned with excessive influence beyond the confines of home and family concerns (Burns 2008).

The satirical comics that lampooned Hillary Clinton as a discontented and domineering FLOTUS—such as *Socialism Trek* and *The Fanatic Four*—were typical of the media framing of her as "co-president" during the Bill Clinton administration (Burns 2008). Michelle Obama was also criticized in the press for not staying within gendered confines, vilified as angry and unpatriotic (Griffin 2011). In her official capacity, she chose to take on the role of "Mom-in-Chief," concentrating on her children and backing initiatives to help other families. As Mary L. Kahl observes, this focus afforded Obama "a nuanced rhetorical platform that is nonthreatening, wholesome, and comprehensible" (2009, 317). Ironically, however, it was Obama's focus on her family history, as a descendent of slaves, that most condemned her in the public as offensive and un-American (Griffin 2011). Obama was unruly—too bold and too Black.

Like Clinton, Obama was depicted in comics as a Political Interloper: driven and unattractively ambitious and forceful. She received two features in the *Female Force* series: "Michelle Obama" and "Michelle Obama: Year One." In the former, which included a multi-panel spread dedicated to her enslaved ancestors, she was described as "meticulous" and as "a woman who does not suffer fools and expects excellence"; it further suggested she "pushed" her husband (Bailey and LaBelle 2009). In "Year One," which focused more on her first year as FLOTUS than her life story, she was described as "fiercely determined." The book also mentioned that she breached royal etiquette by touching Queen Elizabeth during a reception, that she was seen "poop-scooping" after her family's dog, that the press "seemed unnaturally obsessed" with her well-toned arms, and that there were questions about the appropriateness of showing her legs by wearing shorts during a family vacation to the Grand Canyon (Schnakenberg and Fowler 2010). While the comic was largely complimentary of Obama, even suggesting that she was a superhero, the fact that it highlighted these moments at all, even to criticize the media's attention to them, reinforced the unruliness of FLOTUS Obama, challenging her propriety and reestablishing her as a Political Interloper. By contrast, *Female Force: Nancy Reagan* relied more heavily on a personification frame, emphasizing Reagan's placement in the FLOTUS chronology and how her image and activities—fashion icon, Cold War domestic ideal, spiritualist—supported her husband (Burns 2008). The final page glowingly concluded, "Behind every great man is a great woman . . . A great actress . . . A great first lady. A great female force" (Troy and Díaz 2013).

Interestingly, first daughters have also provided comic book material. A 1961 comic introduced *Caroline Kennedy: America's First Young Lady*. The comic depicted Kennedy as an ideal girl who had "a morning kiss for daddy" and "always a smile for her admirers," whose constant companion was a rag doll, whose favorite toys were dolls, and whose activities embraced painting and ballet (Hughston, Giordano, and D'Agostino 1961). She was, in short, a picture of refined femininity. Such depictions of grace, even under fire, continued into Kennedy's adulthood. *Female Force: Caroline Kennedy* waxed that despite excessive privilege and misfortune, she endured familial tragedy and public scrutiny to succeed in motherhood, philanthropy, and politics (Bailey and Howe 2009a). First daughters Malia and Sasha Obama had cameo appearances in *Barack Panther*, a parody of Marvel's Black Panther, depicted as skilled sidekicks to their superheroic dad. Filling the roles of Shuri and Okoye, the innovative princess and honorable general of Wakanda, their appearance was properly feminine in that their activities supported those of their father—in line with the Puppet metaphoric cluster of women as "extensions of" or "mouthpieces for" male politicians (Anderson and Sheeler 2005, 16).[7] Issue #2 of the conservative comic *Liberality for All*, a post-9/11 revenge-fantasy, imagined Chelsea Clinton as president with her son, Willie, playing in the Oval Office at her side, calling attention to the tensions inherent in working motherhood.

Two other comics used the role of "first daughter" as the very foundation for their plots. Red Giant Entertainment introduced *The First Daughter* on Free

Comic Book Day in 2014, though the series never took off. The story focused on Tasha Tasker, the superpowered daughter of a newly elected Black president, who discovered she was part of a centuries old alien initiative that collected first daughters and first sons throughout history to assemble a team that could protect the world from its most dangerous threat ever. The premise was captured on page one in Tasha's words, "Who knew the role of the first daughter would come with so much power and responsibility?" (Crosby and Francisco 2014). The unbearable weight of that responsibility was at the heart of IDW's 2019 *Marilyn Manor*, the spoiled first daughter of a fictional 1980s president, named for her father's illicit affair with Marilyn Monroe. Marilyn embodied her father's recklessness and her martyred mother's belief that "you do what you *have* to do" (Visaggio, Zarcone, and Kniivila 2019); she brashly chose to live her life as she wanted, heedless of the consequences—truly an Unruly Woman and an Interloper.

CONCLUSION

At the end of Donald Trump's first year in office, *Politico* wrote, "Most people who follow politics spent 2016 imagining an America where Mr. President became Madam President. But the reality today looks very different. The highest glass ceiling remains firmly in place, and President Donald Trump's theatrically alpha-male leadership style has made a crack seem even more remote" (2017, para. 1).

Whether activists or action heroes, women are put at a disadvantage when judged by male standards. With superheroics (and politics) frequently defined in masculine terms, "the common interpretation of the action heroine" (and female politician) is usually "as simply enacting masculinity rather than providing legitimate examples of female heroism" (Brown 2011a, 43; Stabile 2009). When female superheroism is exemplified, it appears to focus on traditionally "feminine" traits such as collaboration, love, and mentorship—though it is unclear whether this represents experiences that are distinctly feminine or only those assumed to be feminine (Stuller 2013); either way, in gendered binary discourse, they are viewed as less valuable than masculine experiences. In the words of Clinton's 2008 campaign manager, Patti Solis Doyle, "Sexism costs every woman candidate votes" (in *Politico* 2017, para. 5). Thus, to borrow from the energetic 1977 television theme song, women still need Wonder Woman "fighting for her rights" and society still demands she do so "in her satin tights."

ZOMBAMAS, SOPAPILLAS, DARK HORSES, AND OTHER POLITICIANS OF COLOR

In November 2008, the *Daily Telegraph* revealed that Barack Obama collected *Conan the Barbarian* and Spider-Man comics. This gave the publisher of the Chicago-based Devil's Due Publishing the idea to create the series *Barack the Barbarian*, a gimmicky sword-and-sorcery series featuring Obama and many of his political contemporaries. It also led to Marvel Comics featuring the president-elect in *The Amazing Spider-Man* #583 ("Spidey Meets the President," January 2009). All told, ComicVine indicated that Obama, or his semblance, has appeared in over 350 comic book issues, wherein he interacted with superheroes, zombies, fantasy realms, futuristic technologies, supernatural evils, alien invasions, and mystical powers, but also put himself through school, got married, had a family, ran for the US Senate, and won the presidency.

Although Obama is still the only person of color to hold America's highest elected office in real life, in the comics, there have been others. In 1964, a ten-part story in *Treasure Chest (of Fact and Fun)*, drawn by legendary comics artist Joe Sinnot, imagined Tim Pettigrew for President, a Black candidate at a time when segregation was still legal. The 1997–2001 political manga *Eagle: The Making of an Asian-American President* introduced Japanese American candidate Kenneth Yamaoka. In 2009, DC introduced the Black character Calvin Ellis, based on Barack Obama, as the president of the United States and Superman on an alternate Earth. A 2012 cartoon-coloring book called *Age 4 Prez* presented the presidential vision of the "HipHop raptoonist" Adrian "Age" Scott. Vertigo's 2012 comic *Saucer Country* introduced the first Latina governor Arcadia Alvarado, who became the first Latina president in the 2017 IDW sequel series *Saucer*

State. DC's 2015 *Prez* introduced the racially mixed President Beth Ross. And the 2020 *Yang Gang* from Keenspot envisioned the United States in a futuristic 2028 as it remembered the election of Chinese American Andrew Yang. Other real American politicians of color to appear or even star in comics include Representative John Lewis, Senator Marco Rubio, Representative Alexandria Ocasio-Cortez, Secretary of State Colin Powell, Secretary of State Condoleezza Rice, and Republican presidential candidate and Tea Party activist Herman Cain.

Historically, the image of the American president has been shaped as "the ultimate site where Whiteness, masculinity, and nationhood are fused" (Shome 2000, 369). Similarly, "the genre of the superhero is very much a White-male-dominated power fantasy that is itself very much based in ideas around physical performance and power in relation to the negotiation of identity" (Gateward and Jennings 2015, 170). Frequently serving as proxy for American geopolitical identity, the figure of the superhero is seen as a singular, usually White and masculine, embodiment of the nation, wherein White heroes fight against minority villains or with minority sidekicks establishing a dialectic of minority inferiority (Howard and Jackson 2013; Scott 2006). Recognizing this, this chapter asks how comics present, legitimize, or de-legitimize, a presidency of color in a culture shaped by "racialized understandings of the nation-state" (Dittmer 2013, 49).

The election of Barack Obama was evidence that African American values had come into alignment with American values, and yet the racial tensions that escalated during his presidency triggered expressions of "White fragility," wherein Obama was "a key transitional figure between the racially divided generation of the Baby Boomers and the future generations that will see the decline of the White majority in the United States through immigration," representing "a new kind of blackness" and "a new kind of whiteness" (Smith 2009, 133). This transitional moment paved the way for Obama's successor, Donald Trump, to be called "America's First White President"—the first successful presidential candidate to define his campaign by Whiteness (O'Hehir 2016a). An editorial in the *New York Times* declared that "the election of 2016 marked a turning point in white identity" when "to see yourself as white has fundamentally changed, from unmarked default to racially marked" (Painter 2016, para. 2 and 4). This dynamic was at the heart of the 2012 graphic novel *Right State*, which imagined the 2020 re-election bid of America's second Black president while conservative militias, populated by a broad mix of ideologues and bigots of varying races, attempted a revolution to return America to the way they remembered it from an imagined time before Obama. Likewise, the retro superhero story *The American Way: Those Above and Those Below* depicted a former superhero and wife of former Mississippi governor running for office on a platform of "heritage, not hate" because it was "talk of 'revolution' and 'multiculturalism' that divides" (Ridley and Jeanty 2017).

Whiteness references both identity and ideology (Bucholtz 1999); it is defined by its relation to imaginary Others (Nayak 2007). For example, White imaginaries of Blackness as physical—violent, hypersexual, athletic—simultaneously establish Whiteness as intellectual, clerical, and intangible (Nayak 2007; Gateward and Jennings 2015). Natural, exceptional physical ability of the Black body is assumed and thus problematizes the Black superhero in comics, the Black athlete in sports, and the Black politician in government; Whiteness already defines the Black body as supernatural, thereby condemning Black characters to either fit stereotypes or to be unimpressive (e.g., Scott 2006; Gateward and Jennings 2015). The choice between stereotypical or forgettable is reflected in the costuming of Black superheroes. Blair Davis (2015) remarks,

> A major factor in what sets such heroes as Luke Cage and Black Lightning apart from Superman, Batman, and Captain America is the role of their costume design and the deployment of vague or temporally specific iconography. Superman's cape, Batman's cowl, and their respective chest symbols [. . .] are so visually distinct that they prove highly memorable, along with the fact that such imagery plays an ongoing role in the characterization of each hero. By comparison, the costumes of many black superheroes tell us little about the characters. (211)

Davis further observes that, at best, many of the costume features of Black characters are hokey, such as removable Afros and metal headbands, and, at worst, they are White fetish objects of Blackness, such as animal skins, beads, and nudity. In both cases, costuming draws attention to White ideas of their Blackness over their superheroics.

OUTLANDERS AND OUTSIDERS

Obama's first starring role in comics was the miniseries *Barack the Barbarian*, premised on *Conan the Barbarian*. The character of Conan originated in pulp magazines during the early 1930s, with stories appearing until the late 1960s. It then ran as a Marvel comic from 1970 to 1993 before emerging again in 2019. It was also the basis for three films, two animated series, one live-action series, and several games in different media and genres (Bertetti 2014). Conan and Obama alike defy traditional boundaries and are products of multiple milieus (Selzer 2010; Prida 2013).

Throughout his history, Conan was depicted in assorted variations of the warrior archetype, adept at all necessary skills for survival, with instinctual energy and aggressive might (Wicks 1996; Moore and Gillette 2013). Imola Bulgozdi argues, "Conan's background, however, also links him to the Wildman who stands for man's eternal bond with nature, a type of 'unrefined masculinity'" (2013, 194). The Wildman's closely related antithesis is the brutal Savage; though this role is assigned to Conan's enemies in the stories, in the real world of politics the image of the barbarian and the savage are interchangeable, with the barbarian an oft-employed enemy archetype as "a denier of God and the destroyer of culture. [. . .] rude, crude, and uncivilized [and] irrational" (Keen 1986, 43). The savage lives beyond the bounds of traditions and institutions (Rogin 1987). He is brutal and bestial, domineering and destructive, inexorable and impersonal (Ivie 1980). The image of the savage Other is employed to identify political enemies (Edwards 2008; Edelman 1988). It is an archetype most likely to exist between dissimilar ethnic groups, with the subhuman barbarian or savage image being politically integrated into representations of race (Keen 1986). As Stuart Hall notes, binaries are present in a "racialized discourse," transcribed to the "racialized body," that historically aligned "civilization" with Whiteness and, in juxtaposition, "savagery" with Blackness (1997, 243–44). This is particularly pronounced in cartoons which rely on simplistic stereotypes to quickly summarize ideas and to tap into the collective consciousness of readers helping them to make sense of the content, while reinforcing group beliefs and identities (Eisner 2008; DeSousa and Medhurst 1982; Spears 2002).

The tension of the good-barbarian-warrior/bad-savage-brute into which Obama was placed as "Barack the Barbarian" epitomized the complicated representations of Obama in broader political discourse. The Black body in American history has often served as a living medium upon which various sociopolitical meanings are inscribed (Henderson 2002). Linda F. Selzer (2010) notes that representations of Obama's body during the 2008 election were variously used by opponents to position him as un-American and by supporters as the embodiment of transformative opportunities. In both instances, Obama was depicted as exotic: a Black extremist, an African Muslim, a "Jim Dandy" or "Zip Coon," a skilled athlete, ambiguously racial, or cosmopolitan (Selzer 2010; Zurbriggen and Sherman 2010; Sparks 2009). His "Barack the Barbarian" caricature captured many of these in one text.

The original *Barack the Barbarian* comic ran in 2009, the first year of President Obama's term in office. Barack was written as the driving force of the series, by self-professed Obama-supporter Larry Hama, to be "cool, conscientious, charismatic, contemplative, and cynosural" (in Arrant 2009, para. 18). Obama's cosmopolitanism was captured in the first issue when "Barack of Shikago" ordered lunch in the city of Warshingtun ("Washington")—a tongue-in-cheek land of sword-and-sorcery fantasy, with monsters and mages bearing the names Sorceress Hilaria ("Hillary"), Cha-nee ("Cheney"), the despot Boosh ("Bush"), and his vizier, Harry Burden ("Halliburton"). Amid the trappings of a medieval pub, the so-called Barbarian ordered a multiethnic meal of a "tamale, kielbasa

Figure 9.1. The costuming for Barack the Barbarian, shown here on the Tom Seeley cover for the *Fall of Red Sarah* (Hama and Christmas 2009), emphasizes his African "Otherness."

and schnitzel burger combo with Dijon mustard, and cheese grits on the side. A wonton soup with extra matzo balls to start" (Hama, Schons, and Rosenberg 2009 #1). Meanwhile, his African Otherness, as subhuman savage, was reflected visually as one of the only bare-chested characters; he wore a loin cloth and a necklace of animal teeth with a large gold medallion (see figure 9.1). Such signifiers are also found on mainstream Black superheroes (largely by White creators): Marvel's Luke Cage wears flashy jewelry that aligns him with the culture of drug dealers (Davis 2015); Marvel's Cage, Cyborg, Brother Voodoo, and Black Goliath, as well as DC's Black Lightning all reveal bare muscled chests that emphasize the innate physicality, savagery, and sexuality, of the Black body as defined by Whiteness (Davis 2015; Nayak 2007); and Marvel's Black Panther and DC's Vixen both wear necklaces or necklines that resemble carnivorous teeth, connecting them to the "negro-as-animal discourse" established in the nineteenth century and still engaged in racist rhetoric today (Davis 2015). The satirical comic *Barack Panther* also drew on Obama's Otherness, including an image of his birth certificate as well as a dream sequence with his father, dressed in a traditional African fila and buba, and telling Obama to "cast off the shackles of your imperialist society and take up the mantle you were born to" and become the Barack Panther (Shannon and Denham 2018).

Such problematic racial representations of Obama were also found in the satirical/parodic comic series *President Evil*, a riff on the *Resident Evil* zombie-killing video game franchise. Created by David Hutchison and released from Antarctic Press in 2011, the four-book (plus a one-shot) American-manga series featured a country overrun by swine-flu-infected zombies. After being saved from the zombies by opponents Sarah "Paladin" and John "McPain," "Barot" Obama joined forces with them and fellow Democrat "Killery" Clinton to launch a bipartisan attack on the zombies threatening Obama's family. Along the way, Barot not only faced zombie hordes (including confrontations with undead presidents), but also political adversaries like Dick "Chainsaw" and a mercurial press that alternated between praising him for his heroism in the zombie uprising and condemning him for causing it in the first place, even though it was a problem he inherited from the previous president. Eventually overtaken by right-wing opponents, led by "Crush" Limbaugh, determined to sway public opinion against him, Barot was left facing new zombie troubles in a nuclear wasteland, which he managed to safely protect and rebuild until Trump and Clinton messed everything up with the 2016 election (Hutchison 2010).

As with the paradoxical elements of the warrior-wildman and barbarian-savage imagery inherent in *Barack the Barbarian*, *President Evil* engendered two distinct interpretations. Marc DiPaolo argues that, "*President Evil* depicts Barack Obama as a superhero figure who is the only man standing between the American people and Armageddon," the latter of which falls within the purview of the "evil-to-the-core [. . .] leadership of the Republican Party, and its corporate sponsors" who will stop at nothing to embarrass Obama and destroy democracy (2011, 6683). Laurie Gries (2015) suggests, however, that its zombie imagery—part of what she calls zombama rhetorics—is complicit in those very efforts to discredit Obama.

Zombies are liminal beings: no longer human, but with vestiges of humanness, no longer living, but not yet dead. The figure of the zombie highlights complications in the concept of personhood—how an individual can be a person in one context but not another, or how an individual can be rendered a nonperson (Travis 2015). "Imbued with traits that are already deemed culturally deviant/strange/excessive/unnecessary," the zombie "vilifies, marginalizes, and ostracizes" (Cocarla 2014, 54). As such zombies offer ways to represent and work through fears of Others, or provide the ultimate enemy that must be stopped, contained, and destroyed (Cocarla 2014; Webley 2015). In either case, the zombification of any figure carries ethnic significance. Historically zombies are derived from old African beliefs, used by slave holders in Haiti to terrify slaves into submission. Eventually they became symbolic of White fears of primitive Blackness (Wilentz 2012; Bishop 2006). Thus, connecting Obama to zombie imagery—what Gries labels "zombamicons"—coupled with inflammatory, parodic, or other critical commentary, serves as a rhetoric of dis-identification, estranging him from the public (2015, 7). Gries concludes that zombama rhetorics, such as in *President Evil*, "contribute to a continual marginalization of black men, to a racist legacy that Americans of color have had to endure for generations" (2015, 33).[1]

Efforts by opponents to embarrass, marginalize, or discredit Obama also provided the premise of the "Oh-Bomb-Ah" story arc of *Bomb Queen* from Image Comics. Creator Jimmie Robinson described the series, billed as "not for children (or squeamish adults)," as a satire of politics and pop culture (Sullivan 2009). The titular character was a supervillain, biogenetically created by a shadow government of the United States to be the ultimate prison warden. She ruled over New Port City, a sequestered location along the Eastern seaboard where criminal activity was allowed and law enforcement was not. The city attracted the worst of society, which lowered crime rates throughout the rest of the country. But Bomb Queen's evil and power went beyond anything the authorities anticipated. Writing for *CBR*, Michael Sullivan suggested that although *Bomb Queen* "was brimming with wry observations, social commentary and, between the boobs and booms, leaves you with considerable food for thought" (2009, para. 1). By writing a villain book, Robinson reversed the superhero formula, allowing an evil protagonist to triumph through the debase society that supported her (Speed and Robinson 2008).

The inspiration for the villain protagonist and her city of deviant followers was the post-9/11 American culture under President George W. Bush (Sullivan 2009). The decade following the terrorist attacks produced dark political satire of social unrest, shaped by changes in media production and consumption, public anger and fear, corrupt industries, a faltering economy, and wartime policies (Gournelos and Greene 2011). *Bomb Queen* was part of this atmosphere, designed to reflect the "subtle horror and creepiness of a society gone wrong" (Robinson 2009). Bomb Queen and New Port City, like the zombie virus of *President Evil*, became a problem President Obama inherited from President Bush. She was the embodiment of the society that created her and supported her—both the criminal elements of her New Port City, as well as the unethical government that engineered her (Knopf 2018); as she argued to the American people in an interview, "This country was founded on the action of slave owners, rapists and the genocide of native Indians, so my actions are in good company" (Robinson 2013).

In the "Oh-Bomb-Ah" story arc, collected in *Bomb Queen VI: Time Bomb, Countdown to Armageddon*, New Port City was scheduled to be shut down along with Guantanamo Bay. In retaliation, Bomb Queen set out to undermine President Obama and destroy the country. Her efforts began with a campaign to embarrass and discredit Obama. She stole what she erroneously believed to be a young Obama's donation to a fertility clinic, impregnating herself in order to claim that she carried the president's love child. She used her pregnancy to give legitimacy to a press junket, through a rhetoric of militant motherhood (see chapter eight). The combination of her violent predilections and her pregnancy garnered sympathy from the pro-gun, pro-life right, especially in consort with accusations about Obama's Muslim identity and allusions to stereotypes of the absent, adulterous, Black father (Coles and Green 2010).[2]

Another comic that pit the squeaky-clean image of Obama against the dirty tactics of his opponents, while also drawing on zombama rhetorics, was *Army of Darkness: Ash Saves Obama*. In it, Obama stopped at a comic convention to get some gifts for his daughters and accidentally purchased a copy of the Necronomicon—the book of the dead that turns ordinary humans into demon-possessed zombies. The newly awakened hordes of the undead were soon defeated by the series' hero, Ash J. Williams, selected by fate to protect the world from dark forces, but a copy of the Necronomicon remained in the president's possession. As the story reached its climax, the narrative suggested that the supernatural book would "call to him [. . .] tempting him," which raised the question, "when the President of the United States is tempted with enough power to control the masses . . . What do you think he will do?" (Serrano and Padilla 2010). While the narrative assumption was that he would give in to temptation, the accompanying visuals showed Obama tossing the book into a lighted fireplace in the Oval Office, resisting the corruption of absolute power.

The multifaceted and contested symbols of the Obama presidency and body were also captured in Steven Weissman's *Barack Hussein Obama* (2012) and *Looking for America's Dog* (2016). Both were presented as raw sketchbooks rather than graphic novels and offered, in the words of publisher Fantagraphics, "a dada-esque, surrealistic and satirical vision" of America. Weissman's Obama liked basketball and featured zombie-esque representations of Hillary Clinton and Joe Biden, with yet another zombama allusion; zombifying Obama's secretary of state and vice president fit within the zombama rhetorical strategy suggesting that Obama had hypnotic control over his followers, creating mindlessly devoted "Obamies" (Gries 2015).[3] Nonetheless, critics agreed that Weissman's works were at once apolitical and sharply political. Timothy Callahan suggests *Barack Hussein Obama* focused "on small anxieties blown up large with symbolism," thus presenting "the American Dream as an anxious hallucination" (2012, para. 7), while Woodrow Phoenix calls *Looking for America's Dog* "a kind of existentialist sit-com" that imagined the public, yet mysterious, lives of the First Family in a way that was "sadly banal, weird or ridiculous" (2017, para. 1, para. 3). Phoenix concludes, "This book is a strange confection of craft, beauty, anger, silliness and despair with multiple layers of meaning that you can peel away or just leave alone" (2017, para. 4).

As Weissman's work seemed to both transcend and dive deep into politics, so too did the one-shot story *Drafted: One Hundred Days*. *Drafted* attempted to present a post-racial society and yet reiterated racist perspectives, even if only to criticize them. According to its creator, the *Drafted* series described "the events that unfold after Earth's population is conscripted to fight a galactic war"; the invading aliens did not recognize the socioeconomic status or ethnic identities of individuals, thus everyone on Earth was suddenly rendered equal. *Drafted* endeavored to witness the effects of this newfound equality (Powers 2008, para. 1). *Drafted: One Hundred Days* picked up after the first wave of alien

Figure 9.2. The Obama fist-bump cover by Erik Larsen for *Savage Dragon* #145 (left) is reminiscent of the Obama fist-bump at the DNC (center photo by Dunland/AP), which was referred to as a "terrorist fist jab"—as depicted by Barry Blitt for the *New Yorker* (right).

attacks was repulsed and Chicago was rebuilding, aided by former US Senator Barack Obama, who had lost his ability to speak. Only five pages into the story, a White woman asked Obama, "Is it true you're Muslim?" (Powers 2009). Even though she quickly apologized and explained that the question was "left over from our old lives," planted by Bill O'Reilly (Powers 2009), the moment served to foreground Obama's Otherness even in an imagined, post-apocalyptic, post-racial society. Additionally, Obama's loss of speech effectively reduced him to a more primitive state, so specified when Obama cut his wrist in an apparent suicide attempt and the narration compared him to "an animal gnawing off its own leg to escape a trap" (Powers 2009)—a moment that engaged with the "negro-as-animal discourse" of the nineteenth century.

Obama's Otherness was also found on the cover of *Savage Dragon* #145 (2009), which featured Obama in a friendly exchange with superheroic Chicago police officer Dragon. Drawn in the muted reds and blues of the iconic Obama "Hope" poster by Shepard Fairey, it depicted a fist bump between Dragon and Obama (see figure 9.2). This gesture was a visual reference to the celebratory exchange between Obama and his wife at the Democratic National Convention in 2008, which was subsequently framed by Fox News reporter E. D. Hill as a "terrorist fist jab" and thus became a marker of Obama's un-Americanness, even appearing in cartoon form on the cover of the *New Yorker* (Selzer 2010, 21).

DARK HORSES OF DIFFERENT COLORS

Questions about what is un/American likewise plague Latinxs in politics. The first Democratic primary debate of the 2020 presidential election in June 2019 drew attention when Beto O'Rourke, Cory Booker, Julián Castro (the only Latinx in the race), and Pete Buttigieg gave some responses in Spanish. Additionally, candidate Bill de Blasio used a Spanish quote by Argentine revolutionary Ernesto "Che" Guevara at a rally, Joe Biden occasionally tweeted in Spanish, and most of the twenty-plus candidates seeking the Democratic nomination had Spanish-language versions of their campaign websites (Morin 2019). Young Latinxs, the fastest growing population in the US, were poised to be a key voting bloc in 2020 and beyond, and the Democrats were clearly trying to engage them, but the effort was perceived by some as "Hispandering," especially at a moment when the country was hotly divided over how to respond to migration and immigration from Central America. Although the Democratic candidates were largely praised for using Spanish during the debate, members of the general population have been criticized and harassed for speaking Spanish in public (Contreras and Anderson 2019).

Studies show that Latinxs have more optimistic and trusting attitudes about government, especially naturalized American citizens, than other populations (Uhlaner and Garcia 2002; Lipsitz, Trost, Grossman, and Sides 2005). Keen on civic participation, they respond more positively to campaign messages, even oft-maligned negative advertising, than non-Latinx Whites, and campaign messages directed to Latinx voters tend to be positive, focusing on the Latinx community as a valuable force in American politics (Lipsitz, Trost, Grossman, and Sides 2005; Connaughton and Jarvis 2004). This community-centeredness is likewise found in Latinx superheroes in the comics. "Whereas Anglo superheroes (often characterized as recast Manifest Destiny cowboy types injected with invincibility) tend to defend the nation but are somehow apart from it, Latino superheroes tend to be linked to the community," writes Frederick Luis Aldama (2017, 7). For example, the alter ego of Marvel's Firebird is a social worker, Bonita Juarez. Latinx superheroes are also defined by their difference to Whiteness and are thus more likely to be identified with their bodies and their often raw emotions than with their minds. Furthermore, they must *learn* to be superheroes, whereas White heroes tend to achieve the status through birth, entitlement, or merit. Like Black superheroes, Latinx costumes are likely to represent their ethnic ancestry "in ways that root them in pre-Columbian histories and the Latino community" (Aldama 2017, 8). Their personalities and powers may also be tied to their ethnicity and their struggles "cast within proximate and extended family kinship structures, working-class communities, and a strong presence of Catholicism" (Aldama 2017, 8). Thus, Latinxs in politics and in comics are cast into their own set of double-binds, wherein such identifiers as community are valued but treated as markers of difference and where one's language may be used strategically but not casually—in other words, where one's worth is dependent on one's usefulness, or potential for exploitation.

Enter Arcadio Alvarez, star of the political science-fiction series *Saucer Country* and its sequel *Saucer State* (see chapters seven and eight). The series followed New Mexico Governor Arcadia Alvarado, through a presidential campaign and term threated by extraterrestrial aliens. Alvarado was the granddaughter of illegally immigrated Mexican Americans, running on a pro-immigration platform, while simultaneously, and ironically, fighting what she believed is an imminent invasion of aliens from space. In *Saucer Country*, a radio shock jock called Alvarado "Governor Sopapilla" (Cornell and Kelly 2012) noted the irony in her platform of allowing "aliens in across the border" while purportedly having experienced an alien abduction (Cornell and Kelly 2012). Meanwhile, Alvarado's own incredulous campaign strategist asserted, "Nobody *credible* gets abducted by aliens. Nobody *important* gets abducted by aliens. *Poor people* get abducted by aliens! [. . .] The aliens must be *really* racist!" (Cornell and Kelly 2012).

Racism in contemporary American politics was more explicitly highlighted in the *Saucer State* sequel. Alvarado's Republican opponent Dunfries, who had a passable resemblance to Donald Trump, repeatedly called Alvarado the "chihuahua" (Cornell, Kelly, and Guzowski 2017 #1), alluding to Trump's penchant for using derogatory nicknames for opponents, like calling Senator Elizabeth Warren "Pocahontas" for her claims to have Native American heritage (Lee 2016b). The "chihuahua" nickname marked Alvarado as both a Mexican and as a female-dog, aka a bitch. Dunfries also indicated that she was "like someone you'd hire to clean the pool" (Cornell, Kelly, and Guzowski 2017 #3), calling upon the pop culture stereotype of the Latinx domestic (Brayton 2008). Such racial tensions were emphasized when NASA discovered an alien saucer approaching Earth and a representative of Black Lives Matter stated, "I hope it's an *invasion*. Couldn't be worse than what we have now" (Cornell, Kelly, and Guzowski 2017 #2). Dunfries, too, politicized the approaching saucer, asking in a press conference, "What, are we gonna let the aliens in and give them all green cards?" (Cornell, Kelly, and Guzowski 2017 #3). The presence of Black Lives Matter and debates around green cards clearly placed *Saucer State* in post-2016 political discourse, but unfortunately reiterated many of the stereotypes it attempted to fight (for more, see Knopf 2020b).

Another political Latina found in post-2016 comics included representations of Rep. Alexandria Ocasio-Cortez. In the 2019 *Alexandria Ocasio-Cortez and the Freshman Force: New Party, Who Dis?*, the opening illustration by R. Sikoryak foregrounded AOC's ethnicity and culture. The image adapted Frank Thorne's cover art for *Marvel Feature #4, Red Sonja: She-Devil with a Sword*, depicting AOC as a warrior, with the title "Rep. Ocasio: Puerto Rican Girl from the Bronx." But, unlike the Red Sonja inspiration, clad in a chainmail bikini, AOC was modestly attired in a knee-length, short-sleeved chainmail dress, suggesting a more wholesome, and Catholic, appearance, ala Joan of Arc (see figure 9.3).

Figure 9.3. The *Red Sonja*-inspired artwork (left) by R. Sikoryak for *Alexandria Ocasio-Cortez and the Freshman Force* (center) gives the Puerto Rican the look of Joan of Arc (right: engraving by J. C. Buttre), highlighting her Catholic background.

Asians and Asian Americans are another key demographic in modern American politics. Like Latinx Americans, Asian Americans are more positive in their assessment of campaign messages, optimistic in their attitudes toward government, and interested in civic participation than Whites (Lipsitz, Trost, Grossman, and Sides 2005). Such sentiments are captured in the political *seinen manga*[4] series *Eagle: The Making of an Asian-American President*, which was about the "darkest of dark horse candidates" (Kawaguchi 2000 v1, back cover). Taking place during a fictionalized 2000 presidential election, *Eagle* was the story of a Japanese American senator from New York, Kenneth Yamaoka, a man fiercely committed to becoming president with a knack for inspiring energy and enthusiasm. Beginning with the New Hampshire primary, continuing through his party's nomination to his presidential campaign, and concluding with his inauguration, the story was told through the eyes of a young Japanese reporter, Takashi Jo, covering the campaign for his newspaper in Tokyo. (Spoiler alert! Jo also turned out to be the senator's illegitimate son from a romantic interlude during his tour in Vietnam.) Filled with sex and secrets, intricacies and intrigue, politics and polemics, twists and turns, *Eagle* was nominated for four Eisner Awards in 2001 and 2002, including Best US Edition of Foreign Material. The manga was a favorite of Taiwanese legislator Cho Jung-tai, who found the story's attention to issues such as the transfer of power, political reorganization, and the young revolutionary generation to mirror his own experiences (*CBR* staff 2002).

The *mangaka* (creator), Kaiji Kawaguchi, was inspired to write *Eagle* after seeing the documentary *The War Room* (1993), about the Bill Clinton campaign. Thus, while some characters in *Eagle* were completely fictitious, such as Yamaoka and Jo, others were based on real people: Vice President Al Noah on Al Gore, who was committed to the power of the internet and saving the environment; President Bill Clydon on Bill Clinton, who was from Arkansas and had a scandalized presidency, and his wife, Ellery, on Hillary Clinton; and, campaign advisor George Tuck on political consultant Dick Tuck and reminiscent of James Carville. Kawaguchi, a literary celebrity in Japan, did extensive research for the creation of the series, which totaled an excess of two thousand pages. He read about the American presidency and searched Japanese media for information on the 2000 election and was advised by experts in media and American politics. He also spent time on location throughout the United States, taking hundreds of reference photos, talking with Japanese Americans, and even attending a city council meeting (*CBR* staff 2002).

The series originally ran from 1997 to 2001 in Japan's *Big Comics* and was transformed into an English version in twenty-two monthly installments between 2000 and 2001, before being published in five *tankōbon* (collector's) volumes. The English-language version required not only language translation, which took into consideration regional dialects of American English, but also visual translation, converting the images to be read left-to-right and incorporating more realistic American media and motifs—such as collages of news photos for the covers and readable newspaper clippings. Editor Carl Horn wanted the English version of the book to feel American to not "distance American readers from a story that is meant, after all, to be American" (quoted in *CBR* staff 2002, para. 24). Horn's work on releasing the American version was further shaped by his own political experiences, working for the presidential primary campaigns of Bob Kerrey and Jerry Brown in 1992.

Researchers often characterize Japanese culture as collectivistic: traditional, homogeneous, and group-oriented with a strong emphasis on harmony, in which moral judgements are determined according to context and community (Kubota 1999; Benedict 1946/2005). By contrast, American culture is largely defined as individualistic. Linguistically, these differences appear in the indirect, implicit, and inductive nature of Japanese discourse and the more direct and deductive style of American discourse (Connor 1996; Kubota 1997; Haneda and Shima 1982). Such distinctions can be found within the volumes of *Eagle*. Yamaoka's son Alex, the strategist Tuck, and Vice President Noah had more American personality traits. They were bold, confrontational, and focused on the personal glory of winning. Alex was impatient and wanted the campaign to use all its best material immediately and to go after the biggest targets first, rather than biding its time with more calculated strategy. And Tuck would "only work with winners!" (Kawaguchi 2000 v2, 32).

Jo, along with his friends and associates in Japan, was more traditionally Japanese. He considered how his actions might affect those around him and who might be hurt if he shared the private knowledge he possessed about Yamaoka's past. He made the decision to think and act as a reporter rather than as a son to remain neutral in his judgements, vowing, "I won't be swallowed up in this. I'll figure you [Yamaoka] out not as your son, but as a journalist" (Kawaguchi 2000 v2, 98). Jo was devoted to his family, motivated to do right by the memory of his recently deceased mother and her love for the father he never knew.

Yamaoka, a third-generation Japanese American, fittingly blended American individualism with Japanese community. His political aspirations were at once personal and communal; he was ambitious, choosing to leave a woman he loved in order to launch a political career, but his ambitions served a greater good, motivated by an interest to prevent the country from ever repeating its mistakes with the war in Vietnam. His communication style was one that welcomed confrontation while leaving room for his opponents to save face. For example, when Vice President Noah refused to engage him in a televised debate, Yamaoka challenged him at a dinner with the press. Using table settings and a checkered tablecloth as visual aids, Yamaoka involved Noah in a deliberation about education reform. By the end of the discussion, the reporters realized that the salt and pepper shakers on the table represented the queen and king pieces in a verbalized chess match between the two candidates and declared a stalemate. Noah, however, later admitted that Yamaoka had him in checkmate, but left the game at a draw to invite Noah to become his vice-presidential nominee later in the campaign (Kawaguchi 2000 v3, 70–73).

In American comics, Asians, especially Japanese during and immediately after World War II, were frequently depicted with yellow skin and bestial features (Yizheng 2017; Kunka 2017). Such depictions were consistent with wartime propaganda and attitudes of the "Japs" as treacherous, uncivilized, and fanatical (Benedict 1946/2005). Even with more positive portrayals in recent times, such as Marvel's Asian American superhero Hazmat, visual cues of dark hair, narrow eyes, and darker or yellow-tinted skin remain (Smith 2014). Manga is not as given to visual stereotypes. Matt Thorn has suggested manga character design is, instead, one of individual style and consistency; markers of racial, ethnic, and geographic difference, as well as other forms of stereotyping, are introduced through the narrative and the settings rather than the character images (as referenced in Antononoka 2016 and Berlatsky 2009; see also Phillipps 2001). There were accordingly few visual distinctions among the White American, Japanese, and Japanese American characters in the black-and-white *Eagle*. Black characters, however, *were* visually distinct, therefore allowing *Eagle* to capture coded racism in American political communication.

One common tactic in political campaign communication is the use of implicit racial appeals—messages that indirectly evoke "racial resentments, fears, and stereotypes," often using visual images rather than verbal cues to tap into existing biases (Mendelberg 2001, 9–10). The National Security PAC's "Willie Horton" ad in 1988 did this, visually relating violent crime to Blackness. Donald Trump's midterm election ad featuring Luis Bracamontes in 2018 did this by connecting violence to Brownness and immigration. And, such a strategy was seemingly used in one of Yamoaka's ads in *Eagle*. Responding to the vice president's ideas on education reform, the Yamoaka ad featured a Black boy, with large lips and prominent ears, dressed in a basketball jersey and shorts, backwards hat, and oversized hooded jacket, attempting to hitch a ride to the "21st Century." A sleek sports car whizzed by, and then he was knocked down by a jet that roared past him on the roadway. The visuals cut to an inner-city street, a crowded schoolroom, and a group of mostly Black children, wearing basketball jerseys and hair locs, peering at a powerless desktop computer sitting useless on the floor. The ad's voiceover declared,

> Some call it the Information Superhighway.
> But is it a toll road only for the rich?
> Some talk about our increasingly wired world . . . But what about the American children who aren't even getting a basic education? (Kawaguchi 2000 v3, 80)

As the visuals returned to the hitchhiker, the voiceover asked, "Are they going to be left behind?" At last, a school bus came along to give the boy a ride, and Yamaoka promised, "I won't pass you by" (Kawaguchi 2000 v3, 81). As an attack on the vice president's platform, the ad suggested that Noah is racist and that his plans leave out America's Black community. Yet, at the same time, the ad itself is racist in its stereotypical depictions of Black youth in America—thick lips, hoodies, and dreads on derelict city streets. Written and drawn by an outsider, the manga revealed multiple dimensions of how race is constructed in American culture and politics.

Entrepreneur Andrew Yang's brief run for the 2020 Democratic nomination inspired Keenspot's *Yang Gang* comic, in which the presidential candidate fought the forces of a dystopian future, aided by the machinations of his campaign manager Zach, the sage advice of Whoopi Goldberg, and a super suit built by Elon Musk. Yang's suit—a blue version of Marvel Iron Man's red-and-gold armor—was emblazoned with the word "math" across the chest, alluding to the "MATH" tack-pin the real Yang wore on his blue jacket lapel at the Democratic primary debate on October 15, 2019. The real Yang called himself "the Asian man who likes math," and he "pitched himself as an entrepreneur who understands technology and the economy, the kind of candidate most likely to bring a calculator to the Oval Office" (Timm 2019, para. 1–2). The *Yang Gang*'s superheroic depiction of Yang was in accordance with this campaign image and strategy, but it also played on the racial stereotype of Chinese people being good at math (see Cvencek et al 2014). This kind of positive stereotype can be traced back to the characterization of Asians as the "model minority" that arose in news coverage and political discourse of the 1960s and was perpetuated in subsequent decades through advertising, eventually solidifying an image of Asian Americans as work-oriented, technology-savvy, and intelligent, with little interest in leisure or home life (Taylor, Landreth, and Bang 2005; Taylor, Lee, and Stern 1995). The "model minority myth upholds the American ideologies of meritocracy and individualism, diverts attention away from racial inequality," creates conflict between racial groups, sustains White dominance, and exacerbates economic disparities (Reyes 2009, 44; Larson 2006; Bucholtz 2009). Thus, the *Yang Gang* ostensibly countered some of the very things that Yang's campaign promoted: equitable socioeconomics and fair immigration.

BIPARTISAN, BIRACIAL, BI-OGRAPHY

The blurring of fiction and reality of politics and race raises the question as to how race is framed in *nonfiction* comics (see chapter one). Campaign comics like "Alabama Needs the Little Judge, George Wallace for the Big Job," were explicitly racist with strong pro-segregation messages and anti-Japanese sentiments (Persoff 2007). IDW's "neutral" take on Obama in its 2008 *Presidential Material: Barack Obama* made the Black senator's biracial, international heritage central to its story. The ethnicity of John McCain's ancestry was not so highlighted in *Presidential Material: John McCain* (2008), but ample attention was given to his time opposing the Viet Cong in his war service. Similarly, Obama's 2009 biography from Antarctic Press focused on his biracial heritage and troubled youth—especially as related to his racial identity—before attending to his legal and political career. Michelle Obama's *Female Force* biography devoted several panels to the First Lady's slave ancestry, which was a point of race-based consternation for detractors during the 2008 election (see chapter eight). Children's graphic biographies of Obama, such as *The Boy with the Biggest Dream* (2009, Joyful Stories Press) and *Obama: The Historic Election of America's 44th President* (2012, Capstone Press), foregrounded Obama's race in its historical moment of his becoming the first Black president of the United States. *Obama* was notable, however, in that it let the president himself tell that story by quoting his address to the 2004 Democratic National Convention in which he talked about his Kenyan father and the meaning of his African name.

The *Political Power* biography of 2012 presidential candidate Herman Cain, told after Cain was a mere footnote in presidential campaign history, mentioned that he "grew up poor in the segregated south and all that" but indicated that his story was shaped by his father, not his circumstances (Beard and Belcher 2018). Meanwhile, BlueWater Comics suggested that both Colin Powell and Condoleezza Rice were notable figures specifically *because* of their Blackness. Powell was introduced as "perhaps one of the most prominent African American figures to serve under the United States flag" (Loh and Woodward 2009), and Rice was presented as someone who did not "look like" a Led Zeppelin fan, leading to the suggestion that there might be "more than meets the *eye* to the *first African-American woman Secretary of State*" (Ward and MacNeil 2009). And *Political Power* called out Marco Rubio for building a political identity based on a story that his parents were exiled from Castro's Cuba, when in fact they emigrated in 1956, three years before Castro became Cuba's prime minister and twenty-years before he became its president.

No discussion of race in political comics would be complete without giving due attention to the multiple-award-winning, autobiographical *March* trilogy written by the civil rights leader and congressperson John Lewis with Andrew Aydin, and illustrated by Nate Powell (2013, 2015, and 2016, TopShelf Productions). The trilogy opened and closed with scenes from the protest in Selma, Alabama, on March 7, 1965, known as "Bloody Sunday," when police brutally attacked the nonviolent marchers, including twenty-five-year-old Lewis. The complete story revealed a portion of Lewis's life and painted a picture of the external and internal struggles of the civil rights movement. The medium of the graphic novel was deliberately chosen in relation to its subject matter. Its model was the sixteen-page comic, by the Fellowship of Reconciliation (F.O.R.), *Martin Luther King and the Montgomery Story*, which told about the Montgomery bus boycott. Lewis was introduced to the civil rights movement and the *Montgomery Story* through his mentor James Lawson, who worked for the F.O.R. (Novi 2018). The *Montgomery Story* comic served as a guide used at F.O.R. meetings, so it was fitting that the *New York Times* described its descendent, *March*, as "more movement blueprint than civil rights monument" that speaks to the era of #BlackLivesMatter (Lucas 2016, para. 6).

CONCLUSION

Treasure Chest's 1964 story "Pettigrew for President" tried to envision a color-blind election by building reader support for the unseen candidate throughout the first nine parts of the story, not revealing his race until after the election was won (Feurerherd 2008). But a color-blind election misses the point. For decades, the civil rights political empowerment agenda focused on the election of Black representatives, believing that meaningful enfranchisement is obtained through electoral representation and (was) judicially supported through the Voting Rights Act (Guinier 1991). The election of Barack Obama was supposed to have been an indication of a post-racial era in which the Voting Rights Act (VRA) would no longer be necessary (Clarke 2009). The 2013 *Shelby County v. Holder* decision invalidated protections under the VRA, leaving communities—particularly poor, Black, and Latinx communities—vulnerable to disenfranchisement, setting the stage for a new era of White hegemony (Newkirk II 2018).

In such an environment, comics complicate the legitimacy of politicians of color. Both superhero narratives and pop culture presidencies tend to portray American race relations as good, except for a few misguided individuals. Superheroes and good presidents serve as stand-ins for American idealism as the good Whites defending diversity and modeling inclusion against those who would divide the country or undermine its fragile multiculturalism (Dittmer 2013). Ramona Liera-Schwichtenberg (2000) calls this a strategy of contemporary Whiteness: acknowledging Whiteness as partly corrupt, but separating that characteristic from its larger identity, thus marking racism as an individual flaw rather than a systemic problem. Thus, even comics like *Saucer Country* that attempt to make racism visible, *Bomb Queen*, which flips the script of White-goodness and Black-criminality, or *Political Power*, which highlights the accomplishments of politicians of color, effectively mark racism and racial inequity as problems of individuals rather than of society. Racist sentiments are attributable to shock jocks, not to the citizens who repeat what they hear. Good and bad are matters of perspective, not absolutes. Black leaders are admirable because they overcame the problems of Blackness, not just because they are good leaders. Indeed, even in superhero comics, the idea of a Black, superheroic president—Calvin Ellis, premised on Obama, in DC's "Final Crisis" event—was relegated to an alternate Earth, suggesting that such a thing could not happen here.

10

THE VERY STABLE EVIL GENIUS OF LUTHOR, LOKI, DOOM, AND DONALD

On the evening of November 8, 2016—election night in the United States—political commentator and late-night comedian Stephen Colbert hosted a special broadcast on Showtime called "Stephen Colbert's Live Election Night Democracy's Series Finale." The show

> began with a dark animated sequence in which a seething cartoon version of Mr. Trump reflected angrily on his humiliation by President Obama at the 2011 White House Correspondents Dinner, and the cold, competitive attitude of his father, Fred Trump. Against the backdrop of a stormy night at Trump Tower, he contrives to run for the White House to prove himself to them all. (Itzkoff 2016, para. 3)

Entitled "The Making of Donald Trump," *Cartoon Book Resources* described it as a supervillain origin story that depicted Trump "as an orange, vengeful psychopath worthy of both the DC and Marvel universes" (Tambio 2016, para. 2).

Indeed, earlier in Trump's presidential run, *Salon* released a list of eight evil comic book presidents who resembled the candidate, including Superman's rival, Lex Luthor, and Captain America's nemesis, Red Skull (Peters 2016). The latter of these became a regular stand-in for President Trump on the Pres. Supervillain/@PresVillain Twitter account on which artist @StephenByrne86 posted real Trump quotes he has photoshopped into old comic panels. The banner image for the account (see figure 10.1) depicted Trump speaking on a stage filled with the likes of Marvel supervillains Loki, Green Goblin, Red Skull, Dr. Doom, and Magneto, DC supervillain Joker, a Dalek from *Dr. Who*, and *Star Wars* villain Darth Vader. Actor Mark Hamill, who voiced the Batman villain

The Very Stable Evil Genius of Luthor, Loki, Doom, and Donald   169

Figure 10.1. The Pres. Supervillain Twitter account imagines Trump as a classic comic book supervillain.

Joker in animations, lent his talents to the vilification of Trump by recording a selection of Trump's tweets in the voice of the villainous Clown Prince of Crime (Farber 2017; Melrose 2017a). And *Jimmy Kimmel Live!* redubbed Superman villain Lex Luthor's lines from an episode of the 2003 "Justice League" cartoon with soundbites from an interview Trump did with ABC News' David Muir to demonstrate Kimmel's perspective that Trump's comments were "downright menacing" (Melrose 2017b, para. 2).

Dating back to 1988, when he first floated a presidential bid, Trump's image or name has cameoed in approximately two hundred issues of comic books, including the humor magazines *Cracked* and *MAD*. The first was an appearance of Trump Tower and Trump's Ice Cream in Marvel's *Iron Man*. He was also parodied as MacDonald Crump, owner of a multimillion-dollar fast food chain, and as Donald J. Lofty, a corrupt real estate developer, in the 1980s–90s-era *Teenage Mutant Ninja Turtles* animated cartoon. More recently, he was imagined as a litigious celebrity threatening Marvel's Luke Cage in *New Avengers*, a corrupt politician interacting with DC's Green Arrow, a gang leader in Hanna-Barbera's *Wacky Raceland*, a megalomaniac in *Scooby Apocalypse*, an enemy of diplomacy in the Batman *Dark Knight III* book, as the antihero The Wall in DC's *Suicide Squad*, as a villain opposed to Marvel's Spider-Gwen, and as a stand-in for the supervillain Harvey Dent in *DC Comics Bombshells*, among other appearances (Riesman 2016; Ching 2016; Melrose 2016; Johnston 2016; Shiach 2018). One of the most overtly political cameos, with real-world parallels, was found in *Savage Dragon*, in which Trump's election and immigration policies endangered the welfare of Dragon, a lizardesque-humanoid superhero and Chicago cop who endorsed Barack Obama (in #137), his human Asian American wife, and their interspecies children who must escape to Canada (#218, #226–30).

Such a persistent, widespread view of the president as a villain is notable giving the long-standing tradition of the presidential monomyth in American culture. The myth of the superheroic presidency (see chapter three) took hold at the end of the twentieth century when presidential legend-making developed to imagine the president as a superhuman unification of "physical heroism and moral perfection" capable of single-handedly confronting and exterminating threats to America and humanity (Lawrence and Jewett 2002, 128). Superheroes and presidents are symbolic embodiments of geopolitical identities, civic virtues, and collectivities (Dittmer 2013; Deis 2013; Wanzo 2009; Round 2008; Devarenne 2008; Murphy 2003). In consort, they encapsulate the American monomyth: a narrative in which a heroic individual emerges to vanquish villains that America's ordinary civic and political institutions cannot defeat alone (Lawrence and Jewett 2002).

The distinction between hero and villain, however, is not so clear. When asked at the premier of Marvel's *Thor: The Dark World* if the trickster-villain Loki is "really evil," Loki's actor, Tom Hiddleston (2013), answered, "Every villain is a hero in his own mind." Chris Deis (2013) explains this concept by arguing that the distinction between superheroes and supervillains is sociopolitical context and a matter of perspective. This was seen, for example, in the discussion between actor Josh Brolin, who played the villain Thanos in *The Avengers* cinematic franchise, and late-night host Stephen Colbert in 2018. Colbert asked Brolin if he could see any similarities between Thanos the "Mad Titan" and President Trump. Brolin explained that Thanos's intentions in the film were just; he saw that the world was overpopulated and that resources were limited, so he removed/killed half the population. His goal was good, but his method was callous. Brolin continued that the same could be said of Trump; there are problems with the borders, too many people, and too few resources, but the "manifestation" of how Trump addresses the problem is "extremely callous" (in Graham 2018). The superhero genre reveals "something about a given society's values, struggles, and beliefs" and "because the superhero and supervillain exist as mirrors of one another, the politics of the latter is further highlighted through comparison to the former" (Deis 2013, loc. 1944, 1987–1988). Often the only distinction is that superheroes undertake pro-social missions and supervillains are more likely to pursue the acquisition of power (Coogan 2013; Deis 2013).

Supervillains are described as "egomaniacal and selfish—personal enrichment, personal power, and control over others are their *raisons d'etre*" (Deis

2013, loc. 1956). They may be "super" because of exceptional leverage over organizations and minions, extensive financial resources, special powers or abilities, high intelligence, or mastery of science and technology, along with superior ambition, driven by a vision for the world relevant to their own understandings of justice. They also have some admirable qualities. Comics writer Dirk Manning (2013) explains that villains are the true protagonists of most stories: they have initiative, they take risks, and they make things happen. Heroes, meanwhile, are reactionary and do little but maintain the status quo. Author Michael Crider expands on this idea:

> The government, the Heroes, almost everyone in power, they aren't interested in change, for better or worse. Change is hard to steer. Every once in a while, they might move things forward a bit when it simply can't be resisted, like the Civil Rights movement or the fall of the Wall. But what those people really want, what they crave, is the status quo. The whole edifice of the modern social system is put in place, more or less, to make sure that tomorrow is the same as today. (2015, 5964–5967)

Whereas superheroes narratively depend on villains to externalize their internal struggles to be responsible, to represent the other half of their social identity, and to present them with increasing challenges to push the boundaries of their super abilities, supervillains do not necessarily need heroes (Carpenter 2013; Verano 2013; Levitz 2013). To quote Marvel's Loki in *The Avengers* (2012), villains are already "burdened with glorious purpose."

Outside of comics, we might call supervillains "toxic leaders." These are the bosses, managers, officers, and politicians that Marcia Lynn Whicker defines as "maladjusted, malcontent, and often malevolent, even malicious" (1996, 11) and that Alan Goldman describes as "destructive, disturbing, and dysfunctional" (2009, 139). Analyst Gillian Flynn (1999) argues that these are people who lead through bullying and intimidation, but as Jean Lipman-Bluman (2005) demonstrates, they are also leaders who are charming and charismatic, who earn not only fear but also devotion from followers. Simultaneously loathed and loved, toxic leaders—like supervillains—are individuals of energy and action. "Their drive for a need for recognition, power, and self-promotion" yields higher-than-average productivity (Mehta and Maheshwari 2014, 22), and their initiative and ability are part of their allure.

Toxic leaders can make complicated issues look simple and difficult tasks seem effortless, thus offering a feeling of certainty in an uncertain time and safety in a dangerous world. Their influence gives people at least the semblance of access to the centers of action. Their followers create communities of belonging. Their goals suggest symbolic immortality for those who support them. In these ways, they fulfill powerful psychological needs people have for reassurance, security, specialness, belonging, and agency (Lipman-Blumen 2005; Mehta and Maheshwari 2014). Likewise, Theodor W. Adorno (1982) observed the same psychology at work in propaganda of fascist demagogues. Through repetition of a limited number of ideas, fascist agitators unite people under a common conception of a shared bond under absolute authority, finding a kind of libidinal pleasure in surrendering their individuality to merge with the group. Fascism may appeal to voters who prioritize material interests, who anticipate that democratic political leaders are acting in their own self-interests rather than in those of the people they represent, and who are not integrated into networks of civil society (see Wellhoffer 2003). "Paradoxically, at the same time that we yearn for them, we also feel deeply cynical about toxic leaders," with polls suggesting that the American public has markedly low expectations for the morality of politicians (Lipman-Blumen 2005, 11).

The media is often similarly ambivalent about toxic leaders. Through the combination of its watchdog function and profit drive, both of which preference scandal and excitement, news media often frame these leaders as "rising stars" and "fallen angels," wherein scoundrels are presented as heroes with feet of clay (Lipman-Blumen 2005, 13; also Silk 1998). In entertainment media, the toxic leader shares much in common with the Dark Triad personality traits of antiheroes (see chapter three): narcissism, psychopathy, and Machiavellianism. So, it is not surprising that in the final weeks before the 2012 presidential election, *Gizmodo* released a list of nine reasons to elect a supervillain as president. The reasons included having strong visions for the future, going to great lengths to rebuild the country, not tolerating idiotic interview questions, and eliminating unemployment via enslavement of humankind, as well as already being "part of the shadowy conspiracy that runs the planet" (Davis 2012, para. 9).

THE ART OF THE ZEAL(OT)

Enter ~~Donald Trump~~ Lex Luthor. Alexander Joseph "Lex" Luthor is considered the archenemy of DC Comic's Superman. Introduced in 1940 as a reclusive mad scientist, his character evolved over the decades to become a wealthy American industrialist and business magnate (owner of the multi-industry conglomerate LexCorp), ingenious engineer and inventor, public philanthropist, and politician. Power-mad, he secretly advances his goals through murder, kidnap, extortion, espionage, and organized crime. His opposition to Superman is one rooted in his ideals of humanity, as shaped by his personal drive for success. To Luthor, Superman is a threat to humankind—an alien crutch that keeps people from realizing their own potential. He extrapolates this worldview in *Lex Luthor: Man of Steel* (alternate title: *Luthor*):

Figure 10.2. Donald Trump is compared to Superman supervillain Lex Luthor, with DC Comics alluding to Trump's *Art of the Deal* covers (right) through its own covers (left).

Truth, justice, and the American way. As if that were some inseparable holy trinity.

Truth? That's in the teller. Just calmly massaged words that very well may be nothing but carefully finessed lies.

Justice? Justice belongs to the judge, who sits above those who put him there because they can't trust themselves.

And the American Way? It constantly evolves out of something that proves to be true and a lie, just and more—all men are created equal.... You [Superman] are not a man ... I see something no man can ever be. I see the end. The end of our potential. The end of our achievements. The end of our dreams. You are my nightmare. (Azzarello and Bernejo 2010, 22)

Thus, Lex Luthor, as Ben Dyer suggests, is partly a frustrated and misunderstood humanist (2009, 128).

It is his distrust of Superman and his disgust for the adoration Superman receives that motivates his successful presidential run in the 2000 story arc "President Luthor"—just as Trump's 2016 campaign was supposedly stirred by his humiliation by Obama. In fact, the President Luthor story took inspiration from Donald Trump. In 1987, Trump published *The Art of the Deal* (Random House), which enjoyed forty-eight weeks on the *New York Times* best-seller list. The cover of his book became the model for the one-shot comic *Lex Luthor: The Unauthorized Biography* (1989, DC Comics) and the subsequent trade paperback *President Luthor* (2018, DC Comics; see figure 10.2). In 2000, Trump entered the presidential race as a Reform Party candidate, winning the primaries over conservative Pat Buchanan in California and Michigan (Snell and Kitching 2018). The same year in the comics, Luthor ran for president as a candidate for the Tomorrow Party. Luthor, like Trump, gained his popular fame via land development. Instead of casinos, however, Luthor built futuristic cities designed to make life easier for everyone but the poor. Luthor's presidency became a focal point in the 2009 animated movie *Superman/Batman: Public Enemies,* and his assassination in the White House was a McGuffin in the two-part "A Better World" episode of the *Justice League* cartoon series in 2003. Trump's presidency also became the stuff of animation in the 2018 Showtime series *Our Cartoon President.*

Luthor, however, was not the first, nor the last, supervillain to become president. The malevolent paranormal Philip Nolan Voigt, who captured and exploited unsuspecting citizens with extraordinary powers in Marvel's *D.P.7* title, used his psychic abilities to defeat Bush and Dukakis in the 1988 election (#28–29). In a story stretching across multiple titles of Marvel's short-lived "New Universe," Voigt moved the nation's capital to Denver and was manipulated by South Africa into starting World War III (see Eternal 2002). In 1993, Marvel imagined a drug-war-torn future world in *DOOM 2099*. Doctor Doom/Victor von Doom was originally the cybernetic monarch of the fictional country of Latveria. He first debuted in Marvel's *The Fantastic Four* #5 in 1962, and is considered the archenemy of the superhero team the Fantastic Four, though he has also challenged the Avengers, the X-Men, Spider-Man, Captain America, Iron Man, and others. In 2099, he took the American presidency through revolution to save America from itself and to save the world from America.

Doom's 2099 presidency was eventually usurped by John Anthony Herod, the megalomaniacal corporate head of stockpiled alien technology. Herod installed a reanimated, drug-addled, and tortured Captain America as a puppet president, and replaced the White House with the Red House, before eventually being defeated by Doom who set his sights on world conquest and left a smoldering US without any formal government. Like Herod, other supervillains have also taken control of the presidency from behind the scenes, operating various forms of shadow governments: the mutant Mystique impersonated President Richard Nixon in the 2014 film *X-Men: Days of Future Past*; the mercenary Zartan, on behalf of the Cobra terrorist organization, impersonated the president in the 2009 film *G.I. Joe: The Rise of Cobra* and its 2013 sequel, *G.I. Joe: Retaliation*; in the 2010 animated series *The Avengers: Earth's Mightiest Heroes* and in the 2010 *Avengers: Red Zone* book, the Red Skull infiltrated the US government as Dell Rusk, becoming Secretary of Defense; alien freedom fighters replaced John F. Kennedy with a shape-shifting simulacrum in a retro story of the 2008 *Teen Titans Lost Annual* #8; the villain known as Chameleon attempted to replace Obama at the 2009 inauguration in *The Amazing Spider-Man* #583; the Cobra Commander took control of the White House and Fort Meade in a 2007 story arc in *G.I. Joe: America's Elite*; domestic terrorists replaced George W. Bush with an evil twin in the midst of the 2004 election in *Savage Dragon* #119; Lex Luthor posed as President Rickard via a hologram in the 2001 *Batman: Dark Knight Strikes Again*; and, the evil Dr. Roag and General Ordiz of the Ninth Men replaced Bill Clinton with a shape-shifting doppelganger in the 1993 *Jack Kirby's Secret City Saga*.

In the alternate future of *Earth X*, published by Marvel 1999–2000, Norman Osborn, aka Spider-Man's arch-nemesis Green Goblin, used his corporate control of the US economy to manipulate his way into the presidency. Osborn granted Tony Stark/Iron Man political asylum in exchange for constructing robotic replicas of the fallen Avengers heroes to battle an alien menace known as the Hydra, a parasite collective that controls the minds of its host bodies. Osborn's presidency was terminated, literally, by a young telepath whose moniker "the Skull" was fashioned after Red Skull (the Nazi foe of Captain America) and whose emblem resembled that of the Punisher, a vigilante whose methods include murder, kidnapping, extortion, and torture. The Skull assassinated President Osborn and declared himself in charge but was soon killed by an aging Captain America.

Marvel imagined yet another dystopic future in 2008 with its "Old Man Logan" story arc. In this alternate Earth timeline, superheroes were all but wiped from existence and the US was conquered and divided among supervillains: the West coast was under the control of Abomination (a foe of the Incredible Hulk) and later conquered by a corrupted and cannibalistic Hulk; the Rockies and Southwest belonged to Magneto (nemesis of the X-Men) before being taken over by Kingpin (foe of Spider-Man and arch-enemy of Daredevil) and then "Spider-B****" (a power-mad and blood-thirsty version of Spider-Woman); Doom controlled the Midwest; and Red Skull ruled the Eastern seaboard as a self-declared president of the United States.

Coinciding with the 2016 election, Marvel ran a four-part miniseries *Vote Loki* (see chapter seven) in which the supervillain Loki, half-brother to and frequent enemy of the superhero Thor, ran for president against an unnamed red-tie-clad male candidate and blond female candidate. Other supervillains have run for lesser political offices as part of their nefarious plans, and many of these campaigns also coincided with the 2016 election. Oswald Cobblepot, aka the Penguin—one of Batman's criminal foes—ran for mayor of Gotham City in the TV series *Gotham* in 2016, in the 2016 one-shot comic book *Catwoman:*

Election Night, as well as in the 1992 film *Batman Returns*, and in the *Batman* series starring Adam West in 1966. Marvel's Evil Mutant Magneto was mayor of Sentinel City in a dystopic *Earth X* (2011). Harvey Dent, the Batman supervillain known as Two-Face, ran for mayor of Gotham in various installments of DC franchises; in the alternate 1941 of *DC Comics Bombshells* #13 (2016), he was elected on an anti-immigration platform under the machinations of the supervillain Hugo Strange. Antihero Harley Quinn ran for mayor of New York City in the DC Universe Rebirth *Harley Quinn* #28–32 (2016), in which the incumbent mayor conspired with Gotham's master of fear, the villainous Scarecrow/Dr. Crane, to remove her from the race, alluding to politicians' use of fear tactics to influence the public (see Knopf 2019b).[1] Damien Darhk, immortal gangster in the DC Universe, attempted to control Star City in the CW's *Arrow* via his wife's bid for mayor against Oliver Queen/Green Arrow in a 2015 storyline (see chapter three).

ANY MEANS, OR MEANIES, NECESSARY

Politics and villainy share an affinity. As proclaimed in the opening narration of *The Stainless Steel Rat* #5,

> Personally, I reckon folks ought to *thank* the criminal for this useful role he plays, but there again I would, since I am [. . .] the galaxy's *top* criminal!
> As our tale opens, I am about to try my hand at a racket as old as crime itself . . . Politics! (Gosnell, Ezquerra, Potter, and Landau 1986, 1)

Undeniably, as Jeffrey C. Isaac argues, "Politics is about ends and means—about the values that we pursue and the methods by which we pursue them" (2002, para. 1). For supervillains, political office is often a means to an end: a way to acquire power in their pursuit of control and even more power. But we should not dismiss their presidencies as simple stepping stones on the path to world domination. Presidential supervillains are emblematic of very real dynamics in toxic leadership. "Toxic leaders cast their spell broadly," Lipman-Blumen writes. "Most of us claim we abhor them. Yet we frequently follow—or at least tolerate—them. [. . .] When toxic leaders don't appear on their own, we often seek them out. On occasion, we even create them by pushing good leaders over the toxic line" (2005, ix). She identifies six psychological needs that toxic leaders fill for their followers: authoritarian reassurance, security and certainty, specialness, community membership, belonging and acceptance, and a sense of control. Each of these elements, and their political ramifications, can be found in the stories of supervillain presidents.

In lieu of parental guidance and control, people gravitate towards leaders "who will make us feel safe, protected, and good about ourselves" (Lipman-Blumen 2005, 35). Our need for security and certainty—especially amid rapid change, turbulence, or crises—makes strong leaders particularly attractive. Toxic leaders and fascist demagogues know how to call people to a higher purpose and promise them a special place in history (Lipman-Blumen 2005; Adorno 1982).

Luthor's presidency was all about paternalistic reassurance in changing times. An election night biography feature on Luthor declared,

> On *January 1st, 2000*, at the dawn of the new millennium, it would be Metropolis's darkest hour. Luthor would come to the aid of *Superman*, to save the world from a destructive force from the future, terrorist *Brainiac 13*.
>
> Despite the overnight upheaval of Metropolis, Luthor would once again astonish the world when he harnessed the B13 technology [turning Metropolis into the City of Tomorrow]. Under his Control, Luthor will share it not only with America, but with the entire planet.
>
> [...]
>
> [...]
>
> Time and again, this nation's most inspirational figure would set aside his personal life [including the death of his daughter Lena] to win one more victory for the good of the American people. (David, DeMatteis, Hudnall, Jimenez et al 2018, 96–98)

In short, as Luthor told a reporter in *Superman/Batman: Public Enemies* (2009), "Tough times require a tougher man."

Luthor was also skilled at identifying people's unique qualities and using their talents to his own ends while highlighting their specialness. He compelled Talia Head, daughter of mystical supervillain Rā's Al Ghūl, to come out of hiding and manage LexCorp by offering her protection from the League of Assassins. He chose her because she had experience, was smart, and was suspicious—all qualities he admired and could exploit (David, DeMatteis, Hudnall, Jimenez et al 2000, 23–34). In *Superman/Batman: Public Enemies* (2009), Luthor made a point to recruit members of the superhero community to be part of his administration, reasoning that to have them "working for me [is] to keep them from working against me."

Doom's presidency was about the surrender of freedom for (the illusion of) security. In the year of 2099, formal governments were largely impotent; the real power rested in corporate conglomerates and narco-democracies of the drug trade. Doom observed, "I am reminded of a sentence by a philosopher [...] Noam Chomsky, and the simplicity and power of his statement has forever after haunted me. 'U.S. foreign policy is, in fact, based on the principle that human rights are irrelevant.'" Thus, he concluded, "The greatest threat to this world is *America*. Therefore, I must begin by saving *America from itself*" (Ellis and Moore 2013). Through violent revolution, Doom incapacitated the Senate and took over the White House, thereby investing himself "as the president of what remains" of the United States (Ellis and Moore 2013). People committed themselves to Doom's service because of the promises he made for money and access, allowing them the chance to be part of something bigger than themselves. Individuals known as "netgliders," who could wetwire into the digital scape, worked for Doom, disregarding their fear of him specifically because of the chance to jack themselves into the entirety of the internet—to have complete freedom of and to information. Doom tightened control by restructuring the government into ministries, nationalizing all corporate entities, and instituting public curfews, tithes, and martial law, all in the name of security, salvation, and restitution. He decreed that any act perpetrated "upon the American people will be scrutinized *and* punished by *Doom*" (Ellis and Moore 2013).

Coinciding with people's need for authority figures who can fulfill safety and self-esteem needs, Lipman-Blumen further indicates we need "membership in the human community" to provide us with meaning and purpose and to guard us against isolation (2005, 29). Fears of exclusion make people feel powerlessness to challenge toxic leaders and the dysfunctional system that supports them. "Silent dissenters who believe they are alone—that no other soul shares their opinion—commonly fear the ostracism of their peers. So, they swallow the bile of dissatisfaction and join the toxic leader's wave of followers," adapting to the world or avoiding it, hoping someone else will try to change things (Lipman-Blumen 2005, 40).

Luthor's presidency demonstrated people's sense of impotence under toxic leadership. Superman, arguably the most powerful citizen of America, felt helpless and despondent after Luthor's election. He asked the Martian Manhunter, J'onn J'onzz, if the Justice League of America should have done more to try to stop Luthor. J'onn replied,

> We are *aliens* by birth, you and I. And while I often feel a kinship to being human, this is *not* one of those times. Oddly enough, I am almost grateful. The . . . politics of our adopted world often defy any logic. Without logic, we are left with chaos. (David, DeMatteis, Hudnall, Jimenez et al 2018, 33)

Superman then shared his frustrations with the Green Lantern, who compared American politics to satellites orbiting Earth—they are put into space with the knowledge that at some point, they will fall. "One is no better or worse than the other." He conceded that Luthor was a crook, but then suggests that, "The guy before him mighta been, too. And if we did something to get Luthor kicked out of office ... the guy who replaced him might be, too. No wonder nobody votes" (David, DeMatteis, Hudnall, Jimenez et al 2018, 139).

A similar exchange took place between Superman and Captain Atom in *Superman/Batman: Public Enemies* (2009). Superman refused to join with the other heroes working for Luthor and was branded a traitor—in a display of how toxic leaders prey on fears of social death and establish clear distinctions between a chosen Us and an undesirable Them. He told Atom, "[Luthor]'s a sick man. [And] he's not the first to sit in the Oval Office." Atom replied, "There have been womanizers, drunks, crooks. But Nixon helped turn our worst enemy into our best trading partner and Johnson gave us the voting rights act," pointing to how political toxicity or villainy is inevitable and, perhaps, necessary.

A historical tradition of villainous presidents was likewise found in *DOOM 2099*. As Doom stormed the White House, he thought of the previous residents of "this place: Besuited, quivering American monsters who stabbed the world with sticks for *decades*, unchecked [...]" (Ellis and Moore 2013). Later, as president, Doom confronted the heads of every transnational and mega-corporation in America—people he deemed "worms" because they put profit and personal gain ahead of all else, doing terrible damage to the environment. This meeting very prominently took place in "the Nixon Room" of the White House (Ellis and Moore 2013); Nixon was both an advocate for corporate growth, with policies that severely hurt the economy, and for the environment, establishing the Environmental Protection Agency. He was also a crooked politician and, despite his famous disavowal, a crook. Indeed, Lipman-Blumen argues, "Do not look for saints among formal leaders. Saints rarely seek elected or appointed office. They seldom enter the rough-and-tumble of politics" (2005, 5). This idea was the heart of *Vote Loki*'s 2016 presidential campaign, which echoed the sentiment of the American people that their only choice at the polls is to vote for a "lesser" evil. Likewise, Voigt's telepathically won presidency in *D.P.7.* suggested that the American people had no *choice* at all.

Doom echoed this perspective, noting that, "The American presidency is a vestigial organ. President acts as arbitrator in disputes between the megacorps that truly rule America. 'Presidential elections' are merely circuses disguising the investiture of one sympathetic to certain business interests" (Ellis and Moore 2013). He, however, did not believe that should relieve voters from their responsibility to the collective well-being. A Joseph de Maistre quotation in the pages of *DOOM 2099* proclaimed, "Every country has the government it deserves." Upon discovering that one of the major corporate players in the United States was an alien monster, Doom went on television and chastised the American people. "I won't allow you to point your finger at the alien corpse and say 'It was *him* that did it! America today is *not my fault!*' You *let* him rule you! It *is your fault! You all had a choice!*" (Ellis and Moore 2013). Marvel Comics also imagined what could happen when people abdicate too much of their responsibility for toxic leaders and surrender too much of their freedom for security through the *Earth X* presidency of the Green Goblin and the "Old Man Logan" presidency of Red Skull.

Earth X presented a dystopic future in which all humans had mutated to have superpowers. Because individuals could save themselves, superheroes were no longer needed—and no one stepped up to save the *community*. When food became scarce, those who controlled it also controlled the world, because "What man won't vote his appetite [. . .]?" (Krueger, Leon, Reinhold, and Ross 2011, 78). The extent of Norman Osborn/Green Goblin's corporate holdings thus put him in charge of America. The omniscient narrator of the story, a "watcher" named Uatu, observed,

> Democracy is considered an archaic and obsolete idea. Though some would argue that for the first time, people are truly equal, others cite that that is the very problem. Equality has doomed their race. [. . .] Equality is the nullifier of individuality [. . .] Equality is the despot destroyer of self-worth. In a world of sameness, there can be no heroes. (Krueger, Leon, Reinhold, and Ross 2011, 120)

This speech echoes conditions that give rise to fascism: an atmosphere of emotional aggressiveness, a belief that the democratic principle is ineffective, and a fear that equality undermines individual achievement, exacerbated by a breakdown in the supply chain of food or agri-industry (Adorno 1982; Wellhofer 2003; Schatz 2001).[2]

There is a similar (in)equality of suffering among the masses in *Wolverine: Old Man Logan*, in which people acquiesced to the control of supervillain leaders because an attempt by any to fight back would result in more misery for all. Red Skull's portion of America looked like the country of Oceania in George Orwell's *1984*, with signs proclaiming, "Love with Force," "Work. Family. Hate," "Always Watching YOU," and "Believe in the genius of the President" (Millar and McNiven 2017). Huge monuments depicted the president's deathly visage. The White House was covered in symbols of the Third Reich, its walls lined with the tattered costumes of the country's dead heroes, their patriotic rags a testament to the death of democracy.

PRESIDENT SUPERVILLAIN

So, what was it about the 2016 election that sparked parallels between the crimson-skinned Red Skull and the orange-tinted Donald Trump, Luthor's bald head and Trump's combover, Doctor Doom's cape and "The Donald"'s tie? To answer, let us take another look at Loki's 2016 campaign. The supervillain's dual message about the inherent untrustworthiness of politicians and the active disrepute of the news media reflected the political reality of 2016, when Americans went into the election with their trust in government and the media at record lows (Pew 2015; Byers 2015). Just as frustration with "politics as usual" gave rise to Loki's popularity in *Vote Loki*, so, too, did the surprising Trump phenomenon appear "to have risen from an unusual convergence of an economic and social context that is unsettling for many people, political systems that seem to be permanently unproductive, and a desire for a different style of leadership and politics" (Fitzduff 2017, 2). The Trump campaign responded, uniquely, to this unquiet moment offering "a politics of hope" to people whose wages had stagnated or declined, who were fearful of outside threats of terrorism and economic disruption, who felt disrespected in a changing culture, and who were distrustful of a federal government they felt was ignoring them (Reicher and Haslam 2017, 29; Fitzduff 2017; Glasser and Thrush 2016).

People look to leaders with strong presences to give them a sense of security, belonging, and meaning (Lipman-Bluman 2005; Mehta and Maheshwari 2014; Adorno 1982). The Trump campaign did this. It provided clear definitions of in-groups and out-groups as a foundation for frustrated and/or frightened people to "make sense of their lived experience, to understand their problems, and to entertain the hope of being able to deal with them" (Reicher and Haslam 2017, 37). The pomp and circumstance surrounding his campaign events, for example, encouraged supporters to feel that they were part of something special; they were empowered by their presence there and their association with Trump (Reicher and Haslam 2017). This experience, this connection that Trump made with otherwise disenchanted voters, was captured in *Vote Loki*. Loki decried "a system that has abandoned you. You work hard. You pay your taxes. You cast your votes. And you're left behind by those in power" and he promised, "I'm here to make things sane again!" (Hastings, McCaffrey, and Chuckry 2016). Trump's own promise was to "make America great again."

Both Loki and Trump were seemingly direct in their communications. Loki told voters, "If I were your President, I'd have the guts to lie right to your face. And you'd love it" (Hastings, Foss and Chuckry 2016 #1). This was consistent with headlines that declared, "people are OK with Trump's endless supply of lies" (Chun 2019) and "Trump supporters know Trump lies. They just don't care" (Resnick 2017). Trump's simple speaking style combined with his pragmatic approach to problems appealed to voters more concerned with results than ideologies (Prims, Melton, and Motyl 2017; Goldhill 2017). Such simplicity is especially welcome in times of distress and uncertainty. (It is also worth noting that imagery from the *Vote Loki* comic book appeared in the trailer teasing the 2021

Loki original series on Disney+. The trailer dropped in December 2020 while Trump was still contesting his election loss, further reinforcing Loki's candidacy as shaped by Trump-era politics.)

Research suggests people prefer leaders to speak with confidence regardless of the substance of their address; by contrast, uncertainty, reflection, or consultation suggests weakness (Kessler and Wong-MingJi 2009; Fitzduff 2017). This a strength of villains and a weakness of heroes. In *Earth X*, before the dystopian presidency of the Green Goblin, "Captain America was hailed as a living legend," but

> When asked to become President of the United States, he declined. His conviction, he said, was that he could only represent the American Dream . . . and not a specific generation of citizens.
>
> [. . .] [He] had lost the ability to be a representative of his own people. (Krueger, Leon, Reinhold, and Ross 2011, 49)

Thus, supervillains may find it difficult to masquerade as "good" presidents. In *Jack Kirby's Secret City Saga*, time-traveling villains kidnapped President Bill Clinton and replaced him with a shapeshifter from their own ranks. The shifter struggled, however, with his role, noting, "Some shapes are much harder to hold than others. This one keeps trying to change on me—to be one thing one moment—then another the next!" (Kirby, Thomas, and Ditko 1993). More than just a cheeky poke at Clinton's famous ambivalence, or a wisecrack about political chameleons, the shifter's observation captured the need for diplomacy and flexibility in domestic and world affairs—tact for which supervillains have no need. Villains, toxic leaders, and even antiheroes are admired, or at least enabled, because of their decisive action that produces results (Mehta and Maheshwari 2014; Jonason et al 2012; Barber 1992; Jamieson 1995; McDermott 2016).

Because of the intense loyalty that the supervillain demands, and the supervillainous president achieves, their followers are often suspect to outsiders. As a god, Loki earned worshippers, not just voters. His cult following fervently believed, "Washington is filled with an all-consuming corruption. All who enter its halls must submit. Must become one with the writhing tumorous mass . . . *Loki will burn it! Loki is the fire to destroy the evil that pumps in the heart of democracy!*" (Hastings, Foss, and Chuckry 2016 #1). Likewise, Trump rallies echoed with chants of "drain the swamp!" as supporters counted on him to "make our government honest again" by cleansing Washington, DC, of out-of-touch political insiders and bloated bureaucrats (Harrington 2016, para. 3–4). Loki rebuked "the political machine" because it "can't contain its pleasure in decrying my supporters as crazy and pathetic" (Hastings, Foss, and Chuckry 2016 #2). Opponents exclaimed, "You're *all* either *evil* or *stupid* if you're voting for *him*," while his supporters rejoined, "It's the *establishment* that's *evil!* You're stupid *not* to vote for him!" (Hastings, Foss, and Chuckry 2016 #4). Eventually, the fervent devotion of Loki's followers and the fear it inspired in opponents erupted into violence.

So, too, went the campaign of Donald Trump. Two months before the 2016 election, Trump's main opponent, and Washington insider, Hillary Clinton remarked, "You could put half of Trump's supporters into what I call the basket of deplorables. [. . .] The racist, sexist, homophobic, xenophobic, Islamaphobic—you name it. [. . .] Some of those folks, they are irredeemable" (quoted in Jacobs 2016, para. 1–3). Assorted world leaders and media outlets followed suit, calling Trump's supporters "the stupidest people in the U.S.," bigots, "hideous, disgusting racists," and idiots (Reicher and Haslam 2017, 26). When Trump won the election, post-election protests swept the country, many leading to violence (Mele and Correal 2016). In the bids of both Loki and Trump, the media, untrusted by the people, were viewed as key detractors, working to undermine the legitimacy of the campaigns. Loki's supporters complained, "You know, it's typical, the *media* is doing anything they can to take down Loki. Calling him a vigilante and all that" (Hastings, Foss, Chuckry, and Rosenberg 2016). Likewise, Trump's relationship with the media was classified as war with Trump consistently portraying "the media as a force for evil against him" (*Newsweek* staff 2018, para. 1). Such factors helped to strengthen the communal identity of the "in-group" of supporters, advancing both Loki's and Trump's ability to fulfill followers' social needs while providing opportunities to call out, ostracize, and make examples of dissenters.

As suggested at the outset of this chapter, however, the identities of superheroes and supervillains are defined by, and dependent on, each other, thus the difference between a hero and a villain is often one of context and perspective (Verano 2013; Deis 2013). In *Earth X*, the narrator/watcher Uatu noted of the supervillain Magneto, "He knew that moral behavior was a choice, not a characteristic. Those who claim to be good . . . do evil. And those who cursed and threatened their fellow man have often done so for a perceived greater good" (Krueger, Leon, Reinhold, and Ross 2011, 178). Trump's supervillainous presidency is similarly complicated in the comic book *Trump vs. Time Lincoln*, a one-shot installment of the *Time Lincoln* series, begun in 2010 by Antarctic Press. The steampunk series featured a time-traveling Lincoln fighting those who sow the seeds of oppression throughout history, opposing supervillainous simulacrum of dictators and despots like Stalin, Hitler, Mao, and Castro, whose minions included Nikita Khrushchev, J. Edgar Hoover, Sirhan Sirhan, and Lee Harvey Oswald.

In the 2017 *Trump vs. Time Lincoln*, Lincoln faced the cult leader "Emoj'n Trump"—a parody of the dystopian *Mad Max: Fury Road*'s antagonist Immor-

Figure 10.3. *Trump vs. Time Lincoln*'s villain, Emoj'n Trump (left), is a vile parody of *Mad Max: Fury Road*'s (Warner Brothers, 2015) antagonist, Immortan Joe (right); both are villains to their stories' protagonists but are heroes to their followers.

tan Joe, who rose to power in a post-apocalyptic America through murder and rape (see figure 10.3). Because Immortan Joe controlled many scarce resources, followers flocked to him in hopes of a better life. Likewise, to the followers of Emoj'n Trump, Trump was a hero who offered them access to means of survival. Like Trump's real-world supporters among union workers and traditional Christians (Fitzduff 2017), Emoj'n Trump's followers were described as people who "were hard-working and industrious [. . .] proud of their accomplishments" (Perez and Hutchison 2017). Emoj'n Trump promised them they would be masters of a new, great, world with "riches and food enough to last the rest of [their] natural lives" as long as they obeyed and never questioned his commands (Perez and Hutchison 2017). Emoj'n Trump could thus be read as a toxic leader: his efforts caused harm to others by costing them their freedoms, but he was also a key means to their survival and therefore a savior to his followers. Likewise, the real Trump was an "antiestablishment hero" to his base (Henriques 2017, 107).

CONCLUSION

After Superman, in a parallel universe, killed President Luthor on behalf of the greater good, the Justice Lords (a power-mad variant of the Justice League) took over the US government. Superman controlled the president. Elections were suspended. Free speech was all but dead. Batman reasoned that these measures were a necessity because, "The problem with democracy is that it doesn't keep you very safe" (*Justice League* 2003). Good leaders can do evil in the name of good. Evil leaders can do good in the pursuit of power. Philosopher Ben Dyer observes that it is not necessarily, or at least not always, the goal that makes one a supervillain, but how they go about achieving it. Being a supervillain is about "their means rather than ends" (Dyer 2009, 28). Supervillains cause great suffering to a great many people in pursuit of their perceived destinies. Doom, therefore, was right in his belief that people get the government they deserve, the government they make and choose for themselves. And Loki's voters were right in their beliefs that all candidates are bad, and the establishment is evil. The key in this is that the voters "chose" the candidates and "made" the establishment.

"Politics is about ends and means—about the values that we pursue and the methods by which we pursue them" (Isaac 2002, para. 1). For good or ill, voters often must make decisions about what they value. Unionized coal miners voting for Trump might have been concerned about stagnant wages and unemployment. As Namor, in league with Doom, argued in *Earth X*, "What human won't choose to have food on the table for his or her children?" (Krueger, Leon, Reinhold, and Ross 2011, 78). Food and security provided for families by jobs is a good goal with a moral purpose. The environmental damage wrought by the coal mining—the toxins released into the atmosphere and waterways, the deforestation and erosion of the earth—that provides those jobs nevertheless destroys ecosystems, causes disease, and contributes to the overall pollution that advances climate change, and thus will cause, however indirectly, untold suffering to great numbers of people and animals. From one perspective, this makes those voters who supported a candidate who supports coal mining supervillains, because their goal involved means that will cause suffering. Their opponents were, accordingly, heroes seeking to prevent this suffering. Or were they? Because the voters who opposed that candidate were contributing to the suffering of the coal miners and their families who lacked food on their table, making *them* the supervillains.

Heroism and villainy, like right and left, in politics is messy and complicated. This is the true strength of the supervillain as president; they simplify the complexities. *DOOM 2099* presented Dr. Victor Von Doom's "Contract with America" and "Code of Citizen Conduct for the United States." In it, Doom proclaimed that the critical component of the nation's success and destiny was the citizen. "This responsibility, a cherished product of American strength, comes not from vagueness, but from clarity; not from confusion, but from certainty; not from questions, but from answers" (Ellis and Moore 2013, "2099 Special" 38). The code provided those answers with such provisions as abolishing and prohibiting political parties, and the political expressions they entail. It concluded, "While this Code provides definitive answers, there are no definitive questions" (Ellis and Moore 2013, "2099 Special" 48). This is, indeed, the great strength of the supervillain president. This is also the great danger of the supervillain president, because politics simply isn't that simple.

EX-PRESIDENTS AND DAYS OF FUTURISTIC PASTS

Throughout the preceding chapters, we have encountered various dystopian political futures: post-apocalyptic wastelands in *Ultimates* (chapter three) and *Wacky Raceland* (chapters four and ten); mass corruption in *Transmetropolitan* (chapter four); hopelessness and imminent destruction in *Watchmen* (chapter four); full-corporate sponsorship and control of government, healthcare, and education in *Prez* (chapters four, seven, and eight) and *American Flagg* (chapter four); debate deathmatches in *Campaigners* (chapter seven); drug-cartel-based governments in *DOOM 2099* (chapter ten); and feudal warlords in *Old Man Logan* (chapter ten). Dystopias often present some variation on a theme of "the quasi-omnipotence of a monolithic, totalitarian state demanding and normally exacting complete obedience from its citizens, challenged occasionally but usually ineffectually by vestigial individualism or systemic flaws, and relying upon scientific and technological advances to ensure social control" (Claeys 2010). They are "mirrored if refracted realities" that extrapolate present trends and conditions in one form or another, offering a pessimistic blueprint or nightmarish vision of society's future based on its current trajectory (Claeys 2010; Crook 2000). Dystopian fiction makes guesses "as to which of the plausible alternatives which confront us today will prevail in the years ahead" and thus shape the historical legacy of the present (Ferguson 1997, 8).

Some political comics, however, use the conditions of the present not to imagine the future but to reimagine the past. Allohistories, also known as alternate or alternative histories, alternate universes, uchronias, parahistories, counterfactuals, futurologies, and imaginary histories, are speculative fictions that consider "what if" scenarios at significant moments in history. Such stories may ask, and attempt to answer, what sort of world would exist if all things were possible. They challenge historical record as well as the accepted limits of the physical and social worlds, recognizing the influence of determinist theories in history (Hellekson 2011; Ferguson 1997). Dystopian subgenres, such as steampunk, dieselpunk, and cyberpunk—popular aesthetics in comics that can be classified as "design fictions"—may be understood as considerations of historical legacy in light of contemporary attitudes, and expressions of contemporary anxieties about human nature and resource allocation (Good 2010; Raz 2011; Tanenbaum, Pufal, and Tananbaum 2016).

As explained by Karen Hellekson, allohistory

> speculates about such topics as the nature of time and linearity, the past's link to the present, the present's link to the future, and the role of individuals in the history-making process. [Allohistories] question the nature of history and of causality; they question accepted notions of time and space; they rupture linear movement; and they make readers rethink their world and how it has become what it is. [...] And they foreground the "constructedness" of history and the role narrative plays in this construction. (2011, loc. 132)

These stories may be categorized according to the subject's position in relation to reality, by the moment or timing of the chronological break with historical record, or by authorial motives regarding the perspectives of the present put forth by their authors (Collins 1990; Hellekson 2011; Rosenfeld 2002).

In the latter taxonomy, "nightmare scenarios" are allohistories which depict the past as worse than it appears in actual historical record so to vindicate present conditions. "Fantasy scenarios," conversely, depict the past as better than it appears in actual historical record so to incriminate present conditions (Rosenfeld 2002). These, in turn, may be categorized according to their break with the past. Hellekson (2011) identifies three sorts of allohistories according to their chronological focus: 1) nexus stories, which occur at the moment of the break and focus on key moments in history; 2) true alternate histories, which occur after the break and imagine how the world would be different if different physical laws or sciences existed; and 3) parallel worlds stories, which suggest multiple, simultaneous, alternate realities with different chronologies and outcomes.

Some nexus stories are about time-travel-policing in which efforts are made to keep timelines intact. Antarctic Press's *Time Lincoln* comics are an example of this sort. *Time Lincoln* took place during the final hour of Lincoln's life in Ford's Theater when the president was taken out-of-time to fight evil forces in the past, present, and future in order to keep the world safe for democracy from time-traveling tyrants looking to rewrite history. Some policing stories depict "a ruling body that controls time to its own advantage or to the advantage of the people it rules" (Hellekson 2011, loc. 171). Conspiracy stories, such as the one depicted in *The Red Diaries: The Kennedy Conspiracy*, may be considered a kind of policing story wherein shadowy cabals manipulated people and events to their own ends with networks that were so intricate and convoluted that the truth of the past was both lost and inconsequential. Other nexus stories center on crucial moments in warfare specifically, focusing on military strategy, technology, and leaders. These stories "depend on the Great Man theory of history, relying on the importance of certain key players to shape history" (Hellekson 2011, loc. 193). AfterShock's *Rough Riders* provides a variation on the battle nexus by reimagining Theodore Roosevelt's leadership in the Spanish-American-Cuban-Filipino War as made possible by fantastical steampunk armaments.

True alternate histories focus on causal relationships. They propose different physical laws or alternate sciences and then imagine the repercussions into the present. They suggest that a single historical event having a different result than that of official record will have a domino effect "culminating in worlds dramatically discontinuous with reality" (Hellekson 2011, loc. 203). *The Jekyll Island Chronicles* offered a true alternate history by positing a secret war that occurred between the world wars, headed by President Wilson, weaponized by the great industrialists of the early twentieth century and fought by ordinary citizens with extraordinary technologically enhanced abilities. One subset of true alternate history is the alternate world story, which presents vastly different scientific understandings of humanity, the world, or the universe. *Letter 44* might be considered a type of alternate world story. In it, the forty-third president of the United States was not George W. Bush, but Francis T. Carroll (who looks a bit like George H. W. Bush); like the younger Bush, however, Carroll was perceived as a fool and lied to the American people to involve the country in two costly wars in the Middle East. The forty-fourth president of the United States was not Barack Obama, but Stephen Blades. Blades, like Obama, was a person of color (Latinx), considered the opposite of his predecessor, and promises to close Guantanamo Bay and get the country out of at least one of the Middle East conflicts. Confounding both presidencies, however, was the knowledge of a classified extraterrestrial threat for which research and defense was funded under the cover of prolonged military engagements.

Parallel worlds stories describe multiple allohistories that exist simultaneously. Generally, characters can move or communicate between these parallel worlds. Parallel worlds stories assume that history can change at almost any point, no matter how apparently insignificant. All events in parallel worlds texts exist simultaneously in one timeline or another. Every possible outcome of an event has occurred somewhere. Importantly, parallel worlds texts assume the importance of linear time and are less likely to imply that time is circular. Several parallel worlds stories explicitly base their premises on quantum physics.

The Manhattan Projects was both a true alternate history and a parallel worlds story. It posited that the research and development initiative known as the Manhattan Project during World War II went far beyond the development of nuclear weaponry and included space travel and alien communication at Area 51 and Roswell, New Mexico. Robert Oppenheimer was but one personality of his genocidal, cannibalistic twin Joseph. Franklin D. Roosevelt's brain was hooked into computers. And Albert Einstein had a doppelganger from a parallel dimension. Furthermore, in the tradition of the nexus story, it suggested that Truman was opposed to using the bomb in Japan, but his order was ignored by the megalomaniacal general heading the projects.

OLD FRONTIERS ARE NEW AGAIN

Most of these stories offer a blend of nightmare and fantasy. Depictions of the past as more fantastical than it was in reality may celebrate historical heroism as something sadly unparalleled in the present but can also suggest that those same heroic actions necessarily made present conditions unavoidable. *DC: The New Frontier* by writer/illustrator Darwyn Cooke (see chapters two and four) is an example of this mixed impulse. In his retro, non-canonical history of DC Comics, Cooke used an idealized past to criticize the actual past. The book was critically acclaimed as a celebration of hope in contrast to both the present and to the Cold War realities of paranoia described as an allegory of post-9/11 America and as a critical reflection on what was ignored in pop culture of the 1950s—namely, racism and the excesses of anti-communist rhetoric (Yockey 2012; Naso 2005; Naso 2016; Rikdad 2016). But, as an allohistory, it was also an indictment of the same trends of bigotry, alienation, and nationalism found currently.

"The new frontier" was a phrase coined by John F. Kennedy in his nomination acceptance speech at the Democratic National Convention in July 1960. Not only did Cooke allude to Kennedy's speech through the title of his book, but the epilogue was an extended quotation of the address placed against a backdrop of superhero and villain vignettes. The presidential nomination acceptance address has been described as a secular reformation of the Puritan Jeremiad sermon. Each has five broad features: 1) a general theme of sin-repentance-reform—a warning that the people have deviated from the American dream; 2) organizational pattern to develop the theme—establishment of the significance of the moment/election; 3) application of sacred doctrine to political affairs—a rendering of the national past; 4) an assumption of a special mission and destiny; and 5) a scolding prophet within the community—the speaker/candidate as leader to American greatness (Ritter 1980; Trent and Friedenberg 2008). The same features were found in *DC: The New Frontier*.

A lack of clarity about right and wrong suggested that America has lost its way. Wonder Woman empowered sex slaves of Indo-China to rise up against their captors, and Superman was appalled that she does not stop the women from butchering the men that tortured them. Hourman tried to evade the police who considered him a vigilante, and inadvertently lead them all to their deaths. Batman was branded a criminal for fighting the crime in his city ignored by its corrupt police force. Combat pilot Hal Jordan (aka the superhero Green Lantern) was considered a coward for his pacifist convictions. John Henry killed killers and was betrayed by a child. J'onn J'onzz was brought from Mars to Earth against his will, yet chose to defend its people, knowing they would fear and persecute him if they discovered he was an alien.

The critical moment was established by the sociopolitical context—a warweary world at the threshold of a new age. As historian John Lewis Gaddis (2005) argued, the Cold War created a unique convergence of phenomena that brought the world not only close to the brink of destruction but also comparatively close to consensus regarding democracy. *New Frontier* opened with comic book World War II heroes *The Losers* on what would be their final suicide rescue mission. In recalling the Second World War, the story drew legitimacy from both the Golden Age of comic book history and from a sacred sacrificial moment in American history. In comics and reality, World War II was a time of clarity, purpose, and unquestioned heroism—desirable qualities for uncertain times. At a meta-level, the text also called upon the sacred myth of the Kennedy "Camelot"—an idealistic president that "for one brief shining moment" brought hope to a struggling world. In reconstituting the Kennedy era, with the title and epilogue from Kennedy's 1960 acceptance speech, the book outlined a special mission for the DC heroes, their fans, and Americans in general: a set of challenges to be faced, with the whole world watching and waiting. By superimposing twenty excerpts from Kennedy's speech onto images of the superheroes that make up the "Justice League of America," the League was presented as a leader who could guide America through these challenges.

The jeremiad, in general, is typically a literary work—moralistic prose that laments the current situation and foresees society's imminent demise. Even though *New Frontier* was about the Cold War, it was a product of the twenty-first century, and it closed with words and images that looked across a "New Frontier" of civil rights, economic equity, scientific advancements, and global peace. The imagery of heroes, who were as contemporary in 2004 as in 1960, embarking on a mission of equality, justice, and harmony within a work that resembled a jeremiad may be not only the indictment of political pessimism that Cooke intended but also an indictment of the lack of progress made in charting Kennedy's New Frontier. The graphic novel was heralded as hopeful, but there was an element of despair that American society was clinging to the same hopes as a half a century ago. Indeed, nowhere was the lack of sociopolitical progress more apparent than in one of the special issue stories Cooke developed as a tie-in for the animated movie adaptation of *New Frontier*.

In a story called "Wonder Woman and Black Canary Fight the Gender War," Wonder Woman stormed a strip club to teach the men to respect women. When the club's patrons rejected her message of sisterly love, she beat them senseless with her breastplate (which she lighted on fire, alluding to the symbol of the burning bra in women's liberation). This short story about gender equality was the only narrative in the *New Frontier* title that was presented satirically and comically, rather than nostalgically and seriously. Framing feminism as a joke decades after women's liberation suggested that society was still standing on the edge of that "new" frontier. Likewise, an image in *New Frontier*'s epilogue of a Black child sitting at the grave of John Wilson, aka John Henry Irons or Steel—a hammer-wielding executioner, killed by the Ku Klux Klan—was as salient in 2016, in the midst of the #BlackLivesMatter movement, as it was in 2004, after the racial tensions and riots of the 1990s, and as it would have been in the 1960s during the growing civil rights movement. Despite efforts to bring attention to issues that were often invisible in popular fiction of the 1950s—including nationalism, racism, xenophobia, rape, genocide, and post-traumatic stress—the text's reliance on characters created in the first half of the twentieth century, who interacted with the mass media content of the 1950s, essentially recreated a White patriarchy devoted to an idealized democracy, even if self-consciously so. The politics of Whiteness inherent in the presidency (see chapter nine) is a persistent problem for many political allohistories.

Time Lincoln, from Antarctic Press, and *Rough Riders*, from AfterShock Comics, engaged with the science-fiction subgenre steampunk—a Victoriana aesthetic and subculture, inspired by the work of H. G. Wells and Jules Verne, which focuses on the relationship of man and machine, destabilizing our understanding of the past and the present, and immersing audiences in familiar surroundings made different through the accoutrements of the nineteenth century modified for futuristic purposes (Hantke 1999; Cherry and Mellins 2011). *The Jekyll Island Chronicles*, from TopShelf Productions, employed the related subgenre of dieselpunk, which "draws on the design aesthetics of the early twentieth century, usually inspired by the Art Deco movement and the technologies of the first and second world wars" with an apocalyptic theme befitting the fatalism of war art and literature (Tanenbaum, Pufal, and Tananbaum 2016). Both steampunk and dieselpunk are thought to be motivated less by political inclinations than by nostalgia (Strubel 2014).

A trend of nostalgia permeated cultural products in the early decades of the twenty-first century, arguably as a reaction to modernity, either to recover the past or respond to the present (Niemeyer 2014; Boym 2001). Restorative nostalgia is a desire to reconstruct the past—its institutions, monuments, symbols, and myths—in a quest for truth. "This kind of nostalgia characterizes national and nationalist revivals all over the world, which engage in the antimodern myth-making of history" (Boym 2001, 41). Such nostalgia was at play in the 2016 presidential election, captured by Trump's revival of Reagan's campaign slogan, "Make America Great Again," which resonated with voters' desires to have "an America that used to exist, one they heard about from their fathers and grandfathers and have always longed to go back to" (O'Hehir 2016a, para. 2). This nostalgic impulse was realized, as Andrew O'Hehir argued, when the electorate

> half-consciously voted for an incoherent fantasy of an imaginary American past, perhaps because the American present they inhabit has become so debased. But in one sense the fantasy is [...] a yearning to return to an era when the president was always going to be a white guy and you didn't need to think about it. (2016b, para. 13)

Such nostalgic longings were echoed in the punk allohistories of Lincoln, Roosevelt, and Wilson.

Like the presidency, steampunk and dieselpunk can be linked to performances of a national identity, foregrounding the Eurocentricity of its roots in British, French, and German aesthetics (e.g., Cherry and Mellins 2011). Although steampunk originated as a desire to rebel against the system it portrays, it has evolved into a fetishizing of imagined Victoriana that indulges in imperialist fantasies even while seeking to revise them (Nevins 2008; Bowser and Croxall 2010). Steampunk has engendered much discussion about issues related to gender, class, religion, and war, but issues of race have been a trickier matter (Nevins 2008; Sundén 2014; Jha 2009). Despite what some see as allohistory's potential to explore the possibilities of African Diaspora, Jaymee Goh (2010) notes that there is little room in mainstream steampunk for "nuanced discussions about cultural appropriation, microaggressions or unconscious prejudices made manifest" (2010, 19; see also Balogun 2012). While Patrick Jagoda has argued that "steampunk enables a complex examination of the historical evolution of power structures and control systems," it may also normalize symbols of White identity (2010, 48).

When a dying Lincoln learned that all of history was threatened by the Tyrant of Time, Void Stalin, he joined with a Time Traveler Team, made up of mathematician Sir Isaac Newton, physicist Albert Einstein, diplomat Benjamin Franklin, and inventor George Washington Carver, in the 2010–17 *Time Lincoln*. The team received occasional assistance from futurist Nikola Tesla, aviators Amelia Earhart and Charles Lindbergh, actress Norma Jean Baker, and activist Martin Luther King Jr. in its fight against oppression. The tongue-in-cheek series contained a total of seven stories: the original five-issue run (collected in

Time Lincoln: Fate of the Union) in 2010–11—"Time Lincoln," "Fists of Führer," "Apocalypse Mao," "Cuba Commander," and "Jack to the Future"—plus a single issue of *Time Lincoln: Continental* in 2014, and the more heavily satirical Mad Max parody, *Trump vs. Time Lincoln* in 2017.[1]

In the 2016 debut of *Rough Riders*, Theodore Roosevelt, at the behest of "the Four Horsemen" of J. P. Morgan, Cornelius Vanderbilt, Andrew Carnegie, and John D. Rockefeller, recruited an elite team of up-and-coming legends: magician Harry Houdini, boxer Jack Johnson, cowgirl Annie Oakley, inventor Thomas Edison, and gangster Monk Eastman. Their mission was to acquire alien technology left at the scene of the attack on the USS *Maine* in Cuba in 1898, the event that started the Spanish-American-Cuban-Filipino War. As the series began, America was set to become Earth's most industrious nation, but only if Roosevelt and his Rough Riders could confront Rasputin, dodge Spaniards, and defeat the mind-controlling aliens responsible for the massacre at Little Big Horn. The series was followed by the one-shot *Rough Riders Nation* #1, which claimed to contain the declassified documents proving the existence and legacy of Roosevelt's incredible team—and its continuation through the work of his daughter Alice. According to these files, future teams of "rough riders" included the likes of Babe Ruth and Charlie Chaplin, Franklin D. Roosevelt and Orson Welles, Elvis Presley and Frank Lloyd Wright, Bobby Kennedy and Malcolm X, Muhammad Ali and Evel Knievel, Steve Jobs and Tina Turner, and Colin Powell and RuPaul. The second volume of *Rough Riders* was released in 2017, with the team investigating a conspiracy behind the assassination of William McKinley. In a third volume, released in 2018, Houdini summoned Roosevelt to fight an ancient evil from another realm.

The 2016–18 graphic novel adventure series *The Jekyll Island Chronicles* starred American industrialists Henry Ford and Andrew Carnegie, along with J. P. Morgan, John D. Rockefeller, George Washington Carver, Nikola Tesla, Charles Proteus Steinmetz, and Jack Dempsey, under the guidance of Woodrow and Edith Wilson, as they waged a secret battle against an anarchist league, Zeno, bent on destabilizing a war-weary world (Nedvidek et al 2016). The series' website explained the book's titular premise:

> At the beginning of the 1900's, $1/_6$ of the world's wealth, led by many Captains of Industry, vacationed in and around the tiny Georgia island of Jekyll. Using this place of grandeur and elegance as a backdrop, we developed an alternate history occurring between the World Wars. A time of great social, political and technological upheaval. A time of ingenuity and anarchy. A time for some of the most brilliant, and horrible, minds of the 20th century to confront each other. And a time of great new heroes and incredible new machines.[2] (Lost Mountain Mechanicals 2017, para. 5)

From their Jekyll Island base, these magnates of history assembled a league of extraordinary individuals, including a diesel-powered cyborg and an electrifying woman, while Wilson pursued his League of Nations.

All three comics suggested the Great Man theory of history: they all included Tesla, while *Time Lincoln* and *Jekyll Island* referenced Carver and *Rough Riders* and *Jekyll Island* featured Morgan, Carnegie, and Rockefeller. The comics also all utilized the steampunk aesthetic of Victorian and Edwardian imperialism or the dieselpunk aesthetic of French art deco and German expressionism. They were thus limited in their explorations of history's counterfactuals—the questions about what *might* have been—and thereby suggested that the present, traditionally White and male, version of American politics is the only possible outcome, even if the past held more possibilities.

Across mainstream texts, Whiteness traditionally occupies a position of power and triumph, supported by ethnicity's vulnerability, and maintained through the vilification of racism and inequity as separate, individualistic, and anomalous (Stabile 2009; Walter 2015). In *Time Lincoln* "Continental," for example, the burden of fighting racist evil fell on the victim rather than allies. Martin Luther King, Jr. had to rescue Time Lincoln in a fight against "the Man," saying, "That's why I am here, Mr. President! To blaze a path through the darkness! [. . .] All it takes to move on is to break the circle of hatred that lurks in the hearts of men" (Perry 2014). King's peaceful methods, however, were less effective than Lincoln's violence. In *Rough Riders*, White colonialism was apparent when Roosevelt, larger than life, clad in heavy steam-powered armor, sat astride his armored horse, above a group of Black buffalo soldiers and promised that by *following him* they can have a place in history (Glass 2016) (see figure 11.1). In truth, however, it was the buffalo soldiers who helped establish Roosevelt's historical legacy (Tuccille 2015; Knopf forthcoming). And, in *The Jekyll Island Chronicles* real-life scientists and visionaries Nikola Tesla and Charles Proteus Steinmetz were given prominent roles in the story, while George Washington Carver was only mentioned as a means to introduce the fictional Solomon Taylor, an African American cryptologist, to the Jekyll Island Club's cabal. This narrative choice eschewed giving a voice to a real Black scientist or to highlighting a real groundbreaking cryptologist of the era, such as Elizabeth Smith Friedman. Similarly, the series used a fictional flying ace, the blue-eyed, blonde-haired Billy Colfield when it might have instead engaged the legend of the first African American military pilot Eugene Bullard.

The place of women in history was likewise minimalized in these three series, despite the use of female heroes in each. In *Time Lincoln*, Amelia Earhart never got a close-up action shot like most of the male characters did, and Norma Jean's costume objectified her curvy figure. The *Trump vs. Time Lincoln* one-shot had no female heroes, only female victims. The text proclaimed that

Figure 11.1. The steampunked Theodore Roosevelt in *Rough Riders* #4 (Glass, 2016) underscores White colonialism and imperialism, with heavy armor and European American aesthetics dominating landscapes and bodies.

"*all women* belong to [Emoj'n Trump]," reinforced by visuals of the villainous Trump keeping a harem of naked women (Perez and Hutchison 2017). In *Rough Riders*, Annie Oakley twice risked her own life, once for Roosevelt in Volume I and once for Edison in Volume II, believing her role to be less important than those of her male teammates. An interlude in the first volume of *The Jekyll Island Chronicles* depicted the period of poor health in Wilson's presidency, including his collapse while on a speaking tour for the League of Nations, his subsequent stroke, and Mrs. Wilson's efforts to hide it from the public. But, rather than taking advantage of the opportunity to showcase Edith Wilson's unofficial presidency, the moment became nothing more than a McGuffin for Carnegie advancing the timetable of the club's plans to fight anarchy. It is worth noting that one allohistory *did* flip the patriarchal script: the female-centric elseworlds superhero series *DC Comics Bombshells*, a World War II-era revisioning of DC canon, made Eleanor, not Franklin, Roosevelt the president of the United States, though her administration was mentioned only in passing (*DC Comics Bombshells Annual* #1).

Another genre series that offered a fantastical re-vision of history was *American Legends* from Top Cow Productions. A blending of Western and fantasy, with a touch of horror, *American Legends* may be considered part of the New Weird subgenre of speculative fiction—a hybrid form designed to warp audience's sense of reality (Harvey 2012; Noys and Murphy 2016). Davy Crocket, Mike Fink, and Sally Ann Thunder set out to save the Lewis and Clark expedition from the corrupt machinations of pirate Jean Lafitte and his brother. Aided by the voodoo magic of Marie Laveau, the Lafittes hoped to goad President Thomas Jefferson into a war with the Spanish, allowing Napoleon to conquer America. With cameo appearances by Sacajawea, Johnny Appleseed, and Paul Bunyan, *America Legends* celebrated the Great Men of History, and its closing narration echoed the spirit of allohistory: "There's no telling what would have become of America if it wasn't for Sally and the boys. But that's the thing about history. One small, seemingly insignificant event can alter its course forever" (Schwartz, Schwartz, and Studio Hive 2014). That its course was altered, or maybe preserved, by these American legends is a given.

THE TRUTH IS OUTDATED

Other comic allohistories similarly explore alternative explanations of the past without changing its outcome in the present. Several volumes, for example, offer their own interpretation of historical record and conspiracy theories surrounding the assassination of John F. Kennedy. According to Peter Knight,

> The assassination of President Kennedy in Dallas in 1963 has inspired more conspiracy thinking in America than any other event in the twentieth century. From official government enquiries to amateur websites, and from Hollywood films to literary novels, those seven seconds of mayhem in Dealey Plaza have been relentlessly examined for clues not just to a plot to kill the President, but to the hidden agenda of the last four decades of American history. (2000, 76)

The event is so ingrained in the cultural landscape that "even when not directly there, the assassination seems to be an absent presence in many fictional and factual treatments of recent American history, a ghostly and unspoken moment of hidden causality" (Knight 2000, 77). It is, for example, alluded to in the horror-comedy allohistory *Z-Men: All the President's Men*, a 2015 title from Double Take. One of the publisher's ten series inspired by George A. Romero's 1968 film *Night of the Living Dead*, Z-Men followed Secret Service agents ordered by "LBJ" (President Lyndon B. Johnson) to investigate an undead uprising reported in rural Pennsylvania. LBJ, however, reserved his best agents to protect him in the wake of his predecessor having "his head turned inside out by a high powered rifle" (McComsey and Jemas 2016).[3] And, the "Men in Black" operatives of *Deep State* (2014, BOOM Studios) claimed to know who really killed JFK, as well as what Tesla's final project was, and the real cause of cattle mutilations. Indeed, the assassination provided a foundation for all conspiracy beliefs that followed: the Oklahoma City bombings, the death of Princess Diana, 9/11, swine flu vaccinations, the so-called "Clinton Body Count," and more (Knight 2000; Knight 2008; Aupers 2012; Barkun 2003). It is, therefore, unsurprising that presidential fictions would look to this moment as a pivotal point in history, a moment upon which the country's legacy was transformed.

The Red Diaries: The Kennedy Conspiracy (1997) suggested that the plot was likely devised by multiple parties, including Nixon, Johnson, the mob, and the CIA, but the final kill shot was driven by revenge for the death of Marilyn Monroe. *Badlands* (1991) pointed to a Nixon-Mob-Cuba ring motivated by financial investments. *The Umbrella Academy: Dallas* (2009), the second installment of an Eisner Award-winning superhero series, took the time-policing approach of allohistories and posited, without explanation, that Kennedy had to be eliminated to preserve the authenticity of the timeline. *The X-Files: JFK Disclosure* (2018) proposed that Kennedy was killed by an FBI agent to keep him from revealing the existence of aliens and the government's research in extraterrestrial life and technology.

All four, to varying degrees, based their conspiracy variations on actual historical record—the official findings, sociopolitical contexts, documented incongruities, poorly kept secrets, and long-accepted rumors. The result of the reimagined histories was thus unchanged: Kennedy still died, Johnson still became president, the war in Vietnam still dragged on, and Marilyn Monroe and Camelot became tragic legends. Even the most fictional of the four books, the superhero *Umbrella Academy* and science-fiction *X-Files*, did not transcend the reality of Kennedy's death. *The Umbrella Academy*, in which the assassination was a way to correct historical anomalies, explained, "The point is to *maintain* the status quo. Another frail man of privilege in a dark suit will take Kennedy's place, and another after that . . . Until another *disaffected outcast* decides to change the world with a bullet" (Way and Bá 2009, 157). But it also suggested that Kennedy was "special," that he was "an idea," and that ideas cannot be killed with mere bullets (Way and Bá 2009, 147).

I WANT TO BELIEVE ... IN SOMETHING

Though *The X-Files* drew on several key pieces of JFK conspiracy evidence—the Umbrella Man, the man on the Grassy Knoll, the empty window of the Texas School Book Depository, and the "Fire Ball" gun inspired by the Remington XP-100 model—it was the only one to move beyond the singular event and consider it as part of larger conspiracies by connecting the assassination to the government cover-up of aliens and UFOs (Tipton and Menton3 2018, 3). Around 50 to 70 percent of people believe that the US government is withholding information about the existence of UFOs. Michael Barkun (2003) notes that while early UFO believers did not advance any political agenda beyond seeking the truth from the government, by the end of the twentieth century, as paranoia gave way to cynicism and cynicism to disaffection, belief in UFO cover-ups was linked to a larger political vision of a New World Order (see also Arnold 2008).[4] Alien conspiracies are now perceived as merely one part of the "efforts by an immensely powerful but secret group to seize control of the world" through the subversion of government, subordination of the US to world powers, eradication of religion, domestic mobilization of military, paramilitary, and criminal organizations, mind control, and surveillance (39).

> Belief in conspiracies is central to millennialism in the late twentieth and early twenty-first centuries. [...] Such [perspectives] cast the world in terms of a struggle between light and darkness, good and evil, and hold that this polarization will persist until the end of history, when evil is finally, definitively defeated. (Barkun 2003, 2)

This is the theme at the heart of the alien-centric alternate world and parallel world stories of *Letter 44* and *The Manhattan Projects*.

The Manhattan Projects was an irreverent romp through history, delving into the Nazi rocket program, nuclear mayhem, the supposed Roswell UFO incident, the Soviet space program, Cold War paranoia, Masonic secret societies, cosmonauts, the JFK assassination, the moon landing, and more. Its cast included four US presidents—Franklin D. Roosevelt, Truman, Kennedy, and Johnson; two US Army generals—Leslie Groves and William Westmoreland; three prominent American physicists—J. Robert Oppenheimer, Richard Feynman, and Harry Daghlian; four distinguished scientists from formerly fascist European states—Albert Einstein, Enrico Fermi, Wernher von Braun, and Helmutt Gröttrup; a defense minister and a future premier of the USSR—Dmitriy Ustinov and Leonid Brezhnev; a Cuban president—Fidel Castro; and, two of the earliest cosmonauts—Yuri Gagarin and the dog Laika. "But it is not history," warned critic Nolan Bensen (2015). "It is an alternate history. And in this alternate history, only a few of these figures are depicted with a personality deserving of the secular beatification all of them have received" (Bensen 2015, para. 2). In the twisted, apocalypse-bound biopunk universe of *The Manhattan Projects* (*MP*), Oppenheimer was a serial killer who gained intelligence and multiple personalities by eating the brains of his victims; Einstein had an evil, alcoholic twin from a parallel universe; Daghlian was a being of pure radiation; von Braun was a cyborg; Laika could talk; Westmoreland wore a necklace of human ears; Roosevelt became an artificial intelligence; Truman was an eccentric Masonic priest; Kennedy's Oval Office was awash in cocaine and prostitutes; Groves was behind the Kennedy assassination; and the US and the USSR were co-conspirators in pursuit of interplanetary domination.

As an allohistory, *MP* presented an account of events that differed from the record only in the details. The timeline remained largely intact. Roosevelt died, but was transformed into an AI offering council behind the scenes. Truman assumed office after being notified of the president's death while presiding over an elaborate Masonic ceremony. Oppenheimer helped to develop the atomic bomb, but he was truly the evil twin of the Oppenheimer that history knows. The bomb was dropped on Hiroshima, but not with Truman's approval. Daghlian was irradiated in a nuclear accident at Los Alamos, but rather than killing him it made him superhuman. The Cold War was real, but only insofar as it served as a public relations front for government funding of elaborate research and development programs. The USSR got a man into space before the US, but nonhuman aliens mastered space travel first. Kennedy was assassinated, but it had nothing to do with the mob or the CIA. The US landed on the moon, but only through the assistance of the Soviet cosmonaut program. With shadowy paramilitaries and quasi-governments and whacky historical caricatures, *MP* was a Cold War parody consistent with such absurdist and apocalyptic narratives as *Dr. Strangelove*.

Perceptions of the Cold War as absurd were put forth in the 1950s by opponents of the nuclear arms race, C. Wright Mills and Lewis Mumford. The absurdity was found in the potential to nullify history and to prepare for a war that would result not in victory but in chaotic waste (Seed 1999). Absurdist Cold War narratives thus, like *MP*, highlighted neuroses within military leadership, a denial of death, a kind of sexual perversion linked to technology, and an irrational lust for destruction for its own sake. All are themes found within the characters of the *MP*: the ear-necklace of Westmoreland and rogue insubordination of Groves, the artificially prolonged life of Roosevelt and Dhaglian, the hypersexuality of Kennedy, and Oppenheimer's genocidal impulses. The Cold War parody was visually captured in panels of alternating and competing reds and blues, highlighting scenes of both international tensions and internal struggles (see figure 11.2). Such imagery symbolizes the dichotomous and polarizing Cold

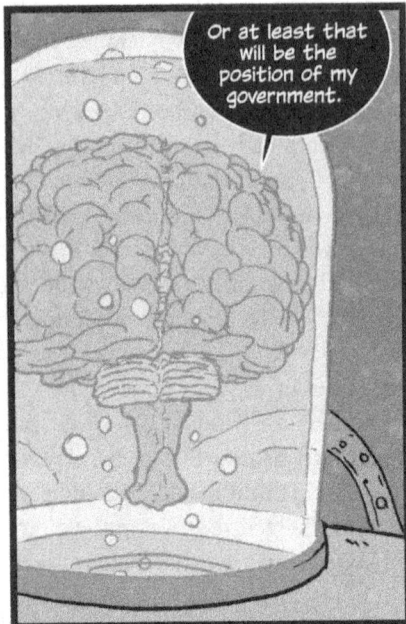

Figure 11.2. The hyperreal *Manhattan Projects* visually punctuates its themes of political interplays and personal struggles with contrasting reds and blues, as alternated between these two panels excerpted from volume 2 (Hickman and Pitarra 2013).

War rhetoric of blue-blooded Americans versus red communists and policy justifications of American exceptionalism and civilization versus non-American barbarism (Esch 2010). It also captured the tension between the "consensual American identity" united in the face of outside hostilities and future uncertainties and "an increasingly unclear personal identity" in which people sought truth and authenticity (Costello 2009, 2).

In much Cold War-era science-fiction, aliens were "deliberate stand-ins for Communists" (Rogin 1984, 9). Alien invasions symbolized the Western political and primal fears "of a society being taken over from the inside by an alien force and thus being made part of a hostile evil collective" (Sardar 2002, 10). Sci-fi invasion narratives resurfaced during George W. Bush's Terror War (Hantke 2010). Numerous pop culture products of the post-9/11 era "featured invasive alien forces, shadowy government conspiracies, and a generalized mood of paranoia and dread" enabled by and responding to heightened anxiety and politics of fear in the era of terrorism (Takacs 2009, 1). One such text was the recent allohistory *Letter 44*.

The book focused on how the actions of the forty-third president of the United States shaped the administration of the forty-fourth president, and it referenced Guantanamo Bay, a housing bubble burst, the need for healthcare reform, and two wars in the Middle East, indicating that the 2012 title was reimagining the recent history of 2001 to 2009, a timeline verified by writer Charles Soule in a 2017 interview (Helvie 2017). But it was written to nearly align with current events "in such a way that readers can see whatever parallels with their own lives (political and otherwise) they might find" (in Helvie 2017, para. 18). Other post-9/11 political thriller comics were similar. *Saucer Country* and *Saucer State* (see chapters seven, eight, and nine) used alien abductions and invasions as metaphors for identity politics of gender, sex, and race in an age of #MeToo and ICE (see Knopf 2020b). *The Homeland Directive* featured a biological, rather than alien, attack, in the "Orwellian present" to offer commentary on the maintenance of freedom and justice in an age of fear (Venditti and Huddleston 2011, inside cover).

For some, the apocalyptic *Letter 44* offered a parallel to the sociopolitical climate of the Trump era "where it feels like a sort of 'end of the world' for many with only a select few who will avoid the negative effects felt by many" (Helvie 2017, para. 17). It was therefore eerily coincidental that a 2014 issue of the series featured Trump's *The Art of the Deal* as the content of the first human communication with encroaching aliens, prompting one human scientist to remark, "Let's hope they don't kill us now on general principles" (Soule, Alburquerque, Major, and Jackson 2015, 73). But, adhering to the tradition of many other presidential allohistories, the underlying message was about the heroism and indomitable spirit of the American people (Helvie 2017).

CONCLUSION

Hellekson argued that allohistories "revolve around the basic premise that some event in the past did not occur as we know it did, and thus the present has changed" (2011, loc. 85). These comics, however, mostly reimagined the past in line with the present as it is. Thus, rather than challenging assumptions of race, gender, class, and power, the steam/diesel/cyber/bio-punked presidencies reinforced a White, patriarchal, and capitalist hegemony. Instead of exploring counterfactuals, these narratives largely assumed determinist forces of power and privilege, even while suggesting such deterministic ideas were unjust (Ferguson 1997). Indeed, they largely suggested that history could not possibly have had a different outcome. Each comic book allohistory also presented some kind of government and/or corporate cover-up: secret underground military bases and laboratories in *DC: The New Frontier*, time-policing to ensure historical continuity in *Time Lincoln*, a secret industrialist cabal in *Rough Riders*, an elite club of influence in *The Jekyll Island Chronicles*, inexplicable phenomena in *The Manhattan Projects*, underground government and criminal machinations in the JFK conspiracy narratives, and classified government enterprises in *Letter 44*.

The combined effect points to Knight's argument that "Conspiracy theories [...] are now less likely to give vent to alarmist fears about an occasional irruption of the normal order of things, than to express a not entirely unfounded suspicion that the normal order of things itself amounts to a conspiracy" (2000, 3). This suspicion is at once concerning and comforting; the former because "it magnifies the power of evil" and the latter because it suggests that the evil is not arbitrary and "gives the conspiracist a definable enemy against which to struggle" (Barkun 2003, 4). The comfort of conspiracy is reinforced by the nostalgic visual aesthetic in many of these titles—including the retro-pop of *DC: The New Frontier*, the steampunk of *Rough Riders* and *Time Lincoln*, the dieselpunk of *The Jekyll Island Chronicles*, the murky photorealism of *The Red Diaries* and *The X-Files: JFK Disclosure*, and the period accoutrements of diners and ice cream carts in *The Umbrella Academy*.

The nostalgic impulses also repurpose and thus reinforce the sociopolitical hegemony of the past, making it impossible to alter the course set by the Great Men of History. This is nostalgia's conservative drive: its refusal to let go of the known past. It is this political and historical orientation that is found not only in the 2016 campaign and election of Trump, a man called a modern version of Theodore Roosevelt (Roosevelt III 2016), but also within the debates surrounding monuments to heroes of the Confederacy and other disreputable leaders of the past (Brooks 2017). Such controversy is found within these allohistories: *American Legends* and *Rough Riders*, for example, contribute to mythmaking of the past's iconic figures, while *The Manhattan Projects* implies that history's giants may have been, at best, power mad. The stories in between, such as those that dream-walk through Dealey Plaza in November of 1963, may be the worst of all. They epitomize the cynical, disaffected conspiracies of presidential allohistory. Rather than offering an enemy to fight, they suggested the enemy, like the past, is unknowable and inescapable. The political disillusionment felt by these backward glances is captured in the closing words *The Red Diaries*:

> Whatever the truth *was*, it couldn't be worse than all the *lies* ... All the theories that have come since then.
>
> *If* the government was involved, the *cover up* has damaged them *more* than the truth would've.
>
> You know, I'm getting to be like *most* other Americans now ...
> *Who* killed Kennedy?
> *I* don't *care*.
> I *just* don't care.
> And that tells you a lot about *what* actually *died* on that day in November of 1963.
> It just doesn't matter. (Reed, Campbell, Jones, and Shuput 1997)

CONCLUSION
THE ART OF THE PEOPLE, BY THE PEOPLE, FOR THE PEOPLE

Comic books are frequently dismissed as children's literature. The superhero genre is repeatedly denigrated by critics as empty escapism; in the words of director Martin Scorsese, superhero movies are "not cinema" because they lack "narrative" and have turned theaters into "amusement parks" (quoted in Clark 2019, paras. 4, 2). But the political power of comics is undeniable. During 2019, especially, "a pattern of writers giving overt voice to their political opinions through superhero comics" emerged—as did very public "controversies where they were] prevented from doing so" (Speelman 2020, para. 3). Independent journalists, including the Investigative Fund, Reveal News, and freelance reporters, have been investigating how comic books are a "new battlefield in the culture wars" (Reveal 2018). The most visible publishers, DC and Marvel, have been at the center of the ideological debate. So far, DC "is happy to allow political subtext become text," with stories like *Lois Lane* facing off against a White House press secretary based on Trump's press secretary, Sarah Huckabee, and senior counselor, Kellyanne Conway (Speelman 2020, para. 7). Marvel, on the other hand, has explicitly expressed a desire to remain apolitical.

With DC leaning left and Marvel staying quiet, or trying to, self-publishing, independent, and small presses are looking to leverage the political power of comics. Through grassroots funding, creators Theodore Robert Beale, better known as Vox Day, and Chuck Dixon, known for his work on Marvel's Punisher and DC's Batman, developed *Alt-Hero*, a superhero comic promoting right-wing politics. *Alt-Hero* presents "Rebel," a White, buxom, Confederate flag-clad superheroine who protects the innocent through a tough approach on border patrol. It is described as an allohistory, taking place in a world where Hitler was overthrown in 1939, Japan attacked Australia instead of Hawaii, the Soviet Union fell in 1956 when the first atomic bomb was dropped in its territories, and the world's power is now dominated by the unmatched military might of China and Russia.

Many conservative comic readers object to what they see as the influence of "social justice warriors" in mainstream comics needlessly changing the demographics of old characters just for a show of identity politics. *Alt-Hero* is perceived by some as a simple backlash to the perceived excessive re-writes of classic heroes (see Arenas 2017). Others see it connected to a larger trend of pushback against diversity, and thus progressivism, in comics and genre media. The "Comicsgate" scandal of 2017 brought this tension to the foreground when proponents of canonical purity/opponents of character and creator diversity released a list of titles and creators to boycott. The Comicsgate blacklist, which included major creators like Larry Hama (*G.I. Joe*), Mark Waid (*The Flash*), Alex de Campi (*Archie vs. Predator*), Kelly Sue DeConnick (*Captain Marvel*), Matt Fraction (*Hawkeye*), Ta-Nehisi Coates (*Black Panther*), and others, was comprised primarily of women, people of color, and the outspokenly left-leaning. It was effectively a social mediated-continuation of charges made by retailers at the 2017 New York Comic-Con that declining comics sales were the fault of Marvel increasing the visibility of female, non-White, and LGBTQAIPD characters by sharing the mantles of Wolverine, Thor, Hulk, and Iron Man with women and people of color (Francisco 2018). The controversy continued into 2019 as Mark Waid fought a legal battle described as a publicity-seeking, nuisance lawsuit against him by Richard C. Meyer, a comics creator and apparent leader of Comicsgate. Meyer's suit claimed that Waid interfered in a publishing agreement Meyer had with Antarctic Press, though the publisher denied any such undue influence. On social media, the tensions mounted between fans and supporters of each creator, fueled in part by Meyer's controversial online presence; under the handle "Diversity & Comics," Meyer is known for comics criticism that is perceived as "targeting minority creators and critics with harassment" (Arrant 2019, para. 3).

Placed in the context of these "reactionary movements and harassment campaigns centered on nerd fandoms," including not only Comicsgate but also GamerGate in games and Sad Puppies in literary science-fiction, which claim "to be fighting against censorship and the politicized groupthink of leftist social justice warriors (SJWs)—antiracists, feminists and marginalized people whom the right characterizes as oppressors" (Berlatsky 2018, para. 2), grassroots and crowdfunded comics like *Alt-Hero*, *My Hero MAGAdemia*, *Liberality for All*, and *President Trump* are not merely right-leaning titles but may also be perceived as part of a concerted effort to co-opt the comics medium for alt-right propaganda. And it proves that what comics say not only has political importance, but that it also has real political consequences, and that real political actors are attentive to and engaged with comic book content.

Other such actions provide further evidence of the political significance of comics. In 2017, an artist worked anti-Semitic and anti-Christian messages in an

Figure 12.1. A 2017 meme from IMgur used Superman—defender of "truth, justice, and the American way"—to argue against Trump's anti-immigration policies as well as his claim that journalists were the "enemy of the American people" (see Taylor 2018).

issue of Marvel's *X-Men*. Artist Ardian Syaf slipped the numbers "212" and "51" into a scene of *X-Men: Gold* #1 that foregrounded the Jewish American character Kitty Pryde. In Syaf's native Indonesia, "212" represented a mass protest against Jakarta's then-Governor Basuki Tjahaja Purnama, a Christian, and "51" points to a verse in the Quran (Chapter Surah 5, verse 51) interpreted by the protestors as a warning that Muslims should not appoint Christian or Jewish people as their leaders (Lovett 2017). A lot of attention has focused on Marvel Comics, especially after Marvel's editor-in-chief Axel Alonso reportedly said in 2017 "There's been this massive discussion about inclusion and diversity ... But Marvel is not about politics. We are about telling stories about the world" (quoted in Opam 2017, para. 3)—DC Comics, however, has also faced its own political identity crisis. In late 2019, several news outlets, including *Variety* and *Forbes*, reported that Warner Bros. "was struggling to find a way to make Superman relevant to modern audiences." The sourced report unleashed a torrent of responses. Newbery and Carnegie Medal-winning author Neil Gaiman suggested on Twitter that the character should not be made relevant but inspirational. Other sources and fans responded with shock that a character known as "the immigrant son of humanity, the protector of the weak, and the fighter of injustice" could be considered irrelevant in 2019 (Williams 2019, para. 4). Fans on Twitter expressed similar sentiments, including "the need for truth in a world of lies." One user described him as "an ethical, principled man fighting against corruption. [...] He's Mr. Smith meets George Bailey in circus tights." Indeed, a meme had been circulating long before his relevance was questioned, one seemingly developed in response to the Trump presidency: a split image featured Christopher Reeve as Clark Kent on the left, beneath the word "Journalist." On the right, Reeve was shown as Superman, beneath the words "Illegal Immigrant."

Across the bottom of the two images was the headline, "Enemy of the American People" (see figure 12.1).

If comics tell stories about the world, then the real world will naturally "leak in," as creator Cecil Castellucci explains (in Herviou 2017, para. 15). Creators Jimmy Palmiotti and Marley Zarcone note that making comics free of politics is "impossible" because even at its "lightest fluffiest basics," a comic is still filtered through the lens and experiences of its creators (in Herviou 2017, para. 16). Cartoonist Chris Ware stated that comics are "a working-class art form" and "the art of the people" (quoted in Sneddon 2013, para. 1). So, whether it is Syaf's numerical expression of his anti-Semitic outlook, the Jewish-created Captain America punching the anti-Semitic Hitler in the face, Joe Sacco giving Palestinian voices agency through his graphic reportage, Paul Cornell spotlighting LGBTQAIPD and immigration issues as byproducts of his plots, Mark Pellegrini presenting Trump's border wall as heroic, or the DNC creating a comic book biography of Harry S. Truman, comics express the varied voices of the people and thus naturally express the people's political or politicized worldviews.

Statistics from 2017 found that nearly 60 percent of comics and graphic novels were bought by readers between the ages of thirteen and twenty-nine, the same demographic that comprised the current and near-future voters of the "youth wave" seen in the 2018 midterm elections (Alverson 2017; Beck and Kitchener 2018). Retailers suggest, however, that their average customer is in their mid-to-late-thirties, an age group historically *less* likely to vote (Rogers 2017; Johnston 2016). Whether they are activists under thirty or apathetics under forty, these comics readers occupy space in key political demographics, and the comic book/graphic novel industry powers multibillion dollar entertainment franchises across multiple mass media that are reaching them (Salkowitz 2019).

As indicated throughout the preceding chapters, entertainment media and pop culture artifacts not only open opportunities for dialogues on civic matters, but can also motivate, educate, and integrate the people to political issues and systems (Foy 2008). The 2017 Women's March, which became an annual event around the world, made the political power of the popular perceptible. The *Independent, Entertainment Weekly, Vox,* and the *Washington Post* all ran stories of the marches that focused on participants' use of pop culture references and imagery. The *Washington Post* suggested that "pop culture gave a lot of people marching [...] the sentiments that helped the crowd seem feisty, energized and defiant, rather than defeated" and further indicated that media creations of "new visions for what the world can be still matter" (Rosenberg 2017, para. 7; see also Leong 2017; Loughrey 2017; Grady 2017). This merger of political symbols and popular markers worked as "memetic signifiers," iconographic "references that because of their inclusive and post-ideological content and their [...] capacity to spread with extreme rapidity, are highly conducive to processes of collective identification" (Gerbaudo 2015, 918). Collective action is the result of purposes and resources oriented within social relationships activated to create a sense of being and working together. The formation of a "we" happens by orienting the ends, means, and the *environment* of action (Melucci 1995). That environment includes a culture of media entertainment.

Active fans of such cult media franchises as *The Lord of the Rings*, *Star Trek*, and *Star Wars*, through the participatory fandom enabled by computer-mediated-communication, are "beginning to be recognized as important contributors to formation of collective belief" because of their close readings and personalization of pop cultural texts (Shefrin 2004, 269). Sarah Thornton argues that fan cultures construct images of the mainstream in order to produce a position of difference; they "carry around images of the social worlds that make up" the culture of their fandom. "These mental maps, rich in cultural detail and value judgement, offer them a distinct 'sense of their place' but also a sense of the other's place" (1995, 99). Fan communities engage various modes of production, consumption, and interaction to establish and reinforce personal and global identities. And, like the political orientations embedded in the texts, these identities are marked by in-groups and out-groups (Hunt 2003; Black 2009; Lyden 2012; Shefrin 2004).

The phenomenon of popular culture icons as political and protest symbols, used across the political spectrum, demonstrates both the persistence of collective identity in a mediated environment and the rising influence of fan cultures to (re)create new forms of collective identification, making use of all available means of production and dissemination. By adopting inclusive and viral "memetic signifiers," like Princess Leia as an avatar of the Women's March or Ms. Marvel as an icon of Muslim immigration, individuals become involved in a process of collective transfiguration which temporarily reverses the experience of isolation and commodification in media consumption (Knopf 2019a). As Gerbaudo has argued, such "memetic signifiers thus constitute the rallying point of political communities that are necessarily transient, but which nonetheless need their own symbols and icons to arise and mobilize people, so to make them perceive their newly found sense of unity and purpose" (2015, 927–28). Pop culture opens avenues for people to declare their participation in a collective project and helps them to shape their understandings of civic responsibility, leadership, communal history, and present concerns (Gerbaudo 2015; Smith 2009).

Research on portrayals of the presidency and campaign politics in broadcast and cinematic entertainment have found that the media present an image of a president who is a flawed hero, an idol with feet of clay (Phalen, Kim, and Osellame 2012; Holbert, Tschida et al 2005). These portrayals also typically reinforce, through appearances and/or behaviors, the historically dominant image of the president as a tough White man (Parry-Giles and Parry-Giles 2006; Parry-Giles and Parry-Giles 2002; Semmler, McKay-Semmler, and Robertson 2013). Graphic media, too, despite the Comicsgate complaints of rampant identity politics, mostly reinforce the presidential patriarchy: from the blonde President Prez Rickard being assisted by a half-naked Native American sidekick (*Prez: The First Teen President*) to President Arcardia Alvarado having to repeatedly endure sexual assault from gray-skinned men and sexual harassment from gray-haired men (*Saucer Country* and *Saucer State*). Political pessimism engendered by such real-world inequities is, however, frequently integral to these stories, as exemplified by the cynical campaigns of the trickster Loki, the demon Etrigan, and the tycoon Lex Luthor.

While comics creators, publishers, and readers continue to debate the appropriate level or types of politics in comics, columnist Ash Griffith had this to say in 2018: "At the end of the day, everyone has a story that deserves to be told, not just the select few. Representation and visibility are so inexplicably important" (2018, para 14). It is no coincidence that the midterm elections of 2018 likewise presented a slate of candidates described by the *New York Times* as "among the most diverse set to run in the history of the United States" (Associated Press et al 2018, para. 1). Comics tell stories about the world, and the world leaks into comics. At the end of the day, everyone wants a voice in their community, whether that community is found in the pages of a "funny book," on the screen of a superhero blockbuster, or in the halls of government.

POSTSCRIPT
POLITICAL PICKS AND PANDEMICS

Final revisions on this book were completed in the midst of the 2020 COVID-19 pandemic. April 2020 was the first month in forty years to not have any popular culture conventions (Delahanty 2020). The two oldest comic-cons in the country, the ITHACON in Ithaca, NY scheduled for March 2020 and the Comic-Con International in San Diego, California, scheduled for July 2020, were both canceled, though San Diego's was replaced with a virtual "Comic Con at Home." Publication and distribution of new comic books ceased for weeks. Artists turned healthcare and frontline workers into superheroes, and on June 7, 2020, more than seventy newspaper cartoon strips recognized front-line workers who had spent five months fighting the virus and ensuring vital services were uninterrupted (Swathwood 2020; CBC 2020; Schwartz 2020).

The historic moment was repeatedly called "challenging," "difficult," "uncertain," and "unprecedented." But it wasn't unprecedented. At least, not exactly. Apocalyptic and post-apocalyptic fictions had long imagined similar scenarios of deadly contagions, quarantined zones, social isolation, mass panic, and economic collapse. As noted by artist Ed Catto, "Geek Culture was way ahead of the curve" with a panel at the 2019 San Diego Comic-Con International called "Art of Infection: Fictional Diseases, Real Life" (2020, para. 2). Panelists—including experts in epidemiology, infection prevention, and popular culture—discussed fictional depictions of viral outbreaks and how they would be handled in the real world, suggesting that science would be able to contain the contagion before it decimated humanity.

Comics are rife with stories of epidemics, pandemics, and plagues.[1] Perhaps one of the best known is *The Walking Dead*, thanks to its popular adaptation to television on AMC. The 2003–2019 zombie apocalypse series by Robert Kirkman "question[ed] what humanity is and what our role is in the evolution of humankind" (Sommers 2016, introduction). It particularly highlighted "apocalyptic economic anxieties" through vignettes that revealed character work histories prior to the zombie outbreak (2018 Fazio). This element of character development created "a space in the narrative for individuals to reflect upon their past lives, and [illustrated] a shared lack of power and dissatisfaction over their former occupations" and demonstrated the "unique opportunity" of a crisis "to establish community among individuals from all walks of life who, prior to the end of the world, would otherwise have remained socially and culturally divided" (Fazio 2018, 50–51). Thus, the comic was prescient of the 20.5 million American jobs lost during the COVID-19 pandemic shutdowns and the refrains that "we are all in this together" (Lee 2020; Fitzpatrick 2020).

DC Comics' *Scooby Apocalypse* (mentioned in chapters four and ten) was a similar tale of survival through alliances that would have been unlikely under normal circumstances. An experiment designed to improve humanity went awry, creating a world full of mutated creatures infected by a nanite virus. While *The Walking Dead* predicted the economic realities of a global pandemic, *Scooby Apocalypse* hinted at the political ramifications. One of the masterminds behind the nanite project was mogul Rufus Dinkley, a red-headed doppelganger of Donald Trump, complete with a gilded tower bearing his name. Despite his role, however unwitting or unintentional it may have been, in the monster plague, Rufus took no responsibility for the deaths and suffering it caused, earning him the description of "sick ... twisted ... egotistic ... narcissistic ... megalomaniacal ..." (Giffen et al 2017). Three years later, the real Donald Trump was criticized for negligence in his handling of the COVID-19 pandemic, with suggestions that his failures, scapegoating, and misinformation may be akin to involuntary manslaughter (Baron 2020).

When the COVID-19 pandemic broke, there were already several current comics with pandemic storylines that offered glimpses of the reality to come. In May 2019, DC Comics launched the first of its *DCeased* titles. IDW released *Pandemica* in September 2019. And, November 2019 introduced *Undiscovered Country* from Image. All of these series were ongoing at the time that both the world and comics publication were disrupted by the coronavirus, and yet all three contained elements that seemed to reflect or comment on the events-to-come.

DCeased, and its follow-ups *DCeased: Unkillables* and *DCeased: Hope at World's End*, featured the spread of the "Anti-Life Equation," a virus that jumped from the cybernetic body of the superhero Cyborg to the internet, infecting people with a techno-organic/biotech variant of the Equation, causing them to suffer a violent transformation into a zombie-like state and to become contagious carriers of the disease. Retrospectively, the superhero-science-fiction-horror story may almost be read as a precursor to the real-world conspiracy theory that connected COVID-19 to emerging 5G technology (Tibken 2020). The concept of a biological virus being transmitted digitally may also be interpreted as analogous to the spread of medical misinformation and fake news via social media (see Waszak, Kasprzycka-Waszak, and Kubanek 2018). A similar concept was introduced in the ironically timed February 2020 release of *Tomorrow* from Dark Horse, in which a Russian computer virus breached the technological-biological barrier and wiped out most of the adult population—calling to mind Russia's interference in the 2016 election and foreshadowing the March 2020 Reuters headline, "Russia deploying coronavirus disinformation to sow panic in West, EU document says" (Emmott 2020).

From its opening scenes at a detention complex in South Texas, *Pandemica* was overtly commenting on racial politics of the late 2010s, such as the growth of immigrant detention under the Trump administration (Kassie 2019). The series quickly became not only provocatively polemic but profoundly prophetic. It offered a dystopian vision of a possible near-future in which the United States was on the verge of war and the world was crippled by a global pandemic. Just a few months after *Pandemica*'s September 2019 release, the US and North Korea alluded to threats of militaristic force, aiming the country toward the brink of war, just days before China reported the first cluster of illnesses that marked the start of the COVID-19 pandemic in December (Kasulis 2019; Taylor 2020). A diegetic newscaster proclaimed, "The death toll continues to mount in what some are calling the *worst epidemic* since the *Spanish Flu of 1918*" (Maberry, Sanchez, and Fotos 2019), and soonafter real world headlines announced COVID-19's deadliest days and historians and epidemiologists alike compared the 2020 coranavirus pandemic to the 1918 influenza pandemic. In the dystopian comic, the pandemic was caused by designer pathogens as part of a shadow government's ethnic cleansing project; non-Aryan populations were the most susceptible to the virus. Likewise, in the real world, COVID-19 disproportionately ravaged Black communities in the United States (Erdman 2020).

Image Comics' *Undiscovered Country* had a similar premise. Set in the near-future, the United States was inexplicably walled off from the rest of the world, until a team seeking a cure for a global pandemic breached the "lost" nation's borders. Like the detention centers in *Pandemica*, the border wall of *Undiscovered Country* hinted at immigration policies under the Trump administration, which ramped up border wall construction ahead of the 2020 election, with projected costs of hundreds of millions, even while Americans suffered the economic downturn of the coronavirus pandemic (Rogers 2020). The comic's visuals of its Sky pandemic foresaw the facemasks, makeshift hospitals, and inadequate protection equipment that would likewise mark the streets of New York during the peak of COVID-19. It also envisioned government complicity in letting the sick die to save the infrastructure, echoed in the words of real-world leaders like Texas Lt. Governor Dan Patrick (Stieb 2020). And it imagined America's leader, "Uncle Sam," leveraging a cure in world affairs, evocative of Donald Trump's efforts to purchase exclusive access to a potential coronavirus vaccine (Colson and Dunn 2020).

The faltering American economy struggled to reopen in late May 2020, even while the COVID-19 death toll mounted. In the midst of this uncertainty, a White Minneapolis police officer killed a Black man, George Floyd, by using excessive force during an arrest. The previous March, a Black Kentucky woman, Breonna Taylor, working as an EMT, was fatally shot eight times by police in her home during a "botched" narcotics raid. A month earlier, an African American man, Ahmaud Arbery, was shot and killed by White residents of a Georgia neighborhood while jogging. Floyd's death sparked protests that began in Minneapolis and soon spread nationwide, with police around the country escalating the violence. Comic books offered context for this, too.

The 2016 debut of *Black*, by Kwanza Osajyefo, told the story of a Black teenager who survived being shot by police and discovered that he was part of a secret faction of Black people with superpowers. *Black*, and its 2019 sequel *White*, tackled race and racism in the United States, but despite the cover of issue four depicting Donald Trump as a "boss" villain in a game of Donkey Kong, with the hoodied hero dodging flaming Klan crosses, police bullets, and judicial gavels, creator Osajyefo warned that his work was not "political" because "I don't like the experiences of marginalized people being dismissed as politics. [...] There's nothing political about not wanting to get shot just because of the color of my skin" (quoted in Kickstarter 2019, para. 1). The cover of *Black*'s 2016 premier issue featured a young Black man standing, hands raised, in front of a line of armed police in full riot gear; similar imagery would later be echoed across the internet during the 2020 George Floyd protests.

Killadelphia (discussed in chapter seven) blended gothic horror with crime drama to explore and expose how society, government, and history impacts current socioeconomic conditions and race relations. As described in *The Beat*, the 2019 comic took "short but deep cuts into the backstory" of Philadelphia to show how "every drug-riddled corner and every forgotten housing project" helped to shape the characters (Denis 2019, para. 5). Creator Rodney Barnes explained,

> For as long as I can remember, folks have questioned how history affects African-American culture. My goal was to answer one aspect of that question [by relating the story] to the ideology of those pockets of uber-passionate folks who don't just rally or vote, they go to extremes politically and form militias. [...] It's no longer about Democrat or Republican, it's about its own ideology forged over centuries. (quoted in Horne 2020, para. 24)

Ultimately, *Killadelphia* argued that America failed its most vulnerable populations: its tired, its poor, its masses yearning to breathe free—or, in the cases of George Floyd and Eric Garner, to just breathe.

As noted elsewhere in this volume, the opening decades of the twenty-first century were punctuated by moments of surprising turbulence: the terrorist attacks of September 11, 2001; the election of America's first Black president in 2008; the increased visibility of social causes through movements such as #BlackLivesMatter in 2013 and #MeToo in 2006/2017; the unanticipated election of reality TV star and real-estate mogul Donald Trump in 2016; and, the pandemic of 2020. Thus, while pandemic comics may seem eerily clairvoyant, they are consistent with the tradition of dystopian, apocalyptic, and post-apocalyptic literature and art. As Kristjan Mavri writes,

> Apocalyptic anxiety has long been noted as a recurring historical pattern. Under the weight of existential pressures apocalyptic rhetoric, prophecies, movements, films, and literary texts proliferate. This fear for and fascination of imagining the end of days has ingrained itself into artistic imagination, with artists envisaging brave new worlds and wastelands. (2013, 1)

But, as Katherine V. Snyder notes, these texts are not purely fictitious or wildly speculative. Instead, the genre "takes what already exists and makes an imaginative leap into the future, following current sociocultural, political, or scientific developments to their potentially devastating conclusions" (2011, 470). The same can be said for the fantasy and horror dramas of *Black* and *Killadelphia*.

Apocalyptic comics present stories of dread and of destruction, and of hope and of survival. The full aftermath of the social and political upheaval of 2020 is yet unclear, but the final pages of *Scooby Apocalypse* may provide a hint about what, hopefully, comes next:

> The human race was beaten, bedraggled, weary beyond imaging...
> But *we were here*.
> [...]
> ...And life as we once knew it is over. But after all we've been through, time is a luxury, and life, in *any* form...
> ...is a blessing.
> [...]
> [...] And we've all been working [...]
> [to] help build a better world on the ashes of the old.
> [...]
> Let's see if we can get it *right* this time. (DeMatteis, Olliffe, and Palmer 2019)

NOTES

PREFACE

1. *I Go Pogo* was also reimagined as a claymation campaign film, headlined by the voices of stars Jonathan Winters, Vincent Price, and Ruth Buzzi. Upon its release in 1980, the *Washington Post* observed, "In a year when American voters from coast to coast have been grousing about the sorry line-up of presidential prospects, one candidate is rapidly emerging as an attractive choice with truly impressive credentials"—Pogo Possum of Okefenokee Swamp and presidential candidate in 1952 and 1956 (Ercolano 1980, para. 1).

CHAPTER 1

1. The American home front was frequently marked by sacrifice, deprivation, and worry, and access to any and all available news and entertainment media was an important aspect of social life. Comic books were plentiful, affordable, and portable, and their fusion of cartoon art and pulp narratives offered a natural fit for the patriotic concerns and fervor of the day. (For more, see Kimble and Goodnow 2017; Wright 2001.)

2. Known campaign comics include: Herbert Hoover *Picture Life of a Great American* (1928, POTUS); *The Story of James Michael Curley* (c1930, MA); *'Erbie and 'Is Playmates* (1932, POTUS); *Story of Brig-Gen William O'Dwyer, Candidate for Mayor* (1945, NYC); *The Life of James Bledsoe* (1948, AR); Cliff Britton for county tax assessor (1948, unknown); *Story of Elpidio Quirino* (1948, Philippines); *Story of Kinley Ray, Candidate for County Court Clerk* (1948, AR); *The Story of Harry S. Truman* (1948, POTUS); *The Story of Royce Upshaw* (1948, AR); *Bill Alexander Leads the Way to a Better Tomorrow* (1950, OK); *Your Governor Chet Bowles* (1950, CT); *Man Against the People: True Record of A. W. Coolidge* (1950, MA); H. Gahagan Douglas *Right! For United States Senator* (1950, CA); *Support and Elect Tyrrell Krum* (1950, VA); *The Story of Al Loveland* (1950, IA); *The Nation's Number One Senator Scott W. Lucas* (1950, IL); *Senator Brien McMahon Statesman from Connecticut* (c1950, CT); *The Story of Sid McMath* (1950, AR); *The Story of James Roosevelt* (1950, CA); *This is Bill Dodd* (1951, LA); *Thrilling True Life Story of the Governor of Massachusetts* (1952, MA); *Career of a Reactionary in Politics: Life Story of CA Herter* (1952, MA); *Ike's Story* (1952, POTUS); Dwight Eisenhower, *The Choice of a Nation* (1952, POTUS); Dwight Eisenhower, *You Never Had It So Good* (1952, POTUS); Adlai Stevenson, *Man with a Plan* (1952; POTUS); *A Man Named Stevenson* (1952, POTUS); *How the Taft-Hartley Law Protects* (1952, POTUS); *Robert B. Meyner for Governor* (1953, NJ); *Re-Elect America's Number 1 Senator Paul Douglas* (1954, IL); *Elect . . . Howell Your Senator* (1954, NJ); *Forward with Eisenhower Nixon* (1956, POTUS); *Wayne Morse the Man* (1956, OR); *Let's Go! Rowe* (c1957, KY); *J. Millard Tawes for Governor* (1958, MD); *Elect Harrison A. Williams U.S. Senator* (1958,

NJ); *Alabama Needs John Patterson for Governor* (1959, AL); *Patterson for Alabama* (c1959, AL); *The Story of Thorn Lord* (1960, NJ); *Alford in Action in Arkansas* (1962, AR); *Sam Boyce* (1962, unknown); *In Good Hands with the Rockefeller Team* (1962, NY); *You Need Rockefeller and Javits* (1962, NY); *Morgenthau Man of Action for Governor* (c. 1962, NY); *Alabama Needs the Little Judge George Wallace for Big Job* (1962, AL); *Our Friend "Ken" Keating* (1964, NY); *Richard B. "Dick" Adkisson* (1966, AR); *Maurice Britt, A Man of Action* (1966, AR); *Milas Hale for county prosecutor* (1966, AR); *Harry Thyng for U.S. Senator!* (1966, NH); *You'll Be the Winner with William Winter* (c1966, unknown); *Cranking Up the Old Machine* (1968, AR); *The Brewer Story* (1970, AL); *Jim Guy Tucker* (1972, unknown); *It's Time for Bagwell* (unknown, MI); *Des Berry The Man Who Beat Hoffa* (unknown, TX); *It's Time for Bryant* (unknown, FL); *Elect David Clark, Democratic Candidate for Congress* (unknown); *Bud Dickison, For One United Sunshine State* (unknown, FL); *Let's Get Things Done for Kansas* (unknown, KS); *Elect Robert F. Ellsworth to the US Congress* (unknown, KS); *Fighting Lawyer* (unknown, NY); *Richard Hughes for Governor of New Jersey* (unknown, NJ); *The Truth on Hume, At Last!* (unknown); *Louisiana Needs Chep Morrison* (unknown, LA); Dennis Roberts, *The Man Who's Done the Most for Rhode Island* (unknown, RI); and Jim Trimble, *Pioneers of Power for the Farm* (unknown). Government-produced biographies for propaganda purposes include: *The Life Story of Franklin Delano Roosevelt* (c. 1941); *John F. Kennedy: The President of the United* States (c. 1963); and *John F. Kennedy: New U.S. President* (1961).

CHAPTER 2

1. A 2012–13 storyline in *Life with Archie* similarly pits the idealism of youth and grassroots campaigning against politics as usual when Kevin Keller decides to run for the Senate to tackle gun control after his partner, Clay, is shot during a robbery. Keller, a veteran, describes campaigning as more brutal than combat when his opponent, the former governor, starts attacking him. Likewise, the 2019–20 story arc in *Archie: The Married Life—10th Anniversary* raised issues of community service versus personal glory in politics, offering some commentary on negative campaigning, when characters Moose Mason, Cheryl Blossom, and Betty Cooper face off in a congressional campaign for different reasons.

2. HUAC is also a passing plot point in DC's *Doomsday Clock* #7 (2018), when Doctor Manhattan, one of the "Watchmen" or superheroes, recalls various events, including testifying before HUAC, in which he inadvertently changed history.

3. The Civil War story arc was certainly not the first time the Avengers, Earth's Mightiest Heroes, had to face Congress, however. In the "Heart of Stone" story, *The Avengers* #190, in 1979 government liaison Peter Gyrich grows frustrated with roster changes to the Avengers so he triggers a Senate investigation as to the team's national security risk in hopes that the special hearing will disband the Avengers initiative, though in this instance it is Gyrich's credibility rather than the superheroes' that is quickly compromised.

4. This creates a timeline fifteen years ahead of the 1969 raid that sparked the Stonewall riots igniting the gay rights movement.

CHAPTER 3

1. Johnson's "Great Society" initiatives involved a series of legislation designed to expand civil rights, education, the arts, urban and rural development, public services, Medicare and Medicaid, and economic opportunity.

2. Another cautionary tale of the superheroic, or excessively empowered, presidency is found in *The Authority*. The hero Hawksmoor and the Authority superteam save America from enemy agents (specifically the Republicans), but in their efforts to create a utopic new world order they "forgot to factor in the human need for *free will*," earning the ire of the people under the revolutionary leadership of "patriotic" post-humans called Paul Revere and the Sons of Liberty (Brubaker and Nguyen 2019).

3. The 2011 graphic novel *Disney's Darkwing Duck: Campaign Carnage* offered a similar message. When masked crime-fighter Darkwing ran for city mayor, the media wondered, "Can the caped candidate convince voters that his role as the 'terror that flaps in the *night*' won't *distract* him from his duties during the *day* as St. Canard's mayor?" (Brill and Silvani 2011, n.p.).

CHAPTER 5

1. For example: Dan O'Neill's (1988) *Farewell to the Gipper* (1988, Eclipse Books), Doug Marlette's (1993, Times Books) *Faux Bubba*, Garry Trudeau's (2005) *Duke 2000: Whatever It Takes* (2005, Andrews McMeel Publishing), and Shannon Wheeler's *Sh*t My President Says: The Illustrated Tweets of Donald Trump* (2017, TopShelf Productions).

CHAPTER 6

1. *Slate* also developed a series of comic strips on the "Whistle Blower" whose report instigated impeachment inquiries on Donald Trump, called *The Whistler*, and on the impeachment proceedings themselves, called *Impeachment Article One*. Both were available online, and the impeachment series was picked up by at least one newspaper.

CHAPTER 7

1. No authorship or publication information about this title is known.

2. Unfortunately, the issue was not released for sale until after Election Day, but the message was broadcast through other media sources, such as the *Los Angeles Times*, *The Geekiary*, *Newsarama*, and *The Mary Sue*. Following Donald Trump's win on Election Day and his 2017 "Muslim ban," the image of Ms. Marvel also became a protest icon opposing the election and policies of Trump (Romano 2017).

3. A decade later, creator Howard Chaykin also imagined foreign interference in US elections. The 1983–89 series *American Flagg* described a Russian satellite launched into orbit for the express purpose of disrupting the 1996 US presidential election.

4. The same sentiment was put forth in the animated prime-time television series *The Simpsons* in 1996. In a short feature within the show's annual Halloween special, two space aliens use bioduplication to replace candidates Bill Clinton and Bob Dole. When exposed they, ironically, declare, "What are you going to do about it? It's a two-party system, you have to vote for one of us!" When one citizen argues that he will vote for a third-party candidate, the aliens laugh at him for throwing away his vote ("Treehouse of Horror VII"). *Vote Loki* likewise pointed to how a popular third-party candidate can split the vote in a way that favors one of the major party candidates that otherwise might not have won. *Army of Darkness: Election Special* also has a line that says, "Typical third party candidate. Waste of a good vote" (Serrano and Galindo 2016).

5. First published in November 2019, Levantine Films had by April 2020 acquired the rights to develop a television adaptation of *Killadelphia* (Dominguez 2020).

6. A demon-possessed president also appears in Marvel's 1986 *Elektra: Assassin*, Ken Wind, whose evilness, for some reason, smells like rotten mayonnaise.

CHAPTER 8

1. It was also reconfigured in a 1980 animated compilation in which Betty is told by her father, in no uncertain terms, that women simply are not as good or as capable as men in areas like politics and sports.

2. Found at https://picclick.com/Lux-Soap-Ad-Dixie-In-Hollywood-Featuring-Ruby-143193721703.html and https://picclick.com/Lux-Soap-Ad-Peggy-Lux-For-President-143193720297.html.

3. AOC was also featured in a comic series from Keenspot, *The Superior AOC*, a Spider-Man/Spider-Gwen parody. Issue #1 in 2019 and issue #2 in 2020 picked on AOC's Twitter fame and criticized her support of big government spending, but they also presented an unflattering image of Fox News and reimagined Senator Ted Kennedy as a Jedi Master, making them parodies of politics rather than political parodies. AOC's gender is mocked, however, by presenting her as a little girl (she is dressed like Dorothy from *The Wizard of Oz* in #2) and by replacing Spider-Man's tingling "Spidey-sense" with the Superior AOC getting a tingling in her vagina, a reference that is also found in her role as foe to an evil Trump doppelganger in *The Donald Who Laughs*, in which she is called "Sex Spider" (Barron, Remulac, and Cortes 2019).

4. The name Olivia Marsdin is presumably a nod to the women who inspired William Moulton Marston's creation of Wonder Woman: Olive Byrne and Elizabeth Marston. In turn, this is a nod to the Lynda Carter's portrayal of Wonder Woman in the 1970s.

5. The Jinxworld series *United States vs. Murder Inc.* (2019, DC Comics) also features an unruly Latina president: Erica Sanchez, the fifth woman president and first Mexican American president, who goes toe-to-toe with mafia families and is assassinated because of it.

6. LGBTQAIPD stands variably for: Lesbian, Gay/Genderqueer/Genderfluid/Gendercreative, Bisexual, Trans/Transgender/Two-spirited, Queer/Questioning, Asexual/Androgynous, Intersex, Pansexual/Panromantic, Demisexual.

7. Another telling example of the political woman-as-puppet is found in the 2019 *Talk Bernie to Me! The Bernie Sanders Special & AOC Surprise* comic book, from Devil's Due Comics. In a story entitled "The Will of the People," the freshman congresswomen known as the Squad (Alexandria Ocasio-Cortez, Ilhan Omar, Ayanna Pressley, and Rashida Tlaib) are imagined as superheroes fighting for justice. When the Republicans take justice out, AOC calls out for Sanders to come to their rescue, thus giving an older, White, male power over younger, ethnic females, reinforcing women at the periphery of politics (Jackson 2019).

CHAPTER 9

1. The Vertigo series *iZombie* both reinforced zombie-as-Other and disrupted the White-patriarchal presidency with its "Dead Presidents" government task force. Led by a wheelchair-bound zombie Lincoln, the other monstrous members of the group are Kennedy in the body of a Black woman, Nixon in the body of a Brown man, Madison in the body of a transgender woman, and Ford without a body at all.

2. Perhaps the least racially stereotyped image of Obama in satirical comics was found in *Blood Feud!* (2014, Parody Brothers), which envisions the Obamas and Clintons as characters in George R. R. Martin's very White sword-and-sorcery fantasy series *Game of Thrones*, with Obama in the role of Robert Baratheon.

3. Obamies were likewise found in the time-warping story *The Adventures of Barry & Joe* with an illustration of the "Night of Living Democrats" (Reid 2019, 86).

4. *Seinen manga* are stories targeted toward young adult men and are frequently published in weekly Japanese manga magazines which collect stories of various genres, such as action, science-fiction, fantasy, comedy, relationships, sports, or politics.

CHAPTER 10

1. We also find the politics of fear in *Smallville*, the WB/CW series about Clark Kent before he becomes Superman. In season 7, episode 18, "Apocalypse" (2008), Clark is shown a world in which he never came to Earth (ala *It's Wonderful Life*). In this alternate reality, Lex Luthor is president, much to the amazement of Clark. His pal, news photographer Jimmy Olsen, explains, "Hey, he played the fear card, got the most votes. End of civics class."

2. Such conditions are reflected in the support Donald Trump received in the 2016 election, particularly among American farmers whose frustrations with policies impacting the agricultural industry, economic hardships, and a sense of alienation from many cultural and social reforms relating to race and gender were captured in the angry rhetoric of Trump (Philpott 2016).

CHAPTER 11

1. Meanwhile, in Image Comics' 2014 *Punks: The Comic*, Lincoln was portrayed as a living-dead president with a dry wit, presently sharing a house with a humanoid skull, dog, and fist. The alternative-style comic was absurdist comedy that tended toward sophomoric humor but nonetheless incorporated historical facts and characterizations into the figure of "Abe."

2. The series built on several key historical aspects of Jekyll Island: in 1886, it was purchased by the newly formed exclusive, elite Jekyll Island Club. Two years later, the club officially opened its doors and became a retreat for America's wealthiest families. In 1910, Senator Nelson Aldrich, under the cover of night, took a group of anonymous American financial leaders to Jekyll Island to conceptualize a federal banking system ("Storied History").

3. Although the series mostly avoided presidential politics, it did take up the racial commentary established by Romero when his sole surviving protagonist, a Black man, was shot by local police who assumed he was a zombie based on his Otherness. In the comic, initial reports of undead uprisings in rural Pennsylvania were blamed on Black militants, and armed citizens wrongfully killed a man trying to get home to his family. *Night of the Living Dead* reflected the climate of police violence against Blacks and civil rights protestors during the 1960s, and *Z-Men*, with its zombie plague and incompetent law enforcement, reflected the "plague of police shootings" against Black communities in the twenty-first century (Holmes 2016, headline).

4. A similar idea is also expressed in the non-science-fiction Kennedy conspiracy comic *The Red Diaries*. As efforts to get to the truth were repeatedly foiled, one spook/spy explained, "It's the *One World Order*. It transcends *nationalities . . . religion . . .* or *family*. It's a world upon *itself* and most of us are *nothing* to them" (Reed, Campbell, Jones, and Shuput 1997, n.p.).

POSTSCRIPT

1. A few of the more prominent tiles in this vein include: *2020 Visions* (1997), *28 Days Later* (2009), *Baltimore* (2007), *The Beauty* (2015), *Black Hole* (1995), *The Bunker* (2013), *Crossed* (2008), *DCeased* (2019), *Eden: It's An Endless World* (1998), *The Empty Man* (2014), *Eugenic* (2017), *Extinction Parade* (2013), *Jeremiah* (1979), *Laid Waste* (2016), *Our Plague Year* (2020), *Pandemica* (2019), *Remote* (2015), *Scooby Apocalypse* (2016), *The Stand* (2008), *The Strain* (2011), *Sweet Tooth* (2009), *Tomorrow* (2020), *Trillium* (2013), *Undiscovered Country* (2019), *The Walking Dead* (2003), *The Wilds* (2019), *Y: The Last Man* (2002), *Z-Men* (2015), and *Zombie Plague: The Day from Hell* (2015). Additionally, viral contagions are found throughout the DC and Marvel superhero universes, as in the Batman "Contagion" (1996) and "Legacy" story arcs (1996), the Spider-Man "Spider-Island" story arc (2011), the "Legacy Virus" of the X-Men franchise (1993), and the "Amazo Virus" of the Justice League franchise (2014).

WORKS CITED

9/11 Commission. 2004. *The 9/11 Commission Report*. Washington, DC: National Commission on Terrorist Attacks Upon the United States. Accessed June 11, 2019. https://www.9-11commission.gov/report/911Report.pdf.
Abad-Santos, Alex. 2017. "The Creators of the Flintstones Comic on Bringing Existential Dread to Bedrock." *Vox.com*, April 6. Accessed January 26, 2019. https://www.vox.com/culture/2017/3/22/15000062/flintstones-comic-interview-russell-pugh.
Abraham, Linus. 2009. "Effectiveness of Cartoons as a Uniquely Visual Medium for Orienting Social Issues." *Journalism and Communication Monographs* 11 (2): 117–65.
Adams, Richard, and Erin McCann. 2012. "America: Elect! The Action-Packed Journey to US Election Day in Graphic Novel Form." *Guardian*, November 6. Accessed June 14, 2019. https://www.theguardian.com/world/interactive/2012/nov/06/america-elect-graphic-novel.
Adorno, Theodor W. 1982. "Freudian Theory and the Pattern of Fascist Propaganda." In *The Essential Frankfurt School Reader*, new edition, edited by Andrew Arato and Eike Gebhardt, 118–37. London: Bloomsbury Academic.
Aguilar, Matthew. 2019. "AOC Comic Creators Unveil New Cover Image After Getting Cease and Desist from DC Comics." *ComicBook*, June 5. Accessed July 1, 2019. https://comicbook.com/dc/2019/06/05/aoc-comic-new-cover-image-after-cease-desist-dc-comics/.
Ahrens, Jörn. 2019. "Joe Sacco and the Quest for Documentation in Comics." *ImageTexT* 11 (1): http://imagetext.english.ufl.edu/archives/v11_1/ahrens/.
Alaniz, José. 2012. "Death, Bereavement, and the Superhero Funeral." In *The Ages of Superman: Essays on the Man of Steel in Changing Times*, edited by Joseph J. Darowski, 177–91. Jefferson, NC: McFarland. Kindle edition.
Aldama, Frederick Luis. 2017. *Latinx Superheroes in Mainstream Comics*. Tucson: University of Arizona Press. Kindle edition.
Aloi, Elizabeth. 2004. "Note: Thirty-Five Years After the 26th Amendment and Still Disenfranchised: Current Controversies in Student Voting." *National Black Law Journal* 18: 283–303.
Alverson, Brigid. 2016. "'Nanjing' and 'Prez' Win Reuben Awards." *CBR.com*, June 1. Accessed January 26, 2019. https://www.cbr.com/nanjing-and-prez-win-reuben-awards/.
Anderegg, David. 2007. *Nerds: Who They Are and Why We Need More of Them*. Los Angeles: Tardier.
Anderson, Karrin Vasby. 1999. "'Rhymes with Rich': 'Bitch' as a Tool of Containment in Contemporary American Politics." *Rhetoric & Public Affairs* 2 (4): 599–623.
Anderson, Karrin Vasby, and Kristina Horn Sheeler. 2005. *Governing Codes: Gender, Metaphor, and Political Identity*. Lanham, MD: Lexington Books.
Antononoka, Olga. 2016. "Blonde is the New Japanese: Transcending Race in *Shōjo Manga*." *Mutual Images* 1 (summer): 22–46.

Arenas, Jorge. 2017. "New Right Wing Comic Publisher Aims to Replace Marvel and DC." *Bounding into Comics*, October 24. Accessed February 22, 2020. https://boundingintocomics.com/2017/10/24/new-right-wing-comic-publisher-aims-replace-marvel-dc/.

Arnold, Gordon B. 2008. *Conspiracy Theory in Film, Television, and Politics*. Westport, CT: Praeger. Kindle edition.

Arnold, Monroe, and Rich Buckler. 1986. "Back to Zero!" *Reagan's Raiders* 1, no. 1. Brooklyn: Solson Publications.

Aronstein, A-J. 2011. "Recovery in Pieces: A Study of the Literature of 9/11." *The Millions*, September 10. Accessed June 11, 2019. https://themillions.com/2011/09/recovery-in-pieces-a-study-of-the-literature-of-911.html.

Arrant, Chris. 2019. "MARK WAID Asks Court to Dismiss RICHARD C. MEYER Lawsuit After ANTARCTIC PRESS' Disposition." *Newsarama*, April 23. Accessed February 22, 2020. https://www.newsarama.com/44896-waid-asks-court-again-to-dismiss-meyer-lawsuit-after-antartic-press-deposition.html.

Arrant, Chris. 2009. "Barack the Barbarian? Behind the Latest Obama Comic." *Newsarama*, May 12. Accessed July 6, 2019. https://www.newsarama.com/2868-barack-the-barbarian-behind-the-latest-obama-comic.html.

Arrant, Chris. 2015. "What if Politicians Were REALLY Evil? CITIZEN JACK Is." *Newsarama*, October 8. Accessed October 22, 2018. https://www.newsarama.com/26231-what-if-politicians-were-really-evil-citizen-jack-is.html.

Arrow. "The Candidate." 2015. Directed by John Behring. Burbank, CA: Warner Bros. Entertainment, 2016.

Arterton, F. Christopher. 1974. "The Impact of Watergate on Children's Attitudes Toward Political Authority." *Political Science Quarterly* 89 (2): 269–88.

Arterton, F. Christopher. 1975. "Watergate and Children's Attitudes Toward Political Authority Revisited." *Political Science Quarterly* 90 (3): 477–96.

Arts. 2019. "Superpowers that Be: Seven Politicians Who Appeared in Comics." BBC, February 28. Accessed June 30, 2019. https://www.bbc.co.uk/programmes/articles/2s43ByttW1qcJYRk2ZYmVRg/superpowers-that-be-seven-politicians-who-appeared-in-comics.

Ashkenas, Jeremy, Hannah Fairfield, Josh Keller, and Paul Volpe. 2014. "7 Key Points from the C.I.A. Torture Report." *New York Times*, December 9. Accessed June 22, 2019. https://www.nytimes.com/interactive/2014/12/09/world/cia-torture-report-key-points.html.

Asselin, Janelle. 2015. "'Symbolia' Comics Magazine Calls it Quits After Current Issue." *Comics Alliance*, March 16. Accessed June 14, 2019. https://comicsalliance.com/symbolia-comics-magazine-calls-it-quits-after-current-issue/.

Associated Press et al. 2018. "The Faces of Change in the Midterm Elections." *New York Times*, November 5. Accessed February 23, 2020. https://www.nytimes.com/interactive/2018/10/31/us/politics/midterm-election-candidates-diversity.html.

Auerbach, David. 2016. "The Bernie Bubble." *Slate*, February 16. Accessed October 26, 2018. https://slate.com/technology/2016/02/the-bernie-sanders-campaign-owes-a-lot-to-social-media.html.

Aupers, Stef. 2012. "'Trust No One': Modernization, Paranoia and Conspiracy Culture." *European Journal of Communication* 27 (1): 22–34.

The Avengers. 2012. Blu-ray. Directed by Joss Whedon. Burbank, CA: Marvel Studios, 2012.

Ayres, Andrea. 2018. "How a Graphic Novel 'Welcome to the New World' Won a Pulitzer." *The Beat*, April 19. Accessed June 22, 2019. https://www.comicsbeat.com/how-a-graphic-novel-welcome-to-the-new-world-won-a-pulitzer/.

Azzarello, Brian, and Lee Bernejo. 2010. *Luthor*. New York: DC Comics. Kindle edition.
Baelo-Allué, Sonia. 2011. "The Depiction of 9/11 in Literature: The Role of Images and Intermedial References." *Radical History Review* 111: 184–93.
Bailey, Neal, and Ryan Howe. 2009. *Female Force: Caroline Kennedy* #1. USA: BlueWater Comics.
Bailey, Neal, and Joshua LaBelle. 2009. *Female Force: Michelle Obama*. USA: Bluewater Comics.
Baker, Kaysee, and Arthur A. Raney. 2007. "Equally Super?: Gender-Role Stereotyping of Superheroes in Children's Animated Programs." *Mass Communications & Society* 10 (1): 25–41.
Balogun. 2012. "The League of Extraordinary Black People: African & African-American Steampunk!" *Chronicles of Harriet*, April 22. Accessed February 19, 2017. https://chroniclesofharriet.com/2012/04/22/the-league-of-extraordinary-black-people-african-african-american-steampunk/.
Balz, Dan, and Emily Guskin. 2016. "In Every State, Pessimism about Trump, Clinton and the Impact of the Election." *Washington Post*, September 7. Accessed October 9, 2016. https://www.washingtonpost.com/politics/in-every-state-pessimism-about-trump-clinton-and-the-impact-of-the-election/2016/09/06/ecff15d0-739a-11e6-b786-19d0cb1ed06c_story.html.
Barber, James David. 1992. *The Presidential Character: Predicting Performance in the White House*, fourth edition. Upper Saddle River, NJ: Prentice Hall.
Barkun, Michael. 2003. *A Culture of Conspiracy: Apocalyptic Visions in Contemporary America*. Berkeley: University of California Press.
Barnes, Rodney, Jason Shawn Alaxender, and Luis NCT. 2020. *Killadelphia—Sins of the Father, Part III*. Portland, OR: Image Comics.
Baron, Neil. 2020. "Could Trump Be Criminally Liable for his Deadly Mishandling of Coronavirus?" *Newsweek*, April 16, 2020. Accessed May 29, 2020. https://www.newsweek.com/could-trump-criminally-liable-his-deadly-mishandling-coronavirus-opinion-1498146.
Barr, Marleen S. 1993. *Lost in Space: Probing Feminist Science Fiction and Beyond*. Chapel Hill: University of North Carolina Press.
Barrington, Greg, and Dom Loise. 1994. *Capital Capers Presents: The Fanatic Four*. Park Ridge, IL: BLT Studios.
Barron, John, and Shawn Remulac. 2017. *Trump's Titans*. Apple Valley, CA: Keenspot.
Barron, John, Shawn Remulac, and Macarena Cortes. 2019. *The Donald Who Laughs*. Apple Valley, CA: Keenspot.
Beard, Jim, and Kurt Belcher. 2018. *Political Power: Herman Cain*. USA: BlueWater Comics.
Bebber, Brett. 2014. "*Till Death Us Do Part*: Political Satire and Social Realism in the 1960s and 1970s." *Historical Journal of Film, Radio and Television* 34 (2): 253–74.
Beck, Julie, and Caroline Kitchener. 2018. "Early Signs of a Youth Wave." *Atlantic*, November 6. Accessed February 23, 2020. https://www.theatlantic.com/politics/archive/2018/11/youth-turnout-midterm-2018/575092/.
Beedle, Tim. 2016. "Hanna-Barbera Beyond: Flintstones, Scooby and more Are Getting Comic Book Reimaginings." *DC Comics*, January 28. Accessed May 3, 2018. https://www.dccomics.com/blog/2016/01/28/hanna-barbera-beyond-flintstones-scooby-and-more-are-getting-comic-book-reimaginings.
Benedict, Ruth. 1946/2005. *The Chrysanthemum and the Sword: Patterns of Japanese Culture*. Boston, MA: Mariner.
Bennett, David. 1985. "Parody, Postmodernism, and the Politics of Reading." *Critical Quarterly* 27 (4): 27–43.
Bennett, W. Lance. 2007. "Relief in Hard Times: A Defense of Jon Stewart's Comedy in an Age of Cynicism." *Critical Studies in Media Communication* 24 (3): 278–83.

Bennett, W. Lance, and David L. Paletz, eds. 1994. *Taken by Storm: The Media, Public Opinion, and U.S. Foreign Policy in the Gulf War*. Chicago: University of Chicago Press.

Bensam, Richard. 2011. "Obsolete Models a Specialty: An Introduction." In *Minutes to Midnight: Twelve Essays on* Watchmen, edited by Richard Bensam, loc. 57–171. Edwardsville, IL: Sequart Research & Literacy Organization. Kindle edition.

Bensen, Nolan. 2015. "The Irreverence of THE MANHATTAN PROJECTS." *Comicverse*, December 1. Accessed August 10, 2019. https://comicsverse.com/the-irreverence-of-the-manhattan-projects-3/.

Berlatsky, Noah. 2015. *Wonder Woman: Bondage and Feminism in the Marston/Peter Comics, 1941–1948*. New Brunswick, NJ: Rutgers University Press.

Berlatsky, Noah. 2018. "The Comicsgate Movement Isn't Defending Free Speech. It's Suppressing It." *Washington Post*, September 13. Accessed February 22, 2020. https://www.washingtonpost.com/outlook/2018/09/13/comicsgate-movement-isnt-defending-free-speech-its-suppressing-it/.

Berlatsky, Noah. 2009. "The Japanese Superman." *The Hooded Utilitarian*, April 7. Accessed July 10, 2019. https://www.hoodedutilitarian.com/2009/04/the-japanese-superman/.

Bertetti, Paolo. 2014. "*Conan the Barbarian*: Transmedia Adventures of a Pulp Hero." In *Transmedia Archaeology*, edited by Carlos Scolari, Paolo Bertetti, and Matthew Freeman, 15–38. New York: Palgrave Macmillan.

Berthiaume, Judy. 2015. "The Politics of Pop Culture in Presidential Campaigns." *University of Wisconsin-Eau Claire*, November 30. Accessed May 12, 2018. https://www.uwec.edu/news/news/the-politics-of-pop-culture-in-presidential-campaigns-924/.

Beyerstein, Lindsay, and Joyce Rice. 2013. "Third Party Politics in the United States: An Eclectic Timeline." *Symbolia Magazine*, February. Accessed June 14, 2019. https://www.facebook.com/SymboliaMag/photos/a.517588064959805/517588284959783/?type=3&theater.

Bishop, Kyle. 2006. "Raising the Dead: Unearthing the Nonliterary Origins of Zombie Cinema." *Journal of Popular Film and Television* 34 (4): 196–205.

Black, James Eric (Jay). 2010. "'Amoozin' but Confoozin': Comic Strips as a Voice of Dissent in the 1950s." *ETC: A Review of General Semantics* 66 (4): 460–77.

Black, James Eric. 2016. *Walt Kelly and* Pogo: *The Art of the Political Swamp*. Jefferson, NC: McFarland. Kindle edition.

Black, Rebecca W. 2009. "Online Fan Fiction, Global Identities, and Imagination." *Research in the Teaching of English* 43 (4): 397–425.

Bontekoe, Ronald. 1996. *Dimensions of the Hermeneutic Circle*. Atlantic Highlands, NJ: Humanities Press.

Books. 2017. "The Senate Torture Report in Graphic-Novel Form." *Slate*, March 6. Accessed June 9, 2019. https://slate.com/culture/2017/03/a-graphic-novel-adaptation-of-the-senate-torture-report.html.

BOOT. 2016. "Golden Age Political Comic Books—No Modern Politics." *CGC* (forum), March 20. Accessed June 1, 2018. https://www.cgccomics.com/boards/topic/388406-golden-age-political-comic-books-no-modern-politics/.

Booth, Wayne C. 1974. *A Rhetoric of Irony*. Chicago: University of Chicago Press.

Borchers, Callum. 2018. "Trump Tweets Another Anti-CNN Cartoon—This One by the Same Artist Who Drew Clinton in Blackface." *Boston Globe*, February 18. Accessed February 22, 2018. https://www.bostonglobe.com/news/politics/2018/02/18/trump-tweets-another-anti-cnn-cartoon-this-one-same-artist-who-drew-clinton-blackface/aHywWmXHMLvKoGqSO4V8KP/story.html.

Bormann, Ernest G., Jolene Koester, and Janet Bennett. 1978. "Political Cartoons and Salient Rhetorical Fantasies: An Empirical Analysis of the '76 Presidential Campaign." *Communication Monographs* 45 (4): 317–29.

Borofsky, Scot, ed. 2003. "Past Masters: Picasso Speaks, 1923." *Gallery Walk* (blog). Accessed August 22, 2019. https://www.gallerywalk.org/PM_Picasso.html

Bowers, Chad, and Jim Towe. 2017. "Youngblood Reborn: Chapter 1." *Youngblood* #1. Portland, OR: Image Comics.

Bowser, Rachel A., and Brian Croxall. 2010. "Introduction: Industrial Evolution." *Neo-Victorian Studies* 3 (1): 1–45.

Boxer, Sarah. 2018. "Why Is Donald Trump So Hard to Caricature?" *Atlantic*, April. Accessed June 26, 2018. https://www.theatlantic.com/magazine/archive/2018/04/donald-trump-caricature/554069/.

Boyer, Lauren. 2016. "Why is Donald Trump Orange?" *US News*, January 14. Accessed October 1, 2018. https://www.usnews.com/news/articles/2016-01-14/why-is-donald-trump-orange.

Boym, Svetlana. 2001. *The Future of Nostalgia*. New York: Basic Books. Kindle edition.

Branham, R. Bracht. 1994. "Defacing the Currency: Diogenes' Rhetoric and the *Invention* of Cynicism." *Arethusa* 27 (3): 329–59.

Brantner, Cornelia, and Katharina Lobinger. 2014. "Campaign Comics: The Use of Comic Books for Strategic Political Communication." *International Journal of Communication* 8: 248–74.

Brayton, Sean. 2008. "'Mexican' Labor in the Hollywood Imaginary." *International Journal of Cultural Studies* 11 (4): 459–76.

Brewer, Paul R., and Xiaoxia Cao. 2006. "Candidate Appearances on Soft News Shows and Public Knowledge about Primary Campaigns." *Journal of Broadcasting and Electronic Media* 50 (1): 18–35.

Brill, Ian, James Silvani, Lisa Moore, and Deron Bennett. 2011. "Campaign Carnage." *Darkwing Duck Annual*. Los Angeles, CA: KABOOM!

Brock, Maria. 2016. "Fantastic Mr. President: The Hyperrealities of Putin and Trump." *Eurocrisis in the Press*. September 9. Accessed November 4, 2017. http://blogs.lse.ac.uk/eurocrisispress/2016/09/09/fantastic-mr-president-the-hyperrealities-of-putin-and-trump/.

Brogan, Jacob. 2017. "Yabba Dabba Depressing." *Slate*, April 12. Accessed January 26, 2019. https://slate.com/culture/2017/04/mark-russell-and-steve-pughs-comic-book-reboot-of-the-flintstones-reviewed.html.

Brooker, Will. 2013. "We Could Be Heroes." In *What is a Superhero?*, edited by Robin S. Rosenberg and Peter Coogan, loc. 435–591. New York: Oxford University Press. Kindle edition.

Brooks, James F. 2017. "Editor's Corner: Monumental Monuments." *Public Historian*, Special Virtual Issue: Monuments, Memory, Politics, and Our Publics. Accessed August 12, 2019. https://tph.ucpress.edu/content/special-virtual-issue-monuments-memory-politics-and-our-publics.

Brown, Clyde, and Gayle K. Pluta Brown. 2004. "'Moo U' and the 26th Amendment: Registering for Peace and Voting for Responsive City Government." *Peace & Change* 29 (1): 48–80.

Brown, Jeffrey A. 2011a. *Dangerous Curves: Action Heroines, Gender, Fetishism, and Popular Culture*. Jackson: University Press of Mississippi. Kindle edition.

Brown, Jeffrey A. 2011b. "Supermoms? Maternity and Monstrous-Feminine in Superhero Comics." *Journal of Graphic Novels and Comics* 2 (1): 77–87.

Brownie, Barbara, and Danny Graydon. 2015. *The Superhero Costume: Identity and Disguise in Fact and Fiction*. New York: Bloomsbury Publishing. Kindle edition.

Brubaker, Ed, and Dustin Nguyen. 2019. *The Authority*. Burbank, CA: DC Comics.

Brubaker, Ed, and Eric Shanower. 2016. "Smells Like Teen President." In *Prez: The First Teen President*, edited by Liz Erickson, 158–214. Burbank, CA: DC Comics.

Brueck, Hillary. 2019. "Alexandria Ocasio-Cortez Now Has Her Own Wonder Woman-Style Comic Book Cover That's Being Auctioned Off for Over $300 Online, and DC Comics Isn't Happy About It." *Insider*, May 19. Accessed July 1, 2019. https://www.insider.com/alexandria-ocasio-cortez-wonder-woman-comic-cover-upsets-dc-comics-2019-5.

Bucholtz, Mary. 1999. "You Da Man: Narrating the Racial Other in the Production of White Masculinity." *Journal of Sociolinguistics* 3/4: 443–60.

Bucholtz, Mary. 2009. "Styles and Stereotypes: Laotian American Girls' Linguistic Negotiation of Identity." In *Beyond Yellow English: Toward a Linguistic Anthropology of Asian Pacific America*, edited by Angela Reyes and Adrienne Lo, 21–42. New York: Oxford University Press.

Bulgozdi, Imola. 2013. "'Barbarian Heroing' and Its Parody: New Perspectives on Masculinity." In *Conan Meets the Academy: Multidisciplinary Essays on the Enduring Barbarian*, edited by Jonas Prida, 193–212. Jefferson, NC: McFarland. Kindle edition.

Bump, Philip. 2013. "How to Spot the Reptilians Running the U.S. Government." *Atlantic*, October 31. Accessed February 1, 2019. https://www.theatlantic.com/national/archive/2013/10/how-spot-reptilians-runing-us-government/354496/.

Bunn, Geoffrey C. 1997. "The Lie Detector, Wonder Woman and Liberty: The Life and Work of William Moulton Marston." *History of the Human Sciences* 10 (1): 91–119.

Burke, Cindy, and Sharon R. Mazzarella. 2008. "'A Slightly New Shade of Lipstick': Gendered Mediation in Internet News Stories." *Women's Studies in Communication* 31 (3): 395–418.

Burke, Kenneth. 1945. *A Grammar of Motives*. Berkeley: University of California Press.

Burke, Kenneth. 1984. *Attitudes Toward History*. Berkeley: University of California Press.

Burlingame, Russ. 2018. "'Arrow': Oliver Queen SPOILERS in 'Fundamentals.'" *Comicbook*, April 12. Accessed March 24, 2019. https://comicbook.com/dc/2018/04/13/arrow-oliver-queen-impeached-in-fundamentals/.

Burns, Lisa M. 2008. *First Ladies and Fourth Estate: Press Framing of Presidential Wives*. DeKalb: Northern Illinois University Press.

Bush, Larry. 2013. "More Than Words: Rhetorical Constructs in American Political Cartoons." *Studies in American Humor* 3 (27): 63–91.

Busse, Kristina. 2013. "Geek Hierarchies, Boundary Policing, and the Gendering of the Good Fan." *Journal of Audience & Reception Studies* 10 (1): 73–91.

Bussel, Rachel Kramer. 2019a. "Why Artist Barbara Slate Made a Graphic Novel Edition of the Mueller Report." *Forbes*, June 26. Accessed June 26, 2019. https://www.forbes.com/sites/rachelkramerbussel/2019/06/26/why-artist-barbara-slate-made-a-graphic-novel-edition-of-the-mueller-report/#2ea00e2068e6.

Bussel, Rachel Kramer. 2019b. "Comic Book About Alexandria Ocasio-Cotez, Inspired by Her Quoting Alan Moore, Coming Out In May." *Forbes*, February 25. Accessed July 2, 2019. https://www.forbes.com/sites/rachelkramerbussel/2019/02/25/alexandria-ocasio-cortez-comic-book/#373697386cae.

Byers, Dylan. 2015. "Americans' Trust in Media at All-Time Low." *CNN Business*, September 30. Accessed July 19, 2019. https://money.cnn.com/2015/09/30/media/media-trust-americans/index.html.

Callahan, Timothy. 2012. "Wally Wood and 'Barack Hussein Obama.'" *CBR*, October 29. Accessed July 8, 2019. https://www.cbr.com/wally-wood-and-barack-hussein-obama/.

Campbell, Karlyn Kohrs. 1996. "The Rhetorical Presidency: A Two Person Career." In *Beyond the Rhetorical Presidency*, edited by Martin J. Medhurst, 179–95. College Station: Texas A&M University Press.

Cantwell, Christopher, and Patric Reynolds. 2020. *The Mask: I Pledge Allegiance to the Mask #4.* Milwaukie, OR: Dark Horse Comics.

Cappella, Joseph N., and Kathleen Hall Jamieson. 1997. *Spiral of Cynicism: The Press and the Public Good.* New York: Oxford University Press.

Capps, Kriston. 2015. "Rand Paul, Superhero." *Atlantic*, April 23. Accessed June 3, 2018. https://www.theatlantic.com/politics/archive/2015/04/dc-comics/391230/.

Carmon, Irin. 2015. "Donald Trump Draws on Long History of Period Stigma." *MSNBC.com*, August 10. Accessed April 30, 2017. http://www.msnbc.com/msnbc/donald-trump-draws-long-history-period-stigma.

Carpenter, Amanda. 2008. "Mommy Palin's Double Standard." *Glamour*, September 3. Accessed June 30, 2019. https://www.glamour.com/story/mommy-palins-double-standard.

Carpenter, Stanford W. 2013. "Superheroes Need Superior Villains." In *What is a Superhero?*, edited by Robin S. Rosenberg and Peter Coogan, loc. 1812–1933. New York: Oxford University Press. Kindle edition.

Carroll, Susan J. 1994. *Women as Candidates in American Politics*, 2nd edition. Bloomington: Indiana University Press.

Carter, Jeff. 2015. "'The Warren Commission Report' Reveals How Much the JFK Assassination Remains a Mystery." *PopMatters*, February 9. Accessed August 25, 2019. https://www.popmatters.com/189868-the-warren-commission-report-by-dan-mishkin-ernie-colon-and-jerry-dr-2495568674.html.

Carter, Phillip. 2017. "The Big Four Scandals of the Trump Administration." *Slate*, July 11. Accessed November 4, 2017. https://www.slate.com/articles/news_and_politics/politics/2017/07/the_four_big_scandals_of_the_trump_administration.html.

Castaneda, Vera. 2017. "'The Torture Report: A Graphic Adaptation' Illustrates the Grim Reality of CIA Interrogation Techniques Post 9/11." *Los Angeles Times*, November 4. Accessed June 9, 2019. https://www.latimes.com/books/jacketcopy/la-ca-jc-torture-report-graphic-2017 1104-story.html.

Catto, Ed. 2020. "With Further Ado #90: The Prescience of Comic-Con." *Pop Culture Squad*, April 15. Accessed April 15, 2020. https://popculturesquad.com/2020/04/15/with-further-ado-90-the-prescience-of-comic-con/#more-13460.

Cavna, Michael. 2019. "The New York Times Cuts All Political Cartoons, and Cartoonists Are Not Happy." *Washington Post*, June 11. Accessed June 22, 2019. https://www.washingtonpost.com/arts-entertainment/2019/06/11/new-york-times-cuts-all-political-cartoons-cartoonists-are-not-happy/.

CBC. 2020. "Front-Line Workers Get the Superhero Treatment in New Comic Book Cover Series." CBC. May. Accessed May 3, 2020. https://www.cbc.ca/player/play/1732657219577.

CBR staff. 2002. "Fly Like an 'Eagle;' Looking Back on the Political Manga Series." *CBR*, June 5. Accessed July 10, 2019. https://www.cbr.com/fly-like-an-eagle-looking-back-on-the-political-manga-series/.

CBS. 2016. "Sen. Elizabeth Warren: Comic Book Hero?" CBS Boston, April 7. Accessed June 16, 2018. http://boston.cbslocal.com/2016/04/07/elizabeth-warren-comic-book-senator-female-force-storm-entertainment-darren-davis/.

CBS/AP. 2008. "McCain, Obama Crack Jokes at Charity Event." CBS News, October 16. Accessed August 21, 2019. https://www.cbsnews.com/news/mccain-obama-crack-jokes-at-charity-event/.

Ceccarelli, Leah. 1998. "Polysemy: Multiple Meanings in Rhetorical Criticism." *Quarterly Journal of Speech* 84 (4): 395–415.

Chaykin, Howard. 2008. *American Flagg! Definitive Collection Trade Paperback, Volume 1.* Berkeley, CA: Image Comics & Dynamic Forces.

Cherry, Brigid, and Maria Mellins. 2011. "Negotiating the Punk in Steampunk: Subculture, Fashion, and Performative Identity." *Punk & Post Punk* 1 (1): 5–25.

Ching, Albert. 2016. "Donald Trump Cameos in 'Dark Knight III: The Master Race' #3." *Comic Book Resources*, February 24. Accessed September 13, 2016. https://www.cbr.com/donald-trump-cameos-in-dark-knight-iii-the-master-race-3/.

Christopher, Tom. N.d. "Malcolm Ater and the Commercial Comics Company." *Tom Christopher* (blog). Accessed April 11, 2018. http://www.tomchristopher.com/comics2/malcolm-ater-and-the-commercial-comics-company/.

Chun, Rene. 2019. "Scientists Are Trying to Figure Out Why People Are OK with Trump's Endless Supply of Lies." *Los Angeles Magazine*, November 14. Accessed May 3, 2020. https://www.lamag.com/citythinkblog/trump-lies-research/.

Claeys, Gregory. 2010. "The Origins of Dystopia: Wells, Huxley and Orwell." In *The Cambridge Companion to Utopian Literature*, edited by Gregory Claeys, 107–134. New York: Cambridge University Press.

Clark, Travis. 2019. "Martin Scorsese Doubled Down on his Marvel Criticism and Called Movie Theaters 'Amusement Parks.'" *Business Insider*, October 14. Accessed February 22, 2020. https://www.businessinsider.com/director-martin-scorsese-criticized-marvel-movies-movie-theaters-2019-10.

Clarke, Kristen. 2009. "The Obama Factor: The Impact of the 2008 Presidential Election on Future Voting Rights Act Litigation." *Harvard Law & Policy Review* 3: 59–85.

Clements, Kendrick A. 2010. *The Life of Herbert Hoover: Imperfect Visionary, 1918–1928*. New York: Palgrave Macmillan.

Cocarla, Sasha. 2014. "A Love Worth Undying for: Neoliberalism and Queered Sexuality in Warm Bodies." In *Zombies and Sexuality: Essays on Desire and the Living Dead*, edited by Shaka McGlotten and Steve Jones, loc. 923–1310. Jefferson, NC: McFarland.

Cocca, Carolyn. 2014. "Re-booting Barbara Gordon: Oracle, Batgirl, and Feminist Disability Theories." *ImageTexT* 7 (4): http://imagetext.english.ufl.edu/archives/v7_4/cocca/.

Cochrane, Emily. 2018. "When Superheroes Battle Evil, Why Does Washington Always Lose?" *New York Times*, April 13. Accessed June 6, 2018. https://www.nytimes.com/2018/04/13/movies/superhero-movies-washington-dc.html.

Cohen, Karl F. 1997. *Forbidden Animation: Censored Cartoons and Blacklisted Animators in America*. Jefferson, NC: McFarland. Kindle edition.

Coles, Roberta L., and Charles Green. 2010. *The Myth of the Missing Black Father*. New York: Columbia University Press.

Collier, Kevin Scott. 2018. *The Animated Administration of James Norcross a.k.a. Super President*. Burbank, CA: Cartoon Research.

Collins, William Joseph. 1990. "Paths Not Taken: The Development, Structure, and Aesthetics of the Alternative History." Ph.D. diss., University of California–Davis.

Colson, Thomas, and Andrew Dunn. 2020. "Trump Reportedly Tried to Poach German Scientists Working on a Coronavirus Vaccine and Offered Cash so it Would Be Exclusive to the US." *Business Insider*, March 15. Accessed May 29, 2020. https://www.businessinsider.com/trump-administration-tried-to-pay-germans-scientists-for-coronavirus-cure-2020-3.

Connaughton, Stacey L., and Sharon E. Jarvis. 2004. "Invitations for Partisan Identification: Attempts to Court Latino Voters Through Televised Latino-Oriented Political Advertisements, 1984–2000." *Journal of Communication* 54 (1): 38–54.

Conners, Joan L. 2005. "Visual Representations of the 2004 Presidential Campaign: Political Cartoons and Popular Culture References." *American Behavioral Scientist* 49 (3): 479–87.

Conners, Joan L. 2007. "Popular Culture in Political Cartoons: Analyzing Cartoonist Approaches." *PS: Political Science & Politics* XL (2): 261–65.

Connor, Ulla. 1996. *Contrastive Rhetoric: Cross-Cultural Implications of Second-Language Writing*. New York: Cambridge University Press.

Conolly, Kaitlin. 2017. "Political Milestones of Christian A. Herter." *State Library of Massachusetts* (blog), May 15. Accessed June 6, 2018. http://mastatelibrary.blogspot.com/2017/05/.

Contreras, Russell, and Curt Anderson. 2019. "Democrats' Use of Spanish in Debate Evokes Praise, Eye Rolls." *Washington Post*, June 27. Accessed July 8, 2019. https://www.washingtonpost.com/national/democrats-use-of-spanish-in-debate-evokes-praise-eye-rolls/2019/06/27/45126efe-991b-11e9-9a16-dc551ea5a43b_story.html.

Conway, Gerry, Carla Conway, Paul Kupperberg, Rafael Kayanan, and Rodin Rodriguez. 1984. "Spelldance." *The Fury of Firestorm* #27. New York: DC Comics.

Conway, Gerry, Rafael Kayanan, and Rodin Rodriguez. 1984. "Give Me Liberty. Give Me Death." *The Fury of Firestorm* #26. New York: DC Comics.

Coody, Elizabeth. 2019. "Wonder Woman as Icon." Paper presented at Page 23 Literary Conference, Denver Pop Culture Con, Denver, Colorado. June 1.

Coogan, Peter. 2013. "The Hero Defines the Genre, the Genre Defines the Hero." In *What is a Superhero?*, edited by Robin S. Rosenberg and Peter Coogan, loc. 243–433. New York: Oxford University Press. Kindle edition.

Cooke, CW, and Luciano Kars. 2012. *Political Power: Michele Bachmann*. N.p.: BlueWater Comics.

Cooke, Darwyn. 2005. *DC: The New Frontier—The Deluxe Edition*. New York: DC Comics.

Cooke, Rachel. 2012. "The Influencing Machine by Brooke Gladstone and Josh Neufeld—Review." *Guardian*, August 4. Accessed June 19, 2019. https://www.theguardian.com/books/2012/aug/05/influencing-machine-gladstone-neufeld-review.

Cornell, Paul. 2017. "The Week of Saucer State." *Paul Cornell: Novelist, Screenwriter, Comics Writer*, May 22. Accessed September 8, 2017. https://www.paulcornell.com/2017/05/the-week-of-saucer-state/.

Cornell, Paul, and Ryan Kelly. 2012. *Saucer Country: Run*. New York: Vertigo.

Cornell, Paul, and Ryan Kelly. 2013. *Saucer Country: The Reticulan Candidate*. New York: Vertigo.

Cornell, Paul, Ryan Kelly, and Adam Guzowski. 2017. *Saucer State* #3 July. San Diego: IDW Publishing.

Cornell, Paul, Ryan Kelly, and Adam Guzowski. 2017. *Saucer State* #2. June. San Diego: IDW Publishing.

Cornell, Paul, Ryan Kelly, and Adam Guzowski. 2017. *Saucer State* #1. May. San Diego: IDW Publishing.

Costello, Matthew J. 2009. *Secret Identity Crisis: Comic Books & the Unmasking of Cold War America*. New York: Continuum.

Costello, Matthew J. 2012. "The Shopping Malls of Empire: Cultural Fragmentation, the New Media, and Consumerism in Howard Chaykin's *American Flagg!*" In *Comic Books and American Cultural History: An Anthology*, edited by Matthew Pustz, 152–68. New York: Continuum Books.

Couto, Anthony. 2018. "Superman Villain Campaigning to Lead Canada's Largest Province." *Comic Book Resources*, June 1. Accessed June 3, 2018. https://www.cbr.com/superman-zod-ontario-canada-election/.

Crider, Michael. 2015. *Good Intentions: A Supervillain Story*. N.p. Kindle edition.
Cronin, Brian. 2016. "16 Comic Book Characters that Ran for President." *Comic Book Resources*, July 26. Accessed July 26, 2016. http://www.comicbookresources.com/article/16-comic-book-characters-that-ran-for-president.
Cronin, Brian. 2019. "Congresswoman Ocasio-Cortez is Humbled, Honored by AOC Superhero Comic." *CBR*, March 1. Accessed April 20, 2019. https://www.cbr.com/alexandria-ocasio-cortez-comic-book-reaction/.
Crook, Stephen. 2000. "Utopia and Dystopia." In *Understanding Contemporary Society: Theories of the Present*, edited by Gary Browning, Abigail Halci, and Frank Webster, London: SAGE Publications.
Crosby, Chris, and Tina Francisco. 2014. "The Last Daughter." *The First Daughter* #0. Clermont, FL: Red Giant Entertainment.
Crowley, Michael, and Dan Goldman. 2009. *08: A Graphic Diary of the Campaign Trail*. New York: Three Rivers Press.
Crowley, Sharon. 1992. "Reflections on an Argument that Won't Go Away: Or, a Turn of the Ideological Screw." *Quarterly Journal of Speech* 78 (4): 450–65.
Culturebox. 2006. "The 9/11 Report." *Slate*, August 8. Accessed June 10, 2019. https://slate.com/culture/2006/08/the-9-11-report.html.
Cupp, S. E. 2016. "The Presidential Candidate who Said he Could Shoot Someone and Still Win." *CNN*, January 25. Accessed October 22, 2018. https://www.cnn.com/2016/01/25/opinions/trump-shoot-somebody-cult-cupp/index.html.
Cvencek, Dario, Na'ilah S. Nasir, Kathleen O'Connor, Sarah Wischnia, and Andrew N. Meltzoff. 2014. "The Development of Math–Race Stereotypes: 'They Say Chinese People Are the Best at Math.'" *Journal of Research on Adolescence* 25 (4): 630–37.
D'Amore, Laura Mattoon. 2012. "The Accidental Supermom: Superheroines and Maternal Performativity, 1963–1980." *Journal of Popular Culture* 45 (6): 1226–48.
Danesi, Marcel. 2000. *Encyclopedic Dictionary of Semiotics, Media and Communications*. Toronto: University of Toronto Press.
Daniels, Mitch. 2019. "Sadly, Political Cartooning is Becoming a Lost Art." *Washington Post*, July 31. Accessed August 29, 2019. https://www.washingtonpost.com/opinions/sadly-political-cartooning-is-becoming-a-lost-art/2019/07/31/1513a8d6-aa5e-11e9-9214-46e594de5d5_story.html.
Danjoux, Ilan. 2007. "Reconsidering the Decline of the Editorial Cartoon." *PS: Political Science & Politics* XL (2): 245–48.
David, Peter, J. M. DeMatteis, James D. Hudnall, Phil Jimenez, et al. 2018, *Superman: President Luthor*. Burbank, CA: DC Comics.
Davies, Dominic. 2017. "Comics Activism: An Interview with Comics Artist and Activist Kate Evans." *Comics Grid: Journal of Comics Scholarship* 7 (1): 1–12.
Davis, Blair. 2015. "Bare Chests, Silver Tiaras, and Removable Afros: The Visual Design of Black Comic Book Superheroes." In *The Blacker the Ink: Construction of Black Identity in Comics and Sequential Art*, edited by Frances Gateward and John Jennings, 193–212. New Brunswick, NJ: Rutgers University Press. Kindle edition.
Davis, Julie. 2009. "Power to the Cubicle-Dwellers: An Ideological Reading of *Dilbert*." In *Comics & Ideology*, vol. 2, edited by Matthew P. McAllister, Edward H. Sewell Jr., and Ian Gordon, 275–300. New York: Peter Lang.
Davis, Lauren. 2012. "9 Reasons to Elect a Supervillain President." *Gizmodo*, October 21. Accessed November 16, 2016. https://io9.gizmodo.com/9-reasons-to-elect-a-supervillain-president-5953525.

Dawe, Ian. 2013. "Lee Harvey Oswald: A Comics Villain?" *Sequart Organization Magazine*, November 20. Accessed September 9, 2015. http://sequart.org/magazine/34564/lee-harvey-oswald-a-comics-villain/.

DCE Editorial. 2016. "Get to Know Hanna-Barbera Beyond." *DC Comics*, May 18. Accessed December 9, 2018. https://www.dccomics.com/blog/2016/05/18/get-to-know-hanna-barbera-beyond.

de Heer, Margreet. 2017. "Not My President." *NBM Blog*, January 9. Accessed June 19, 2019. https://blog.nbmpub.com/2017/01/09/not-my-president/.

Deis, Chris. 2013. "The Subjective Politics of the Supervillain." In *What is a Superhero?*, edited by Robin S. Rosenberg and Peter Coogan, loc. 1934–2034. New York: Oxford University Press. Kindle edition.

Delahanty, Patrick. 2020. "April 2020 is the First Conventionless Month in Over 40 Years." *FanCons*, April 9. Accessed May 29, 2020. https://fancons.com/news/post/1527/april-2020-is-the-first-conventionless-month-in-over-40-years.

Delbanco, Andrew. 1995. *The Death of Satan: How Americans Have Lost the Sense of Evil*. New York: Farrar, Straus, and Giroux.

DeMatteis, J. M., and Don Perlin. 1982. "Moon Madness." *The Defenders* #113. New York: Marvel Comics Group.

DeMatteis, J. M., Pay Olliffe, and Tom Palmer. 2019. "The End is Here." *Scooby Apocalypse* #36. Burbank, CA: DC Comics.

Denevi, Timothy. 2017. "The Origins of Hunter S. Thompson's Loathing and Fear." *Paris Review* (blog), July 18. Accessed June 22, 2019. https://www.theparisreview.org/blog/2017/07/18/hunter-s-thompson-origins-of-his-fear-and-loathing/.

Denham, Brian. 2010. "Rogue Warrior." In *Sarah Palin Rogue Warrior*, edited by Doug Dlin and Joe Wight, 16–17. San Antonio, TX: Antarctic Press.

Denis, Ricardo Serrano. 2019. "Review: Killadelphia #1 Opens What Could be the Best Vampire Comic in Years." *Comics Beat*, November 17. Accessed April 10, 2020. https://www.comicsbeat.com/review-killadelphia-1-best-vampire-comic-in-years/

Dennis, Steven T., Chris Strohm and David McLaughlin. 2019. "Top Takeaways from the Mueller Report." *Bloomberg*, April 18. Accessed June 22, 2019. https://www.bloomberg.com/news/articles/2019-04-18/mueller-report-takeaways.

DeSousa, Michael A., and Martin J. Medhurst. 1982. "Political Cartoons and American Culture: Significant Symbols of Campaign 1980." *Studies in Visual Communication* 8: 84–97.

Devarenne, Nicole. 2008. "'A Language Heroically Commensurate with His Body': Nationalism, Fascism, and the Language of the Superhero." *International Journal of Comic Art* 10 (1): 48–54.

Devere, Heather, and Sharon Graham Davies. 2006. "The Don and Helen New Zealand Election 2005: A Media A-Gender?" *Pacific Journalism Review* 12 (1): 65–85.

Devitt, James. 2002. "Framing Gender on the Campaign Trail: Female Gubernatorial Candidates and the Press." *Journalism and Mass Communication Quarterly* 79 (2): 445–63.

de Vreese, Claes. 2005. "The Spiral of Cynicism Reconsidered." *European Journal of Communication* 20 (3): 283–301.

Diebler, Matthew. 2006. "'I'm Not One of *Them* Anymore': Marvel's X-Men and the Loss of Minority (Racial) Identity." *International Journal of Comic Art* 8: 406–413.

Dinschel, Elizabeth (education specialist). N.d. "Using Political Cartoons to Understand Historical Events." *Herbert Hoover Presidential Library and Museum.* Accessed May 30, 2018. https://hoover.archives.gov/sites/default/files/using-political-cartoons.pdf.

DiPaolo, Marc. 2011. *War, Politics and Superheroes: Ethics and Propaganda in Comics and Film*. Jefferson, NC: McFarland. Kindle Edition.

Dirksen Congressional Center Staff. N.d. "The Comic Book Campaign: The Illinois U.S. Senate Race, 1950." *The Dirksen Congressional Center*. Accessed May 27, 2018. http://www.dirksencenter.org/print_lp_lucas.htm.

Dittmer, Jason. 2005. "Captain America's Empire: Reflections on Identity, Popular Culture, and Post-9/11 Geopolitics." *Annals of the Association of American Geographers* 95 (3): 626–43.

Dittmer, Jason. 2013. *Captain America and the Nationalist Superhero: Metaphors, Narratives, and Geopolitics*. Philadelphia: Temple University Press.

Dixon, Chuck, and Brett R. Smith. 2016. *Clinton Cash: A Graphic Novel*. Washington, DC: Regnery Publishing.

Dlin, Doug, and Paul Kilpatrick, eds. 2004. *You Can Vote!* San Antonio, TX: Antarctic Press.

Dlin, Doug, and Joe Wight, eds. 2010. *Sarah Palin Rogue Warrior*. San Antonio, TX: Antarctic Press.

Dmitry, Baxter. 2016. "Guccifer: Hillary Clinton is a High Priestess of the Illuminati." *YourNewsWire*, September 25. Accessed October 6, 2016. http://yournewswire.com/guccifer-hillary-clinton-high-priestess-illuminati/.

Dodson, P. Claire. 2016. "How Comic Fans Got Their Faith Back." *Atlantic*, April 15. Accessed July 2, 2019. https://www.theatlantic.com/entertainment/archive/2016/04/faith/478386/.

Doherty, Thomas. 2018. *Show Trial: Hollywood, HUAC, and the Birth of the Blacklist*. New York: Columbia University Press. Kindle edition.

Dominguez, Noah. 2020. "*Killadelphia*: TV Series Based on Image Comic in Development at Levantine." *CBR*, April 16. Accessed April 26, 2020. https://www.cbr.com/killadelphia-tv-adaptation-levantine-films-rodney-barnes/.

Dougall, Alistair, senior ed. 2014a. "Captain America." In *Marvel Encyclopedia: Updated and Expanded*, 70–75. New York: DK.

Dougall, Alistair, senior ed. 2014b. "The Hulk." In *Marvel Encyclopedia: Updated and Expanded*, 172–75. New York: DK.

Dow, Bonnie J., and Mari Boor Tonn. 1993. "Feminine Style and Political Judgment in the Rhetoric of Ann Richards." *Quarterly Journal of Speech* 79: 286–303.

Drum, Nicole. 2020. "Marvel Addresses Police Wearing Punisher Skull Logo While Confronting Protestors." *ComicBook*, June 7. Accessed June 7, 2020. https://comicbook.com/marvel/news/police-wearing-punisher-skull-logo-during-protests-marvel-respon/.

Dumaroag, Ana. 2019. "Armie Hammer Calls Out Marvel's Ike Perlmutter for Supporting Trump." *ScreenRant*, August 10. Accessed August 30, 2019. https://screenrant.com/marvel-armie-hammer-ike-perlmutter-trump/.

Duncan, Randy. 2012. "Image Functions: Shape and Color as Hermeneutic Images in *Asterios Polyp*." In *Critical Approaches to Comics: Theories and Methods*, edited by Matthew J. Smith and Randy Duncan, 43–54. New York: Routledge.

Duncan, Randy, Matthew J. Smith, and Paul Levitz. 2015. *The Power of Comics: History, Form, and Culture*, second edition. New York: Bloomsbury.

Dunn, Joe, and Ben Dunn. 2018. "I Built My Wall of . . ." *Tremendous Trump: World War T*. San Antonio, TX: Antarctic Press.

Dunn, Patrick. 2015. "Cartoonist Mark Russell on his Reboot of *Prez*, Comics' First Teen President." *A.V. Club*, June 17. Accessed September 20, 2015. http://www.avclub.com/article/cartoonist-mark-russell-his-reboot-prez-comics-fir-220736.

Dunn, Susan. 2016. "Trump's 'America First' Has Ugly Echoes from U.S. History." *CNN*, April 28. Accessed September 30, 2018. https://www.cnn.com/2016/04/27/opinions/trump-america-first-ugly-echoes-dunn/index.html.

Dunn, Will. 2019. "Art of Offence: The Political Cartoon Controversy." *New Statemen*, July 3. Accessed August 30, 2019. https://www.newstatesman.com/culture/2019/07/art-offence-political-cartoon-controversy.

Dyer, Ben. 2009. *Supervillains and Philosophy: Sometimes Evil is Its Own Reward.* Chicago: Open Court. Kindle edition.

Edelman, Murray. 1988. *Constructing the Political Spectacle.* Chicago: University of Chicago Press.

Edelman, Murray. 1995. *From Art to Politics: How Artistic Creations Shape Political Conceptions.* Chicago: University of Chicago Press.

Edelstein, Sally. 2013. "LBJ's Comic Great Society." *Envisioning the American Dream* (blog), May 16. Accessed July 20, 2018. https://envisioningtheamericandream.com/2013/05/16/lbjs-comic-great-society/.

Edgar, Timothy H. N.d. "ACLU Analysis of the 9–11 Commission's Recommendations for Intelligence Reform." ACLU. Accessed June 22, 2019. https://www.aclu.org/other/aclu-analysis-9-11-commissions-recommendations-intelligence-reform.

Edwards, Janis L. 2001. "Running in the Shadows in Campaign 2000: Candidate Metaphors in Editorial Cartoons." *American Behavioral Scientist* 44 (12): 2140–51.

Edwards, Janis L., and Carol K. Winkler. 1997. "Representative Form and the Visual Ideograph: The Iwo Jima Image in Editorial Cartoons." *Quarterly Journal of Speech* 83: 289–310.

Edwards, Janis L., and C. Austin McDonald II. 2010. "Reading Hillary and Sarah: Contradictions of Feminism and Representation in 2008 Campaign Political Cartoons." *American Behavioral Scientist* 54 (3): 319–29.

Edwards, Jason A. 2008. "Defining the Enemy for the Post-Cold War World: Bill Clinton's Foreign Policy Discourse in Somalia and Haiti." *International Journal of Communication* 2: 830–47.

Eisner, Will. 2008. *Expressive Anatomy for Comics and Narrative: Principles and Practices from the Legendary Cartoonist.* New York: Norton.

Ellingson, Laura L. 2009. *Engaging in Crystallization in Qualitative Research: An Introduction.* Thousand Oaks, CA: Sage.

Ellis, Warren, and John Francis Moore. 2013. *DOOM 2099: The Complete Collection.* New York: Marvel Entertainment.

Emad, Mitra C. 2006. "Reading Wonder Woman's Body: Mythologies of Gender and Nation." *The Journal of Popular Culture* 39 (6): 954–84.

Emmott, Robin. 2020. "Russia Deploying Coronavirus Disinformation to Sow Panic in West, EU Document Says." *Reuters*, March 18. Accessed May 30, 2020. https://www.reuters.com/article/us-health-coronavirus-disinformation/russia-deploying-coronavirus-disinformation-to-sow-panic-in-west-eu-document-says-idUSKBN21518F.

Englehart, Steve, and Joe Staton. 1986. "See Red!" *The Green Lantern Corps* #210. New York: DC Comics.

Eno, Vincent, and El Cswaza, 1988. "Alan Moore Interview, 1988." *Internet Archive WaybackMachine*, February 20, 2006. Accessed January 26, 2019. https://web.archive.org/web/20181008212606/http://www.johncoulthart.com/feuilleton/2006/02/20/alan-moore-interview-1988/.

Ercolano, Patrick. 1980. "Doesn't Everybody Go Pogo?" *Washington Post*, September 5. Accessed May 30, 2020. https://www.washingtonpost.com/archive/lifestyle/1980/09/05/doesnt-everybody-go-pogo/bd4d0ad6-565d-431b-a170-34ba2f4ce772/.

Erdman, Shelby Lin. 2020. "Black Communities Account for Disproportionate Number of COVID-19 Deaths in the US, Study Finds." CNN, May 6. Accessed May 29, 2020. https://www.cnn.com/2020/05/05/health/coronavirus-african-americans-study/index.html.

Esch, Joanne. 2010. "Legitimizing the 'War on Terror': Political Myth in Official-Level Rhetoric." *Political Psychology* 31 (3): 357–91.

Estren, Mark James. 2012. *A History of Underground Comics*, anniversary edition. Berkeley, CA: Ronin Publishing.

Eternal, Prime. 2002. "Philip Nolan Voigt." Marvunapp.com, August 1. Accessed July 18, 2019. http://www.marvunapp.com/Appendix/voigt.htm.

Evans, Zach. 2016. "Batman, Jesus, Axl Rose, Winnecke Among Presidential Write-In Candidates." *Courier & Press*, November 20. Accessed July 21, 2018. https://www.courierpress.com/story/news/2016/11/20/batman-jesus-axl-rose-winnecke-among-presidential-write—candidates/94166656/.

Eveland, William P., Jr. 2002. "The Impact of News and Entertainment Media on Perception of Social Reality." In *The SAGE Handbook of Persuasion: Developments in Theory and Practice*, second edition, edited by James Price Dillard and Lijiang Shen, 691–727. Thousand Oaks, CA: Sage.

Fahey, Sean, Borja Peña, and Evan Keeling. 2012. "The Man in the Green Hat." In *District Comics: An Unconventional History of Washington, DC*, edited by Matt Dembicki, 112–21.

Falk, Erika. 2008. *Women for President: Media Bias in Nine Campaigns*. Urbana: University of Illinois Press.

Farber, Madeline. 2017. "Mark Hamill Reads Donald Trump's Tweet as The Joker." *TIME*, January 8. Accessed April 27, 2019. http://time.com/4627755/mark-hamill-joker-donald-trump-tweet/.

Fazio, Michele. 2018. "Past Lives: Memory and the Meaning of Work in *The Walking Dead*." In *Working-Class Comic Book Heroes*, edited by Marc DiPaolo, 49–80. Jackson, MS: University Press of Mississippi. Kindle edition.

Feinberg, Leonard. 1967. *Introduction to Satire*. Ames: Iowa State University Press.

Felker, Jim, and Ben Dunn. 2010. "Sarah Palin: Steam Machine." In *Steampunk Palin*, edited by Doug Dlin and Joe Wight, 1–15. San Antonio, TX: Antarctic Press.

Felkins, Patricia K., and Irvin Goldman. 1993. "Political Myth as Subjective Narrative: Some Interpretations and Understandings of John F. Kennedy." *Political Psychology* 14 (3): 447–67.

Ferguson, Niall. 1997. "Introduction: Virtual history: Towards a 'Chaotic' Theory of the Past." In *Virtual History: Alternatives and Counterfactuals*, edited by Niall Ferguson, 1–90. New York: Basic Books. Kindle edition.

Feuerherd, Joe. 2008. "In 1964, a Candidate Emerges from the Catholic Imagination." *National Catholic Reporter*, October 12. Accessed August 10, 2019. https://www.ncronline.org/news/politics/1964-candidate-emerges-catholic-imagination.

Finch, Meredith, and Shane Davis. 2017. *Catwoman: Election Night*. Burbank, CA: DC Comics.

Fitzduff, Mari. 2017. "Introduction: All Too Human: The Allure of Donald Trump." In *Why Irrational Politics Appeals: Understanding the Allure of Trump*, edited by Mari Fitzduff, 1–24. Santa Barbara, CA: ABC-CLIO. Kindle edition.

Fitzpatrick, Lisa. 2020. "Coronavirus and the Underserved: We Are Not All in this Together." *Forbes*, April 2. Accessed May 29, 2020. https://www.forbes.com/sites/lisafitzpatrick/2020/04/02/covid-19-and-the-underserved-we-are-not-all-in-this-together/#a0b00395a71e.

Fletcher, Louis. 2013. *Presidential War Power*, third edition, revised. Lawrence: University Press of Kansas.

Flood, Joe. 2018. "There Are No Superheroes in DC." *Washington Post*, June 29. Accessed July 17, 2018. https://www.washingtonpost.com/opinions/there-are-no-superheroes-in-dc/2018/06/29/cd03412a-7636-11e8-b4b7-308400242c2e_story.html.

Flor, Rachel. 2014. "Rare JFK Superman Comic Book Story 'Superman's Mission for President Kennedy' at JFK Library." JFK Library, March 20. Accessed July 17, 2018, https://www.jfklibrary.org/About-Us/News-and-Press/Press-Releases/2014-March-20-Superman-Exhibit.aspx.

Flynn, Gillian. 1999. "Stop Toxic Managers Before They Stop You." *Workforce* (August): 44–46.

Foss, Sonja K. 2009. "Ideological Criticism." In *Rhetorical Criticism: Exploration and Practice*, fourth edition, 209–266. Long Grove, IL: Waveland.

Fox, Alison. 2019. "An AOC Comic Book Finds the Congresswoman Leading 'The Freshman Force.'" *AMNewYork*, May 7. Accessed July 2, 2019. https://www.amny.com/entertainment/aoc-comic-book-1.30785754.

Fox & Friends Weekend. 2015. "Trump: 'We're Going to Take the Country Back.'" *Fox News Insider*, July 12. Accessed October 1, 2018. http://insider.foxnews.com/2015/07/12/donald-trump-phoenix-speech-were-going-take-country-back.

Fox, M. Steven. 2013. "Bobman and Teddy." *Comixjoint* (blog). Accessed July 20, 2018, https://comixjoint.com/bobmanandteddy.html.

Foy, Joseph J. 2008. "American Idle: Politics and Popular Culture." In *Homer Simpson Goes to Washington: American Politics through Popular Culture*, edited by Joseph J. Foy, 9–18. Lexington: University Press of Kentucky.

Francisco, Eric. 2015. "'Arrow' Skewers the 2016 Election with Oliver Queen's Mayoral Candidacy." *Inverse*, November 19. Accessed February 18, 2017, https://www.inverse.com/article/8321-arrow-skewers-the-2016-election-with-oliver-queen-s-mayoral-candidacy.

Francisco, Eric. 2018. "Comicsgate is GamerGate's Next Horrible Evolution." *Inverse*, February 9. Accessed February 22, 2020. https://www.inverse.com/article/41132-comicsgate-explained-bigots-milkshake-marvel-dc-gamergate.

Franklin, Daniel P. 2006. *Politics and Film: The Political Culture of Film in the United States*. Lanham, MD: Rowman & Littlefield.

Friends of George C. Wallace. N.d. *Alabama Needs "The Little Judge" George C. Wallace for the Big Job*. N.p.

Gaddis, John Lewis. 2005. *The Cold War: A New History*. New York: Penguin Press.

Gaiman, Neil, Michael Allred, Bryan Talbot, and Mark Buckingham. 2016. "The Golden Boy." In *Prez: The First Teen President*, edited by Liz Erickson, 133–57. Burbank, CA: DC Comics.

Gaines, William M. 1954. "Testimony of William M. Gaines, Publisher, Entertaining Comics Group, New York, N.Y." thecomicbooks.com. Accessed May 28, 2019. http://www.thecomicbooks.com/gaines.html.

Garcia, Kevin, Dan Lauer, and Walt Barna. 2016. *The Unconstitutional Actions and Adventures of the Dead Presidents*, part one. Orange County, CA: comiXology.

Garcia, Vanessa. 2017. "Wonder Woman and the Double Binds of the First Female President." *BitchMedia*, November 10. Accessed July 1, 2019. https://www.bitchmedia.org/article/wonder-woman-and-double-binds-first-female-president.

Garger, Kenneth. 2019. "President Trump Depicted as 'Avengers' Supervillain Thanos in New Campaign Video." *New York Post*, December 10. Accessed June 4, 2020. https://nypost.com/2019/12/10/president-trump-depicted-as-avengers-supervillain-thanos-in-new-campaign-video/.

Garry, Patrick M. 1992. *Liberalism and American Identity*. Kent, OH: Kent State University Press.

Gateward, Frances, and John Jennings. 2015. "Introduction: The Sweeter the Christmas." In *The Blacker the Ink: Constructions of Black Identity in Comics and Sequential Art*, edited by Frances Gateward and John Jennings, loc. 87–421. New Brunswick, NJ: Rutgers University Press. Kindle edition.

Gathara, Patrick. 2019. "The Death of the Political Cartoon." *Al Jazeera*, July 2. Accessed August 30, 2019. https://www.aljazeera.com/indepth/opinion/death-political-cartoon-190702083907178.html.

Genter, Robert. 2007. "'With Great Power Comes Great Responsibility': Cold War Culture and the Birth of Marvel Comics." *Journal of Popular Culture* 40 (6): 953–76.

Gerbaudo, Paolo. 2015. "Protest Avatars as Memetic Signifiers: Political Profile Pictures and the Construction of Collective Identity on Social Media in the 2011 Protest Wave." *Information, Communication & Society* 18 (8): 916–29.

Gerber, Steve, and Gene Colon. 1976. "Open Season!" *Howard the Duck* #8. New York: Marvel Comics Group.

Gianos, Phillip L. 1999. *Politics and Politicians in American Film*. Westport, CT: Praeger.

Gibbons, Dave. 2008. "Illustrating Watchmen." *WATCHMENComicMovie.com*. October 23. Accessed January 26, 2019. http://www.watchmencomicmovie.com/102308-dave-gibbons-watchmen-comic-illustrator.php.

Giffen, Keith, J. M. DeMatteis, Dale Eaglesham, Tom Derenick, and Hi-Fi. 2017. "Brotherly Hate." *Scooby Apocalypse* #13. Burbank. CA: DC Comic

Gilsinan, Kathy. 2020. "C-SPAN is So Hot Right Now." *Atlantic*, January 27. Accessed March 15, 2020. https://www.theatlantic.com/politics/archive/2020/01/c-span-impeachment-trump/605602/.

Giroux, Henry A. 2009. *Youth in a Suspect Society: Democracy or Disposability*. New York: Palgrave MacMillan.

Giroux, Henry A. 2012. *Disposable Youth: Racialized Memories, and the Culture of Cruelty*. New York: Routledge.

Gladstone, Brooke, and Josh Neufeld. 2011. *The Influencing Machine: Brooke Gladstone on the Media*. New York: W. W. Norton & Company.

Glass, Adam. 2016. "The Bull Moose." *Rough Riders* #4. Sherman Oaks, CA: AfterShock Comics.

Glasser, Susan B., and Glenn Thrush. 2016. "What's Going on with America's White People?" *Politico*, September/October. Accessed October 26, 2018. https://www.politico.com/magazine/story/2016/09/problems-white-people-america-society-class-race-214227.

Glidden, Sarah. 2016. "Spoiler: On the Campaign Trail with Jill Stein." *The Nib*, August 8. Accessed June 19, 2019. https://thenib.com/jill-stein-spoiler.

Goh, Jaymee. 2010. "On Race and Steampunk: A Quick Primer." *SteamPunk Magazine* 7: 16–21.

Goldenberg, Suzanne, and Richard Adams. 2008. "The Tears Over Coffee that Turned Round Poll." *Guardian*, January 10. Accessed October 1, 2018. https://www.theguardian.com/world/2008/jan/10/hillaryclinton.uselections20082.

Goldhill, Olivia. 2017. "Rhetoric Scholars Pinpoint Why Trump's Inarticulate Speaking Style is So Persuasive." *Quartz*, April 22. Accessed June 26, 2018. https://qz.com/965004/rhetoric-scholars-pinpoint-why-trumps-inarticulate-speaking-style-is-so-persuasive/.

Goldman, Alan. 2009. *Transforming Toxic Leaders*. Stanford, CA. Stanford Business Books. Kindle edition.

Goldstein, Hilary. 2006. "The 9/11 Report: Graphic Novel Adaptation Review." *IGN*, September 11. Accessed June 10, 2019. https://www.ign.com/articles/2006/09/12/the-911-report-graphic-novel-adaptation-review.

Good, Joseph. 2010. "'God Save the Queen, for Someone Must!': *Sebastian O* and the Steampunk Aesthetic." *Neo-Victorian Studies* 3 (1): 208–215.

Gosnell, Kelvin, Carols Ezquerra, Jack Potter, and Janet Landau. 1986. "The Stainless Steel Rat for President: Part One." *The Stainless Steel Rat* #5. London: Eagle Comics.

Gournelos, Ted, and Viveca Greene. 2011. "Introduction: Popular Culture and Post-9/11 Politics." In *A Decade of Dark Humor: How Comedy, Irony, and Satire Shaped Post-9/11 America*, edited by Ted Gournelos and Viveca Greene, 74–545. Jackson: University Press of Mississippi. Kindle edition.

Grady, Constance. 2017. "The Women's March Shows How Intertwined Pop Culture and Politics Have Become." *Vox*, January 24. Accessed May 12, 2018. https://www.vox.com/culture/2017/1/24/14358000/womens-march-washington-pop-culture-politics.

Graham, Phil. 2018. "Infinity War's Josh Brolin Reads Trump Tweets as Thanos." *ScreenRant*, June 20. Accessed June 4, 2020. https://screenrant.com/infinity-war-thanos-josh-brolin-trump-tweets/.

Gries, Laurie. 2015. "Obama Zombies and Rhetorical (Dis)Identifications in an Era of Dog Whistle Politics and Political Polarization." *ImageTexT* 8 (1): http://imagetext.english.ufl.edu/archives/v8_1/gries/.

Griffin, Farah Jasmine. 2011. "At Last . . . ?: Michelle Obama, Beyoncé, Race & History." *Daedalus* 140 (1): 131–41.

Griffith, Ash. 2018. "Comics Will Always Be Political." *RVA*, September 14. Accessed February 23, 2020. https://rvamag.com/art/zines-books/comics-will-always-be-political.html.

Gring-Pemble, Lisa, and Martha Solomon Watson. 2003. "The Rhetorical Limits of Satire: An Analysis of James Finn Garner's *Politically Correct Bedtime Stories*." *Quarterly Journal of Speech*. 89 (2): 132–53.

Groensteen, Thierry. 2007. *The System of Comics*, translated by Bart Beaty and Nick Nguyen. Jackson: University Press of Mississippi.

Guggenheim, Marc, John Romita Jr., and Barry Kitson. 2010. *The Amazing Spider-Man: Election Day*. New York: Marvel Publishing.

Guinier, Lani. 1991. "The Triumph of Tokenism: The Voting Rights Act and the Theory of Black Electoral Success." *Michigan Law Review* 85 (5): 1077–1154.

Guinilling, Nicole Marie. 2014. "#ISA2014 Mixer and Launch of Journal for Narrative Politics." *Ad Astra Comix*, March 27. Accessed June 22, 2019. https://adastracomix.com/2014/03/27/isa2014-mixer-launch-of-journal-for-narrative-politics/.

Gunn, Joshua. 2008. "Father Trouble: Staging Sovereignty in Spielberg's *War of the Worlds*." *Critical Studies in Media Communication* 25 (1): 1–27.

Gutiérrez, Miren, María Pilar Rodríguez and Juan Manuel Díaz de Guereñu. 2018. "Journalism in the Age of Hybridization: *Los Vagabundos de la Chatarra*—Comics Journalism, Date, Maps, and Advocacy." *Catalan Journal of Communication & Cultural Studies* 10 (1): 43–62.

Haber, Matt. 2012. "Symbolia Tablet Magazine Aims to Turn News into a Comic." *Fast Company*, December 4. Accessed June 14, 2019. https://www.fastcompany.com/1682043/symbolia-tablet-magazine-aims-to-turn-news-into-a-comic?position=1&campaign_date=06092019.

Hafer, Dick. 1993. *Shafted! Bill and Hillary's Excellent Adventure*. Falmout, VA: A.K.A., Inc.

Hahn, Dan F. 2003. *Political Communication: Rhetoric, Government, and Citizens*, second edition. State College, PA: Strata Publishing.

Hajdu, David. 2009. *The Ten-Cent Plague: The Great Comic-Book Scare and How it Changed America*. New York, NY: Picador.

Hall, Stuart. 1997. "The Spectacle of the 'Other.'" In *Representation: Cultural Representations and Signifying Practices*, edited by Stuart Hall, 223–79. Thousand Oaks, CA: Sage Publishing.

Hama, Larry, and John Christmas. 2009. *Barack the Barbarian: The Fall of Red Sarah*. Chicago: Devil's Due Publishing.

Hama, Larry, Christopher Schons, and Rachelle Rosenberg. 2009. "Quest for the Treasure of Stimuli." *Barack the Barbarian* #1. Chicago: Devil's Due Publishing.

Haneda, Saburo, and Hirosuke Shima. 1982. "Japanese Communication Behavior as Reflected in Letter Writing." *Journal of Business Communication* 19 (1): 19–32.

Hanley, Tim. 2014. *Wonder Woman Unbound: The Curious History of the World's Most Famous Heroine*. Chicago: Chicago Review Press.

Hanna, Natalie. 2017. "Why Donald Trump's 'Pussy Grabbing' Sexist Banter Would Be More at Home in Medieval Times." *Newsweek*, October 13. Accessed November 4, 2017. http://www.newsweek.com/donald-trump-grab-em-pussy-geoffrey-chaucer-683976.

Hantke, Steffen. 1999. "Difference Engines and Other Infernal Devices: History According to Steampunk." *Extrapolation* 40 (3): 244–54.

Hantke, Steffen. 2010. "Bush's America and the Return of Cold War Science Fiction: Alien Invasion in *Invasion, Threshold,* and *Surface.*" *Journal of Popular Film and Television* 38 (3): 143–51.

Harich, Jack. 2014. *The Dueling Loops of the Political Powerplace: Why Progressives are Stymied and How They Can Find Their Way Again.* N.p.: Lulu.com.

Hariman, Robert. 2008. "Political Parody and Public Culture," *Quarterly Journal of Speech* 94 (3): 247–72.

Harper, Jennifer. 2016. "Price of Bias: America Now Shunning News Media After 2016 Election." *Washington Post,* November 15. Accessed October 26, 2018. https://www.washingtontimes.com/news/2016/nov/15/america-avoiding-the-news-media-after-2016-electio/.

Harrington, Rebecca. 2016. "Here's What Trump Means When He Says 'Drain the Swamp'—Even Though It's Not an Accurate Metaphor." *Business Insider,* November 11. Accessed July 19, 2019. https://www.businessinsider.com/what-does-drain-the-swamp-mean-was-dc-built-on-a-swamp-2016-11.

Harrison, Jaime. 2019. "Character." YouTube video, May 29. Accessed May 31, 2019. https://youtu.be/qGL5dclzjHo.

Hart, Roderick P., and E. Johanna Hartelius. 2007. "The Political Sins of Jon Stewart." *Critical Studies in Media Communication* 24 (3): 26372.

Harter, Lynn M. 2004. "Masculinity(s), the Agrarian Frontier Myth, and Cooperative Ways of Organizing: Contradictions and Tensions in the Experience and Enactment of Democracy." *Journal of Applied Communication Research* 32 (2): 89–118.

Harvey, Jonathan R. 2012. "The Wild West and the New Weird in K.J. Bishop's 'The Etched City' and China Miévelle's 'Iron Council.'" *Contemporary Literature* 53 (1): 87–113.

Harvey, Robert C. 1994. *The Art of the Funnies: An Aesthetic History,* Studies in Popular Culture. Jackson: University Press of Mississippi.

Hastings, Christopher, Langdon Foss, and Chris Chuckry. 2016. *Vote Loki* #1. New York: Marvel Worldwide.

Hastings, Christopher, Langdon Foss, and Chris Chuckry. 2016. *Vote Loki* #4. New York: Marvel Worldwide.

Hastings, Christopher, Paul McCaffrey, and Chris Chuckry. 2016. *Vote Loki* #2. New York: Marvel Worldwide.

Hastings, Christopher, Langdon Foss, Chris Chuckry, and Rachelle Rosenberg. 2016. *Vote Loki* #3. New York: Marvel Worldwide.

Hayner, Chris E. 2017. "It's Not 'The West Wing' but Mayor Queen is Vital to Star City, Says 'Arrow' EP." *Screener,* February 15. Accessed February 16, 2017. http://screenertv.com/television/arrow-spectre-of-the-gun-mayor-oliver-queen-more-important-green-arrow/.

Helfer, Andrew, Steve Buccellato, and Joe Staton. 2007. *Ronald Reagan: A Graphic Biography.* New York: Hill and Wang.

Hellekson, Karen. 2011. *The Alternate History: Refiguring Historical Time.* Kent, OH: Kent State University Press. Kindle edition.

Hellman, John. 1979. "Corporate Fiction, Private Fable, and Hunter S. Thompson's *Fear and Loathing: On the Campaign Trail '72.*" *Critique: Studies in Contemporary Fiction* 21 (1): 16–29.

Helvie, Forrest. 2017. "The Final Days of LETTER 44 as U.S. PRESIDENT Preps for Alien First Contact." *Newsarama,* ebruary 21. Accessed August 10, 2019. https://www.newsarama.com/33241-its-the-end-of-the-world-as-we-know-it-with-letter-44s-charles-soule.html.

Henderson, Carol E. 2002. *Scarring the Black Body: Race and Representation in African American Literature.* Columbia: University of Missouri Press.

Henriques, Gregg. 2017. "Trump: An Antiestablishment Hero?" In *Why Irrational Politics Appeals: Understanding the Allure of Trump*, edited by Mari Fitzduff, 107–120. Santa Barbara, CA: ABC-CLIO. Kindle edition.

Herman, Ian, Ron Goulart, Sean Joyce, and Malena Molina. 2017. *The Phantom*. Neshannock, PA: Hermes Press.

Hermes Press. N.d. "The Phantom: President Kennedy's Mission Issue #1A." *Hermes Press* (retail). Accessed July 30, 2018. https://hermes-press.myshopify.com/products/the-phantom-president-kennedys-mission-issue-1a-pre-order.

Herviou, Nicole. 2017. "Superhero Comics Creators: We're Political, and Always Have Been." *Mashable*, March 16. Accessed February 23, 2020. https://mashable.com/2017/03/16/politics-in-comics/.

Hess, Aaron. 2011. "Breaking News: A Postmodern Rhetorical Analysis of *The Daily Show*." In *The Daily Show and Rhetoric: Arguments, Issues, and Strategies*, edited by Trischa Goodnow, loc. 3781–4213. Lanham, MD: Lexington. Kindle edition.

Hibbard, James. 2018. "James Comey Gets a Heroic Comic Book 'Origin Story.'" *Entertainment Weekly*, April 25. Accessed June 16, 2018. http://ew.com/books/2018/04/25/james-comey-comic-book/.

Hickman, Jonathan, and Nick Pitarra. 2013. *The Manhattan Projects*, volume 2. Berkeley, CA: Image Comics.

Hiddleston, Tom. 2013. "Tom Hiddleston Interview—Is Loki Really Evil?—*Thor the Dark World* Premiere." *Red Carpet News TV*, October 20. YouTube video. Accessed July 11, 2019. https://youtu.be/Unc6dPWEx8E.

Hill, Megan R. 2013. "Developing a Normative Approach to Political Satire: A Critical Perspective." *International Journal of Communication* 7: 324–37.

Hoerger, Michael, Mia Partlow, and Nate Powell. 2010. *Edible Secrets: A Food Tour of Classified US History*. Bloomington, IN: Microcosm Publishing.

Holbert, R. Lance, Dhavan V. Shah, and Nojin Kwak. 2004. "Fear, Authority, and Justice: The Influence of TV News, Police Reality, and Crime Drama Viewing on Endorsements of Capital Punishment and Gun Ownership." *Journalism and Mass Communication Quarterly* 81 (2): 343–63.

Holbert, R. Lance, Owen Pillion, David A. Tschida, Greg G. Armfield, Kelly Kinder, Kristin L. Cherry, and Amy R. Daulton. 2003. "*The West Wing* as Endorsement of the U.S. Presidency: Expanding the Bounds of Priming in Political Communication." *Journal of Communication* 53: 427–43.

Holbert, R. Lance, Dhavan V. Shah, and Nojin Kwak. 2003. "Political Implications of Prime-Time Drama and Sitcom Use: Genres of Representation and Opinions Concerning Women's Rights." *Journal of Communication* 53 (1): 45–60.

Holbert, R. Lance, David A. Tschida, Maria Dixon, Kristin Cherry, Keli Steuber, and David Airne. 2005. "*The West Wing* and Depictions of the American Presidency: Expanding the Domains of Framing in Political Communication." *Communication Quarterly* 53 (4): 505–522.

Holmes, Malcolm D. 2016. "Plague of Police Shootings." *U.S. News*, September 23. Accessed October 10, 2016. http://www.usnews.com/opinion/articles/2016-09-23/whats-really-behind-plague-of-fatal-police-shootings-of-unarmed-black-men.

Horne, Karama. 2020. "Indie Comics Spotlight: Killadelphia is Rodney Barnes' Ode to Dracula and The Wire." *SyFy Wire*, January 31. Accessed May 31, 2020. https://www.syfy.com/syfywire/indie-comics-spotlight-killadelphia-is-rodney-barnes-ode-to-dracula-and-the-wire.

Howard, Sheena C., and Ronald L. Jackson II. 2013. "Introduction." In *Black Comics: Politics of Race and Representation*, edited by Sheena C. Howard and Ronald L. Jackson II, 1–9. New York: Bloomsbury. Kindle edition.

Hudson, John. 2011. "Why Are Comic Books Obsessed with Sarah Palin?" *Atlantic*, January 24. Accessed June 30, 2019. https://www.theatlantic.com/entertainment/archive/2011/01/why-are-comic-books-obsessed-with-sarah-palin/339110/.

Hughes, Jamie A. 2006. "'Who Watches the Watchmen?': Ideology and 'Real World' Superheroes." *Journal of Popular Culture* 39 (4): 546–57.

Hughes, Richard T. 2005. *Myths America Lives By*. Urbana: University of Illinois Press.

Hughston, Louise, Dick Giordano, and Jon D'Agostino. 1961. *Caroline Kennedy: America's First Young Lady*. Derby, CT: Charlton Comics Group.

Humphries, Sam, and Joe Bennett. 2013. "Reconstruction." *Ultimate Comics: The Ultimates #24*. New York: DC Comics.

Humphries, Sam, and Billy Tan. 2012. "Divided We Fall—Part Three: By the Time I Get to California." *Ultimate Comics: The Ultimates #15*. New York: Marvel Comics.

Humphries, Sam, Tommy Patterson, Jon Alderink, and Rachel Deering. 2015. "Once Upon a Time in Minnesota . . ." *Citizen Jack #1*. Berkeley, CA: Image Comics.

Humphries, Sam, Tommy Patterson, Jon Alderink, and Rachel Deering. 2015. "The Return of the Goon." *Citizen Jack #2*. Berkeley, CA: Image Comics.

Humphries, Sam, Tommy Patterson, Jon Alderink, and Rachel Deering. 2016. "The Abyss." *Citizen Jack Issue #5*. Berkeley, CA: Image Comics.

Humphries, Sam, Tommy Patterson, Jon Alderink, and Rachel Deering. 2016. "Devil Inside." *Citizen Jack Issue #4*. Berkeley, CA: Image Comics.

Humphries, Sam, Tommy Patterson, Jon Alderink, and Rachel Deering. 2016. "The End of the Road." *Citizen Jack Issue #6*. Berkeley, CA: Image Comics.

Hunt, Nathan. 2003. "The Importance of Trivia: Ownership, Exclusion and Authority in Science Fiction Fandom." In *Defining Cult Movies: The Cultural Politics of Oppositional Taste*, edited by Mark Jancovich, Antonio Lázaro Reboll, Julian Stringer, and Andy Willis. 185–201. New York: Manchester University Press.

Hutchison, David. 2010, *President Evil Pocket Manga*. San Antonio, TX: Antarctic Press.

IDW Publishing. N.d. "About." *Presidential Material Comics*. Accessed June 3, 2018. http://www.presidentialcomics.com/about.html.

Ignatius, David. 2016. "Donald Trump is the American Machiavelli." *Washington Post*, November 10. Accessed November 5, 2017. https://www.washingtonpost.com/opinions/donald-trump-is-the-american-machiavelli/2016/11/10/8ebfae16-a794-11e6-ba59-a7d93165c6d4_story.html.

Illing, Sean. 2016. "Bernie Sanders is Right that 2016 is a 'Lesser of Two Evils' Election: But No One Should Be Shocked by the Truth." *Salon*, May 23. Accessed October 24, 2018. https://www.salon.com/2016/05/23/bernie_sanders_is_right_that_2016_is_a_lesser_of_two_evils_election_but_no_one_should_be_shocked_by_the_truth/.

"Industry Wide Records." N.d. *Comichron*. Accessed July 21, 2018. http://www.comichron.com/vitalstatistics/diamondrecords.html.

Ingold, David, John McCormick, Chloe Whiteaker, Arit John, Mira Rojanasakul, and Allison McCartney. 2018. "Record Numbers of Women Running for Office May Not Mean Big Gains in Congress." *Bloomberg*, May 7. Accessed June 23, 2019. https://www.bloomberg.com/graphics/2018-women-candidates/.

Isaac, Jeffrey C. 2002. "Ends, Means, and Politics." *Dissent Magazine* (Spring). Accessed July 19, 2019. https://www.dissentmagazine.org/article/ends-means-and-politics.

Itzkoff, Dave. 2016. "For Stephen Colbert, a Very Uncomfortable Election Night." *New York Times*, November 10. Accessed April 24, 2019. https://www.nytimes.com/2016/11/10/arts/television/stephen-colbert-showtime-uncomfortable-election.html.

Ivie, Robert. 1980. "Images of Savagery in American Justifications of War." *Communication Monographs* 47 (4): 279–94.
Iyengar, Shanto. 2016. *Media Politics: A Citizens Guide*, third edition. New York: W. W. Norton & Company.
Jackson, Shepard. 2019. "The Will of the People." *Talk Bernie to Me!* Chicago: Devil's Due Comics.
Jacobs, Ben. 2016. "Hillary Clinton Regrets 'Basket of Deplorables' Remark as Trump Attacks." *Guardian*, September 11. Accessed October 25, 2018. https://www.theguardian.com/us-news/2016/sep/10/hillary-clinton-basket-of-deplorables-donald-trump.
Jacobson, Sid, and Ernie Colón. 2006. *The 9/11 Report: A Graphic Adaptation*. New York: Hill and Wang.
Jagoda, Patrick. 2010. "Clacking Control Societies: Steampunk, History, and the Difference Engine of Escape." *Neo-Victorian Studies* 3 (1): 46–71.
Jamieson, Kathleen Hall. 1995. *Beyond the Double Bind: Women and Leadership*. New York: Oxford University Press.
Jay. 2017. "The Unconstitutional Actions and Adventures of the Dead Presidents #1 Comes to Comixology!" *Comic Frontline* (blog), January 4. Accessed July 1, 2019. https://comicfrontline.blogspot.com/2017/01/the-unconstitutional-actions-and.html.
Jenkins, Henry. 2013. "'Super-Powered Fans': The Many Worlds of San Diego Comic-Con." *Boom: A Journal of California* 2 (2): 22–36.
Jenkins, Paul et al. 2010. *Civil War: Front Line*. New York: Marvel Worldwide.
Jha. 2009. "The Intersection of Race and Steampunk." *Silver Goggles* (blog), October 20, 2009. Accessed February 19, 2017. http://silver-goggles.blogspot.com/2009/10/intersection-of-race-and-steampunk.html.
Johnston, Angus. 2016. "Why We Should Lower the Voting Age in America. *Rolling Stone*, November 3. Accessed February 23, 2020. https://www.rollingstone.com/politics/politics-features/why-we-should-lower-the-voting-age-in-america-190319/.
Johnston, Deirdre D., and Debra H. Swanson. 2003. "Undermining Mothers: A Content Analysis of the Representation of Mothers in Magazines." *Mass Communication & Society* 6 (3): 243–65.
Johnston, Rich. 2019. "DC Sends Cease and Desist Demand Over Woman AOC Cover." *Bleeding Cool*, May 17. Accessed July 2, 2019. https://www.bleedingcool.com/2019/05/17/dc-sends-cease-and-desist-over-wonder-woman-aoc-cover/.
Johnston, Rich. 2018. "Jesus Should Have Been a Superhero—Talking to Mark Russell." *Bleeding Cool*, August 25. Accessed January 27, 2019. https://www.bleedingcool.com/2018/08/25/jesus-superhero-mark-russell/.
Johnston, Rich. 2020. "Will Brain Bendis Get Superman Directly Involved in Politics?" *Bleeding Cool*, January 1. Accessed March 15, 2020. https://www.bleedingcool.com/2020/01/01/brian-bendis-superman-politics-action-comics-1018-spoilers/.
Johnston, Rich. 2016. "Oliver Queen Gets into Bed with Donald Trump . . ." *Bleeding Cool*, December 9. Accessed November 3, 2017. https://www.bleedingcool.com/2016/12/09/oliver-queen-gets-bed-donald-trump/.
Jolles, Marjorie. 2012. "Going Rogue: Postfeminism and the Privilege of Breaking Rules." *Feminist Formations* 24 (3): 43–61.
Jonason, Peter K., Gregory D. Webster, David P. Schmitt, Norman P. Li, and Laura C. Crysel. 2012. "The Antihero in Popular Culture: Life History Theory and the Dark Triad of Personality Traits." *Review of General Psychology* 16: 192–99.
Jones, Jeffrey P. 2010. *Entertaining Politics*, second edition. Lanham, MD: Rowman & Littlefield.

Jurgens, Dan, Karl Kesel, William Messner-Loebs, Jerry Ordway, Louise Simpson, Roger Stern, et al. 2016. *Superman: Funeral for a Friend*. Burbank, CA: DC Comics.

Justice League. 2003. "A Better World." DVD. Directed by Dan Riba. Burbank, CA: Warner Bros. Entertainment, 2010.

Kahl, Mary L. 2009. "First Lady Michelle Obama: Advocate for Strong Families." *Communication and Critical/Cultural Studies* 6 (3): 316–20.

Kaneya, Rui. 2014. "How Comics Journalism Brings Stories to Life." *Columbia Journalism Review*, September 19. Accessed June 14, 2019. https://archives.cjr.org/united_states_project/illustrated_press_chicago_comics_journalism.php.

Kassie, Emily. 2019. "Detained." *Guardian*, September 24. Accessed May 29, 2020. https://www.theguardian.com/us-news/2019/sep/24/detained-us-largest-immigrant-detention-trump.

Kasulis, Kelly. 2019. "US, North Korea Allude to War Ahead of Pyongyang's Deadline." *VOA*, December 5. Accessed May 29, 2020. https://www.voanews.com/east-asia-pacific/us-north-korea-allude-war-ahead-pyongyangs-deadline.

Kawaguchi, Kaiji. 2000. *Eagle: The Making of an Asian-American President*, vol. 1: "The Candidate," adapted by Carl Gustav Horn. San Francisco, CA: Viz Communication.

Kawaguchi, Kaiji. 2000. *Eagle: The Making of an Asian-American President*, vol. 2: "Scandal," adapted by Carl Gustav Horn. San Francisco, CA: Viz Communication.

Kawaguchi, Kaiji. 2000. *Eagle: The Making of an Asian-American President*, vol. 3: "The Vice-President," adapted by Carl Gustav Horn. San Francisco, CA: Viz Communication.Keen, Sam. 1986. *Faces of the Enemy: Reflections of the Hostile Imagination*. San Francisco, CA: Harper & Row.

Keith, Jed W. 2016. "Recapturing the Magic: Mark Russell on The Flintstones." *FreakSugar*, July 12. Accessed January 23, 2019. http://www.freaksugar.com/mark-russell-the-flintstones-interview/.

Kelly, John. 2016. "What's With All Trump's Talking about 'Draining the Swamp'?" *Slate*, October 26. Accessed October 1, 2018. http://www.slate.com/blogs/lexicon_valley/2016/10/26/why_do_trump_and_his_supports_keep_talking_about_draining_the_swamp.html.

Kemnitz, Thomas Milton. 1973. "The Cartoon as a Historical Source." *Journal of Interdisciplinary History* IV (1): 81–93

Kennedy, Michael. 2016. "Batman Supported by Write-In Votes During 2016 Election." *ScreenRant*, November 27. Accessed July 21, 2018. https://screenrant.com/batman-votes-write-in-united-states-presidential-election-2016/.

Kessler, Eric H., and Diane J. Wong-MingJi. 2009. *Cultural Mythology and Global Leadership*. Northampton, MA: Edward Elgar.

Khouri, Andy. 2011. "BOOM!'s Presidential Straw Poll to be Determined by Comics Pre-Orders." *Comics Alliance*, August 18. Accessed June 3, 2018. http://comicsalliance.com/boom-studios-presidential-straw-poll-comics/.

Kickstarter. 2019. "'In 'BLACK,' Kwanza Osajyefo Created a World Where Only Black People Have Superpowers. The Sequel, 'WHITE,' Is about What Happens When America Finds Out." *Kickstarter Magazine*, March 13. Accessed May 31, 2020. https://medium.com/kickstarter/In-black-kwanza-osajyefo-created-a-world-where-only-black-people-have-superpowers-da7cfebaf6d9.

Kieffer, Bill, and Joe Paradise. 1992. *Great Morons in History Featuring Dan Quayle*. San Diego, CA: Revolutionary Comics.

Kimble, James J., and Trischa Goodnow. 2017. "Introduction." In *The 10th War: Comic Books, Propaganda, and World War II*, edited by Trischa Goodnow and James J. Kimble, 1–25. Jackson: University Press of Mississippi.

Kimmel, Michael. 2011. *Manhood in America: A Cultural History*, third edition. New York: Oxford.

Kirby, Jack, Roy Thomas, and Steve Ditko. 1993. "When Titans Crash." *Jack Kirby's Secret City Saga* #2. Brooklyn, NY: TOPPS Comics.

Kitch, Carolyn. 2002. "'A Death in the American Family': Myth, Memory, and National Values in the Media Mourning of John F. Kennedy Jr." *Journalism & Mass Communication Quarterly* 79 (2): 294–309.

Knight, Peter. 2000. *Conspiracy Culture: From the Kennedy Assassination to the* The X-Files. London: Routledge. Kindle edition.

Knight, Peter. 2008. "Outrageous Conspiracy Theories: Popular and Official Responses to 9/11 in Germany and the United States." *New German Critique* 35 (1): 156–93.

Knopf, Christina M. 2017. "Hey, Soldier!—Your Slip is Showing!": Militarism vs. Femininity in WWII Comic Pages and Books." In *The 10 Cent War: Comic Books, Propaganda, and World War II*, edited by James Kimble and Trisha Goodnow, 26–45. Jackson: University Press of Mississippi.

Knopf, Christina M. 2018. "Queen of Burlesque: The Subtle (as a Hammer) Satire of *Bomb Queen*." In *Gender and the Superhero Narrative*, edited by Michael Goodrum, Tara Prescott, and Phillip Smith, 101–123. Jackson: University Press of Mississippi.

Knopf, Christina M. 2019a. "'Carrie Fisher Sent Me': Princess Leia as an Avatar of Resistance in the Women's March(es)." *Unbound: A Journal of Digital Scholarship* 1 (1): https://journals.library.unt.edu/index.php/unbound/article/view/103/66.

Knopf, Christina M. 2019b. "Politics as 'the Sum of Everything You Fear': Scarecrow as Phobia Entrepreneur." In *Politics in Gotham: The Batman Universe and Political Thought*, edited by Damien D. Picariello, 159–76. Switzerland: Palgrave Macmillan.

Knopf, Christina M. 2020a. "Living the American Nightmare: The Graveyard Vote, Demon Sheep, Zombie PACs, and Devil Women." In *The Politics of Fear: Horror and Political Thought*, edited by Damien Picariello, 3–16. Switzerland: Palgrave Macmillan.

Knopf, Christina M. 2020b. "UFO (Unusual Female Other) Sightings in *Saucer Country/State*: Metaphors of Identity and Presidential Politics." In *Monstrous Women in Comics*, edited by Samantha Langsdale and Elizabeth Coody, 257–73. Jackson: University Press of Mississippi.

Knopf, C. M. forthcoming. "AfterShock's *Rough Riders* and the Reification of Race Reimagined." In *Drawing the Past: Comics and the Historical Imagination*, edited by Michael Goodrum, D. Hall, and Phillip Smith. Jackson: University Press of Mississippi.

Knopf, Christina M. in preparation. "Caped Crusaders and Cartoon Crossovers: A Nostalgic Look 'Beyond' DC Superheroes." In *The DC Universe*, edited by Doug Brode.

Koenig, Bryan. 2013. "The New Storytellers: For-Profit News Startups Look to Harness Latest Tech, Starting with Mobile." *Online Journalism Review*, May 30. Accessed June 14, 2019. http://www.ojr.org/the-new-storytellers-for-profit-news-startups-look-to-harness-latest-tech-starting-with-mobile/.

Kotz, Dean, and Lisa Moore. 2011. *Decision 2012: Ron Paul*. Los Angeles, CA: BOOM! Studios.

Kovach, Bill, and Tom Rosentiel. 2001. *The Elements of Journalism: What Newspeople Should Know and the Public Should Expect*. New York: Three Rivers Press.

Kremer, Warren, and Al Avison. 1952. *Your Vote is Vital!* New York: Harvey Publications.

Kretsch, Ron. 2016. "'Reagan's Raiders': Insane '80s Ultra-Patriot Superhero Comics." *Dangerous Minds*, October 18. Accessed December 20, 2018. https://dangerousminds.net/comments/reagans_raiders_insane_80s_ultra_patriot_superhero_comics.

Krishef, Zachary. 2017. "Mark Russell Discusses the Flintstones." *Critical Writ*, April. Accessed January 23, 2019. http://www.criticalwrit.com/2017/04/mark-russell-flintstones-interview.html.

Krueger, Jim, John Paul Leon, Bill Reinhold, and Alex Ross. 2011. *Earth X*. New York: Marvel Comics. Kindle edition.

Krugman, Paul. 2017. "Trump's Deadly Narcissism." *New York Times*, September 29. Accessed November 5, 2017. https://www.nytimes.com/2017/09/29/opinion/trumps-deadly-narcissism.html.

Kubiak, Dan. 1971. "Youth and Their Vote: A New Day is Coming." *Theory into Practice* 10 (5): 321–22.

Kubota, Ryuko. 1997. "A Reevaluation of the Uniqueness of Japanese Written Discourse: Implications to Contrastive Rhetoric." *Written Communication* 14: 460–80.

Kubota, Ryuko. 1999. "Japanese Culture Constructed by Discourses: Implications for Applied Linguistics Research and ELT." *TESOL Quarterly* 33 (1): 9–35.

Kunka, Andrew J. 2017. "Comics, Race, and Ethnicity." In *The Routledge Companion to Comics*, edited by Frank Bramlett, Roy T. Cook, and Aaron Meskin, 275–84. New York: Routledge. Kindle edition.

Lake, Thomas. 2015. "'I am Batman,' Trump Tells Boy on Helicopter Ride." CNN, August 17. Accessed July 20, 2018. https://www.cnn.com/2015/08/16/politics/donald-trump-iowa-state-fair/index.html.

LaMarre, Heather L., Kristen D. Landreville, and Michael A. Beam. 2009. "The Irony of Satire: Political Ideology and the Motivation to See What You Want to See in the *Colbert Report*." *International Journal of Press/Politics*. 14 (2): 212–31.

Landon, Richard. 2008. "A Half-Naked Muscleman in Trunks: Charles Atlas, Superheroes, and Comic Book Masculinity." *Journal of the Fantastic in the Arts* 18: 200–216.

Larson, Stephanie G. 2006. *Media and Minorities: The Politics of Race in the News and Entertainment*. Oxford: Rowman & Littlefield.

Lawrence, John Shelton, and Robert Jewett. 2002. *The Myth of the American Superhero*. Grand Rapids, MI: William B. Eerdmans Publishing Company.

Lee, Don. 2020. "Unemployment Hits 14.7% in April. How Long Before 20.3 Million Lost Jobs Come Back?" *Los Angeles Times*, May 8. Accessed May 29, 2020. https://www.latimes.com/politics/story/2020-05-08/jobs-report-labor-market-shock.

Lee, Michelle. 2016. "Fact Check: Has Trump Declared Bankruptcy Four or Six Times?" *Washington Post*, September 26. Accessed August 17, 2018. https://www.washingtonpost.com/politics/2016/live-updates/general-election/real-time-fact-checking-and-analysis-of-the-first-presidential-debate/fact-check-has-trump-declared-bankruptcy-four-or-six-times/.

Lee, Michelle Ye Hee. 2016. "Why Donald Trump Calls Elizabeth Warren 'Pocahontas.'" *Washington Post*, June 28. Accessed May 2, 2020. https://www.washingtonpost.com/news/fact-checker/wp/2016/06/28/why-donald-trump-calls-elizabeth-warren-pocahontas/.

Lee, Stan et al. 2017/1966–1968. *Iron Man Epic Collection: By Force of Arms*. New York: Marvel.

Lefèvre, Pascal. 2012. "Mise en Scène and Framing: Visual Storytelling in *Lone Wolf and Cub*." In *Critical Approaches to Comics: Theories and Methods*, edited by Matthew J. Smith and Randy Duncan, 71–83. New York: Routledge.

Lehoczky, Etelka. 2016. "'Faith' Makes Fat a Force to Reckon With." NPR, July 6. Accessed July 2, 2019. https://www.npr.org/2016/07/06/484012379/faith-makes-fat-a-force-to-reckon-with.

Leong, Tim. 2017. "Women's March: The Best Pop-Culture-Themed Signs." *Entertainment Weekly*, January 23. Accessed February 7, 2019. https://ew.com/news/womens-march-pop-culture-signs/#the-womens-march-on-washington.

Lepore, Jill. 2015. *The Secret History of Wonder Woman*. New York: Vintage Books. Kindle edition.

Lequidre, Zorikh, and Evan Azriliant. 2006. "The HUAC, McCarthyism, and Witch-Hunts Through Captain Marvel Comics." *Captain Marvel Culture*. Accessed May 22, 2019. http://www.captainmarvelculture.com/witchhunt.html.

Levitz, Paul. 2013. "Why Supervillains?" In *What is a Superhero?*, edited by Robin S. Rosenberg and Peter Coogan, loc. 1654–1714. New York: Oxford University Press. Kindle edition.
Lewis, Danny. 2016. "Victoria Woodhull Ran for President Before Women Had the Right to Vote." *Smithsonian Magazine*, May 10. Accessed July 1, 2019. https://www.smithsonianmag.com/smart-news/victoria-woodhull-ran-for-president-before-women-had-the-right-to-vote-180959038/.
Liefeld, Rob, and Matt Yackey. 2009. *Youngblood* 4 #9. Berkeley, CA: Image Comics.
Liera-Schwichtenberg, Ramona. 2000. "Passing or Whiteness on the Edge of Town." *Critical Studies in Media Communication* 17 (3): 371–74.
Lifeforce Comics. 2011. "The New Teen Titans—Drug Awareness Comic Book Series." *Lifeforce* (blog), January 22. Accessed July 28, 2018. http://lifeforcecomics.blogspot.com/2011/01/new-teen-titans-drug-awareness-comic.html.
Lim, Timothy, Mark Pellegrini, and Brett R. Smith. 2018. *My Hero MAGAdemia: Wall Might*. San Antonio, TX: Antarctic Press.
Lipman-Bluman, Jean. 2005. *The Allure of Toxic Leaders: Why We Follow Destructive Bosses and Corrupt Politicians—and How We Can Survive Them*. New York: Oxford University Press.
Lipsitz, Keena, Christina Trost, Matthew Grossman, and John Sides. 2005. "What Voters Want from Political Campaign Communication." *Political Communication* 22: 337–54.
LoGiurato, Brett, and Colin Campbell. 2015. "'Is this a Comic-Book Version of a Presidential Campaign?'" *Business Insider*, October 28. Accessed October 23, 2018. https://www.businessinsider.com/donald-trump-confronted-by-john-harwood-2015–10/.
Loh, Wy-Yuih, and M. Scott Woodward. 2009. *Political Power: Colin Powell*. USA: BlueWater Productions.
Loise, Dom, and Greg Barrington. 1994. *Capital Capers Presents: Socialism Trek: The Search for Health Care*. Park Ridge, IL: BLT Studios.
Long, Heather. 2016. "Voters Say This is the Ultimate 'Lesser of Two Evils' Election." *CNN Business*, October 13. Accessed October 24, 2018. https://money.cnn.com/2016/09/25/news/economy/donald-trump-hillary-clinton-lesser-of-two-evils/index.html.
Lost Mountain Mechanicals. 2017. "What is The Jekyll Island Chronicles?" *Jekyll Island Chronicles*. Accessed August 10, 2019. https://jekyllislandchronicles.com/about/series.
Lou, Michelle. 2019. "A Publisher is Turning the Mueller Report into a Graphic Novel." CNN, June 23. Accessed June 23, 2019. https://www.cnn.com/2019/06/23/politics/muller-report-graphic-novel-trnd/index.html.
Loughrey, Clarisse. 2017. "Women's March: How Star Wars' Princess Leia Became a Potent Symbol of Resistance." *Independent*, January 22. Retrieved February 6, 2019. https://www.independent.co.uk/arts-entertainment/films/news/womens-march-on-washington-star-wars-princess-leia-carrie-fisher-a-womans-place-is-in-the-resistance-a7539916.html.
Lovett, Jamie. 2017. "Marvel Releases Statement on Controversial X-Men Gold Art." *ComicBook*, September 5. Accessed February 23, 2020. https://comicbook.com/marvel/2017/04/08/marvel-releases-statement-on-controversial-x-men-gold-art/.
Loyd, John. 2011. "The Last Laugh: Understanding *Watchmen*'s Big Joke." In *Minutes to Midnight: Twelve Essays on* Watchmen, edited by Richard Bensam, loc. 1515–1742. Edwardsville, IL: Sequart Research & Literacy Organization. Kindle edition.
Lucas, Julian. 2016. "John Lewis's National Book Award-Winning Graphic Memoir on the Civil Rights Movement." *New York Times*, November 17. Accessed July 10, 2019. https://www.nytimes.com/2016/11/27/books/review/john-lewis-march.html.
Lunbeck, Elizabeth. 2017. "The Allure of Trump's Narcissism." *LARB*, August 1. Accessed November 5, 2017. https://lareviewofbooks.org/article/the-allure-of-trumps-narcissism/#!.

Lyden, John C. 2012. "Whose Film is it Anyway? Canonicity and Authority in *Star Wars* Fandom." *Journal of the American Academy of Religion* 80 (3): 775–86.

Lyons, Kim. 2018. "Pittsburgh Post-Gazette Cartoonist Fired as Paper Shifts Right." *New York Times*, June 15. Accessed August 30, 2019. https://www.nytimes.com/2018/06/15/business/media/pittsburgh-cartoonist-fired.html.

Maberry, Jonathan, Alex Sanchez, and Jay Fotos. 2019. *Pandemica #3*. San Diego, CA: IDW Publishing.

MacDonald, Heidi. 2019. "Marvel Rejects 'Orange Skull' Reference in Art Spiegelman's Historical Essay." *ComicsBeat*, August 19. Accessed August 30, 2019. https://www.comicsbeat.com/marvel-rejects-orange-skull-reference-in-art-spiegelmans-historical-essay-ike-perlmutter/.

Macdonald, Isabel. 2015. "Drawing on the Facts: Comics Journalism and the Critique of Objectivity." In *The Comics of Joe Sacco: Journalism in a Visual World*, edited by Daniel Worden, 54–66. Jackson: University Press of Mississippi. Kindle edition.

Mackay, Brad. 2016. "Comics Journalism: A Guest Post by Brad Mackay." *Ad Astra Comix*, April 7. Accessed June 22, 2019. https://adastracomix.com/2016/04/07/comics-journalism-a-guest-post-by-brad-mackay/.

MacNaughton, Wendy. 2019. "Behind Bars, and Pixels Too: How Technology Makes Jail Even Bleaker." *New York Times*, August 29. Accessed August 31, 2019. https://www.nytimes.com/2019/08/29/business/video-visit-jail-prison.html.

Mahrt, Nina. 2008/2009. "A Comic Approach to Politics? Political Education via Comics." *Journal of Social Science Education* 718 (2/1): 119–31.

Mann, Thomas E., and Norman J. Ornstein. 1994. "Introduction." In *Congress, the Press, and the Public*, edited by Thomas E. Mann and Norman J. Ornstein, 1–14. Washington, DC: American Enterprise Institute and the Brookings Institution.

Manning, Dirk. 2013. "How I Learned to Stop Worrying and Love the Bomb (Queen): A Public Confession Masking as a Forward." In *Bomb Queen VI: Time Bomb Countdown to Armageddon*, by Jimmie Robinson. Berkeley: Image Comics.

Manning, Shaun. 2016. "DC Cancels Second 'Prez' Series, Releasing 12-Page Election Special in November." *Comic Book Resources*, August 11. Accessed August 11, 2016. http://www.comicbookresources.com/article/dc-cancels-second-prez-series-releasing-12-page-special-in-november.

Marshall, Bridget M. 2012. "Comics as Primary Sources: The Case of *Journey into Mohawk Country*." In *Comic Books and American Cultural History: An Anthology*, edited by Matthew Pustz, 26–39. New York: Continuum.

Marston, George. 2020. "Democratic Presidential Candidates Come to Comic Books with POLITICAL POWER Biographies." *Newsarama*, February 25. Accessed May 31, 2020. https://www.newsarama.com/49182-democratic-presidential-candidates-come-to-comic-books-with-political-power-biographies.html.

Maveal, Chloe. 2019. "Marvel Depoliticizes Captain America in Marvel Comics #1000." *ComicsBeat*, August 27. Accessed August 31, 2019. https://www.comicsbeat.com/marvel-depoliticizes-captain-america-marvel-comics-1000/.

Mavri, Kristjan. 2013. "Cormac McCarthy's *The Road* Revisited: Memory and Language in Post-Apocalyptic Fiction." *Politics of Memory* 2 (3): 1–14.

Mazziotta, Julie. 2015. "Meet Faith, the Plus-Size Superhero We Can All Admire." *People*, November 16. Accessed July 2, 2019. https://people.com/books/meet-faith-the-plus-size-superhero-we-can-all-admire/.

McAllister, Matthew Paul. 1990. "Cultural Argument and Organizational Constraint in the Comic Book Industry." *Journal of Communication* 40 (1): 55–71.

McCarthy, Joseph. 1950. "Speech of Joseph McCarthy, Wheeling, West Virginia, February 9, 1950." *History Matters*. Accessed June 9, 2019. http://historymatters.gmu.edu/d/6456.

McClelland-Nugent, Ruth. 2012. "The Amazon Mystique: Subverting Cold War Domesticity in *Wonder Woman* Comics, 1948–1965." In *Comic Books and the Cold War: Essays on Graphic Treatment of Communism, the Code and Social Concerns*, edited by Chris York and Rafiel York, loc. 1524–1703. Jefferson, NC: McFarland. Kindle edition.

McCloud, Scott. 1993. *Understanding Comics: The Invisible Art*. New York: Harper Perennial.

McComsey, Jeff, and Bill Jemas. 2016. *Z-Men: All the President's Men*, volume 1. New York: Double Take.

McDermott, Jim. 2016. "Electing a President in an Age of Superheroes." *Eureka Street* 26 (2): 26–28.

McDuffie, Dwayne and Val Semeiks. 1992. "Political Asylum Part 1: Damage Control." *The Demon* #26. New York, NY: DC Comics.

McDuffie, Dwayne, Val Semeiks, and Bob Smith. 1992. "Political Asylum Part 2: Etrigan, He's Our Man, If He Can't Do It, No One Can!" *The Demon* #27. New York, NY: DC Comics.

McDuffie, Dwayne, Val Semeiks and Bob Smith. 1992. "Political Asylum Part 3: Spin Control." *The Demon* #28. New York: DC Comics.

McDuffie, Dwayne, Val Semeiks, and Bob Smith. 1992. "Political Asylum Part 4: Out of Control." *The Demon* #29. New York, NY: DC Comics.

McIntosh, Samuel. 2017. *President Trump*, January 11. N.p: comiXology.

McKerrow, Raymie E. 1989. "Critical Rhetoric: Theory and Praxis." *Communication Monographs* 56 (2): 91–111.

McKerrow, Raymie E. 1991. "Critical Rhetoric in a Postmodern World." *Quarterly Journal of Speech* 77 (1): 75–78.

McLuhan, Marshall. 1964. *Understanding Media: The Extensions of Man*. New York: McGraw-Hill.

McMillan, Graeme. 2015. "'Action Presidents' Signed for Four Book Deal by Harper Collins." *Hollywood Reporter*, January 13. Accessed June 13, 2018. https://www.hollywoodreporter.com/heat-vision/action-presidents-signed-four-book-763527.

McMillan, Graeme. 2017. "DC Reviving Hanna-Barbera's 'Snagglepuss' as Gay Playwright." *Hollywood Reporter*, October 16. Accessed January 27, 2019. https://www.hollywoodreporter.com/heat-vision/dc-reviving-hanna-barberas-snagglepuss-as-gay-playwright-1048870.

Medhurst, Martin J., and Michael A. DeSousa. 1981. "Political Cartoons as Rhetorical Form: A Taxonomy of Graphic Discourse." *Communication Monographs* 48: 197–236.

Mehta, Sunita, and G. C. Maheshwari. 2014. "Toxic Leadership: Tracing the Destructive Trail." *International Journal of Management* 5 (10): 18–24.

Melder, Keith. 1989. "Creating Candidate Imagery: The Man on Horseback." In *Campaigns and Elections, A Reader in Modern American Politics*, edited by Larry J. Sabato, 5–11. Boston: Scott, Foresman and Company.

Mele, Christopher, and Annie Correal. 2016. "'Not Our President': Protests Spread After Donald Trump's Election." *New York Times*, November 9. Accessed October 26, 2018. https://www.nytimes.com/2016/11/10/us/trump-election-protests.html.

Melucci, Alberto. 1995. "The Process of Collective Identity." In *Social Movements and Culture*, edited by Hank Johnston and Bert Klandermans, 41–63. Minneapolis: University of Minnesota Press.

Melrose, Kevin. 2016. "Donald Trump Becomes a Marvel Supervillain in 'Spider-Gwen.'" *Comic Book Resources*, July 2. Accessed September 13, 2016. https://www.cbr.com/donald-trump-becomes-a-marvel-supervillain-in-spider-gwen/.

Melrose, Kevin. 2017a. "Mark Hammill's Joker Returns to Read Trump's Meryl Streep Tweets." *Comic Book Resources*, January 14. Accessed January 21, 2017. https://www.cbr.com/mark-hamills-joker-returns-to-read-trumps-meryl-streep-tweets/.

Melrose, Kevin. 2017b. "Trump Chillingly Reimagined as Justice League's President Luthor." *Comic Book Resources*, January 27. Accessed January 29, 2017. https://www.cbr.com/trump-justice-league-president-luthor/.

Mendelberg, Tali. 2001. *The Race Card: Campaign Strategy, Implicit Messages, and the Norm of Equality*. Princeton, NJ: Princeton University Press.

Mendelson, Scott. 2018. "'Black Panther' is $99k Away From One Last Box Office Milestone." *Forbes*, July 16. Accessed July 21, 2018. https://www.forbes.com/sites/scottmendelson/2018/07/16/box-office-marvel-black-panther-700m-chadwick-boseman-ryan-coogler/#5424d5694c99.

Menin, Julie. 2009. "Women and the 2008 Election: A New Majority." *HuffPost*, January 1. Accessed June 23, 2019. https://www.huffpost.com/entry/women-and-the-2008-electi_b_146580.

Merino, Ana. 2012. "Interextuality: Surrealist Intertextualities in Max's *Bardín*," translated by Elizabeth Polli. In *Critical Approaches to Comics: Theories and Methods*, edited by Matthew J. Smith and Randy Duncan, 252–64. New York: Routledge.

Messner-Lobe, William, and Peter Gross. 1992. "Testimony to the World." *Doctor Fate* #39. New York: DC Comics.

Meyer, John. 2000. "Humor as a Double-Edged Sword: Four Functions of Humor in Communication." *Communication Theory* 10 (3): 310–31.

Mickwitz, Nina. 2019. "'True Story': The Aesthetic Balancing Acts of Documentary Comics." *ImageTexT* 11 (1): http://imagetext.english.ufl.edu/archives/v11_1/mickwitz/.

Microcosm Publishing. 2010. "Edible Secrets: A Food Tour of Classified U.S. History." Accessed June 19, 2019. https://food-history.org/edible-secrets-a-food-tour-of-classified-u-s-history/.

Millar, Mark, and Steve McNiven. 2017. *Wolverine: Old Man Logan*. New York: Marvel Comics.

Miller, Elaine K. 2009. "Sarah Palin in the '08 Campaign: Political Cartoon Portrayals." *ek miller Productions*. Accessed June 26, 2019. http://ekmillerproductions.com/108-2/.

Mooney, Jadwiga E. Pieper. 2007. "Militant Motherhood Re-Visited: Women's Participation and Political Power in Argentina and Chile." *History Compass* 5 (3): 975–94.

Moore, Alan, and Dave Gibbons. 2014. *Watchmen*, new edition. Burbank, CA: DC Comics.

Moore, Robert, and Douglas Gillette. 2013. *King, Warrior, Magician, Lover: Rediscovering the Archetypes of the Mature Masculine*. New York: HarperCollins. Kindle edition.

Moore, Rose. 2017. "Supergirl: Lynda Carter's President Marsdin is a Durlan." *ScreenRant*, March 28. Accessed July 1, 2019. https://screenrant.com/supergirl-lynda-carter-president-marsdin-durlan-alien/.

Moran, Lee. 2017. "Donald Trump Aces Keith Olbermann's Screening Test for Psychopaths." *Huffington Post*, March 30. Accessed November 5, 2017. https://www.huffingtonpost.com/entry/keith-olbermann-donald-trump-sanity-test_us_58dcaa2ee4b08194e3b7438b.

Morin, Rebecca. 2019. "Some 2020 Democrats Spoke in Spanish During Their First Debate. Was it 'Hispandering'?" *USA Today*, June 30. Accessed July 8, 2019. https://www.usatoday.com/story/news/politics/elections/2019/06/30/dnc-debate-spanish-beto-booker-castro-latinos-hispandering/1592517001/.

Morreale, Joanne. 1991. "The Political Campaign Film: Epideictic Rhetoric in a Documentary Frame." In *Television and Political Advertising, Vol. 2*, edited by Frank Biocca, 187–201. Hillsdale, NJ: Lawrence Erlbaum Associates.

Morreale, Joanne. 1996. "Playing Politics: Mythical Portraiture in Presidential Campaign Film." *Visual Communication Quarterly* 3 (1): 8–12.

Morris, Jonathan S., and Rosalee A. Clawson. 2005. "Media Coverage of Congress in the 1990s: Scandals, Personalities, and the Prevalence of Policy and Process." *Political Communication* 22 (3): 297–313.

Morrison, Grant. 2003. *Animal Man: Deus Ex Machina*. New York: DC Comics.

Morrison, Matthew C. 1969. "The Role of the Political Cartoonist in Image Making." *Central States Speech Journal* 20: 252–60.

Moses, Lucia. 2017. "'Politics is Pop Culture News': In the Trump Era, Political News is Everyone's Beat." *Digiday*, April 10. Accessed July 20, 2018. https://digiday.com/media/politics-pop-culture-news-trump-era-political-news-everyones-beat/.

Moulton, Charles. 1943. *Wonder Woman #7*. New York: Wonder Woman Publishing Co.

Mount Holyoke. N.d. "Man Against the People." *Five Colleges Libraries*. Accessed June 6, 2018. https://fcaw.library.umass.edu/F/IFFKS6BFBTP1LFDC48FDNX72LAQECS44JUBKXXQIIT554IF36G-00989?func=find-b&find_code=035&request=ocm47956890&pds_handle=GUEST.

Moy, Patricia, and Michael Pfau. 2000. *With Malice Toward All? The Media and Public Confidence in Democratic Institutions*. Westport, CT: Praeger.

Murphy, Brenda. 1999. *Congressional Theatre: Dramatizing McCarthyism on Stage, Film, and Television*. Cambridge, UK: Cambridge University Press.

Murphy, Chris. 2013. "Think for Yourself and Question Authority: Politics in Transmetropolitan." In *Shot in the Face: A Savage Journey to the Heart of* Transmetropolitan, edited by Chad Nevett, 24–31. Edwardsville, IL: Sequart Research & Literacy Organization. Kindle edition.

Murphy, John M. 2003. "'Our Mission and Our Moment': George W. Bush and September 11th." *Rhetoric and Public Affairs* 6 (4): 607–632.

Myers, Sheri Leigh, and Sophie Goldstein. 2006. *Cheated!* Los Angeles: Wake Up and Save Your Country.

Nabi, Robin L., Emily Moyer-Gusé, and Sahara Byrne. 2007. "All Joking Aside: A Serious Investigation into the Persuasive Effect of Funny Social Issue Messages." *Communication Monographs* 74 (1): 29–54.

Nama, Adilfu. 2011. *Super Black: American Pop Culture and Black Superheroes*. Austin: University of Texas Press.

Nash, George H. 2003. "Herbert Hoover: Political Orphan." In *Uncommon Americans: The Lives and Legacies of Herbert and Lou Henry Hoover*, edited by Timothy Nash, 9–18. Westport, CT: Praeger.

Naso, Markisan. 2005. "Darwyn Cooke: Toward the Heavens." *Comics Bulletin*. Accessed September 18, 2016. http://comicsbulletin.com/features/110950048942545.htm.

Naso, Markisan. 2016. "Darwyn Cooke, 1962–2016." *Comics Journal*, May 19. Accessed September 18, 2016. http://www.tcj.com/darwyn-cooke-1962-2016/.

Nayak, Anoop. 2007. "Critical Whiteness Studies," *Sociology Compass* 1/2: 737–55.

Nedvidek, Steve, Ed Crowell, Jack Lowe, J. Moses Nester, and S. J. Miller. 2016. *The Jekyll Island Chronicles: A Machine Age War*. Marietta, GA: TopShelf Productions.

Nelson, Blake. 2018. "An Illustrated Guide to Making Comics Journalism." *IRE Journal* (3): 20–21.

Nelson, Dana. 2008. *Bad for Democracy: How the Presidency Undermines the Power of the People*. Minneapolis: University of Minnesota Press.

Nelson, John S. 2005. "Horror Films Face Political Evils in Everyday Life." *Political Communication* 22: 381–86.
Neufeld, Josh. 2017. "The Trump-Russia Memos." *Columbia Journalism Review* (Fall). Accessed July 18, 2018. https://www.cjr.org/special_report/trump-russia-memos-dossier-buzzfeed.php.
Nevins, Jess. 2008. "Introduction: The 19th-Century Roots of Steampunk." In *Steampunk*, edited by Ann VanderMeer and Jeff VanderMeer, 3–11. San Francisco: Tachyon Publications.
Newkirk, Vann R., II. 2018. "How *Shelby County v. Holder* Broke America." *Atlantic*, July 10. Accessed May 2, 2020. https://www.theatlantic.com/politics/archive/2018/07/how-shelby-county-broke-america/564707/.
Newsweek staff. 2018. "Donald Trump vs. the Media: Who Will Win the War?" *Newsweek*, August 5. Accessed July 19, 2019. https://www.newsweek.com/donald-trump-vs-media-who-will-win-war-analysis-1057661.
Nicolle, Malachai, and Ethan Nicolle. 2013. *Axe Cop: President of the World*, comiXology edition. Milwaukie, OR: Dark Horse Books.
Niemeyer, Katharina. 2014. "Introduction: Media and Nostalgia." In *Media and Nostalgia: Yearning for the Past, Present and Future*, edited by Katharina Niemeyer, 1–24. New York: Palgrave Macmillan. Kindle edition.
Niven, David, and Jeremy Zilber. 2001. "How Does She Have Time for Kids and Congress?" *Women & Politics* 23 (1–2): 147–65.
Niven, David, S. Robert Lichter, and Daniel Amundson. 2003. "The Political Content of Late Night Comedy." *Harvard International Journal of Press/Politics* 8 (3): 118–33.
NMG. 2012. "EXTRACTION! COMIX REPORTAGE": A Gallery of Radical Canadian Comics Journalism." *Ad Astra Comix*, August 13. Accessed June 22, 2019. https://adastracomix.com/2012/08/13/a-review-of-extraction-comix-reportage/.
Noon, David Hoogland. 2016. "Barack Obama and the Myth of the Superheroic Presidency." *Canadian Review of American Studies/ Revue canadienne d'études américaines* 46 (3): 432–54.
Novi, Luigi. 2018. "Review: The 'March' Trilogy by John Lewis, Andrew Aydin, & Nate Powell." *Comic Mix*, November 6. Accessed July 10, 2019. https://www.comicmix.com/2018/11/06/review-the-march-trilogy-by-john-lewis-andrew-aydin-nate-powell/.
Noys, Benjamin, and Timothy S. Murphy. 2016. "Introduction: Old and New Weird." *Genre* 49 (2): 117–34.
Nyberg, Amy Kiste. 1998. *Seal of Approval: The History of the Comics Code*. Jackson: University Press of Mississippi.
Nyberg, Amy Kiste. 2006. "Theorizing Comics Journalism." *International Journal of Comic Art* 8 (2): 98–112.
Nyberg, Amy Kiste. 2012. "Comics Journalism: Drawing on Words to Picture the Past in *Safe Area Goražde*." In *Critical Approaches to Comics: Theories and Methods*, edited by Matthew J. Smith and Randy Duncan, 116–28. New York: Routledge.
Nyberg, Amy Kiste. 2017. "The Comics Code." In *The Routledge Companion to Comics*, edited by Frank Bramlett, Roy T. Cook, and Aaron Meskin, 25–33. New York: Routledge. Kindle edition.
O'Brien, Edward. 2018. "Montana Voters Talk Campaign Fatigue, 2018 Priorities." *Montana Public Radio*, April 4. Accessed October 29, 2018. http://www.mtpr.org/post/montana-voters-talk-campaign-fatigue-2018-priorities.
O'Hehir, Andrew. 2016a. "America's First White President." *Salon*, December 10. Accessed January 24, 2017. http://www.salon.com/2016/12/10/americas-first-white-president/.

O'Hehir, Andrew. 2016b. "Fake News, a Fake President and Fake Country: Welcome to America, Land of No Context." *Salon*, December 3. Accessed August 10, 2019. https://www.salon.com/control/2016/12/03/fake-news-a-fake-president-and-a-fake-country-welcome-to-america-land-of-no-context/.

O'Leary, Stephen D. 1994. *Arguing the Apocalypse: A Theory of Millennial Rhetoric*. New York: Oxford University Press.

Opam, Kwame. 2017. "Of Course Your Comics Are Political, Marvel." *Verge*, April 3. Accessed February 23, 2020. https://www.theverge.com/2017/4/3/15161012/marvel-comics-sales-diversity-politics.

Ormrod, Joan. 2014. "Cold War Fantasies: Testing the Limits of the Familial Body." In *The Ages of Wonder Woman: Essays on the Amazon Princess in Changing Times*, edited by Joseph J. Darowski, loc. 979–1265. Jefferson, NC: McFarland. Kindle edition.

O'Shea, Shane, and Ogden Whitney. 1964. "Herbie and the Purloined Pops." *Herbie* #2. Sparta, IL: Best Syndicated Features.

Ott, Brian L. 2010. "The Visceral Politics of V for Vendetta: On Political Affect in Cinema." *Critical Studies in Media Communication* 27 (1): 39–54.

Owens, Katharine A., Victor Eno, Jocelyn Abrams, and Danielle Bedney. 2019. "Comic-Con: Can Comics of the Constitution Enable Meaningful Learning in Political Science?" *PS: Political Science and Politics*: 1–6.

Painter, Nell Irvin. 2016. "What Whiteness Means in the Trump Era." *New York Times*, November 12. Accessed January 24, 2017. https://www.nytimes.com/2016/11/13/opinion/what-whiteness-means-in-the-trump-era.html.

Paleologos, David. 2018. "Paleologos on the Poll: Ask Voters About Trump and Get an Earful, Regardless of Party." *USA Today*, June 21. Accessed October 24, 2018. https://www.usatoday.com/story/news/politics/2018/06/21/democrats-republicans-think-other-deplorable-trump-midpoint-presidency/722352002/.

Palin, Sarah. 2008. "Palin's Speech at the Republican National Convention." *New York Times*, September 3. Accessed June 30, 2019. https://www.nytimes.com/elections/2008/president/conventions/videos/transcripts/20080903_PALIN_SPEECH.html.

Paoletta, Rae. 2015. "This Plus-Size Superhero is Here to Save Us All from Lame Comic Book Stereotypes." MTV, November 10. Accessed July 2, 2019. http://www.mtv.com/news/2423809/faith-valiant-plus-size-superhero/.

Papenfuss, Mary. 2019. "Alexandria Ocasio-Cortez Quotes 'Watchmen' Author Alan Moore, Slays Nerd Hearts." *HuffPost*, January 11. Accessed February 1, 2019. https://www.huffingtonpost.com/entry/ocasio-cortez-quotes-watchmen-author-alan-moore-nerd-hearts_us_5c39231be4b0922a21d4fd6e.

Parker, Jeff, and Miguel Mendonca. 2020. "Perfect World." *The Flash: Fastest Man Alive* #6. Burbank, CA: DC Comics. Comixology edition.

Parry-Giles, Trevor, and Shawn J. Parry-Giles. 2002. "*The West Wing's* Prime-Time Presidentiality: Mimesis and Catharsis in a Postmodern Romance." *Quarterly Journal of Speech* 88: 209–227.

Parry-Giles, Trevor, and Shawn J. Parry-Giles. 2006. *The Prime-Time Presidency: The West Wing and U.S. Nationalism*. Urbana: University of Illinois Press.

Patrick, Kevin. 2017. *The Phantom Unmasked: America's First Superhero*. Iowa City: University of Iowa Press.

Perez, Alfred, and Ben Dunn. 2017. *President Pence*. San Antonio, TX: Antarctic Press.

Perez, Alfred, and David Hutchison. 2017. *Trump vs. Time Lincoln*. San Antonio: Antarctic Press.

Perez, Alfred, Ben Dunn, and Tony Galvan. 2017. *The Tremendous Trump*. San Antonio, TX: Antarctic Press.

Perez, Maria. 2017. "Trump's Defining Feature is His 'Overcompensating' Long Ties, Cartoonists Say." *Newsweek*, December 26. Accessed June 21, 2019. https://www.newsweek.com/trump-defining-feature-long-red-tie-cartoonists-759335.

Perry, Fred. 2014. *Time Lincoln: Continental #1*. San Antonio, TX: Antarctic Press.

Persoff, Ethan. 2007. "Segregation: George Wallace for the Big Job." *Comics with Problems* (blog) 19 (August). Accessed April 11, 2018. http://www.ep.tc/problems/nineteen/01.html.

Persoff, Ethan. 2012. "Election Day Comics from 1960." *Comics with Problems* (blog) 53 (November). Accessed July 14, 2018. http://www.ep.tc/problems/53/.

Peters, Mark. 2016. "Donald Trump, Supervillain? Here are 8 Evil Comic Book Presidents Who Resemble the GOP Front-Runner." *Salon*, April 3. Accessed November 16, 2016. https://www.salon.com/2016/04/03/donald_trump_supervillain_here_are_8_evil_comic_book_presidents_who_resemble_the_gop_front_runner/.

Peters, Mark. 2017. "Comics as Interpretive Journalism: Three Ways Trump's Tweets Have Landed in Panels." *Paste Magazine*, July 12. Accessed June 26, 2018. https://www.pastemagazine.com/articles/2017/07/comics-as-interpretive-journalism-three-ways-trump.html.

Petersen, Anne Helen. 2017. *Too Fat, Too Slutty, Too Loud: The Rise and Reign of the Unruly Woman*. New York: Plume.

Peterson, Geoff, and J. Mark Wrighton. 1998. "Expressions of Distrust: Third-Party Voting and Cynicism in Government." *Political Behavior* 20 (1): 17–34.

Pew Research Center. 2015. "Beyond Distrust: How Americans View Their Government." *People Press*, November 23. Accessed October 26, 2018. http://www.people-press.org/2015/11/23/beyond-distrust-how-americans-view-their-government/.

Pfau, Michael, Patricia Moy, and Erin Alison Szabo. 2001. "Influence of Prime-Time Television Programming on Perceptions of the Federal Government." *Mass Communication and Society* 4 (4): 437–54.

Phalen, Patricia F., Jennie Kim, and Julia Osellame. 2012. "Imagined Presidencies: The Representation of Political Power in Television Fiction." *Journal of Popular Culture* 45 (3): 532–50.

Phillipps, Susanne. 2001. "Images of Asia in Japanese Best-Selling Manga." *Electronic Journal of Contemporary Japanese Studies*. Papers presented at ICAS 2, Berlin, Germany, August 9–12. http://www.japanesestudies.org.uk/ICAS2/Phillipps.pdf.

Philpott, Tom. 2016. "Farmers Are Huge Trump Supporters. Here's Why." *Mother Jones*, October 31. Accessed May 3, 2020. https://www.motherjones.com/environment/2016/10/trump-farmers/.

Phoenix, Woodrow. 2017. "Looking for America's Dog." *Slings and Arrows*. Accessed July 8, 2019. https://theslingsandarrows.com/looking-for-americas-dog/.

Pilkington, Ed. 2018. "'He's My Guy': Donald Trump Praises Gianforte for Assault on Guardian Reporter." *Guardian*, October 19. Accessed October 24, 2018. https://www.theguardian.com/us-news/2018/oct/18/trump-greg-gianforte-assault-guardian-ben-jacobs.

Podlas, Kimberlianne. 2013. "Funny or No Laughing Matter? How Television Viewers Interpret Satire of Legal Themes." *Seton Hall Journal of Sports and Entertainment Law* 21 (2): 289–331.

Polgreen, Erin, and Joyce Rice. 2014. "Comic: How Big Media Drowned Out the Rest of Us." *YES! Magazine*, May 23. Accessed June 14, 2019. https://www.yesmagazine.org/issues/the-power-of-story/the-power-of-story-1.

Politico Magazine. 2017. "Will America Ever Have a Woman President?" *Politico*, November/December. Accessed June 23, 2019. https://www.politico.com/magazine/story/2017/11/03/will-america-have-woman-president-politics-2017-215769.

Politics. 2016. "How to Draw Donald Trump." *Vanity Fair*, October 19. Accessed June 26, 2018. https://video.vanityfair.com/watch/caricature-artists-draw-donald-trump.

Powell, Gary N., D. Anthony Butterfield, and Xueting Jiang. 2018. "Why Trump and Clinton Won and Lost: The Roles of Hypermasculinty and Androgyny." *Equality, Diversity and Inclusion: An International Journal* 37 (1): 44–62.

Powers, Mark. 2008. "Commentary Track: Drafted #12." *CBR*, November 26. Accessed July 8, 2019. https://www.cbr.com/commentary-track-drafted-12/.

Powers, Mark. 2009. *Drafted: One Hundred Days*. Chicago: Devil's Due Publishing.

Press, Charles. 1981. *The Political Cartoon*. Toronto: Associated University Presses.

Prida, Jonas. 2013. "Introduction." In *Conan Meets the Academy: Multidisciplinary Essays on the Enduring Barbarian*, edited by Jonas Prida, 5–12. Jefferson, NC: McFarland. Kindle edition.

Prims, J. P., Zachary J. Melton, and Matt Motyl. 2017. "Tweeting Morals in the 2016 Election." In *Why Irrational Politics Appeals: Understanding the Allure of Trump*, edited by Mari Fitzduff, 171–90. Santa Barbara, CA: ABC-CLIO. Kindle edition.

Prince, Michael J. 2011. "Alan Moore's America: The Liberal Individual and American Identities in *Watchmen*." *Journal of Popular Culture* 44 (4): 815–30.

Publisher's Weekly. 2008/2009. "08: A Graphic Diary of the Campaign Trail." Accessed June 19, 2019. https://www.publishersweekly.com/978-0-307-40511-1.

Rafter, Dan, and Nathan Carson. 2010. *Female Force: Sarah Palin, the Sequel*. USA: BlueWater Comics.

Raz, Carmel. 2011. "Wagnerpunk: A Steampunk Reading of Patrice Chéreau's Staging of *Der Ring des Nibelungen* (1876)." *Neo-Victorian Studies* 4 (2): 91–107.

Reagan, Nancy. 1983. "Dear Friend." Keebler Company Presents DC Comics' *The New Titans*, inside front cover. New York: DC Comics.

Reed, Bill. 2007. "365 Reasons to Love Comics #74." *Comic Book Resources*, March 15. Accessed September 21, 2015. http://goodcomics.comicbookresources.com/2007/03/15/365-reasons-to-love-comics-74/.

Reed, Gary, Laurence Campbell, Chris Jones, and Larry Shuput. 1997. *The Red Diaries: The Kennedy Conspiracy*. Wayne County, MI: Caliber Comics.

Reeve, Elspeth. 2015. "How Donald Trump Evolved from a Joke to an Almost Serious Candidate." *New Republic*, October 27. Accessed October 1, 2018. https://newrepublic.com/article/123228/how-donald-trump-evolved-joke-almost-serious-candidate.

Rehak, Bob. 2011. "Adapting *Watchmen* after 9/11." *Cinema Journal* 51 (1): 154–59.

Reicher, Stephen and S. Alexander Haslam. 2017. "The Politics of Hope: Donald Trump as an Entrepreneur of Identity." In *Why Irrational Politics Appeals: Understanding the Allure of Trump*, edited by Mari Fitzduff, 25–40. Santa Barbara, CA: ABC-CLIO. Kindle edition.

Reid, Adam. 2019. *The Adventures of Barry & Joe: Obama & Biden's Bromantic Battle for the Soul of America*. New York: Dey St.

Reid, Jeff. 2015. "Crossing the Streams: Superman and JFK." *BookRiot*, April 10. Accessed July 18, 2018. https://bookriot.com/2015/04/10/crossing-streams-superman-jfk/.

Resnick, Brian. 2017. "Trump Supporters Know Trump Lies. They Just Don't Care." *Vox*, June 10. Accessed May 3, 2020. https://www.vox.com/2017/7/10/15928438/fact-checks-political-psychology.

Reveal & PRX. 2018. "Never Meet Your (Super) Heroes." RevealNews.org, September 22. Accessed February 22, 2020. https://www.revealnews.org/episodes/never-meet-your-super-heroes/.

Reyes, Angela. 2009. "Asian American Stereotypes as Circulating Resource." In *Beyond Yellow English: Toward a Linguistic Anthropology of Asian Pacific America*, edited by Angela Reyes and Adrienne Lo, 43–62. New York: Oxford University Press.

Richardson, Laurel. 2000. "Writing: A Method of Inquiry." In *Handbook of Qualitative Research*, second edition, edited by Norman K. Denzin and Yvonna S. Lincoln, 923–43. Thousand Oaks, CA: Sage.

Ridley, John, and Georges Jeanty. 2017. *The American Way: Those Above and Those Below* #2. Burbank, CA: Vertigo.

Rieder, Travis N. 2016. "Is the 'Lesser of Two Evils' an Ethical Choice for Voters?" *Washington Post*, August 13. Accessed October 24, 2018. https://www.washingtonpost.com/posteverything/wp/2016/08/13/is-the-lesser-of-two-evils-an-ethical-choice-for-voters/.

Riesman, Abraham. 2016. "Donald Trump Has Had 20 Comic-Book Cameos, and Lost His Head in Many of Them." *Vulture*, November 8. Accessed November 18, 2016. http://www.vulture.com/2016/11/donald-trump-comics.html.

Rifas, Leonard. 2012. "Ideology: The Construction of Race and History in *Tintin in the Congo*." In *Critical Approaches to Comics: Theories and Methods*, edited by Matthew J. Smith and Randy Duncan, 221–34. New York: Routledge.

Riggs, Ben. 2016. "Why Reading Comics Makes You Smarter." *Geek and Sundry*, ebruary 15. Accessed August 11, 2019. https://geekandsundry.com/science-proves-reading-comics-makes-you-smarter/.

Rikdad. 2016. "Retro Review: DC: The New Frontier." *Rikdad's Comic Thoughts* (blog), June 18. Accessed September 18, 2016, http://rikdad.blogspot.com/2016/06/retro-review-dc-new-frontier.html.

Ritchie, William. 2011. "At Play Amidst Strangeness and Charm: *Watchmen* and the Philosophy of Science." In *Minutes to Midnight: Twelve Essays on* Watchmen, edited by Richard Bensam, loc. 1069–1325. Edwardsville, IL: Sequart Research & Literacy Organization. Kindle edition.

Ritter, Kurt W. 1980. "American Political Rhetoric and the Jeremiad Tradition: Presidential Acceptance Addresses, 1960–1976." *Central States Speech Journal* 31: 153–71.

Rivera, Joshua. 2015. "DC Comics Skewers Right-Wing Politics in this New Comic Where Teen is Made President." *Business Insider*, June 17. Accessed September 20, 2015. http://www.businessinsider.com/dc-comics-prez-2015-6.

Robbins, Frank, and Don Heck. 1972. "Candidate for Danger." *Detective Comics* #423. New York: National Periodical Publications.

Robbins, Frank, and Don Heck. 1972. "The Unmasking of Batgirl." *Detective Comics* #422. New York: National Periodical Publications.

Robbins, Trina. 2001a. *The Great Women Cartoonists*. New York: Watson-Guptill Publications.

Robbins, Trina. 2001b. *Nell Brinkley and the New Woman in the Early 20th Century*. Jefferson, NC: McFarland.

Robbins, Trina. 2009. *The Brinkley Girls: The Best of Nell Brinkley's Cartoons*. Lake City Way, NE: Fantagraphics Books. Kindle edition.

Robbins, Trina. 2016. "Of Presidents and Pantsuits." *Trina's Blog*, December 1. Accessed August 1, 2018. https://trinarobbins.wordpress.com/2016/12/01/of-presidents-and-pantsuits/.

Roberts, Elizabeth. 2016. "UN Drops Wonder Woman as Honorary Ambassador." CNN, December 13. Accessed May 15, 2019. https://www.cnn.com/2016/12/13/health/wonder-woman-un-ambassador-trnd/index.html.

Robinson, Jimmie. 2009. *Bomb Queen: WMD*. Berkeley, CA: Image Comics.

Robinson, Jimmie. 2013. *Bomb Queen VI: Time Bomb*. Berkeley, CA: Image Comics.

Rogers, David. 2020. "Trump Administration Ducks and Dodges to Justify Wall Spending." *Politico*, April 24. Accessed May 29, 2020. https://www.politico.com/news/2020/04/24/trump-border-wall-spending-204606.

Rogers, Vaneta. 2017. "Is the Average Age of Comic Book Readers Increasing? Retailers Talk State of the Business 2017." *Newsarama*, February 2. Accessed February 23, 2020. https://www.newsarama.com/33006-is-the-average-age-of-comic-book-readers-increasing-retailers-talk-state-of-the-business-2017.html.

Rogin, Michael. 1984. "Kiss Me Deadly: Communism, Motherhood, and Cold War Movies." *Representations* 6 (Spring): 1–36.

Rogin, Michael. 1987. *Ronald Reagan, the Movie and Other Episodes of Political Demonology*. Berkeley, CA: University of California Press.Romano, Aja. 2017. "Muslim American Superhero Kamala Khan has become a Real-World Protest Icon." *Vox*, February 2. Accessed February 4, 2017. https://www.vox.com/culture/2017/2/2/14457384/kamala-khan-captain-america-protest-icon.

Roosevelt, Kermit, III. 2016. "Theodore Roosevelt's Lessons for Today's Politics." *TIME*, July 25. Accessed February 9, 2018. http://time.com/4421539/theodore-roosevelt-lessons/.

Rose, Margaret A. 1999. *Parody: Ancient, Modern, and Post-Modern*. New York: Cambridge University Press.

Rosenkranz, Patrick. 2003. *Rebel Visions: The Underground Comix Revolution, 1963–1975*. Seattle, WA: Fantagraphics Books.

Rosenberg, Alyssa. 2017. "The Women's March Served Notice that Pop Culture Still Has Political Power." *Washington Post*, January 25. Retrieved February 7, 2019. https://www.washingtonpost.com/news/act-four/wp/2017/01/25/the-womens-march-served-notice-that-pop-culture-still-has-political-power/.

Rosenfeld, Gavriel. 2002. "Why Do We Ask 'What If?' Reflections on the Function of Alternate History." *History and Theory* 41 (4): 90–103.

Rossiter, Clinton. 1966. *1787: The Grand Convention*. New York: Macmillan.

Rossiter, Clinton. 1987. *The American Presidency*. Baltimore, MD: Johns Hopkins University Press.

Rothman, Lily. 2018. "Exclusive: Congressman John Lewis' Next Book, *Run*, Will Pick Up Where Award-Winning *March* Left Off." *TIME*, February 15. Accessed March 28, 2019. http://time.com/5135822/john-lewis-book-announcement/.

Round, Julia. 2008. "London's Calling: Alternate Worlds and the City as Superhero in Contemporary British-American Comics." *International Journal of Comic Art* 10 (1): 24–31.

Rowe, Kathleen. 1995. *The Unruly Woman: Gender and the Genres of Laughter*. Austin: University of Texas Press.

Rowland, Robert C., and Thea Rademacher. 1990. "The Passive Style of Rhetorical Crisis Management: A Case Study of the Superfund Controversy." *Communication Studies* 41: 327–42.

Rubin, Jennifer. 2013. "Why Popular Culture Matters in Politics." *Washington Post*, October 28. Accessed May 12, 2018. https://www.washingtonpost.com/blogs/right-turn/wp/2013/10/28/why-popular-culture-matters-in-politics/.

Rushing, Janice Hocker. 1986. "Mythic Evolution of 'The New Frontier' in Mass Mediated Rhetoric." *Critical Studies in Mass Communication* 3 (3): 265–96.

Russell, Jeffrey Burton. 1977. *The Devil: Perceptions of Evil from Antiquity to Primitive Christianity*. Ithaca, NY: Cornell University Press.

Russell, Mark, Ben Caldwell, and Mark Morales. 2016. *Prez, Volume 1: Corndog-in-Chief*. Burbank, CA: DC Comics.

Russell, Mark, Mike Feehan, Sean Parsons, and Jose Marzán Jr. 2018. "Opening Night." *Exit Stage Left: The Snagglepuss Chronicles* #5. Burbank, CA: DC Comics.

Russell, Mark, and Steve Pugh. 2017. "Election Day." *The Flintstones* #5. Burbank, CA: DC Comics.

Russell, Mark, Steve Pugh, and Chris Chuckry. 2017. "The End of the World as We Know It." *The Flintstones* #6. Burbank, CA: DC Comics.

Ryan, Shane. 2019. "Politics is Not a Comic Book." *Paste*, January 29. Accessed January 29, 2019. https://www.pastemagazine.com/articles/2019/01/politics-is-not-a-comic-book.html.

Sabato, Larry J. 2000. *Feeding Frenzy: Attack Journalism & American Politics*. Baltimore, MD: Lanahan Publishers.

Sacco, Joe. 2013. *Journalism*. New York: Metropolitan Books.

Salkowitz, Rob. 2019. "As Comics' Direct Market Struggles, a Surprising Publisher Rises." *Forbes*, January 18. Accessed February 23, 2020. https://www.forbes.com/sites/robsalkowitz/2019/01/18/as-comics-direct-market-struggles-a-surprising-publisher-rises/#5348831f33a6.

Sanderson, Peter. 2011. "Bringing Light to the World: *Watchmen* from Hiroshima to Manhattan." In *Minutes to Midnight: Twelve Essays on* Watchmen, edited by Richard Bensam, 2233–3617. Edwardsville, IL: Sequart Research & Literacy Organization. Kindle edition.

Sardar, Ziauddin. 2002. "Introduction." In *Aliens R Us: The Other in Science Fiction Cinema*, edited by Ziauddin Sardar and Sean Cubitt, 1–17. London: Pluto Press.

Schaffenberger, Kurt, Leo Dorfman, and Milt Snapinn. 1958. *Superman's Girl Friend Lois Lane* #62. New York: National Periodical Publications.

Schatz, Sar. 2001. "Democracy's Breakdown and the Rise of Fascism: The Case of the Spanish Second Republic, 1931–6." *Social History* 26 (2): 145–65.

Scheff, Thomas. 2008. "Who, Me, Angry?" *PsycCRITIQUES* 53 (41): http://www.soc.ucsb.edu/faculty/scheff/main.php?id=68.html.

Schnakenberg, Robert, and Tess Fowler. 2010. *Female Force: Michelle Obama, Year One*. BlueWater Comics.

Schneck, Robert Damon. 2005. *The President's Vampire: Strange-but-Tue Tales of the United States of America*. San Antonio, TX: Anomalist Books.

Scholwater, Dana. 2012. "Financialization of the Family: Motherhood, Biopolitics, and Paths of Power." *Women & Language* 35 (1): 39–56.

Schwartz, Bill, Zachary Schwartz, and Studio Hive. 2014. *American Legends* #5. Berkeley, CA: Image Comics.

Schwartz, Kenneth. 2020. "Comic Strips Thank Front-Line COVID-19 Workers." *VOA News*, June 6. Accessed June 7, 2020. https://www.voanews.com/usa/comic-strips-thank-front-line-covid-19-workers.

Scott, Anna Beatrice. 2006. "Superpower vs. Supernatural: Black Superheroes and the Quest for a Mutant Reality," *Journal of Visual Culture* 5 (3): 295–314.

Scott, Kim Allen, and Susan Parks. 1992. "Comics and Candidates." *Arkansas Historical Quarterly* 51 (3): 247–53.

Scott, Suzanne. 2013. "Fangirls in Refrigerators: The Politics of (In)visibility in Comic Book Culture." *Transformative Works and Cultures* 13: doi:10.3983/twc.2013.0460.

Seaquist, Carla. 2017. "Pop Culture Captures Campaign Politics." *Huffington Post*, April 4. Accessed May 12, 2018. https://www.huffingtonpost.com/carla-seaquist/popular-culture-meets-cam_b_9607064.html.

Seed, David. 1999. *American Science Fiction and the Cold War: Literature and Film*. Edinburgh: Edinburgh University Press.

Selzer, Linda F. 2010. "Barack Obama, the 2008 Presidential Election, and the New Cosmopolitanism: Figuring the Black Body." *MELUS* 35 (4): 15–37.

Semmler, Shane M., Kelly McKay-Semmler, and Terry Robertson. 2013. "Gendered Issue Depictions in *Commander in Chief* Versus *The West Wing*." *Atlantic Journal of Communication* 21 (5): 247–62.
Sergi, Joe. 2013. "Tales from the Code: The Christmas *Panic*." *CBLDF*, December 23. Accessed May 22, 2019. http://cbldf.org/2013/12/tales-from-the-code-the-christmas-panic/.
Serrano, Elliott, and Diego Galindo. 2016. *Army of Darkness: Election Special*. Mt. Laurel, NJ: Dynamite Entertainment.
Serrano, Elliott, and Ariel Padilla. 2010. *Army of Darkness: Ash Saves Obama*. Runnemede, NJ: Dynamite Entertainment.
Seven, John. 2019. "INDIE VIEW: 'Mueller Report Graphic Novel' and 'Minus' Capture Secrets and Lies." *Comics Beat*, June 21. Accessed June 21, 2019. https://www.comicsbeat.com/indie-view-mueller-report-graphic-novel-and-minus-capture-secrets-and-lies/.
Shafer, Jack. 2016. "How Trump Took Over the Media by Fighting It." *Politico*, November 5. Accessed October 26, 2018. https://www.politico.com/magazine/story/2016/11/2016-election-trump-media-takeover-coverage-214419.
Shah, Dhavan V. 1998. "Civic Engagement, Interpersonal Trust, and Television Use: An Individual-Level Assessment of Social Capital." *Political Psychology* 19 (3): 469–96.
Shannon, Kelsey, and Brian Denham. 2018. *Barack Panther*. San Antonio, TX: Antarctic Press.
Shefrin, E. 2004. "*Lord of the Rings*, *Star Wars*, and Participatory Fandom: Mapping New Congruencies between the Internet and Media Entertainment Culture." *Critical Studies in Media Communication* 21 (3): 261–81.
Shiach, Kieran. 2018. "Suicide Squad Introduces a Patriotic New Hero to Make America Great Again." *CBR*, February 15. Accessed July 11, 2019. https://www.cbr.com/suicide-squad-new-superhero-donald-trump/.
Shome, Raka. 2000. "Outing Whiteness." *Critical Studies in Media Communication* 17 (3): 366–71.
Shugart, Helene A. 1999. "Postmodern Irony as Subversive Rhetorical Strategy." *Western Journal of Communication* 63 (4): 433–55.
Silk, Mark. 1998. *Unsecular Media: Making News of Religion in America*. Urbana: University of Illinois Press.
Simon, Joe, and Jerry Grandenetti. 2016. "Oh Say Does That Star Spangled Banner Yet Wave?" In *Prez: The First Teen President*, edited by Liz Erickson, 7–31. Burbank, CA: DC Comics.
The Simpsons. "Treehouse of Horror VII." 1996. DVD. Directed by Mike B. Anderson. Los Angeles, CA: 20th Century Fox, 2006
Slate, Barbara. 2019. "Welcome to the Mueller Report Graphic Novel Blog." *Mueller Report Graphic Novel*, May 19. Accessed June 19, 2019. https://muellerreportgraphicnovel.blogspot.com/2019/05/welcome-to-mueller-report-graphic-novel.html.
Slaughter, Anne-Marie. 2012. "Why Women Still Can't Have It All." *Atlantic*, July/August 2012. Accessed August 28, 2019. https://www.theatlantic.com/magazine/archive/2012/07/why-women-still-cant-have-it-all/309020/.
Smigel, Robert, and Adam McKay. 2000. *X-Presidents*. New York: Random House Comics Group.
Smith, Jeff. 2009. *The Presidents We Imagine: Two Centuries of White House Fictions on the Page, on the Stage, Onscreen and Online*. Madison: University of Wisconsin Press.
Smith, Philip. 2014. "Wiz Kids, Nuclear Bombs, and Marvel's Hazmat." *Journal of Graphic Novels and Comics* 5 (4): 1–14.
Sneddon, Laura. 2013. "'The Art of the People': How Comics Got Political." *New Statesman America*, August 21. Accessed February 23, 2020. https://www.newstatesman.com/culture/2013/08/art-people-how-comics-got-political.

Snell, Andrew, and Chris Kitching. 2018. "Donald Trump Tried to be President in 2000 but Campaign Flopped and Now He Doesn't Seem to Remember It." *Mirror*, January 6. Accessed July 15, 2019. https://www.mirror.co.uk/news/politics/donald-trump-tried-president-2000-11807012.

Snyder, Katherine V. 2011. "'Time to Go': The Post-Apocalyptic and the Post-Traumatic in Margaret Atwood's *Oryx and Crake*." *Studies in the Novel* 43 (4): 470–89.

Sobowale, Julie. 2009. "Review—'08: A Graphic Diary of the Campaign Trail." *Curled Up with a Good Book*. Accessed June 22, 2019. http://www.curledup.com/08presid.htm.

Sodaro, Robert J. 2020. "Satire in Not So Dead." In *Bronx Heroes in Trumpland*. By Ray Felix, Tom Sciacca, and Tom Ahearn, 9–12. Vancouver, BC: Arsenal Pulp Press.

Sommers, Joseph Michael. 2016. "When the Zombies Came for Our Children: Exploring Posthumanism in Robert Kirkman's *The Walking Dead*." *Comics Grid: Journal of Comics Scholarship* 6 (p.2). DOI: http://doi.org/10.16995/cg.40.

Soule, Charles, Alberto J. Alburquerque, and Dan Jackson. 2015. *Letter 44 Volume II: Redshift*. Portland, OR: Oni Press.

Sparks, Anthony. 2009. "Minstrel Politics or 'He speaks Too Well:' Rhetoric, Race, and Resistance in the 2008 Presidential Campaign." *Argumentation and Advocacy* 26 (Summer): 21–38.

Spears, Russell. 2002. "Four Degrees of Stereotype Formation: Differentiation by Any Means Necessary." In *Stereotypes as Explanations: The Formation of Meaningful Beliefs about Social Groups*, edited by Craig McGarty, Vincent Y. Yzerbyt, and Russel Spears, 125–56. Cambridge, UK: Cambridge University Press, 2002.

Speed, Andrea, and Jimmie Robinson. 2008. "Shop Talk: Talking the Origins of Evil with Jimmie Robinson." In *Bomb Queen II: Dirty Bomb*, by Jimmie Robinson, n.p. Berkeley, CA: Image Comics.

Speelman, Tom. 2020. "The Divide Between Marvel and DC Over Politics." *Polygon*, January 9. Accessed January 25, 2020. https://www.polygon.com/comics/2020/1/9/20995875/politics-in-comics-dc-marvel-superman-trump-lois-lane-art-spiegelman.

Spiegelman, Art. 2019. "Art Spiegelman: Golden Age Superheroes Were Shaped by the Rise of Fascism." *Guardian*, August 17. Accessed August 19, 2019. https://www.theguardian.com/books/2019/aug/17/art-spiegelman-golden-age-superheroes-were-shaped-by-the-rise-of-fascism.

Stabile, Carol A. 2009. "'Sweetheart, This Ain't Gender Studies': Sexism and Superheroes." *Communication and Critical/Cultural Studies* 6 (1): 86–92.

Stäheli, Urs. 2003. "The Popular in the Political System." *Cultural Studies* 17 (2): 275–99.

Stanley, T. L. 2016. "Abe Lincoln Trashes Clinton and Trump in this Insane Ad for Libertarian Gary Johnson." *AdWeek*, August 29. Accessed February 3, 2019. https://www.adweek.com/creativity/abe-lincoln-trashes-clinton-and-trump-insane-ad-libertarian-gary-johnson-173174/.

Stewart, Charles J., Craig Allen Smith, and Robert E. Denton Jr. 2012. *Persuasion and Social Movements*, sixth edition. Long Grove, IL: Waveland Press. Kindle edition.

Stieb, Matt. 2020. "Texas Lt. Gov. Dan Patrick: 'Lots of Grandparents' Willing to Die to Save Economy for Grandchildren." *New York Magazine*, March 23. Accessed May 30, 2020. https://nymag.com/intelligencer/2020/03/dan-patrick-seniors-are-willing-to-die-to-save-economy.html.

Stone, Sam. 2019. "Alexandria Ocasio-Cortez is Getting Her Own Comic Book." *CBR*, February 22. Accessed July 2, 2019. https://www.cbr.com/alexandria-ocasio-cortez-comic-book/.

Strachan, J. Cherie, and Kathleen E. Kendall. 2004. "Political Candidates' Convention Films: Finding the Perfect Image—An Overview of Political Image Making." In *Defining Visual*

Rhetorics, edited by Charles A. Hill and Marguerite Helmers, 135–54. Hillside, NJ: Lawrence Erlbaum Associates.

Stripling, Jack. 2016. "Trump: The College Years." *Chronicle of Higher Education*, July 3. Accessed November 4, 2017. http://www.chronicle.com/article/Trump-The-College-Years/237013.

Strömberg, Frederik. 2010. *Comic Art Propaganda: A Graphic History*. New York: St. Martin's Griffin.

"Storied History." *Jekyll Island Club Resort*. Accessed August 10, 2019. https://www.jekyllclub.com/about/jekyll-island-history/.

Strubel, Jessica. 2014. "Victorian Gear Heads and Locomotive Zealots: Vicarious Nostalgia, Retro-Futurism and Anachronisms of Steampunk and Dieselpunk." *Fashion, Style & Popular Culture* 1 (3): 377–93.

Stuller, Jennifer K. 2010. *Ink-Stained Amazons and Cinematic Warriors: Superwomen in Modern Mythology*. New York: I. B. Tauris & Co. Kindle edition.

Stuller, Jennifer K. 2013. "What is a Female Superhero?" In *What is a Superhero?*, edited by Robin S. Rosenberg and Peter Coogan, loc. 592–705. New York: Oxford University Press. Kindle edition.

Sullivan, Michael Patrick. 2009. "Jimmie Robinson Talks Bomb Queen Vs. Obama!" *Comic Book Resources*, August 20, 2009. Accessed February 17, 2016. http://www.comicbookresources.com/?page=article&id=22607.

Sundén, Jenny. 2013. "Corporeal Anachronisms: Notes on Affect, Relationality, and Power in Steampunk." *Somatechnics* 3 (2): 369–86.

Sundén, Jenny. 2014. "Steampunk Practices: Time, Tactility, and a Racial Politics of Touch." *Ada* 5: http://adanewmedia.org/2014/07/issue5-sunden/.

Sundén, Jenny. 2015. "Clockwork Corsets: Pressed Against the Past." *International Journal of Cultural Studies* 18 (3): 379–83.

Superman/Batman: Public Enemies. 2009. DVD. Directed by Sam Liu. Burbank, CA: Warner Home Video, 2009.

Suson, Esther Elizabeth. 2015. "Is Donald Trump Too Controversial for Election 2016?" *POTUS 2016*, July 1. Accessed October 1, 2018. http://potus2016.org/donald-trump-too-controversial-election-2016/.

Swathwood, Sheridan. 2020. "Artist Draws Healthcare Workers as Superheroes Fighting COVID-19." *25 News/Week*, April 28. Accessed June 8, 2020. https://week.com/2020/04/28/artist-draws-healthcare-workers-as-superheroes-fighting-covid-19/.

Swierczynski, Duane, Jason Pearson, and Dexter Vines. 2011. *Deadpool: Wade Wilson's War*. New York: Marvel Worldwide.

Takacs, Stacy. 2009. "Monsters, Monsters Everywhere: Spooky TV and the Politics of Fear in Post-9/11 America." *Science Fiction Studies* 35: 1–20.

Tambio, Megan. 2016. "WATCH: Stephen Colbert Gives Donald Trump a Supervillain Origin Story." *Comic Book Resources*, November 10. Accessed November 14, 2016. https://www.cbr.com/stephen-colbert-gives-donald-trump-a-supervillain-origin-story/.

Tanenbaum, Joshua, Marcel Pufal, and Karen Tanenbaum. 2016. "The Limits of Our Imagination: Design Fiction as a Strategy for Engaging with Dystopian Futures." *LIMITS '16*. DOI: 10.1145/2926676.2926687.

Taveira, Rodney. 2016. "The US Election Doesn't Just Feed Pop Culture—It Is Pop Culture." *Conversation*, October 12. Accessed December 11, 2016. http://theconversation.com/the-us-election-doesnt-just-feed-pop-culture-it-is-pop-culture-66554.

Taylor, Charles R., Stacy Landreth, and Hae-Kyong Bang. 2005. "Asian Americans in Magazine Advertising: Portrayals of the Modern Minority." *Journal of Macromarketing* 25 (2): 163–74.

Taylor, Charles R., Ju Yung Lee, and Barbara B. Stern. 1995. "Portrayals of African, Hispanic, and Asian Americans in Magazine Advertising." *American Behavioral Scientist* 38 (4): 608–21.

Taylor, Chris. 2018. "Democrats, It's Time to Fight like Superman for Truth, Justice, and the American Way." *Yahoo! News*, January 23. Accessed June 8, 2020. https://news.yahoo.com/democrats-apos-time-fight-superman-150000271.html.

Taylor, Derrick Bryson. 2020. "How the Coronavirus Pandemic Unfolded: A Timeline." *New York Times*, May 26. Accessed May 29, 2020. https://www.nytimes.com/article/coronavirus-timeline.html.

Terrill, Robert E. 1993. "Put on a Happy Face: *Batman* as Schizophrenic Savior." *Quarterly Journal of Speech* 79: 319–35.

Terror, Jude. 2017. A New Comic Called "Trump's Titans" is Some Kind of Parody, But of What, And Why? *Bleeding Cool*, August 23. Accessed November 3, 2018. https://www.bleedingcool.com/2017/08/23/trumps-titans-kind-parody/.

Thibodeau, Ruth. 1989. "From Racism to Tokenism: The Changing Face of Blacks in *New Yorker* Cartoons." *Public Opinion Quarterly* 53 (4): 483–94.

Thiessen, Marc. A. 2017. "Yes, Trump Can Make Mexico Pay for the Border Wall. Here's How." *Washington Post*, January 17. Accessed October 1, 2018. https://www.washingtonpost.com/opinions/yes-trump-can-make-mexico-pay-for-the-border-wall-heres-how/2017/01/17/7edf7872-dcbf-11e6-ad42-f3375f271c9c_story.html.

Thomas, Roy, and Sal Buscema. 1971. *The Avengers* #92. New York: Marvel Comics.

Thomas, Roy, Jerry Orway, Rafael Kayanan, et al. 2015/1985. *America vs. The Justice Society of America*. Burbank, CA: DC Comics. Kindle edition.

Thompson, Ethan. 2009. "'I Am Not Down with That': *King of the Hill* and Sitcom Satire." *Journal of Film and Video* 61 (2): 38–51.

Thompson, Hunter S. 2012/1972. *Fear and Loathing on the Campaign Trail '72*, reprint edition. New York: Simon & Schuster.

Thompson, Matt. 2018. "Is Politics Ruining Pop Culture?" *Radio Atlantic*, May 4. Accessed July 20, 2018. https://www.theatlantic.com/entertainment/archive/2018/05/radio-atlantic-is-politics-ruining-pop-culture/559637/.

Thompson, Paul. 1990. "Agrarianism and the American Philosophical Tradition." *Agriculture and Human Values* 7: 3–8.

Thornton, Sarah. 1995. *Club Cultures: Music, Media and Subcultural Capital*. Oxford: Blackwell.

Thrush, Glenn, and Maggie Haberman. 2017. "Trump is Criticized for Not Calling Out White Supremacists." *New York Times*, August 12. Accessed March 10, 2018. https://www.nytimes.com/2017/08/12/us/trump-charlottesville-protest-nationalist-riot.html.

Tibken, Shara. 2020. "5G Has No Link to COVID-19 as Social Media Aims to Squash False Conspiracy Theory." *CNet*, May 29. Accessed May 29, 2020. https://www.cnet.com/news/5g-has-no-link-to-covid-19-as-social-media-aims-to-squash-false-conspiracy-theory/.

Tilley, Carol L. 2018. "Superheroes and Identity: The Role of Nostalgia in Comic Book Culture." In *Reinventing Childhood Nostalgia: Books, Toys, and Contemporary Media Culture*, edited by Elisabeth Wesseling, 51–65. New York: Routledge. Kindle edition.

TIME. 2008. "The Reptilian Elite." November 20. Accessed July 2, 2019. http://content.time.com/time/specials/packages/article/0,28804,1860871_1860876_1861029,00.html.

Timm, Jane C. 2019. "Andrew Yang's Campaign is All About 'Math/' But His Numbers Don't Always Add Up." NBC News, October 20. Accessed May 2, 2020. https://www.nbcnews.com/politics/2020-election/andrew-yang-s-campaign-all-about-math-his-numbers-don-n1068651.

Timmerman, David. 1996. "1992 Presidential Candidate Films: The Contrasting Narratives of George Bush and Bill Clinton." *Presidential Studies Quarterly* 26 (2): 364–73.

Tipton, Denton J., and Menton3. 2018. *The X-Files: JFK Disclosure*. San Diego, CA: IDW.
Todd, Mort, and Cliff Mott. 2004. *Political Action Comics Presents Major Flip Flop*. New York: Comicfix.
Tolbert, Matt, Neil Grahame, and Mark Braun. 1992. *Read My Lips: The Unofficial Cartoon Biography of George Bush*. Westlake Village, CA: Malibu Graphics Publishing Group.
Tongco, Tricia. 2016. "Meet Faith, the Body-Positive Superhero of Our Dreams." *HuffPost*, February 18. Accessed July 2, 2019. https://www.huffpost.com/entry/meet-faith-the-body-positive-superhero-of-our-dreams_n_56c3bd9de4b0b40245c865f1.
Tonn, Mari Boor. 1996. "Militant Motherhood: Labor's Mary Harris 'Mother' Jones." *Quarterly Journal of Speech* 82 (1): 1–21.
Tornoe, Rob. 2013. "Visual Storytelling: Thanks to Online Tools, Comics Do Much More Than Entertain." *Editor & Publisher*, February 12. Accessed June 9, 2019. https://www.editorandpublisher.com/columns/digital-publishing-visual-storytelling-does-more-than-entertain/.
Traister, Rebecca. 2010. *Big Girls Don't Cry: The Election That Changed Everything for American Women*. New York: Free Press.
"Transcript: Donald Trump's Taped Comments about Women." 2016. *New York Times*, October 8. Accessed November 4, 2017. https://www.nytimes.com/2016/10/08/us/donald-trump-tape-transcript.html.
Travis, Mitchell. 2015. "We're All Infected: Legal Personhood, Bare Life and *The Walking Dead*." *International Journal for the Semiotics of Law* 28 (4): 787–800.
Treat, Shaun. 2019. "Superheroes, the Original AntiFa." *Superhero Rhetoric Fortress of Blogitude!* (blog), August 18. Accessed August 23, 2019. https://rhetoricsuperhero.wordpress.com/2019/08/18/superheroes-the-original-antifa/.
Trent, Judith S., and Robert V. Friedenberg. 2008. *Political Campaign Communication: Principles and Practices*, sixth edition. Lanham, MD: Rowman & Littlefield.
Troy, Michael and Manuel Díaz. 2013. *Female Force: Nancy Reagan*. Bluewater Comics.
Trujillo, Nick. 1991. "Hegemonic Masculinity on the Mound: Media Representations of Nolan Ryan and American Sports Culture." *Critical Studies in Media Communication* 8: 290–308.
Truman Library Institute. 2016. "The Story of Harry S. Truman." *Tru Blog*, July 25. Accessed May 27, 2018. http://www.trumanlibraryinstitute.org/trumancomicbook/.
Turnquist, Kristi. 2020. "Portland Publisher Teams with Stormy Daniels, of Trump Scandal Fame, for 'Space Force' Comic Book Series." *Oregon Live*, May 26. Accessed May 31, 2020. https://www.oregonlive.com/entertainment/2020/05/portland-publisher-teams-with-stormy-daniels-of-trump-scandal-fame-for-space-force-comic-book-series.html.
Uhlaner, Carole Jean, and F. Chris Garcia. 2002. "Latino Public Opinion." In *Understanding Public Opinion*, edited by Barbara Norrander and Clyde Wilcox, 77–101. Washington, DC: Congressional Quarterly Press.
Unknown. 1964. *Alvin for President*. New York, NY: Dell Publishing.
Valentino, Nicholas A., Matthew N. Beckmann, and Thomas A. Buhr. 2001. "A Spiral of Cynicism for Some: The Contingent Effects of Campaign News Frames on Participation and Confidence in Government." *Political Communication* 18: 347–67.
Van Dijk, Teun A. 1998. *Ideology: A Multidisciplinary Approach*. New York: Sage.
Van Zoonen, Liesbet. 2005. *Entertaining the Citizen: When Politics and Popular Culture Converge*. Lanham, MD: Rowman & Littlefield.
Van Zoonen, Liesbet, and Dominic Wring. 2012. "Trends in Political Television Fiction in the UK: Themes, Characters and Narratives, 1965–2009." *Media, Culture & Society* 34 (3): 263–79.
Venditti, Robert, and Mike Huddleston. 2011. *The Homeland Directive*. Marietta, GA: TopShelf Productions.

Verano, Frank. 2013. "Superheroes Need Supervillains." In *What is a Superhero?*, edited by Robin S. Rosenberg and Peter Coogan, loc. 1715–1811. New York: Oxford University Press. Kindle edition.

Vice, Samantha. 2011. "Cynicism and Morality." *Ethical Theory and Moral Practice* 14 (2): 169–84.

Vidmar, Neil, and Milton Rokeach. 1974. "Archie Bunker's Bigotry: A Study in Selective Perception and Exposure." *Journal of Communication.* 26 (1): 36–47.

Visaggio, Magdalene, Marley Zarcone, and Irma Kniivila. 2019. *Marilyn Manor #1.* San Diego, CA: IDW Publishing.

Waldman, Paul. 2012. "The Return of the Green Lantern Theory of Geopolitics." *American Prospect*, September 14. Accessed August 1, 2018. http://prospect.org/article/return-green-lantern-theory-geopolitics.

Walker, Tristam. 2010. "Graphic Wounds: The Comics Journalism of Joe Sacco." *Journeys* 11 (1): 69–88.

Wander, Philip. 1983. "The Ideological Turn in Modern Criticism." *Central States Speech Journal* 34 (1): 1–18.

Wanzo, Rebecca. 2009. "The Superhero: Meditations on Surveillance, Salvation, and Desire." *Communication and Critical/Cultural Studies* 6 (1): 93–97.

Ward, Chris, and Azim Akberali. 2009. *Political Power: Barack Obama.* USA: BlueWater Comics.

Ward, Chris, and Dave MacNeil. 2009. *Female Force: Condoleezza Rice.* USA: BlueWater Productions.

Warner, Andy. 2017. "The Voting Rights Act Was Gutted. Here's What Happened Next." *The Nib*, January 9. Accessed June 19, 2019. https://thenib.com/voting-rights-act.

Waszak, Przemyslaw M., Wioleta Kasprzycka-Waszak, and Alicja Kubanek. 2018. "The Spread of Medical Fake News in Social Media—The Pilot Quantitative Study." *Health Policy and Technology* 7 (2): 115–18.

Way, Gerard, and Gabriel Bá. 2009. *The Umbrella Academy: Dallas.* Milwaukie, OR: Dark Horse Comics.

Webley, Steve. 2015. "The Supernatural, Nazi Zombies, and the Play Instinct: The Gamification of War and the Reality of the Military." In *Horrors of War: The Undead on the Battlefield*, edited by Cynthia Miller and A. Bowdoin Van Riper, 201–217. Lanham, MD: Rowman & Littlefield.

Weiner, Robert G., and Shelley E. Barba. 2012. "Obama and Spider-Man: A Meta-Data Media Analysis of an Unlikely Pairing." In *The Iconic Obama, 2007–2009: Essays on Media Representations of the Candidate and New President*, edited by Nicholas A. Yanes and Derrais Carter, 113–27. Jefferson, NC: McFarland.

Weissman, Steven. 2012. *Barack Hussein Obama.* Seattle, WA: Fantagraphics Books.

Welch, Kyle. 2019. "Christopher Cantwell and Patric Reynolds Stump Speech on 'The Mask: I Pledge Allegiance to the Mask.'" *Multiversity Comics*, September 23. Accessed September 24. http://www.multiversitycomics.com/interviews/the-mask-interview/.

Wellhofer, E. Spencer. 2003. "Democracy and Fascism: Class, Civil Society, and Rational Choice in Italy." *American Political Science Review* 97 (1): 91–106.

Whicker, Marcia Lynn. 1996. *Toxic Leaders: When Organizations Go Bad.* New York: Doubleday.

Wicks, Stephen. 1996. *Warriors and Wildmen: Men, Masculinity, and Gender.* Westport, CT: Praeger.

Wilde, Lukas R. A. 2019. "9/11, Comics, and the Threatened Orders of Pictorial Media: Non-Fictional Comics as Historical Re-Enactment." *ImageTexT* 11 (1): http://imagetext.english.ufl.edu/archives/v11_1/wilde/.

Wilentz, Amy. 2012. "A Zombie is a Slave Forever." *New York Times*, October 30. 2012. Accessed August 25, 2019. https://www.nytimes.com/2012/10/31/opinion/a-zombie-is-a-slave-forever.html.

Williams, Brett. 2013. "From Helix to Vertigo: The Unusual Publication History of *Transmetropolitan*." In *Shot in the Face: A Savage Journey to the Heart of* Transmetropolitan, edited by Chad Nevett, 1–6. Edwardsville, IL: Sequart Research & Literacy Organization. Kindle edition.

Williams, Kristian. 2005. "The Case for Comics Journalism: Artist-Reporters Leap Tall Conventions in a Single Bound." *Columbia Journalism Review* (March/April): 51–55.

Williams, Maren. 2017. "Lowlights from Comics Censorship History." *CBLDF*, June 2. Accessed June 2, 2017. http://cbldf.org/2017/06/lowlights-from-comics-censorship-history/.

Williams, M. H. 2019. "Superman is Still Super: Finding his Relevance in 2019." *Medium*, December 3. Accessed February 9, 2020. https://medium.com/into-the-discourse/finding-the-heart-of-superman-making-a-hero-relevant-in-2019-322aff03aae2

Wills, Garry. 2010. *Bomb Power: The Modern Presidency and the National Security State*. New York: Penguin Press.

Wilson, G. Willow, Mirka Andolfo, Ian Herring, and VC's Joe Caramagna. 2016. *Ms. Marvel* #13. Marvel Comics. New York, NY: Marvel Worldwide.

Wilz, Kelly. 2016. "Bernie Bros and Woman Cards: Rhetorics of Sexism, Misogyny, and Constructed Masculinity in the 2016 Election." *Women's Studies in Communication* 39 (4): 357–60.

Witt, Linda, Karen M. Paget, and Glenna Matthews. 1995. *Running as a Woman: Gender and Power in American Politics*. New York: The Free Press.

Wodak, Ruth, and Bernhard Forchtner. 2014. "Embattled Vienna 1683/2010: Right-Wing-Populism, Collective Memory and the Fictionalisation of Politics." *Visual Communication* 13 (2): 231–55.

Wolk, Douglas. 2007. *Reading Comics: How Graphic Novels Work and What They Mean*. Cambridge, MA: Da Capo Press. Kindle edition.

Woo, Elaine. 2012. "Screenwriter Molded by Blacklist." *Los Angeles Times*, June 28. Retrieved May 22, 2019. https://www.latimes.com/archives/la-xpm-2012-jun-28-la-me-joan-scott-20120628-story.html.

Worcester, Kent. 2007. "Symposium—The State of the Editorial Cartoon: Introduction." *PS: Political Science & Politics* XL (2): 223–27.

Worcester, Kent. 2011. "New York City, 9/11, and Comics." *Radical History Review* 111: 139–54.

Wright, Bradford W. 2001. *Comic Book Nation: The Transformation of Youth Culture in America*. Baltimore, MD: The Johns Hopkins University Press.

Wuerker, Matt. 2017. "Drawing Trump." *Politico*, December 24. Accessed June 21, 2019. https://www.politico.com/interactives/2017/drawing-trump/.

Yancey-Bragg, N'dea. 2019. "A Canadian Political Cartoonist's Drawing of Donald Trump Went Viral. Two Days Later, He Was Fired." *USA Today*, June 30. Accessed August 30, 2019. https://www.usatoday.com/story/news/world/2019/06/30/canadian-cartoonist-loses-contract-viral-donald-trump-drawing/1612647001/.

Yanes, Nicholas A. 2012. "Comics and Politics: An Interview with Larry Hama, Creator of *Barack the Barbarian*." In *The Iconic Obama, 2007–2009: Essays on Media Representations of the Candidate and New President*, edited by Nicholas A. Yanes and Derrais Carter, 128–30. Jefferson, NC: McFarland.

Yezbick, Daniel F. 2009. "The Joy of Plex: Erotic Athrology, Tromplographic Intercourse, and 'Interspecies Romances' in Howard Chaykin's *American Flagg!*" *ImageTexT* 4 (3): http://imagetext.english.ufl.edu/archives/v4_3/yezbick/.

Yizheng, Zou. 2017. "Flying Tigers and Chinese Sidekicks in World War II American Comic Books." In *The 10 Cent War: Comic Books, Propaganda, and World War II*, edited by James Kimble and Trisha Goodnow, 46–65. Jackson: University Press of Mississippi.

Yockey, Matt. 2012. "Retopia: The Dialectics of the Superhero Comic Book." *Studies in Comics* 3 (2): 349–70.

Yoe, Craig. 2020. *Voting is Your Superpower*. Algonquin, IL: Clover Press.

Yoos, George E. 1985. "The Rhetoric of Cynicism." *Rhetoric Review* 4 (1): 54–62.

York, Chris, and Rafiel York. 2012. "Introduction: Frederic Wertham, Containment, and Comic Books." In *Comic Books and the Cold War: Essays on Graphic Treatment of Communism, the Code and Social Concerns*, edited by Chris York and Rafiel York, 63–190. Jefferson, NC: McFarland. Kindle edition.

York, Rafiel. 2012. "*The Fantastic Four*: A Mirror of Cold War America." In *Comic Books and the Cold War: Essays on Graphic Treatment of Communism, the Code and Social Concerns*, edited by Chris York and Rafiel York, 2642–2835. Jefferson, NC: McFarland. Kindle edition.

Young, Bryan. 2012. "Paul Cornell Talks About His New Political Comic Book, Saucer Country." *HuffPost*, March 13. Accessed April 28, 2017. https://www.huffingtonpost.com/bryan-young/paul-cornell-saucer-country_b_1339009.html.

Young, Dannagal Goldthwaite. 2004. "Late-Night Comedy in Election 2000: Its Influence on Candidate Trait Ratings and the Moderating Effects of Political Knowledge and Partisanship." *Journal of Broadcasting and Electronic Media* 48 (1): 1–22.

Zakaria, Fareed. 2016. "Why Donald Trump Could Never Be a Normal Candidate." *Washington Post*, November 3. Accessed October 1, 2018. https://www.washingtonpost.com/opinions/why-donald-trump-could-never-be-a-normal-candidate/2016/11/03/68483dd4-a203-11e6-a44d-cc2898cfab06_story.html.

Zilber, Jeremy, and David Niven. 2000. "Stereotypes in the News: Media Coverage of African-Americans in Congress." *International Journal of Press/Politics* 5 (1): 32–49.

Zillman, Dolf and Joanne R. Cantor. 1972. "Directionality of Transitory Dominance as a Communication Variable Affecting Humor Appreciation." *Journal of Personality and Social Psychology*. 24 (2): 191–98.

Zimmer, Troy A. 1979. "The Impact of Watergate on the Public's Trust in People and Confidence in the Mass Media." *Social Science Quarterly* 59 (4): 743–51.

Zurbriggen, Eileen L., and Aurora M. Sherman. 2010. "Race and Gender in the 2008 U.S. Presidential Elections: A Content Analysis of Editorial Cartoons." *Analyses of Social Issues and Public Policy* 10 (1): 223–47.

INDEX

Page numbers in *italics* refer to illustrations.

Action Comics, 4, 38, 40, 49, 58
activism, 99, 109; and comics, xxiii, 101, 112; messages, 106
activists, 14, 34, 56, 61, 98, 112, 134, 135, 147, 149, 151, 192, 206
Ad Astra Comix, 112
Adams, John, 130
Adder, Michael de, xi
Adorno, Theodor W., 172, 177, 180, 181
Adventure Time: President Bubblegum, 117
Adventures of Barry & Joe: Obama & Biden's Bromantic Battle for the Soul of America, The, 219ch9n3
Algonquin Round Table, 33, 70
Ali, Muhammad, 193
aliens (human), 123
aliens (space), 24, 123–24, 143, 157–58, 160, 178, 193, 197–201, 217n4
All the Shah's Men: An American Coup and the Roots of Middle East Terror (Kinzer), 97
allohistory, 186–89, 193, 196–202
Alt-Hero, 203–4
alt-history. *See* allohistory
alternate history. *See* allohistory
alternative history. *See* allohistory
Alvarado, Arcadia (fictional character), 123–24, 143–44, 150–51, 160, 208
Alvin and the Chipmunks, xv, 115
Amell, Stephen, 50, 52
"America First," 122
America We Deserve, The (Trump), 121–22, *122*
American Flagg!, 66–68, *68*, 186, 217ch7n3
American Legends, 196, 202

American monomyth, xii, 40, 42, 52, 77, 80, 170
American way, 19, 82, 173, *205*
American Way: Those Above and Those Below, The, 151
Anderson, Karrin Vasby, 134, 136, 145, 148
Anderson, Nick, 76
Andersonville Trial, The (play), 24
Ant-Man & the Wasp, 55
Antarctic Press, 154, 165, 183, 187, 191, 204
antiheroes, xvi, 50, 128, 169, 176; defined, xvi, 52–53
apathy, 35, 58, 131
apocalyptic fictions, 48, 191, 199, 201, 209, 213
Appleseed, Johnny, 196
Aquaman (fictional character), 43
Aquaman (film), 55
Archie: The Married Life, 146–47, 216ch2n1
Armed Forces Information and Education Division of the Office of the Secretary of Defense, 114
Army of Darkness, 117, 127, 156–57, 217n4
Arnold, Gordon, 26, 35, 36, 198
Arnold, Monroe, 75, 83
Art of the Deal, The (Trump), xxv, 173–74, *173*, 201
Ater, Malcolm, 3, 4
athletics. *See* sports
Atlantic (magazine), 106, 132, 142
atomic: age, 40; bombs, 34, 199, 203; powers, 46, 87; weapons, 86
Authority, The, 217ch3n2
Avengers (fictional group), xvii, 28, *28*, 47, 170, 174–75, 216n3
Avengers, The (film), 171
Avengers: Endgame, xii
Avengers: Infinity War, 55

Bachmann, Michele, 6, 11–13, 18
Badlands, 197
Bagley, Pat, 106
Baker, Norma Jean. *See* Monroe, Marilyn
Banner, Bruce. *See* Incredible Hulk
Barack Hussein Obama (book), 90–91, 157
Barack Panther, 80, 82, 84, 148, 154
Barack the Barbarian, 47, 79, 145, 150, 152–55, *154*
Barnes, Rodney, 130, 212
Batgirl (character), 24, 25, 26–28
Batman, 10, 23, 30–31, 43, 44, 47, 49, 52, 54, 80, 93, 117, 142, 152, 168, 169, 174, 175, 176, 177, 179, 184, 190, 203, 220n1
Batman (TV series), 42
Batman, Keith, 10
Batman: Brave and the Bold, 48, 58, 60
Batman Family, 27
Batman Returns, 176
Batman: The Animated Series, 10
Batman: The Dark Knight Strikes Again, 58, 60, 175
Berman, Ari, 101–2, *102*
Bernstein, Carl, 56
Biden, Joe, 6, 18, 47, 157, 159
Bilirakis, Gus, 98
Bill and Ted's Excellent Adventure (film), 15
Bin Laden, Osama, *104*
biopunk, xxiv, 199, 201
Bitch Planet, 117, 144
Black (comic), 212, 213
Black Canary, 191
Black Goliath, 154
Black Lightning, 154
Black Lives Matter, xvi, 160, 166, 191, 213
Black Panther (fictional character), 82, 148
Black Panther (film), xix, 55
Black Panthers (activists), 97
Black Widow (fictional character), 33
blacklist, 23–24, 34, 204
blackness, 151–54, 164
Bleeding Cool (entertainment news site), 86
Blossom, Cheryl (fictional character), 147, 216ch2n1
Bobman and Teddy, 42, 77, 79
Bomb Queen, 47, 155–56, 167
Bonaparte, Napoleon, 196
Booker, Cory, 159

BOOM! Studios, 6, 10, 98, 197
Boop, Betty (fictional character), xxiii, 137, *137*, 218ch8n1
Booth, Wayne C., 85
Boss Smiley (fictional character), 57, 59, 60, 63, 119
Boxer, Sarah, 106
Boys, The (comic), xii
Bracamontes, Luis, 164
Brantner, Cornelia, xiv, xv, 5, 89
Brezhnev, Leonid, 198
Brinkley Girls, 136
Brinkley, Nell, 136
Brolin, Josh, xviii, 170
Bronx Heroes in Trumpland, 93, 119
Brother Voodoo, 154
Brubaker, Ed, 58, 72–73, 217ch4n2
Buchanan, Pat, 121, 174
Bullwinkle Moose (fictional character), xv, 115, 119
Bunyan, Paul, 196
Burke, Kenneth, 85, 86
Burns, Lisa M., 147
Bush, George H. W., 15, 32, 43, 57, 89, 90, 120–21, 174, 188
Bush, George W., 18, 45–47, 50, 64, 80–81, 96, 107, 109, 123, 156, 175, 188, 200; as "Boosh," 153
Bush, Jeb, 5, 12, 13
Bush, Prescott, 13
Buttigieg, Pete, 5, 159
BuzzFeed, 99, 132

Cage, Luke (fictional character), 152, 154, 169
Cain, Herman, xxiv, 6, 12, 18–19, 151, 166
campaign, xiv, xvii, 27, 113–31, 143, 165, 181; advertisements, xii, 15, 121, 131, 159, 164; announcement, xxv; comics, xxii, 3–19, 89, 114, 165; communication, 5, 164; contributions or donations, xxii, 30, 132; events, xiii, 89; fatigue, 131; logos, 51, 59; mailers, 10; media coverage, 98, 102–4, 108–10; messages, 109, 120; platforms, 26, 57; promises, 120, 121; slogans, 25, 50–51, 60, 128, 138, 192; websites, 10, 159
Campaigners (comic), 117, 186
Campbell, Karlyn Kohrs, 147
candidate film, 15–19

Capitol (building), 13, 19
Captain America, xi–xii, xv, xvii, xxv, 40, 42, 47, 48, 49–50, 55, 75, 77, 85, 87–88, 93, 142, 152, 168, 174, 175, 182, 206: and *Captain America: Winter Soldier*, 32, 33
Captain Atom (fictional character), 179
Captain Britain (fictional character), 85
Captain Canuck (fictional character), 85
Captain Marvel (fictional character), 24, 28, 204
Carnegie, Andrew, 193–95
Caroline Kennedy: America's First Young Lady, 148
Carter, Jimmy, 42, 43, 49, 120, 218n4
Carter, Lynda, 142–43
Carver, George Washington, 192–94
Carville, James, 162
Castro, Fidel, 34, 166, 183, 198
Castro, Julián, 159
Catwoman (fictional character), 47, 69, 117, 119, 175–76
CBR (*Comic Book Resources*), 156, 161, 162
Centennial Congress—1876 Democratic House of Representatives Illustrated by Cash Thomas, xiv, *xv*, 77
Chaplin, Charlie, 193
Chappaquiddick (scandal), 89
Chaykin, Howard, 67, 217ch7n3
Cheated!, xxiii, 113–14, 130
Cheney, Dick, 80, 107; as "Chainsaw," 155; as "Cha-nee," 153
Chisholm, Shirley, 142
Christie, Chris, 12–13, 18
CIA (Central Intelligence Agency), 96, 97, 107, 112, 120, 197, 199
Citizen Jack, 117, 124–27, *126*, 130
civil rights, 4, 96, 167, 190, 216ch3n1, 219ch11n3; commission, 9; era, 57; and John Lewis, 166; movement, 171, 191
Clinton, Bill, 5, 18, 43–44, 57, 80, 82, 89–90, 91–92, 120, 121, 147, 161–62, 175, 182, 197, 217n4
Clinton Cash: A Graphic Novel, 89, 144
Clinton, Chelsea, 148
Clinton, Hillary, xvi, xxiii, 5, 13, 14, 44, 50–51, *51*, 80–81, 82–83, 88, 89–90, 91, *104*, *104*, 117, 119, 127, 132, 135, 143–46, 147, 154–55, 157, 162, 183, 197; as "Hilaria," 153

CNN, 125
Coates, Ta-Nehisi, 204
Cobblepot, Oswald (fictional character). *See* Penguin
Cocca, Carolyn, 27
Colbert, Stephen, 168, 170
Cold War, xii, xxiv, 22–23, 32, 33, 40–41, 43, 44–45, 66, 75, 92, 148, 190, 199; and conspiracies, 26, 29, 35; ideologies, 65, 79; paranoia, xxii, 23, 35–36, 45, 70, 71, 189, 198; science-fiction, 200
collective action, 207
Colón, Ernie, 94, 95, 96, 99, *100*, 102, 103, 106, 108
comic cons: Ithaca, 209; New York, 204; San Diego, 47, 209
Comics Beat (media outlet), 97, 117, 212
Comics Code, 22, 23, 31, 36–37
Comics Code Authority (CCA), xxii, 21–24, 35, 37
Comicsgate, 204, 208
ComicVine (wiki), xv, 150
comix (underground comics), 23, 76, 77
Conan the Barbarian, 150, 152–53
conspiracy, xxiii, xxiv–xxv, 24, 26, 27, 29, 30, 33, 35–37, 56, 113–14, 119, 120, 124, 130, 172, 188, 193, 196–98, 199, 200–202, 210, 219ch11n4
convention film. *See* candidate film
Conway, Kellyanne, 203
Coody, Elizabeth, 142
Coogan, Peter, 77–78, 79, 81, 83, 84, 170
Cooke, Darwyn, 22, 39, 44–45, 189–91
Cooper, Betty (fictional character), 216ch2n1
Cornell, Paul, 123–24, 143–44, 160, 206
coronavirus. *See* COVID-19
Costello, Matthew, xix, 41, 68, 200
costume, xxi, 10, 23, 45, 47, 50, 65, 79, 83–84, 139, 140, 146, 152, 159, 180, 194
COVID-19, 98, 209–11; and Black communities, 211
Cracked, 169
Crane, Jonathan (fictional character). *See* Scarecrow
Crider, Michael, 171
Crocket, Davy, 196
Cronkite, Walter, 121
Crucible, The (play), 24

C-SPAN, 27
cyberpunk, 187, 201
Cyborg (fictional character), 154, 210
cyborgs, 54, 75, 92, 145, 154, 194, 199, 210
cynicism (political), xxii, xxiv, 27, 28, 35–36, 37, 52, 55, 59, 71–73, 120, 128, 198

Daffy Duck (fictional character), 115, 217ch4n3
Daghlian, Harry, 198, 199
Daniels, Stormy, 13–14
Dark Horse Comics, 117, 211
Dark Knight Returns: The Golden Child, 117, 119
Darkwing Duck (fictional character), 115
Dastardly and Muttley, 29
Dave (film), xiv, 25
Davis, Blair, 152, 154
DC Comics, xii, 22, 26, 30, 33, 38, 39, 42–43, 44, 48, 50, 53, 56, 58, 69, 119, 120, 142, 173–74, 189, 210, 218ch8n5; and political ideology, 205
DC Comics: Bombshells, 170, 176, 196
DC: The New Frontier, 22–23, 39, 40, 44–45, 189–91, 201–2
DC Universe, 144, 176
DC Universe: Decisions, 49
DCeased, 210
Deadpool (fictional character), 32, 33, 49–50, 55
Dean, Howard, 83
Deathlok, 29
DeConnick, Kelly Sue, 204
Deep State, 197
Deis, Chris, 40, 170–71, 183
Democrats: administrations, 44, 46, 48; candidates, xvi, 10, 12, 42, 117, 121, 128, 143, 159, 164; Committees, xxii, 3, 4, 5, 56, 206; National Conventions, 39, 44, 158, 158, 165, 189; Party, 41; politicians, 75, 89; primaries, 5, 117, 158, 164; rallies, 127
Demon, The. *See* Etrigan the Demon
demons, 120–23, 125–27, 129–31, 157, 208, 218ch7n6
Dempsey, Jack, 193
Dent, Harvey (fictional character), 169, 176
Dever, Paul, 9, 15
Devil's Due, 47, 140–42, *141*, 150, 218n7

Diehard (fictional character), 54
dieselpunk, xxiv, 187, 191, 192, 194, 201, 202
DiMaggio, Joe, 34
Dimples (fictional character), 136–37
DiPaolo, Marc, xvi–xix, 5, 44, 49, 80–81, 155
Dirksen, Everett M., 4
disenfranchisement, xxiii, 113, 167. *See also* voter suppression
Disney (company), 23, 182
District Comics: An Unconventional History of Washington, DC, 36
Dittmer, Jason, 40, 77, 84, 88, 151, 167, 170
Dixon, Chuck, 90, 203
Doctor Fate (fictional character), 24, 31–32
Dole, Bob, 79, 217n4
Doom, Dr. Victor von (fictional character), xv, 168, 174–75, 177–78, 179–81, 185, 186
DOOM 2099, 174, 179–80, 185, 186
Doomsday Clock, 65, 66, 67, *67*, 216ch2n2
Doonesbury (comic strip), 76
D.P.7, 174, 179
Drafted: One Hundred Days, 157–58
Dr. Strangelove or: How I Learned to Stop Worrying and Love the Bomb (film), 199
Dr. Who (TV series), 168
"Drain the Swamp," 25, 122, 182
Dukakis, Michael, 121, 174
Duke, David, 121, 217ch5n1
Dynamite Comics, 47
dystopias, 58, 64, 65, 68, 117, 144, 164, 182, 183, 186–87, 211, 213

Eagle: The Making of an Asian-American President, xxiv, 150, 161–64
Earhart, Amelia, 192, 194
Earth X, 175, 176, 180, 182, 183, 185
Eastman, Monk, 193
E. C. Comics, 20–22, *21*, 23
Edelman, Murray, xiii, 153
Edible Secrets: A Food Tour of Classified U.S. History, 97, 103, 105, 108
Edison, Thomas, 193, 195
editorial cartoons, xi, 5, 76, 77, 79, 91–93; and caricature, 106
Edwards, Janis, 76, 91, 145
Edwards, John, 80
Einstein, Albert, 189, 192, 198, 199

Eisenhower, Dwight "Ike," 4, 15, 16, 44, 46, 109, 215n2
Eisner, Will, 105, 153
Eisner Awards, 161, 197
Ellis, Calvin (fictional character), 47, 58, 150, 167. *See also* Superman
Ellis, Warren, 63, 178, 179, 180, 185
"enemies from within" speech (McCarthy), 28, *28*
enemy archetypes, 153, 155
Entertainment Weekly (news outlet), 206
Equal Rights Party, 136
Etrigan the Demon (fictional character), 120–23, *122*, 126, 208
Exit Stage Left: The Snagglepuss Chronicles, 25, 33–36, 69, 70–71, 73, 74

Fairey, Shepard, 158
Faith (comic series), 117, 144
fake news, 46, 210
Fanatic Four, The, 79, 82, 84, 147
fandom, 133, 207
Fantastic Four (fictional group), 41, 45, 82, 84, 174
fascism, xi–xii, xix, 26, 45, 172, 177, 180, 198
FBI, 13, 106, 197
Female Force (comic series), 5, 13, 14, 132, 147–48, 165
femininity, 52, 132, 134, 136, 137–38, 143, 144, 146–49
feminism, 67, 77, 83, 97, 126, 133, 136, 139, 140, 146, 191, 204
Fermi, Enrico, 198
Feynman, Richard, 198
Fink, Mike, 196
Firebird (fictional character). *See* Juarez, Bonita
Firestorm (fictional character), 29
First Lady (FLOTUS), 38, 43, 144, 147–48, 165
Flash (fictional character), 29, 204
Flintstones, The (comic), xii, 69–70, 71, 72, 73, 117
Floyd, George, xvi, 212
Ford, Gerald, 42, 120, 218ch9n1
Ford, Henry, 193
Foreman, Carl, 24
Fox News, 158, 218n3
Fraction, Matt, 204

Franklin, Benjamin, 192
Front, The (film), 24

Gabriel Over the White House (film), 25
Gaddis, John Lewis, 190
Gadot, Gal, 140, 142–43
Gagarin, Yuri, 198
Gaiman, Neil, 57, 60, 63, 66, 205
Gaines, William (Bill), 21, 22, 23, 34, 35
Gardner, Guy (fictional character). *See* Green Lantern (fictional character)
Garfield, James A., 14
gender: depictions, 144; and double-binds, 133; norms, 136, 140, 146–47; Western citizenship, 138. *See also* femininity; masculinity; women
G. I. Joe (franchise), 174, 175, 204
Gianforte, Greg, 125
Gingrich, Newt, 6
Ginsberg, Ruth Bader, 13
Gizmodo (website), 172
Gladstone, Brooke, 98, 100–101, 102, 110
Glidden, Sarah, 98, 101, 109–10
Going Rouge: The Sarah Palin Rogue Coloring & Activity Book, 88, 136, 145
Goldwater, Barry, 88, 109
Goldwater Made Simple from A to Z with BMG, 88
good government comics, xxiii, 114–16, 123
Gordon, Barbara (fictional character). *See* Batgirl (character)
Gore, Al, 13, 18, 145, 162
Gorilla Grodd (fictional character), 29
Gotham (TV show), 175
Gotham City (fictional place), 27, 119, 175–76
Governator, The, 84, 85, *85*
governors (US state), 3, 4, 8, 9, 12, 13, 15, 84, 98, 110, 120, 121, 123, 137, 143, 150, 151, 160, 211, 215n2
Graphic History Collective, 112
Great Depression, xi, 25, 40
Great Morons in History featuring Dan Quayle, 15, 89, 90
Great Society, 42, 216ch3n1
Great Society Comic Book, The, 42, 77, 79, 82
Great War, 8, 191
Green Arrow (fictional character), 169; and *Arrow*, 50–54, *51*, 176

Green Goblin (fictional character), 168, 175, 180, 182
Green Lantern (fictional character), 43, 44, 142, 178, 190
"Green Lantern Theory," 53
Green Party, 109–10
Gröttrup, Helmutt, 198
Groves, Leslie, 198
Guardian (newspaper), xi, 98, 103, 109, 125

Hafer, Dick, 89
Halpern, Jake, 110
Hama, Larry, 153–54, 204
Hamill, Mark, 168
Hamilton, Alexander, 130
Hamilton (musical), 142
Hanna-Barbera, 25, 29, 33, 69–71, 169
Harper's, 95, 135, 136
Harrison, Jaime, 10, *11*
Harrison, William Henry, 17, 51
Harwood, John, 124
Hazmat (fictional character), 163
Heer, Margreet de, 98, *101*, 108, 110
hermeneutics, xx
Hiddleston, Tom, 170
Higgins, D. M., 92–93
High Noon (film), 24
Hill, E. D., 158
Hippolyta (fictional character), 139–40
Hitler, Adolf, xxv, 30, 31, 46, 60, 81, 87, 88, 183, 203, 206
Homeland Directive, The, 201
Hoover, Herbert, xiv, 3, *7*, 7, 18, 19, 137, *137*, 215n2
Hoover, J. Edgar, 183
horror (genre), xix, 21, 36, 37, 117, 156, 196, 212, 213; and comedy, 80, 124, 197, 217n4
Horton, Willie, 164
Houdini, Harry, 193
House of Representatives. *See* Congress
House Un-American Activities Committee (HUAC), 23–25, 26, 27, 31, 32, 34, 35, 72, 216ch2n2
Houston Chronicle, 76
How the Trump Stole Christmas, 88
Howard the Duck (fictional character), 119–20
Huckabee Sanders, Sarah, 203

Huckleberry Hound (fictional character), 34, 70
Humphrey, Hubert, 79
humor, 85–86, 89, 92, 93, 219ch11n1; political, 76; publications, 77, 169; satiric, 90–91
Huntsman, Jon, 6
HYDRA (fictional organization), 33, 128
hypermasculinity, 42, 51–52, 85, 133

ideology: Cold War, 23, 65; and conspiracy, 35; political in comics, xv, xviii–xix, 5, 92, 203; ideological criticism, xix–xx; and race, 152, 165
IDW, xiv, 6, 12, 97, 98, 143, 150, 210
Image Comics, 47, 54, 117, 124, 129, 144, 155, 210, 211, 219ch11n1
image function, xx
ImageTexT, 99
imitatio, *51*
immigrant, xii, 7, 18, 48, 71, 140, 205, 211. *See also* aliens (human)
immigration, xxv, 80, 92, 96, 123, 151, 159, 160, 164, 165, 170, 176, 205, 206, 207, 211
impeachment, xxiii, 53, 57, 125; of Nixon, 15; of Trump, xvii, 97, 106, 217ch5n1
Incident at Vichy (play), 24
Incredible Hulk, 41, 83, 86–87, *87*, 92, 175, 204
Incredibles 2, The (film), 55
Independent (newspaper), 206
Insider (news site), 97, 106
intertextuality, xxi, 77
Iron Man (fictional character), 24, 32–33, 48, 164, 169, 174, 175
Irons, John Henry (fictional character). *See* Steel (fictional character)
irony, 59, 79, 89, 160
Isaac, Jeffrey C., 176, 185
iZombie (comic series), 218ch9n1

Jack Kirby's Secret City Saga, 175, 182
Jackson, Andrew, 46
Jacobson, Sid, 94, 95, 96, 99, *100*, 102, 103, 106, 108
Jagoda, Patrick, 192
Jamieson, Kathleen Hall, 53, 71, 72, 133, 182
Jefferson, Thomas, 18, 196
Jekyll Island Chronicles, The, 188, 191, 193–94, 195, 201–2

Index

Jerusalem, Spider (fictional character), 64, 73
Jewett, Robert, 39–40, 41, 43, 77, 170
Jewish people, 205; as creators, xi, xii, 206; characters, 205
Jimmy Kimmel Live! (TV show), 169
Jobs, Steve, 193
John F. Kennedy: New U.S. President, 9, 17
Johnson, Andrew, 130
Johnson, Gary, xvi
Johnson, Jack, 193
Johnson, Lyndon B. (LBJ), xxii, xxiv, 38, 42, 79, 82, 179, 197, 198
Joker (fictional character), xvi, 93, 117, 168–69
J'onzz, J'onn (fictional character), 178, 190
Jordan, Hal (fictional character). *See* Green Lantern (fictional character)
journalism, xii, xxiii, 13, 104–12
journalists, 64, 73, 96, 98, 99, 101, 107, 108, 110, 129, 134, 163, 203, 205
Juarez, Bonita (fictional character), 159
Justice League (fictional group), 44, 49, 169, 174, 178, 184, 190, 220n1
Justice Society (fictional group), 24, 29, 30–31, 36

Kahl, Mary L., 147
Kallaugher, Kevin, 106
Kawaguchi, Kaiji, 161–64
Kazan, Elia, 24
Keenspot Press, xii, 48, 75, 151, 164, 218n3
Keller, Kevin (fictional character), 216ch2n1
Kelly, Senator Robert (fictional character), 24, 32
Kelly, Walt, xii
Kendall, Kathleen E., 16, 19
Kennedy, Bobby, 79, 193
Kennedy, Caroline, 13, 148
Kennedy, John F., xxii, 9–10, 14, 16, 17, 18, 38–39, 41–46, *46*, 49, 57, 175, 198, 199, 216ch1n2, 218ch9n1; assassination of, 38, 96, 188, 196, 197, 199, 202, 219ch11n4; and Camelot, xxii, 190; and "new frontier," 189, 190
Kennedy, Robert, Jr., 115
Kennedy, Ted, 18, 79, 83, 218n3
Kent, Clark, 38, 47, 49, 55, 205, *205*, 219ch10n1. *See also* Superman
Kerry, John, xvi, 79, 82, 83

Khan, Kamala (fictional character). *See* Ms. Marvel (Kamala Khan) (fictional character)
Killadelphia, 117, 129–30, 212, 213, 218ch7n5
Kimmel, Jimmy, 169
Kimmel, Michael, 17, 51, 132
King, Martin Luther, Jr., 14, 82, 192, 194
Kinzer, Stephen, 97
Kirby, Jack, 182
Knievel, Evel, 193
Knight, Peter, 196–97, 202
Knute Rockne All American (film), 17
Kyle, Selena. *See* Catwoman (fictional character)

Lafitte, Jean, 196
Laika, 198, 199
Lane, Lois (fictional character), 24, 26, 38, 203
Larsen, Erik, *158*
Late Show with Stephen Colbert, The, xviii
Laveau, Marie, 196
Lawrence, John Shelton, 39–40, 41, 43, 77, 170
League of Nations, 194, 195
Lee, Stan, 23, 33
Legally Blonde 2: Red, White, and Blonde (film), 24
Lego Batman, 10
Letter 44, 188, 198, 200–201
Levitt, Saul, 24
Lewinsky, Monica, 92
Lewis, John, xxiv, 15, 151, 166, 190
Lewis and Clark Expedition, 196
LGBTQAIPD, 146, 204, 206, 218ch8n6
"Libarro World," 79
Liberality for All, 79, 148, 204
Libertarian candidate, xvi
Life with Archie, 216ch2n1
Limbaugh, Rush, 14, 79, 155
Lincoln, Abraham, xxiv, 14, 15, 46, 48, 60, 82, 109, 130, 183–84, 187, 192, 194, 218ch9n1, 219ch11n1
Lindbergh, Charles, 192
Lipman-Bluman, Jean, 171–72, 176, 177, 178, 179, 181
lizard people. *See* reptilians
Lobinger, Katharine, xiv, xv, 5, 89
Logan. *See* Wolverine (fictional character)

Loki (fictional character), xv, xxiv, 128–29, 130, 168, 170, 171, 175, 181–83, 185, 208
Looking for America's Dog, 90–91
Lord of the Rings, 207
Los Angeles Times, 104
Losers, The, 190
Lucas, Scott, 4
Luckovich, Mike, 5
Luthor, Lex (fictional character), 60, 168–69, 172–74, *173*, 175, 177–79, 180, 184, 208, 219ch10n1
Lux Soap, and Peggy Lux for President, 137–38

MAD Magazine, xii, 97, 142, 169
Mad Max (franchise), 142, 183–84, *184*, 193
Magneto (fictional character), 168, 175, 176, 183
"Make America Great Again," 51, 122, 181, 192
Manchurian Candidate (film), 26
manga, 48, 80, 150, 154, 161, 164; and visual stereotypes, 163; *seinen manga* defined, 219ch9n4
Manhattan Project, 189
Manhattan Projects, The, 189, 198–200, *200*, 201–2
March (trilogy), 15, 166
Marilyn Manor, 149
Mars Attacks! (film), 25
Marsdin, Olivia (fictional character), 143, 218n4
Marston, William Moulton, 137, 139, 218n4
Martian Manhunter (fictional character). *See* J'onzz, J'onn
Martin Luther King and the Montgomery Story, 166
Marvel Comics, 32, 40, 42, 43, 48, 86, *87*, 97, 119, 128, 150, 152, 168, 174, 175, 180; and political ideology, xii, 203, 204, 205
masculinity, xiv, xix, xxiv–xxv, 16–18, 19, 53, 80, *85*, 132–33, 134, 136, 137, *137*, 146, 149, 151, 153. *See also* hypermasculinity
Mask: I Pledge Allegiance to the Mask, The, 117, 129, 130
Mason, "Moose" (fictional character), 147–48, 216ch2n1
Mavri, Kristjan, 213

mayors, 5, 12, 49, 50, 53–54, 57, 59, 115, 119, 125, 137, 146, 175–76, 215n2, 217ch4n3
McCain, John, xiv, 6, 12, 13, 47, 98, 109, 136, 145, 165; as "McPain," 81, 154
McCarthy, Joseph, xii, 23, 24, 28, *28*, 30; and McCarthyism, xxii, 23, 74
McCloud, Scott, 16, 106, 111–12
McLuhan, Marshall, 111
media: and campaigns, 126, 127, 128–29, 132, 136, 143; consumption, 207; criticism, 100–101, 110; entertainment, 207, 215ch1n1; fandoms, 133, 206; franchises, 32, 80, 81, 154, 170, 176, 206, 207; genre, 204; journalism, 98–99, 172; mainstream, 80, 128; multi-media, 86, 97, 111, 152, 206; political coverage, 75, 92, 107, 109, 110, 156, 162, 183; public trust of, 181; social, 96, 102, 147, 204, 210
Meet John Doe (film), 25
MeToo, 147, 201, 213
Metropolis (fictional city), 24, 49, 177
Meyer, Richard C., 204
Meyner, Robert, 9, 15, 215n2
military: leadership, 199; service, 6, 8, 9, 10, 11, 12, 16–17, 19, 45, 83, 87, 140, 194; strength, 83, 121, 203; technology, 82, 188, 201; threats, 71, 198
Miller, Arthur, 24
Miller, Elaine K., 144–45
Miller, Frank, 117
Mills, C. Wright, 199
mimesis, *51*
Mondale, Walter, 60
Monica's Story, 92
Monroe, Marilyn, 34, 149, 192, 194, 197
monster, 43, 83, 179, 210
Moore, Alan, xvi, 39, 65, 66, *67*, 140
Moore, Arda, 52, 139, 140
Moore, Michael, 80
Morgan, J. P., 193–94
Morreale, Joanne, 16, 18
motherhood: as activism, 134, 149, 156; and politics, 133, 134, 148; and superheroes, 133–34
mothers, 12, 33, 138, 163
Moulton, Charles. *See* Marston, William Moulton
Mr. Smith Goes to Washington (film), 24, 25

Mr. Terrific, 24, 29
Ms. Marvel (Kamala Khan) (fictional character), 116–17, *116*, 207, 217ch7n2
Mueller, Michael, xviii, 119
Mueller Report, xxiii, 105
Mueller Report Graphic Novel, 95, 96–97, 102, 104, 107, 108
Mueller Report Illustrated: The Obstruction Investigation, 97
Mumford, Lewis, 199
Muslim, 205; belief that Obama is, 153, 156, 158; immigration ban, 207, 217ch7n2. *See also* Khan, Kamala (fictional character)
My Hero Academia, 48, 80
My Hero MAGAdemia, 80, 82, 84, 204
My Little Pony: Friendship is Magic, 117

Nast, Thomas, *135*, 136
National Association for the Advancement of Colored People (NAACP), 115
national identity: in Cold War, 65; and presidency, 40, 41, 192; in steampunk performances, 192; and superheroes, 41
National Periodical Publications, 38. *See also* DC Comics
Nazis, xii, 24, 29, 30, 33, 83, *84*, 86, 88, 93, 175, 198
Necronomicon, 47, 127, 157
Neufeld, Josh, 98, 99, 101, 102, 105, 110
New Avengers, 169
New York Times, xi, xii, 55, 107, 110–11, 112, 151, 166, 173, 208
New Yorker, 95, 97, 158, *158*
Newton, Sir Isaac, 192
Nib, The, 98
9/11 (event), xiii, 45, 94–96, 99–100, 102–4, 106–7, 112, 197; and post-9/11 culture, 148, 156, 189, 200–201
9/11 Commission Report, The, 94, 100, 107
9/11 Report: A Graphic Adaptation, The, 94–96, 99–100, *100*, 102–4, *104*, 106–7, 112
1984 (Orwell), 180
Nirvana (band), 58
Nixon, Richard, xxii, 18, 42, 56, 57, 64, 65, 66, 109, 174, 179, 197, 251n2, 218ch9n1
Noon, David Hoogland, 39–40, 46, 49, 54
Northworthy, Jack (fictional character), 124–26

NPR, 144
Nyberg, Amy Kiste, 20, 21, 22, 23, 24, 36–37, 95

Oakley, Annie, 193, 195
Obama, Barack, xiii, xiv, xviii, xxiv, 6, 11, 12, 13, 14, 18, 19, 46–47, 48, 49, 54, 80–81, 84, 88, 89, 90–91, 98, 103, 115, 142, 150–58, *154*, *158*, 165, 167, 168, 170, 173, 175, 188, 219ch9n2; as "Barot," 81, 84, 154–55; as "Robama," 145; and "zombamicons," 155
Obama, Malia, 91, 148
Obama, Michelle, xxiii, 13, 14, 147–48, *158*
Obama, Sasha, 91, 148
"obamies," 157, 219ch9n3
Ocasio-Cortez, Alexandria "AOC", xvi, xvii, 79, 140, *141*, 151, 160, *161*, 218n3, 218ch8n7
Olive Oyl (fictional character), 137
Olsen, Jimmy (fictional character), 219ch10n1
Omar, Ilhan, 218ch8n7
On the Waterfront (film), 24
Operation Ajax: The Story of the CIA Coup that Remade the Middle East, 97, 105, 112
Oppenheimer, J. Robert, 189, 198, 199; and fictional evil twin Joseph, 189, 199
Opper, Frederick, 3–4
O'Reilly, Bill, 158
O'Rourke, Beto, 159
Orwell, George, 180; "Orwellian," 201
Osborn, Norman (fictional character). *See* Green Goblin (fictional character)
Oswald, Lee Harvey, 105, 183
Our Cartoon President (TV series), 174

Palin, Sarah, xxiii, 6, 11–12, 13, 14, 18, 47, 79, 84, 85, 88, 111, 132, 134–36, 144–46; as "Paladin," 81, 154; as "Red Sarah," 145
Palmiotti, Jimmy, 206
pandemic, 98, 209–13. *See also* COVID-19
Pandemica, 210–11, 220n1
Parker, Dorothy, 34
Parker, Peter. *See* Spider-Man (fictional character)
Parks, Susan, xv, 3, 4, 5, 6, 8
parody, xii, 6, 15, 48, 183–84, 193; and Cold War, 199–200; defined, 77, 79; workings of, 79, 85–86

Parry-Giles, Shawn J., xiii–xiv, xix, xxv, 25, 40, 208
Parry-Giles, Trevor, xiii–xiv, xix, xxv, 25, 40, 208
patriarchy, 17–18, 52, 101, 139, 146, 191, 196, 201, 208, 218ch9n1
Patrick, Dan, 211
Patterson, John, 4
Paul, Rand, 5, 12
Paul, Ron, 6, 10, 11, 18
Peanuts, 117
Pelosi, Nancy, xvii, 13, 106
Pence, Mike, 77, 79, 83, 84, 98
Penguin, The (fictional character), 47, 175
Perlmutter, Isaac "Ike," xi, xii
Perry, Rick, 6
Peters, Mark, 106
Phantom, The, 39, 45, 46
Picture Life of a Great American, xiv, 3, 7, 7, 215n2
Pirates vs. Ninjas: Debate in 08, 116
Pogo (fictional character), xii, xv, 215n1; in *I Go Pogo*, 215n1
politainment, xviii
Political Action Comics: Major Flip Flop, 79–80, 82, 144
political advertisements. *See* campaign advertisements
political cartoons. *See* editorial cartoons
political debates, 91, 117, 128, 158–59
political fiction, narrative types, 113–14
Political Power (comic series), 5, 12–14, 17–18, 19, 166, 167
Politico (news magazine), xvi, 105, 149
Popeye (fictional character), 137
popular (pop) culture: as allusion, 79, 142; and apocalypse, 209; audiences, 88, 207; Cold War, xxii, 26, 45, 189; comics, xviii; conspiracies, 35; conventions, 209; education, 15; post-9/11, 189, 200; protest symbols, 206, 207; US politics, xiii–xiv, xxv, 39, 72, 79, 93, 113, 156, 167
post-apocalyptic fictions, 158, 184, 186, 209, 213
Powell, Colin, xxiv, 151, 166, 193
Pres. Supervillain (Twitter feed), 92–93, 168, 169
presidential election (years): 1928 campaigns, xiv, 3, 7, 19; 1948 campaigns, 3–4, 7, 137; 1952 campaigns, 9, 16, 114, 130, 215n1; 1956 campaigns, 137, 215n1; 1960 campaign, 39, 44, 114–15, 189, 190; 1964 campaigns, 109, 115, 150, 166–67; 1968 campaigns, 41; 1972 campaigns, 56, 142; 1976 campaigns, xii, 119–20; 1980 campaigns, 42, 49, 79, 215n1; 1988 campaigns, 115, 121, 164, 169, 174; 1992 campaigns, 120–21, 162; 1996 campaigns, 5, 92, 217ch7n3, 217n4; 2000 campaigns, 13, 46, 61, 109, 122, 132, 161, 162, 174; 2004 campaigns, xvi, xxiii, 5, 14, 80, 113–14, 115, 130, 165, 175; 2008 campaigns, 14, 98, 109, 115, 116, 123, 132, 134, 135, 136, 142, 144, 145, 149, 150, 153, 158, 165, 213; 2012 campaigns, 6, 10, 11, 12, 13, 14, 90, 98, 103, 108, 109, 110, 123, 135, 142, 143, 166, 172; 2016 campaigns, xii, xvi, 5, 13, 14, 48, 50–51, 69, 98, 108, 109–10, 117, *118*, 119, 120, 122–29, 135, 142, 143–44, 149, 151, 155, 168, 173–74, 175–76, 179, 180–81, 183, 192, 211, 213; 2020 campaigns, xvi–xvii, xviii, 5–6, 93, 98, 117, 119, 129, 151, 158–59, 164, 182, 211
President Evil, 6, 47, 80–81, 85, *85*, 144, 154–55, 156
President Pence (comic book), 77, 79, 83, 84
President Trump (comic book), 48, 204
Presidential Affairs (comic book), 92, 93
Presley, Elvis, 193; impersonator ("Black Elvis"), 104, *104*
Pressley, Ayanna, 218ch8n7
Prez (fictional character), xxii–xxiv, 56–65, *61*, *63*, *66*, 68–69, *70*, *71*, *72*–73, 117, 119, 146, 151, 186, 208
Prime-Time Presidency: The West Wing and U.S. Nationalism, The (Parry-Giles and Parry-Giles), xiii
Prince, Diana (fictional character). *See* Wonder Woman
Princess Leia (fictional character), 207
propaganda, xv, 172, 204; and political campaigns, 5, 114, 216ch2n2; wartime, 163
Pryde, Kitty (fictional character), 205
PS: Political Science and Politics, xxv
Punisher (fictional character), xvi, 175, 203

Quayle, Dan, 15, 89, 90
Queen, Oliver (fictional character). *See* Green Arrow (fictional character)

Quick Draw McGraw (fictional character), 33, 34, 69, 70
Quinn, Harley (fictional character), 176

race, 153, 201; appeals of, 164; in comics and culture, 31, 165–66, 192; in politics, 27, 31, 164, 165–66; and racism, 18, 45, 160, 163, 167, 189, 191, 194, 212; relations, 28, 48, 58, 130, 151, 167; stereotypes, 153; specific to Asians, 150, 151, 161–65, 170; specific to Blacks, xxiv, 25, 48, 49, 77, 82, 104, 142, 143, 147, 149, 150–56, 159, 163–64, 165–67, 213, 218ch9n1, 219ch11n3; specific to Latinx, 159; and Whiteness, 151–52
Rall, Ted, 14
Rasputin, 193
"read my lips," 121
Read My Lips: The Unofficial Cartoon Biography of George Bush, 15, 89, 90
Reagan, Nancy, 13, 43, 49, 60, 148
Reagan, Ronald, 14, 17–18, 32, 42–43, 67, 75, 79, 83, 88, 92, 115
Reagan's Raiders, xxiii, 43, 75, 77, 79, 83, 86, 87–88, 92
Red Diaries: The Kennedy Conspiracy, The, 188, 197, 202, 219ch11n4
Red Guardian (fictional character), 85
Red Scare, 23, 33, 71, 103. *See also* McCarthy, Joseph
Red Skull (fictional character), xi, xv, xxiv, 93, 168, 174–75, 180
Red Sonja, 160, *161*
Reeve, Christopher, 205, *205*
Reno, Janet, 82
reporters, 26, 55, 98, 102, 120, 125, 158, 161, 163, 177. *See also* journalists
reptilians, 143
Republicans, 5, 125, 128, 212, 217ch4n2, 218ch8n7; administrations, 44, 45, 46, 48–49, 79; candidates, 3, 4, 6, 11, 12, 16, 42, 84, 98, 109, 151; Committees, 5; National Conventions, 103; Party (GOP), 81, 125, 140; politicians, 42, 45, 89, 160; primaries, 121, 124; rallies, 127; Women's Club, 28
Resident Evil, 81, 154
Revere, Paul, 217ch4n2
Rice, Condoleezza, xxiv, 13, 18, 151, 166
Right State, 151

Right Stuff, The, 142
Robbins, Trina, 137, 138
Rockefeller, John D., 193, 194
Romanoff, Natasha. *See* Black Widow (fictional character)
Romney, Mitt, 6, 13, 103, 109
Ronald Reagan: A Graphic Biography, 18
Roosevelt, Eleanor, 196
Roosevelt, Franklin Delano, xxiv, 4, 9, 14, 40, 46, 198, 199
Roosevelt, Theodore, xxiv, 14, 46, 48, 192, 193, 194, 195, *195*, 202
Rough Riders (comic series), 48, 188, 191, 193, 194–95, *195*, 201, 202
Round, Julia, xvi, 40, 170
Ross, Alex, 47
Rubio, Marco, xxiv, 5, 151, 166
RuPaul, 193
Rushing, Janice Hocker, 113
Russell, John, 98
Russell, Mark, xxiii, 34, 58–59, 62–63, 69–73, 117, 146
Ruth, Babe, 193

Sacajawea, 196
Sacco, Joe, 95, 96, 99, 103, 206
Sanders, Bernie, xviii, 6, 13, 14, 18, 127, 218ch8n7
Sandman, 57, 60, *61*, 62–63, 66
Santorum, Rick, 6
Sarah Palin: Rogue Warrior, 136, 145
Sarah Palin versus the World, 79, 136
satire, xii, xxiii, 15, 21, 42, 65, 75–76, 77, 81–82, 88–89, 91–93, 142, 156; techniques of, 79, 82, 85–86, 89
Saturday Night Live, 80
Saucer Country, 123–24, 130, 143–44, 150, 160, 167, 201, 208
Saucer State, xxiv, 143, 160, 201, 208
Savage Dragon, 47, 158, *158*, 170, 175
Scarecrow (DC Comics fictional character), 176
Schwarzenegger, Arnold, 18, 84
science-fiction, 160, 191, 197, 200, 204
Scooby Apocalypse, 69, 169, 210, 213
Scooby-Doo! Mystery Incorporated, 58
Scorsese, Martin, 203
Scott, Adrian, 23

Scott, Adrian "Age," 150
Scott, Kim Allen, xv, 3, 4, 5, 6, 8
Seduction of the Innocent (book), 20
Seeley, Tom, *154*
semiotics, xxi
Sessions, Jeff, 98
Shafted! Bill and Hillary's Excellent Adventure, 89
Sheeler, Kristina Horn, 134, 136, 145, 148
Showtime, 168, 174
Sikoryak, R., 92–93, 160, *161*
Silver Deer (fictional character), 29
Simpsons, The (TV show), 217n4
Sinnot, Joe, 150
Slate, Barbara, 95, 96–97, 102, 104, 105, 108, 217ch6n1
Smallville (TV show), 33, 219ch10n1
Smigel, Rob, 80, 82
Smiler (fictional character), 64
Snagglepuss ("S. P."), 25, 33–34, 35, 69, 70–71, 72
Snowden, Edward, 14
Socialism Trek, 79, 80, 84, 144, 147
Soros, George, 80, 81
Soviet Union, 65, 203; as Cold War enemy, 35; hammer and sickle, 67; space program, 198, 199
Spanish-American-Cuban-Filipino War, 188, 193
Sparta, U.S.A., 123
speculative fiction, xxiv; and allohistory, 186; New Weird subgenre of, 196
Spider-Man (fictional character), xii, xvi, 23, 41, 47, 88, 115–16, 130, 142, 150, 174, 175, 218n3, 220n1
Spiegelman, Art, xi–xii
sports, 42, 91, 219ch9n4; candidate achievements in athleticism, 6, 11–12, 16–17, 18, 19; and masculinity, 17, 47, 218ch8n1; and race, 152, 153
Squadron Supreme (fictional group), 43
Stainless Steel Rat, 176
Stalin, Joseph, 183, 192
Stark, Tony (fictional character). *See* Iron Man (fictional character)
Star Trek, 14, 80, 84, 207
Star Wars, 81, 168, 207
steampunk, xxiv, 85, 145–46, 183, 187, 188, 191, 192, 194, 202

Steampunk Palin, 6, 47, 84, 85
Steel (fictional character), 191
Stein, Jill, 98, 101, 108, 109–10
Steinmetz, Charles Proteus, 193, 194
Stewart, Jon, 14
Strachan, J. Cherie, 16, 19
Strange, Hugo (fictional character), 176
Super Mario Bros. (media franchise), 142
Super President (animated cartoon), 41–42
Supergirl (fictional character), 38, 57, 142
Supergirl (TV show), 143
superheroes: as anti-fascist, xi; costumes of, 83, 85; defined, xvi, 77–78, 81–82; and gender, 133–34; genre, xv, xxii, 36–37, 65, 170, 203; as political symbols, xvi; and/as politicians, 13, 26, 43, 53–54, 140, 145; parodies of, 77–80, 84–85, 93; and race, xxiv, 151–52, 167; style of, 95; and US Congress, 28–33; and US presidency, 39–40, 41–43, 44, 45–46, 48–49, 52, 55
Superman, xiii, xv, xvi, xxii, 4, 19, 24, 26, 29, 31, 33, 38–39, 40, 41, 42, 43–44, 47, 49, 52, 54, 58, 77, 83, 123, 150, 152, 169, 172–74, 177, 178, 184, 190, 205, *205*, 219ch10n1. *See also* Kent, Clark; Ellis, Calvin
Superman/Batman: Public Enemies (animated film), 174, 177, 179
supervillains: and civics, 116; defined, 170, 184–85; as politicians, 172, 174–76, 182–83, 185; as protagonist, 156
Syaf, Ardian, 205
Symbolia Magazine, 95, 98–99, 103, 108, 110, 112

Taft, William Howard, 46
Tea Party, 14, 58
Teen Titans (fictional group), 43, 175
Teenage Mutant Ninja Turtles (animated cartoon), 169
Tesla, Nikola, 192, 193, 194
third party candidates, 98, 108, 109–10, 217n4
Third Reich, 29, 83, 86, 180. *See also* Nazis
Thor (fictional character), xv, 45, 48, 49, 50, 128, 175, 204
Thor: The Dark World (film), 170
Three Little Pigs Buy the White House, The, 88
Three Stooges: Red White and Stooge, The, 117, 119

Thump: The First Hundred Days, 88
Thunder, Sally Ann, 196
TidalWave Productions, 5–6
Time Lincoln (comic series), 48, 82, 84, 85, 183–84, *184*, 187, 191, 192–93, 194, 201, 202
Timely Comics, 40. *See also* Marvel Comics
Tlaib, Rashida, 218ch8n7
Top Cow Productions, 196
Torture Report: A Graphic Adaptation, The, 95, 96, 99–100, 102, 106, 107, 108
toxic leadership, xxiv; allure of, 176; defined, 171–72; and fascism, 177; followers, 178; media coverage of, 172
Transmetropolitan, 63, 64, 73, 186
Treasure Chest (of Fact and Fun), xxiv, 150, 166
Tremendous Trump, 6, 48, 83, 84, 85, *85*, 86, 87, *87*, 92
Trevor, Steve (fictional character), 139, 140
Trudeau, Garry, 76
True Comics, 8
Trujillo, Nick, 16, 17–18
Truman, Harry S., xxii, 3–4, 7–8, *8*, 20, 46, 189, 198, 199, 206
Trump, Donald J., xi, xii, xiii, xvi, xvii–xviii, xxiii, xxiv, xxv, 5, 6, 12, 13–14, 18, 25, 45, 46, 48, 50–53, 55, 58, 69, 75, 77, 79, 80, 81, 82, 83–84, 85, 86–88, *87*, 91–93, 97, 98, 99, 101, 105–6, 108, 109, 117, 119, 121–23, *122*, 124–25, 127, 129, 144, 149, 151, 155, 160, 164, 168–70, *169*, 172, 173–74, *173*, 180–84, *184*, 185, 192, 193, 194–95, 201, 202, 203, 204, 205, 206, 210, 211, 212, 213, 217ch5n1, 217ch6n1, 217ch6n2, 218n3, 219ch10n2
Trump vs. Clinton Adult Coloring Book, 88
Trump's Titans (comic series), xxiii, 48, 75, 77, 79, 80, 81, 83–84, *84*, 86, 87, 88, 91–92, 144
Tuck, Dick, 162
Turner, Tina, 193
12 Angry Men (film), 24
Two-Face (fictional character). See Dent, Harvey (fictional character)

UFOs, 198
Ultimate Fantastic Four, 45
Ultimates, The, 48, 50, 186
Umbrella Academy, The, 197, 202
Unconstitutional Actions and Adventures of the Dead Presidents, The, 45–46
Undiscovered Country, 210, 211
United States vs. Murder Inc., 218ch8n5
Unquotable Trump, 87, 92–93
unruly woman metaphor, 134, 136, 140, 143, 144–45, 146, 147, 149, 218ch8n5
US Congress (House and Senate), xiv, *xv*, xxii, 24, 25–26, 28–36, 72, 77, 108, 119, 178, 216ch2n2; campaigns for, 4, 10–11, 14, 24, 25, 26–27, 29, 59, 98, 132, 146–47, 150, 215n2, 216ch2n1; committees of, 20, 24, 31, 33, 34, 94, 96; hearings in, 20, 22–24; representatives of, xiii, xvi, xxii, 4, 6, 11, 12, 13, 14, 15, 22, 23, 24, 26, 27, 28, 29, 30, 31–33, 34, 61, 119, 125, 139–40, 142, 146, 151, 158, 160, 161, 165, 166, 218ch8n7
US presidency: attitudes toward, 57; as heroic, 39–41, 43, 49, 52, 54–55, 80–81, 170, 217ch3n2; masculinity in, 17, 52, 137; and political myth, 39, 54; in popular culture, xiii–xiv, 207–8; and race, 151, 191
USSR, 198, 199
Ustinov, Dmitriy, 198

vampires, 117, 130
Van Buren, Martin, 17, 51
Van Zoonen, Liesbet, 113–14
Vanity Fair, 105
variant covers, 60, 140–42, *141*, 145
Venom (film), 55
Verano, Frank, 171, 183
Vertigo Comics, 57, 123, 143, 150, 218ch9n1
Vietnam War (Second Indo-China War), xxii, 12, 28, 41, 42, 65, 79, 82, 89, 161, 163, 197
Vixen (fictional character), 154
Voigt, Philip Nolan (fictional character), 174, 179
von Braun, Wernher, 198, 199
Vote Loki, 117, 128–29, 130, 175, 179, 181, 217n4
voter suppression, 113, 115, 130
voters, xxiii, 50, 53, 56, 72, 129, 131, 172, 179, 180–81, 185, 192, 206, 215n1; Latinx as, 159; women as, 132, 138; youth as, 73
voting, 114–15, 128, 130–31
voting fraud, xxiii, 113
voting rights, 101–2, 110; Act, xxii, 56, 72, 98, 101, *102*, 105, 113, 167, 179
Vox (media outlet), 69, 206

Wacky Raceland, 69, 169, 186
Waid, Mark, xii, 204
Wakanda (fictional country), 148
Wallace, George, 4, 8–9, 15, 18, 165
Walters, Barbara, 14
Wanzo, Rebecca, xvi, 5, 19, 40, 170
war on drugs, xvi, 43, 75, 92; and Drug Awareness Campaign, 42–43
Ware, Chris, 206
Warner, Andy, 98, 101–2, 110
Warner Brothers, 17, 23, 58, *184*, 205
Warren Commission Report, xxiii
Warren Commission Report: A Graphic Investigation into the Kennedy Assassination, The, 96, 104, 105
Warren, Elizabeth, 5, 6, 14, 160
Washington, DC, xi, 12, 18, 25, 29, 36, 55, 56, 60, 182; as "Warshingtun," 153
Washington, George, 14, 16, 46, 130
Washington Post, xi, 56, 97, 105, 125, 206, 215n1
Watchmen, The, xvi, xxiii, 39, 65–66, *67*, 71, 72, 73, 140, 186, 216ch2n2
Watergate (scandal), xxii, 15, 35, 56–57, 73; and public distrust, 59, 71
Weissman, Steven, 90–91, 157
Welles, Orson, 193
Wertham, Frederic, 20, 31
West, Adam, 176
West, Kanye, 80
West Wing, The (TV show), xiv, 25
Westmoreland, William, 198–99
Wheeler, Shannon, 97, 217ch5n1
Whicker, Marcia Lynn, 171
White (comic), 212
White House (place), xv, 38, 88, 92, 129, 145, 174, 179, 180
Whiteness, 151–52, 153, 154, 159, 167, 191, 194; and White fragility, 151
Williams, Ash J. (fictional character), 47, 117, 127, 157
Williams, Serena, 143
Williamson, Marianne, xvi–xvii, *xvii*
Wilson, Edith, 193, 195
Wilson, G. Willow, 117
Wilson, John (fictional character). *See* Steel
Wilson, Wade (fictional character). *See* Deadpool
Wilson, Woodrow, xxiv, 188, 192, 194, 195

Wilz, Kelly, 144
Wolverine (fictional character), 204
Wolverine: Old Man Logan, 175, 180, 186
Woodhull, Victoria Claflin, xxiii, 135–36, *135*
Woodward, Bob, 56
women, xxiii, 11; as comics fans, 133, 204; liberation, 142, 147, 191; media coverage of, 133–34, 136, 143, 147; as Other, 143; in politics, xxiv, 27, 52, 132–33, 134, 138, 148, 149, 218ch8n1; sexualization of, 67; and suffrage, 136; as superheroes, 132–33, 149; UNICEF campaign for, xvi; in US history, 194–95
Women's March, 206, 207
Wonder Wart-Hog (fictional character), 79, 81
Wonder Woman, xv, xvi, xxiii, 30, 31, 43, 44, 52, 137, 138–40, *141*, 142–43, 145, 149, 190, 191, 218n4
World War I. *See* Great War
World War II, xxv, 3, 4, 7, 8, 9, 10, 23, 24, 29, 35, 40, 45, *46*, 54, 163, 189, 190, 191, 196
Wright, Frank Lloyd, 193

X, Malcolm, 14, 193
X-Files: JFK Disclosure, The, 197, 198, 202
X-Men (fictional group), 24, 32, 41, 80, 174, 175, 205, 220n1
X-Men: Dark Phoenix (film), 55
X-Men: Days of Future Past (film), 174
X-Presidents, 80, 82

Yang, Andrew, 151, 164–65
Yang Gang, 151, 164–65
Yezbick, Daniel F., 67–68
Yglesias, Matthew, 53
Youngblood, 54
youth movement, xxii, 27, 56–59, 62, 64, 70, 73
youth vote, 69, 119

Zarcone, Marley, 149, 206
Zedong, Mao, 183
Zelensky, Volodymyr, 106
'08: A Graphic Diary of the Campaign Trail, 98, 102, 104, *104*, 105, 108–9
Z-Men: All the President's Men, 197, 219ch11n3
zombies, 47, 84, 144, 155, 156, 157, 209–10; as Other, 155, 217ch9n1, 219ch11n3

ABOUT THE AUTHOR

Credit: Roger Theise of Roger William Photography (Cortland, NY)

Christina M. Knopf is associate professor of Communication and Media Studies at the State University of New York, Cortland. The author of multiple articles on political rhetoric, representations of war and the military, gender in the public sphere, and comics, Dr. Knopf is a Distinguished Research Fellow of the Eastern Communication Association.

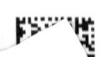
www.ingramcontent.com/pod-product-compliance
Lightning Source LLC
Chambersburg PA
CBHW070301240426
43661CB00057B/2612